World labour report 1

*Employment, incomes, social protection,
new information technology*

International Labour Office   Geneva

ISBN 92-2-103604-9

First published 1984
Second impression 1986

II

Preface

This work is the first of its kind to be published by the International Labour Office. It is concerned mainly with facts, and aims at giving an overall picture of recent developments concerning major labour problems in the contemporary world. It is intended for people everywhere who are concerned about these problems – trade unionists, managers, politicians, educators, the layman pondering the future of society. We hope that it will help to refresh or supplement their knowledge and will thus serve as food for thought. By and large, the facts reviewed in it are known to the specialists, but they are not always readily available to the general public.

This work is a synthesis of the vast amount of information which the International Labour Office receives from the 150 member States of the Organisation and is permanently engaged in analysing. In preparing it, we have also availed ourselves of the work carried out by the Office itself and the lessons drawn from its operational activities in many countries.

This synthesis, made pursuant to the function of "the collection and distribution of information on all subjects relating to the international adjustment of conditions of industrial life and labour", assigned to the Office by the Constitution of the ILO, does not in any way commit the Organisation or its member States. It has been prepared by the Office under my responsibility.

It has not been an easy task. Few are the pages where the facts presented might not have called for fuller or deeper analyses, or perhaps deserved different explanations. Three temptations have had to be avoided in the process: to paint a broad social canvas, which would have gone beyond our intentions; to write a sort of condensed treatise on each subject; and to draw up a dry inventory of unquestionable facts. I trust that the middle way chosen is both free of that dryness and not too objectionable to the specialists, and yet provides food for thought to all those who require better information about labour questions for the sake of advancing knowledge – or simply for the sake of progress.

Another word of caution: this report does not put forward ready-made solutions to the problems it describes. To do so would be beyond its ability as an analytical exercise that commits the Office alone; it would also be beyond its intention as an endeavour to present facts and basic data.

It may of course be objected that implicit in any presentation of facts is a theory, whether consciously formulated or not. If theory there is, it can only derive from the principles of a world-wide, tripartite organisation – bringing together governments, workers and employers – that is striving to promote greater social justice. However objective they attempt to be, our analyses cannot call those principles in question. Our bias is that.

This initial volume begins with an examination of employment in the world today. Three chapters are devoted to this major subject. The first analyses the phenomena of labour underutilisation and poverty in the least advanced countries – which, it should be remembered, include two-thirds of the world's population – from the economic standpoint. Employment problems in the industrialised market economies are analysed in the second chapter. The third chapter is devoted to an examination of employment and labour questions in the countries of Eastern Europe.

The fourth chapter briefly analyses the phenomenon of economic migration for employment at the international level.

These analyses of employment are followed in the fifth chapter by a general picture of incomes and wages in the world.

The sixth chapter takes stock of current social security problems in the industrialised countries, after briefly reviewing their achievements in the field of social protection.

In the seventh and last chapter, an attempt is made to assess the impact of new information technology.

The volume concludes with a statistical annex containing international data on the world's labour force, income distribution in a number of countries and social security costs.

Employment, income, social protection, new information technology – these, then, are the central themes of this first volume.

The second volume, to be published in 1984, will, after discussing training for employment, look into several major areas in connection with conditions of work: working hours, safety and health, work organisation, leave. Significant aspects of the social dialogue will then be described: the social partners, labour relations, labour disputes. The second volume will conclude with an examination of major human rights questions in relation to labour: freedom of association, forced labour, discrimination.

These two volumes will thus have attempted to provide some tentative answers to the major questions one cannot fail to ask at the beginning of the eighth decade of this century in the field of labour: What jobs are available for whom? What income do they provide? To what social protection do they entitle workers? How are people trained for them? What are the conditions of work? Who determines and negotiates these conditions, and how? What human rights do they protect?

This work will be followed by two further reports, to be published at regular intervals during the decade. These publications, taken as a whole, will constitute the fresco of labour questions the first panel of which I have the honour to present today.

In short, this is the vast undertaking which this first volume attempts to delimit.

□

It is also hoped that this programme will serve as an incentive for studies of greater depth on the major theme of labour and its future, which our Organisation does not have the means to implement.

Though human labour is as old as mankind, our conception of work is new as measured against the scale of history.

Made possible by the outstanding events in the cultural, economic, technical and political fields which have marked world civilisation since the fifteenth century, this conception – and we have not yet fully grasped all its implications nor really know where it will eventually lead – is in reality no more than two centuries old. The semantic field of the words denoting it has been both enlarged and unified. This new idea has given rise to an immense vocabulary, which would have been incomprehensible even during the last century. In their current senses, such terms as employment and its regrettable negative have a history of scarcely 100 years. The word unemployment appeared in English in only about 1890.

If we do not sufficiently appreciate the newness of our conception of work, it is perhaps because we tend to forget the underlying nature of our contemporary civilisations: industrious civilisations, civilisations of doing, civilisations of know-how, obsessed by the production and distribution of wealth.

Among the many causes that may account for these phenomena, two to which the modern notion of work is closely linked are fundamental. They have to do with both intentions and means.

The first is in fact the objective of growing wealth set by our societies. The rulers of the past were preoccupied with the attainment of power and glory. Today the economic growth of their States and the economic prosperity of their people are among their major occupations.

The second is the enormous technological power acquired by man. The Chinese junks in the days of the last Ming emperors in the sixteenth century were no faster than the Athenian triremes during the time of Pericles. Napoleon moved at the same speed – or just as slowly – as Caesar. But Kruschev and Kennedy had the means – and the will – to send men and machines into outer space.

These unprecedented changes would not have been possible if wealth-creating work had not been placed at the centre of society's scale of values.

The tendency to forget this great novelty is understandable enough. We tend to see our wealth-creating activity as a natural function because the lesson was not brought home to us that it has not always been natural or, at least, has seldom been man's principal function.

In the vast literature of world history, little space has been devoted to man's labour. There are few good histories of the subject. There are still fewer books describing the evolving notion of work over time. This is hardly surprising for the centuries up to modern times since human work was neither the centre nor the object of history. But that there should be so few works in our time – as both those directly concerned and outside observers know and can testify – to enable us to appreciate better the nature of a value so central to our civilisations and the ideology it implies, is a paradox that cannot fail to surprise and a gap that needs to be filled. This indispensable undertaking would make us understand better the operation of our societies and would also show us where work is taking us.

In addressing the International Labour Conference in 1974, I recommended that a general inquiry into human labour should be carried out. The main purpose of such an inquiry would, of course, have been to acquaint us better with work in order to improve it. But I also hoped that it would help to shed light on our choices. Lack of means prevented us from going ahead with that inquiry. I hope that major research institutes, foundations, disinterested bodies will now join efforts and back those of the ILO for the purpose of carrying out the inquiries and research needed to meet the challenge of our time.

And I hope that the work which I have the honour to present today may serve as encouragement to take part in this great undertaking.

Francis Blanchard

V

Contents

Chapter 1

Labour underutilisation and poverty in the developing countries

In 1980, according to ILO estimates, the so-called developing world had an economically active population of about 1,245 million men and women, over two-thirds living in Asia. A whole book would be needed to summarise the employment problems of so vast and varied a part of mankind.

This chapter attempts merely to show how these problems stand at present, and how they have evolved in recent years as the domestic structures of countries have changed and the international environment has become inhospitable.

The first section reviews the diversity of the developing world, the type of changes taking place in the various countries and their effects on employment. A warning is made against too narrow an interpretation – modelled on facts and trends in the Western countries – of "employment" and "unemployment" in the developing countries, and an attempt is made to bring out the cause-and-effect relationship between employment and poverty and to show how general development policies affect that relationship.

The next three sections contain a detailed analysis of the impact on the level and "quality" of employment of some of the major processes at work at various stages of development and of how they affect the underutilisation of labour and poverty. We shall consider in turn the transition from subsistence agriculture to commercialised and mechanised agriculture; industrialisation; and the urban informal sector. The last section contains

some suggestions for international and national action.

The general pattern of development

The notion of employment

In the developing countries employment cannot be equated with the enjoyment of a full-time job under regulated conditions of work and pay. Nor can unemployment be said to be a period of semi-activity while waiting for such a job. To paraphrase A. K. Sen, employment may be viewed under a number of headings. It is an activity which yields an income or gives a right to share in a collective income. But since delinquency and crime also yield an income, employment must be an activity which produces a socially and legally accepted output. Furthermore, since employment cannot be slavery, specific relations must be established between the worker and the employer embodying commonly accepted principles of personal freedom and mobility. Employment also implies recognition from the standpoint of society. Some activities are "recognised" and accepted as forms of employment. Others, however worth while and essential they may be (for example, women's work in the home), are not. Conversely, many boring, repetitive and unpleasant jobs are regarded as employment: not to have even such a job may be a source of shame and felt inadequacy, even for persons with secondary sources of income.

1.1

Women's work

Women, especially those who are poor, work hard. Women's productive work is often underestimated because of the many tasks they perform, some of which are not visible, and because a household's status may be lowered by appearing to depend on women's earnings. Yet in Nepal, for example, women contribute 50 per cent of household income, compared with 43 per cent by men, and the balance by children. Even secluded women in Nigeria and Bangladesh engage in extensive productive work. In the Andes rural women perform a substantial part of agricultural work despite the image to the contrary given by census data. And in Africa women are the principal producers of food.

The contribution that women make to total household earnings is significantly higher in poor households. Many women work for pitiful returns as wage labourers or traders. When all work is counted paid and unpaid (such as collecting water and fuel, preparing food, etc.) data from the Third World as a whole indicate substantially longer working hours for women than for men, especially in poor rural households. That women's work is of marginal importance is a lingering and dangerous myth.

Although today there is a better understanding of the nature of employment in the Third World and of the complexity of work relations which go to make up one aspect of employment, observers are too often prisoners of the oversimplified means by which employment is recorded. It may be said, for example, that an important aspect of employment is the work status, i.e. the worker's relationship to his or her work. Traditional measures of work status divide active persons into employers, self-employed workers, wage earners and unpaid (normally family) workers. Within each of these groups, however, there are differences in the control which the individual exercises over his other work. Employers may have one employee or hundreds; the self-employed may be autonomous small-scale producers, or insecure tenants (and, indeed, the apparently self-employed may be as dependent as or more than any wage earner on a "patron"); wage labour ranges from almost total subjugation of the worker (as in various forms of debt bondage) to freely entered contracts; unpaid family labour may imply egalitarian sharing of work burdens, or it may involve exploitation of domestically available labour. The evolution of employment cannot be properly grasped without an understanding of the processes whereby individuals move from one activity to another within these categories. These shifts are as important as – if not more than – shifts from one conventional category of employment to another. However, they are not measured, nor perhaps always measurable.

In addition, there are the many problems of labour force measurement in the developing countries, which are discussed in box 1.2. Approaches to measurement vary according to the perceived needs of data users. Thus, the concept of labour force participation associated with a person's usual economic activity during the year gave way, during the Great Depression of the 1930s, to the activity or labour supply approach, concerned with work and unemployment during a short, specific reference period (such as the last week). Similarly, in recent years increasing attention has been given to underemployment and the relationship between income, economic hardship and employment as governments have become more concerned with poverty alleviation and the satisfaction of basic needs.

Change in the developing world

Before reviewing the structural change taking place in the developing countries – first in domestic and then in international terms – it is necessary to recall the great diversity of these countries (see box 1.3).

Certainly much structural change points everywhere in the same direction, partly because in the final analysis tastes and technologies tend to converge. However, the same consequences for labour and employment cannot be expected in countries as diverse as India and Mexico. Furthermore, in developing countries with a centrally planned economy many key linkages (e.g. the role

1.2

Labour force measurement

The conventional labour force approach classifies people as employed, unemployed or economically inactive. Economically active persons are those above a specified age (often 10 or 15 years) who have worked for pay or profit during a particular reference period (frequently one week) or sought work. With the exception of unpaid family workers (i.e. those who "assist" the household head in generating some economic output, such as farm crops) who, at least according to previous recommendations concerning the definition of employment, have to work at least 15 hours during the reference week, others are considered to be employed if (a) they were engaged in some economic activity, e.g. for at least one hour during the reference period or (b) they were temporarily absent from their job.

This definition raises many problems. At present, the most widely accepted view of an "economic activity" is something recorded in the national income statistics. As a result, many essential activities, including housework, preparing food for family use and gathering fuel, are not usually included despite their contribution to the economic welfare and survival of the poor.

Another problem is that encountered in trying to achieve a reliable measurement of female employment. There is no doubt that in many developing areas the number of women in the labour force – even according to the strictest definition of economic activity – is much larger than that given in the official statistics. This applies particularly to help on family farms and in the Middle East. Other difficulties include pinning down major seasonal fluctuations in employment,

especially where most agricultural work is concentrated over a period of a few months. The growing extent of part-time employment also raises a problem since statistics frequently fail to distinguish between part-time workers and full-time workers.

The labour force approach thus divides economically active persons into two categories: the employed and the unemployed. But there are many persons who do not clearly come within one of these categories or the other. Many are visibly underemployed in the sense of working less than full time. Others work full time but earn less than a subsistence income. Some of the unemployed may even be voluntarily idle. To clarify some of these issues, recommendations have been made for more elaborate data gathering such as time-use surveys and/or modifying the length of the reference period. Such suggestions may solve some problems but they create others in the process. Other analytical frameworks to replace the labour force approach have been proposed. Again, these generally replace one set of normative judgements by another and raise new, and sometimes more acute, measurement problems. All said and done, it appears that a flexible approach to data collection which, while preserving international comparability, allows the user to arrange the data for a number of alternative uses, is the most useful.

Such an approach was adopted at the international level by the Thirteenth International Conference of Labour Statisticians convened by the Governing Body of the ILO in October 1982 (see box 2.1 in Chapter 2).

3

of internal migration) and distributive processes are different. Lastly, the data on performance are averages which serve only to hide the diversity of individual country experience. This last trap cannot be totally avoided but this review will try to give also a notion of the range of values of different indicators.

Changes in domestic structures

The first characteristic of domestic structural transformation is the change in the composition of the gross domestic product (GDP) by sector of activity. Table 1.1 gives data by developing regions. As a general rule, the importance of agriculture declines in time although Burma, Chad, Uganda, Zaire and Zambia have apparently had the opposite experience since 1960. The average, however, fell considerably, from 31 per

cent to 18 per cent for all developing countries and, as regards the two major groups identified in World Bank statistics, from 50 to 36 per cent for the low-income countries (below US$500 per capita in 1978) and from 24 to 15 per cent for so-called middle-income countries (GNP per capita between US$500 and US$1,000 in 1978). The converse of a rise in the share of industry and services held good. However, in a few countries, such as Brazil, El Salvador and Jamaica, the share of industry rose by only two percentage points or less.

The second characteristic is the fact that the location of population has also changed rapidly, and changed uniformly in favour of urban areas. By 1980 urban populations had reached about 70 per cent or more of the total in Argentina, Brazil,

1.3

The diversity of developing economies

The importance of the creation of the Organisation of the Petroleum Exporting Countries (OPEC) led most observers to separate the net oil exporters (OECD), or major petroleum exporters (UNCTAD), or capital surplus oil exporters (World Bank), from the bulk of the developing countries. At the other end of the range is a tendency to separate the low-income or least developed countries. These countries have in common a low per capita income, a low degree of industrialisation and a low degree of literacy; they are a rather special group, mainly found in Africa. The World Bank also makes a distinction between "poor" and "middle-income" countries.

Among the middle-income countries another group is usually singled out: the newly industrialising countries, semi-industrial countries (World Bank), or fast-growing exporters of manufactures (UNCTAD). The number of countries included in this group varies according to the criteria applied. A relatively large absolute and relative size of the manufacturing sector and a rapid increase of exports of manufactures are the criteria most often used.

There is thus a tendency to deal with subgroups of developing countries: the oil exporters, least developed countries (for which exports of raw materials are most important) and newly industrialising countries where access to new loans and technology and markets for their manufactured goods are of overriding importance.

Table 1.1
Structure of GDP: developing regions, 1960–80
(in percentage)

Group	Agriculture 1960	Agriculture 1980	Industry 1960	Industry 1980	Services 1960	Services 1980
All developing countries	31.0	17.3	29.9	38.5	39.1	44.2
Latin America and Caribbean (low-income countries)	26.2	17.2	27.7	32.0	46.1	51.0
Latin America and Caribbean (middle-income countries)	16.2	10.0	36.7	39.0	47.1	51.0
China	..	..	..	..	..	..
India	51.0	37.0	19.4	25.0	29.5	38.0
Asia (other low-income countries)	48.1	33.0	17.5	27.0	34.4	40.0
Asia (middle-income countries)	34.8	18.0	21.0	36.0	44.2	46.0
Africa and Middle East (low-income countries)	54.4	41.0	13.3	17.0	32.4	42.0
Africa and Middle East (middle-income countries)	33.0	20.0	28.3	35.0	38.8	45.0
Africa and Middle East (capital surplus oil producers)	25.8	8.0	51.1	63.0	23.2	29.0

.. = not available.

Source: United Nations: *Handbook of world development statistics* (New York, Oct. 1982).

Colombia, Chile, Iraq, Mexico, Peru and Venezuela. In Bangladesh, China, Ethiopia and Tanzania it was still about 12 to 14 per cent.

These two indicators of transformation give an idea of the changes taking place in some features of employment. Table 1.2 gives a breakdown of employment by sector. The share of the labour force in agriculture is seen to have fallen from 73 per cent to 59 per cent on an average, less than the fall in the share of agriculture in the GDP. To the extent that very crude calculations based on World Bank data on output and employment shares can be trusted, output per worker in agriculture in relation to the national average had, by 1980, fallen to 0.5 per cent in the poorest countries and to 0.33 per cent in middle-income countries.

Agricultural employment seems highly resilient. Thus in Iraq, while only 20 per cent of the population lives in rural areas, 42 per cent of the labour force still works in agriculture. In Venezuela the comparable figures are 17 and 18 per cent respectively. A corollary is that the share of employment in industry has usually risen slowly, on an average from 13 per cent of the labour force to 20 per cent. It has not risen at all in Paraguay and Sri Lanka, and has fallen in Chile and Peru. Finally, the share of employment in services has risen throughout the developing world (on an average from 14 to 21 per cent of the labour force) and is particularly high in urbanised higher-income developing countries. The share of service employment estimated for Brazil in 1980 is higher than that of Spain or Italy.

A final indicator of domestic transformation is education. Even in 1960 the average figure for primary school enrolment was about 76 per cent for all developing countries (and by 1980 may have reached 95 per cent). Even more significant has been the increase in secondary school enrolment and, in the more prosperous developing countries, enrolment in higher education. Indeed, progress in these last two educational stages has quite probably been at the expense of the quality of primary education. (Furthermore, in many countries, particularly in Africa, even primary school enrolment is still low.) Changes in the education profile have tended to produce a better educated, perhaps more personally independent labour force, often with high aspirations. They have also frequently resulted in the waste of educated people through unemployment and their use in tasks for which their education would hardly seem relevant. However, the emphasis given to secondary and higher education has often implied an increasing educational gap between the rural worker, who has probably never completed primary education (in any case of low quality), and more privileged modern sector employees.

International factors contributing to the modification of domestic structures

For domestic transformation to take place and for the structure of employment to change, all but the most self-reliant of developing countries need a steady stream of imports of goods and services. Sudden falls in import availability are likely to lead to an underutilisation of capital goods and labour alike. A gradual slow-down in availability will constrain the process of growth, closing a number of options and making development more difficult. Between 1960 and 1970 the purchasing power of exports from poorer countries grew at 3.6 per cent per annum. For "middle-income" countries it grew nearly twice as fast (6.5 per cent). These rates resulted from similar increases in export volume for both groups, but from a terms-of-trade gain for one group and loss for the other. For the period 1970-80 the terms of trade for both groups rose in the early part of the decade, but have

Table 1.2
Labour force structure: developing regions, 1960-80 (in percentage)

Group	Agriculture 1960	Agriculture 1980	Industry 1960	Industry 1980	Services 1960	Services 1980
All developing countries	72.6	59.1	12.8	19.9	14.5	21.0
Latin America and Caribbean (low-income countries)	63.5	49.3	14.8	19.8	21.7	30.9
Latin America and Caribbean (middle-income countries)	45.6	31.8	20.7	25.8	33.6	42.4
China	74.8	60.0	15.4	25.8	9.8	14.2
India	74.0	62.2	11.3	17.2	14.7	20.6
Asia (other low-income countries)	76.4	65.5	8.1	11.8	15.5	22.7
Asia (middle-income countries)	68.0	52.5	12.2	19.4	19.8	28.1
Africa and Middle East (low-income countries)	87.6	80.0	5.1	8.6	7.3	11.4
Africa and Middle East (middle-income countries)	69.8	55.6	12.2	19.0	18.0	25.4
Africa and Middle East (capital surplus oil producers)	68.8	51.8	11.2	18.3	20.0	29.9

Source: Figures for 1960: ILO: *Labour force estimates and projections* (Geneva, 1977). Figures for 1980 were estimated on the basis of the trends for 1960 to 1970 at country level.

5

been falling badly since 1979. However, while the volume of exports from middle-income countries expanded at the same rate as before, that for the poorest countries rose by a mere 16 per cent in ten years. The oil prices naturally hit most developing countries both directly through their own needs for petroleum products and indirectly (and probably more severely) by the slow-down of growth in OECD countries.

Consequently, exports from the poorest developing countries have been able to buy only a volume of exports which has steadily diminished in relation to income per capita. Furthermore, the industrialised Western countries have considerably reduced their demand for Third World agricultural products and minerals. Western consumption of tropical foods and beverages and of agricultural raw materials such as jute, cotton and rubber fell during the 1970s, though it is not really known whether this was caused primarily by a slow-down in the growth of Western economies, by an increase in their self-sufficiency or by supply problems in some developing countries.

The recession at the beginning of the 1980s has had serious consequences for the developing countries. First, it has intensified their balance-of-payments problems. While apparently they share this fate with the developed countries, in fact their export prices have been weakening quickly. Export earnings are thus decreasing rapidly owing to both lower prices and a lower export volume. Secondly, the debt and repayment position of most developing countries is rapidly becoming critical. As interest rates rise, old debts become expensive to service and new loans almost impossible. Thirdly, there is an unmistakable tendency for protection to increase in the industrialised countries. Developing countries, largely because of their limited power of retaliation, have been the victims. Fourthly, the recession has led to a change of attitude in the industrialised countries. Governments feel forced to attend more to national problems and the importance given to North-South issues is decreasing accordingly.

Whether a country can finance its current account deficit determines the extent to which its imports can exceed its exports. Three inflows have traditionally filled this gap: direct investment, loans and aid. A fourth source has also become important: remittances from workers employed abroad. The solution to problems of external finance tends to depend heavily on each country's level of development and past experiences. Unfortunately, there is a tendency for both success and failure to become cumulative.

The poorest countries in fact depend heavily on aid. The World Bank estimates that in 1978 aid inflows for the poorest countries provided about 60 per cent of all external finance (i.e. net capital inflows plus workers' remittances). In contrast, for all middle-income oil exporters, official development assistance accounted for little over 10 per cent of external finance in 1978. These countries have become ever more dependent on commercial loans. In many of them the first oil crisis suddenly and considerably reduced their foreign exchange resources, jeopardising their investment plans and putting jobs at risk. Many then borrowed their way out of trouble, helped by commercial banks recycling OPEC funds. This allowed growth to continue but debts and debt-servicing costs (yearly interest plus repayments) have increased tremendously. The total outstanding debt of developing countries was about US$460,000 million in 1980, of which US$280,000 million was owed to private commercial lenders. For 1981 the total outstanding debt was estimated at US$520,000 million and annual repayment and annual repayment and interest obligations by the end of 1981 at US$110,000 million, equal to almost one-quarter of developing countries' export earnings.

Debts are concentrated among the middle-income oil importers (such as Brazil) and some oil exporters (such as Mexico). Countries with the highest debts are not the worst off. The poorest countries on the whole have borrowed little, but even relatively small repayments can cause serious problems since their capacity to generate foreign exchange is so limited. In many low-income countries imports have already been cut to the bone and further austerity measures are hardly possible without long-term damage to their economies. A further limitation on food imports, essential spare parts and industrial inputs would lead both to higher prices for consumer goods and thus a fall in real incomes and to capacity underutilisation in industry and a subsequent contraction in employment levels.

The evolution of employment and anti-poverty policies

In the 1950s and 1960s the main problem perceived by economic policy-makers was to maximise the rate of growth of output. Efforts were made to stimulate the high productivity and modern industrial sector, assuming that it would absorb surplus labour from rural areas within a reasonable period. Lower income groups were expected to benefit from faster economic growth through their gradual incorporation into the mainstream of economic development. By the end of the 1960s, however, it was becoming clear that this pattern of development was not having the desired effects. Despite high rates of growth of industrial production and continued general economic growth, too much of the labour force remained in low-productivity and low-income employment. The benefits of growth were not being widely spread to the lower-income groups.

The extent of the problem is only partially shown by available indicators of open unemployment. Aggregate data are given in table 1.3 and show an average figure of 6 per cent in 1980 for the whole developing world, excluding China. Some unemployment rates, particularly in countries with a great deal of wage employment, had reached high levels in the early 1960s, as in Sri Lanka and some Caribbean countries. And, indeed, where rates were high in the 1960s, they have generally remained so. In most countries, however, recorded unemployment has been far higher for urban than for rural areas, higher for the young than for the old and frequently higher for the better educated (secondary school and university graduates) than for those who have never completed primary education. This fits a pattern where it might be thought that the incidence of open unemployment responds to the perceived range of job opportunities. Nevertheless, it is also true that, for males at least, the picture in South Asia is that school-leaving children from poor families are more at risk from unemployment than those from better-off groups.

Table 1.3

Open unemployment: developing regions, percentage of labour force

Group	Total	Male	Female
All developing countries	6.0[a]	5.2[a]	7.8[a]
Latin America and Caribbean (low-income countries)	8.1	7.4	10.3
Latin America and Caribbean (middle-income countries)	5.6	7.8	8.4
China	..	..	..
India	4.6	3.3	7.3
Asia (other low-income countries)	4.5	2.3	10.2
Asia (middle-income countries)	3.4	3.4	3.4
Africa and Middle East (low-income countries)	14.8	15.9	12.6
Africa and Middle East (middle-income countries)	7.7	4.7	8.7
Africa and Middle East (capital surplus oil producers)	5.4	6.1	4.0

.. = not available.

[a] Excluding China.

Source: ILO Bureau of Statistics (estimated on the basis of replies from 61 countries to a special survey conducted by the ILO in 1980).

In Latin America the statistical series of unemployment rates available show no particular pattern over time. In only five out of 14 countries did rates rise unequivocally. The unweighted average for all these countries rose slightly, from 3.4 per cent in 1950 to 3.9 per cent in 1980.

These concepts and statistics clearly say very little about the underutilisation of labour. Over the past decade increased attention has therefore been paid to pinpointing the facts more closely through the use of a different analytical framework concentrating on problems of poverty and income inequality.

While it is frequently difficult to determine in which direction the share of a given population in poverty, or the absolute number of the poor, has moved, there is no doubt that poverty is widespread, and not only in the apparently poorest countries. Economic growth is not a simple process by which the fruits of development are equitably spread. In a number of Asian countries, such as India, the share of population below a given poverty line has fluctuated but shown no long-term tendency to fall, while in others, such as Bangladesh, there is probably a long-term tendency for poverty to increase. In Africa south of the Sahara the income position of the rural poor has almost certainly deteriorated since agricultural growth has experienced a marked deceleration, in the context of considerable inequality in land use and ownership. And in Latin America the share of the population in poverty certainly remains high, although in some Latin American countries – as in certain South-East Asian countries – high growth and improved income distribution have led to a considerable reduction of poverty.

In a search for more direct approaches for promoting employment and combating poverty, throughout the 1970s the ILO organised several employment missions, each of which stressed the need for a co-ordinated attack on poverty and unemployment. Without underestimating the usefulness of such measures as public works programmes, they showed that levels of poverty and unemployment are the end result of a host of economic and social relationships and political decisions. Often measures such as agrarian reform, exchange and interest rate policy, etc., though not directly aimed at alleviating unemployment and poverty, can be more important than conventional direct measures. In short, employment promotion and poverty alleviation are part of the whole process of economic development.

These ILO missions encompassed a wide range of issues but, precisely because of this, implementation of their recommendations was not always easy, often because they included changing some of the fundamental assumptions on which development policies are based.

A recent ILO report, commenting on the implementation of the 1972 mission to Kenya, observes:

". . . While it is true that many of the ILO reports' recommendations were implemented, implementation was distinctly selective. Some of the measures taken are perhaps surprising in the extent to which they confront vested interests (e.g. the capital gains tax, taxation of luxury goods, abolition of investment allowance), but on the whole measures implying structural upheaval, such as planned ceilings and redistribution, land tax and a freeze on the incomes of the higher paid, have been avoided. The problem is that the ILO strategy, while perhaps not constituting a totally indivisible package, contains a *core* of mutually reinforcing recommendations. In particular, the recommendations on the structure of rewards, land policy, technology, protection, the informal sector and education seem to be closely linked to each other."

The conclusion to be drawn is that far more recognition must be given to the forces which impede the achievement of equitable growth and, by extension, to means of overcoming these obstacles. Post-war thinking on economic development largely failed to take into account the widespread and substantial wage and income differentials both within and between economic sectors, between people with different education levels, from different ethnic backgrounds, etc. Explanations of the distribution of employment incomes have come to call more and more on "institutional features" rather than on the operation of market forces.

The behaviour of employment in the course of economic development is very closely bound up with the shape and pattern of the growth of output and the means by which this increase in output is distributed. As growth proceeds, certain factors of production, i.e. financial capital, human skills, access to fertile land and use of foreign exchange, become critical. Not surprisingly, those who control the use of these factors are those who benefit primarily from growth. Others benefit only indirectly through a secondary demand for the goods and services they can supply. At critical points in development a new key resource becomes important and the pattern of the distribution of employment incomes changes.

However, it is probably a mistake to view processes of growth as solely sequential. In primitive peasant communities with ample land widely distributed, labour itself maybe the scarce resource. If land becomes scarce, or is rendered scarce by political action, then control of land becomes crucial. This may lead to "feudal" forms of labour exploitation with a subsistence labour class subservient to a land-based élite. This pattern may then either disappear or become modernised with a country's partial integration into the world economy. Later, the promotion of urban industrial development singles out a capital accumulation as the essential factor. This process may well be accompanied by large capital inflows from abroad. But these are not separate stages in development. Access to capital and foreign exchange may be crucial in urban industrial development at the same time as "feudal" forces determine the pattern of agricultural growth.

The various processes at work in development can best be illustrated by some country examples. A first one is that of countries which underwent a structural reform in agriculture, such as the Republic of Korea or China. In Korea a first step was to transform tenurial conditions and redistribute land. This was followed by technological and institutional innovations that raised productivity. Then a massive investment was made in primary education to achieve universal education in rural areas, later followed by an expansion of secondary and university education. Korea thus found itself with an abundance of highly educated human resources, though it had no natural resources to speak of. An acceleration of growth could therefore be based only on labour-intensive industrialisation. At first this was oriented towards import substitution; because of the earlier rural development, internal markets had already been created. By the late 1960s, however, import substitution possibilities were exhausted, and there was a shift

towards export-oriented, labour-intensive development. That effort, which also depended on large foreign capital inflows, was successful as regards both growth and distribution.

Chinese development strategy has been shaped by two major constraints: an extreme shortage of arable land in relation to population and isolation from the mainstream of world technological developments. The Chinese response to these constraints has been twofold. Following an initial phase of property redistribution, poverty reduction – mainly through rural development and the provision of basic social services, but also through food security by means of large-scale food transfers – has been based largely on local resources and initiative, with a strong emphasis on economy and technical improvisation. Communes have established some industries in rural areas but industrialisation has been based primarily on centrally mobilised resources, using mainly technologies developed in the 1950s. Through the initial distribution of assets and by controlling to some extent the distribution of the gains from productivity, China has achieved a per capita growth rate which is probably significantly above the average for other low-income countries.

A large country which followed a different policy option is Brazil. The bulk of Brazil's development effort was put into the modern, urban sector and exports were seen as an immediate panacea. No initial distribution of income and asssets in rural areas took place, nor were human resources equally developed. This model has resulted in a substantial per capita growth rate but the benefits of growth have been very uneven among sectors, regions and urban and rural locations and certainly among households. As a result, large differences in economic welfare among population groups still exist.

While simplified, the idea of a critical constraint to explain the pattern of labour use and poverty at different levels of productivity and industrialisation is helpful in understanding change. But it is also helpful in formulating policy, for the extent to which ownership of the critical resource is concentrated can be the most important single factor in determining levels of poverty in the longer term.

To understand in detail how employment and incomes are determined requires an analysis of particular patterns of development. It is within a particular development process that labour market structures determine the level of labour utilisation and poverty. Such an analysis will be given in the following parts.

Processes in agriculture

This section will review trends in rural and, above all, agricultural employment in recent years against a background of increasing commercialisation in agriculture – i.e. sales of both edible and non-edible crops on foreign and domestic markets – and of increasing modernisation in farming techniques and the sophistication of agricultural inputs available. The effects of these phenomena on the employment of the rural poor and on the levels of living that employment can bring them will be examined.

Employment and unemployment in rural areas

The nature of employment in rural areas is very diverse. In the statistics, self-employment and unpaid family worker categories are both important. But these categories are not simple groupings. The employment conditions of the self-employed and to a large extent of their family members depend mainly on their access to land and their consequent security and ability to survive inevitable crop and market failures. Both the amount of land farmed in relation to family responsibilities and the degree of ownership are crucial. Tenants may well be unable to renew their

lease and have to forfeit any claim to the land they farm. Self-employed peasants practising shifting cultivation on customary land (or frequently squatting on state land) have, of course, no realisable land assets and may be forced to forfeit tools, equipment or seed grain.

The self-employed can also be grouped in terms of their participation in wage employment for others. At peak seasons some kind of exchange labour was historically common in communities of small farmers. However, as differentiation has proceeded, wage labour has come to predominate. This is the case of full-time wage labour on large farms and plantations: in some "modern style" plantations conditions of work may indeed be up to common urban standards. Elsewhere plantation labour may be isolated geographically and ethnically and work under conditions of extreme discrimination. Pure wage labour is also a village phenomenon, although the range runs from the entirely landless labourer to labourers with below subsistence landholding (or indeed minor handicraft activities). Paradoxically, labourers owning minor capital assets may find themselves less mobile and less able to take advantage of full-time work offered (see box 1.4). The experience of India, for example, suggests that fully landless workers may frequently be paid a higher daily wage than the semi-landless. Nevertheless, ownership of something, perhaps of a cow and grazing rights, should give rural workers the slight amount of independence needed to escape from the most feudal and onerous labour conditions. In many developing areas the employment link of labourer to farmer is paralleled by relations of social hierarchy and dependence.

In these circumstances, data on rural unemployment cannot be expected to indicate accurately changes in rural employment. The rural unemployment rates published are certainly generally low and fairly stable. Unfortunately, little can be read from them. Rural underemployment has, of course, been frequently measured according to seasonal fluctuations (which may be

1.4

The changing pattern of labour underutilisation and poverty in rural Egypt

In rural Egypt the pattern of distribution of landholdings seems to be moving towards increased inequality, with subdivisions at the bottom of the landholding distribution and the reappearance of large landholdings at the top. This pattern of landholding has important implications for employment generation. Smallholdings act as a "trap" for family labour, where male workers tend to be "locked in" to service these small areas without, however, being fully employed. Data generated by the farm management survey carried out in 1977 show that, on an average, the head of the family works about 90 days a year, which means that he is employed for one-third of his time. It may appear paradoxical that such a situation exists where underemployment coincides with rising agricultural wage rates. One possible explanation is that family labour is usually reserved for the family farm, especially during the peak season. Thus, while adult males remain idle during the slack season, they are fully employed during the peak season and therefore cannot be hired out for work on other farms. By contrast, adult females appear to be occupied the year round since livestock care is almost exclusively a female occupation and the livestock intensity is high on small farms.

Some features of the Egyptian rural labour market are very recent. Prominent among these are the effects of the tight labour market on increased rural wages, leading to an improvement in the lot of wage earners over the past five years. This improvement, though limited to wage labourers who account for 12 per cent of the total rural labour force or 24 per cent of the agricultural labour force, has raised the standard of living of at least a part of the landless labourers. These changes have affected the nature of the poverty groups. Wage earners are no longer the "poorest of the rural poor". Poor households are now those with no, or little, diversity of income sources. For instance, a very small farmer with a migrant member in one of the Gulf States may be better off. It appears therefore that, apart from the disabled and the old, the poor are those "locked in" in very small farms and those working in the low-productivity tertiary sector in the village.

considerable), the theoretically possible labour displacement from agriculture (which is usually irrelevant) and earnings (which are low). Low earnings are an immediate indicator of conditions of employment, to which should be added indicators of the development of employment, including changes in landlessness (or the share of the wage labour force in the total); access to land in terms of *(a)* concentration (i.e. of unequal distribution) and *(b)* fragmentation; and finally, changes in rural wage rates.

It is important to consider these variables together. A rise in landlessness, for example, needs to be evaluated in the light of real wage changes and changes in land fragmentation (since fragmentation may be the consequence either of land deprivation or of a voluntary relinquishment of an uneconomical smallholding). Some data must be interpreted with great caution. A high degree of land concentration may reflect a dualistic (plantation/small farm) pattern of development, while a low level of concentration of operated holdings may mask a high level of concentration of owned holdings.

Data on changes in the extent of paid labour in the agricultural labour force over time are not available for all countries. The share of wage employment rose in ten of the 27 countries on which some information is available for the early to mid-1960s and the early to mid-1970s (see table 1.4). It changed quite drastically, for example, in Egypt, where it rose to nearly 50 per cent in 1976 (from 35 per cent in 1960) and in the Philippines, where it rose to 17 per cent in 1975 (from 11 per cent in 1960). In Asia the pattern was extremely mixed, with a rise in the share in India, Indonesia and Thailand and a fall in Sri Lanka (caused by a drop in the importance of plantation agriculture) and Pakistan and, very slightly, in the Republic of Korea. The share increased in both Morocco and Egypt but fell in Algeria.

In nine of the 15 Latin American countries in the example, the share of agricultural wage employment actually fell. Admittedly, in Latin American countries the incidence of landlessness is generally higher than elsewhere, which is a reflection of the importance of large-scale plantation agriculture in their agrarian structures. It is difficult to give an

Table 1.4
The share of wage labour in agriculture

Country	Year	%	Year	%
Argentina	1960	50.0	1970	53.2
Bolivia	1950	10.0	1976	11.7
Brazil	1960	25.5	1970	25.4
Costa Rica	1963	52.8	1973	59.7
Chile	1960	67.0	1970	61.8
Dominican Republic	1960	24.6	1970	29.7
Ecuador	1962	39.9	1974	36.7
El Salvador	1961	63.8	1971	47.4
Honduras	1961	27.5	1974	29.0
Mexico	1960	53.6	1970	50.0
Nicaragua	1963	48.1	1971	45.7
Panama	1960	15.5	1970	20.8
Peru	1961	31.0	1972	22.3
Uruguay	1962	53.6	1975	50.8
Venezuela	1961	33.0	1971	27.7
Algeria	1966	59.3	1977	48.3
Egypt	1960	34.7	1976	49.9
Morocco	1960	19.9	1971	21.1
India	1961	23.1	1971	36.5
Indonesia	1964	20.3	1971	23.6
Iran	1960	25.2	1976	18.6
Republic of Korea	1966	9.7	1975	9.1
Pakistan	1961	14.0	1976	8.0
Philippines	1960	11.1	1975	17.1
Sri Lanka	1963	54.8	1971	51.0
Syria	1960	37.5	1970	18.6
Thailand	1960	3.1	1970	4.1

Source: ILO: *Year Book of Labour Statistics* (Geneva, 1977, 1982).

sector is not generating sufficient employment to absorb the growing labour force, even allowing for rural-urban movement. This slow growth in modern agricultural employment puts pressure on the land resources of the peasant. As will be seen below, it is largely due to the spread of labour-saving mechanisation.

The information available shows that, from 1960 to 1970, the concentration of landholdings in Asia increased in India and Bangladesh and remained fairly stable elsewhere. An increased degree of concentration is compatible with a movement both towards the consolidation of middle-sized into larger holdings by modernising farmers' methods and towards increasing fragmentation and a spread of mini-holdings among the poor. In India the trend towards consolidation has been definitely shown in surveys. As regards the second trend, the share of farms under 1 hectare in size in fact increased in Bangladesh, India and the Philippines. The share had already reached 70 per cent in Indonesia in 1963. In the Republic of Korea it declined as, presumably, very small holdings were gradually consolidated.

In Latin America measures of land concentration are consistently much higher than elsewhere. Furthermore, they increased in Costa Rica, the Dominican Republic, Honduras, Nicaragua and Panama, of the eight countries for which clear data are available. The little information available for sub-Saharan Africa shows that, contrary to general belief, the concentration of land is as high as in most of Asia. High degrees of concentration may well be a feature of areas of export crop production, but a significant extent of differentiation seems present everywhere.

This picture of employment in agriculture gives no grounds for optimism. There seems rather to have been an increase in landlessness for negative reasons, i.e. workers pushed out of the smallholding sector to find village wage employment in some countries like Indonesia, while in Latin America labour is pushed from the

unambiguous interpretation to any trend in landlessness in these countries. A fall in landlessness may be caused by a relative contraction in plantation employment. Indeed, it seems that in most Latin American countries peasant employment has expanded faster than full-time wage employment (although casual wage employment as a source of income is increasing). However, in most Latin American countries the average size of smallholdings has clearly diminished and employment conditions in peasant agriculture have almost certainly worsened. The modern agricultural mechanising and labour-saving large farm sector into smallholdings. There is evidence of land fragmentation, not in any equalising sense, but in a way compatible with the continuation or even increase in the number of large holdings.

Low per capita agricultural output

Agricultural output per capita has experienced positive but halting rates of growth since 1960. Indeed it would appear that inequality in assets and incomes works to slow down agricultural growth. Growth in per capita agricultural output and in food production has been uniformly well below growth in overall GNP per capita. For the World Bank's low-income economies, growth in agriculture per capita from 1960 to 1970 was at 0.1 per cent. The same rate continued from 1970 to 1980. For the "middle-income" countries rates were somewhat higher, 1.0 per cent and 0.5 per cent. Such rates are low and give little opportunity to increase average consumption of agricultural products. Furthermore, out of 43 developing countries for which data exist, per capita agricultural growth from 1962 to 1970 was zero or negative for 13. From 1970 to 1980 it was zero or negative for as many as 30 out of 67 developing countries (in 20 other countries the rate was between zero and one). Clearly, the scope for rural employment to be stimulated by any increase in the physical volume of agricultural output has been negligible in very large parts of the developing world. Africa is perhaps the best known region in this respect: throughout the 1970s per capita agricultural growth was negative in the vast majority of sub-Saharan African countries.

In Africa there are two corollaries of this poor growth record. First, by the end of the 1970s food aid imports to low-income countries amounted to over 5 kilograms of grain per person per year, while grain imports increased at over 10 per cent annually throughout the decade. Secondly, in virtually every country in Africa domestic food prices increased more quickly during the 1970s than the price of basic manufactures (e.g. clo-

thing). The relative profitability of export crops may thus have fallen and been a factor accounting for the lower volume of virtually all African agricultural exports.

The faster rise in food prices than in clothing prices by the end of 1970s has also applied virtually across the board in Latin America (Mexico, Peru and Venezuela seem to be the only exceptions out of 16 countries for which the ILO has information). In Asia, however, the pattern is more mixed. Out of the nine countries for which information is at hand, in three – India, Bangladesh and the Philippines – prices of manufactures rose faster than food prices, which indicates a more satisfactory rate of agricultural growth. Nevertheless, there seems no doubt that Third World food output in general has apparently kept up with a constant volume of demand and has certainly not kept up with the increase in demand which might have been expected to accompany even a minor increase in average incomes or a redistribution of consumption towards the poor.

Rural poverty

The FAO has estimated the share of persons suffering from undernourishment in the total population of 24 African countries: the share in rural areas is certainly the highest. In 1972-74 it reached a high of 54 per cent for Chad, but was no less than 30 per cent for Kenya, where it had apparently risen over the previous three years. Only for the Ivory Coast (8 per cent in 1972-74) was the share less than 10 per cent. Food shortages in Africa are widespread even in relatively well-endowed regions and those with a history of cash cropping. In addition, the incomes of over half of the rural population frequently impose consumption patterns which in any society would be considered unacceptable, including a predominance of starchy foods.

In Latin America even calculations using a conservative "subsistence" poverty line based on the cost of a minimal diet show that one-third of the

13

1.5

Rural poverty in Bangladesh, Thailand and West Bengal

An ILO regional team has investigated the nature and extent of rural poverty in a number of Asian countries. Some of the results are given here.

In Bangladesh a major feature of rural poverty is the high degree of landlessness, estimated at 26 per cent of the total labour force in 1977. In addition to this group, another 11 per cent is almost totally dependent on wage labour. Changes in the poverty level of this group can be charted through information on daily wages which, in real terms, were lower at the end of 1970s than they had been 30 years earlier. Real wages were determined mainly by a long-term trend of increasing pressure on the land and a fall in agricultural output per worker. However, this trend was interrupted by upward fluctuations in output per hectare and by shifts in the internal terms of trade in favour of agriculture. The positive "trickle-down" effects resulting from output growth and favourable price changes were insufficient (adding on an average some 1.7 per cent to average wages annually) to combat the trend effect, which decreased wages by over 2 per cent annually.

In Thailand the trend in rural poverty has been downwards. Thailand is, however, a special case in that output growth in agriculture has come far more from expansion of the cultivated area

than from higher yields, since the rural poor have been able to open up farms on the land frontier. Rural wages also grew in real terms in the late 1970s, a phenomenon which does not seem to be due merely to growth in output per worker, which was a continuing feature, but to a shift in relative prices in favour of agriculture and away from other economic activities.

In West Bengal, where landlessness is also widespread, real wages increased fairly steadily during the late 1970s, despite increasingly unfavourable land-man ratios. The real wage increases followed a better agricultural performance. However, there were also found to be the positive effects of *(a)* official protection of the rights of over 1 million share-croppers (Operation Barga), previously tenants-at-will, *(b)* the distribution of nearly 300,000 hectares of land to 1.28 million beneficiaries, half of whom belonged to scheduled tribes and castes, and *(c)* the over 50 million work-days of employment that were created by public works schemes, averaging over 15 days of employment per agricltrual worker annually. From this example, the ILO team concludes that both output growth and structural reform are necessary to prevent declining income levels in a rural society characterised by poverty and inequality.

---

rural population lives in poverty. Such an extent of poverty (affected of course by the relatively high proportion and numbers of poor in Brazil) in a subcontinent with generally high average income levels points to the ineffectiveness of "trickle down" as a means of distributing the benefits of growth. Lastly, rural poverty in Asia affects an extremely high proportion of the population, over 50 per cent in India according to official estimates, and comparable shares elsewhere.

In countries such as India, most of the rural poor belong to the following categories: agricultural households without land, or only a small amount of land; "other" rural households (i.e. engaged in small-scale handicrafts); and farmers with very small holdings. Landless labour households normally have the lowest per capita incomes of any rural group; in the early 1960s they accounted for some 20 per cent of all rural households. Households relying on labour outside agriculture accounted for another 5 per cent. Families operat-

ing small holdings are a less homogeneous group. In the early 1960s the 58 per cent of land operating households that farmed under 1 hectare held only 7 per cent of the total land area and fell mostly below the poverty line. However, the same households had 11 per cent of the irrigated land and 27 per cent of the milk cattle. In contrast to this picture of rural poverty, in Chile it was found that 51 per cent of rural workers on large farms, 84 per cent of workers on "medium" to "large" farms and 63 per cent of smallholders and peasants fell below the poverty line. Some information on rural poverty in three Asian countries is given in box 1.5.

This, then, is the overall picture: high and continuing levels of rural poverty; highly unequal access to land; slow rates of labour absorption in the large farm sector; and extremely unevenly distributed rates of growth of output. In these circumstances, what are the effects on employment when agriculture is opened up to trade and is modernised?

Commercialisation of agriculture and employment

Commercialisation has definitely increased, at least for three reasons: *(a)* the need to supply urban demand for foodstuffs, fibres, etc.; *(b)* greater trade and specialisation within rural areas; and *(c)* increasing exports of food and agricultural raw materials. Only the last two of these can be quantified. In the 1960s the volume of exports from developing countries of the two groups, food and agricultural raw materials, rose by 3.5 and 3.8 per cent annually. In the 1970s the rates dropped to 1.1 and 0.6 per cent respectively.

It is difficult to say whether the process of commercialisation world-wide has increased faster in recent years than before. Africa, for instance, experienced quite considerable growth in output of a number of non-food crops in the 1960s, more than in the 1970s. Some African success stories, such as the agricultural performance of the Ivory Coast or Malawi, are based on production for export, applying well-known techniques to increased amounts of land. In some Asian countries – Thailand is the obvious example – the spread of export agriculture in recent years has been phenomenal.

In Africa the differential returns to land from producing for export or producing domestic food crops (e.g. maize or millet) are more decisive in positively affecting an area's overall income level than, for example, in Asia. Given that colonial governments frequently limited export cash cropping, the spread of export crop cultivation in recent years was bound to have a major impact on the distribution of incomes and employment. Labour demand increased in some areas which, coupled with inhospitable conditions in many regions, has encouraged labour movement even across national boundaries. The result has almost certainly increased inequality and social stratification among the peasantry. Thus in West Africa export crop production is associated with a greater degree of stratification in landholding sizes than is

domestic food production. While tree crops can, in principle, be cultivated on any holding size, in fact, because smaller cultivators also grow food crops, the bulk of exports comes from larger holdings. An extension of export agriculture is therefore likely to increase inequality.

Indeed, a dualistic pattern of agricultural development tends to emerge or to be reinforced. Even in areas where land is plentiful, as the population has increasingly gathered into settlements to use social services, so rights to neighbouring land have acquired a monetary value at a time when shifting cultivation still applies to areas farther afield. With higher population density, surplus production for the domestic market naturally increases. However, smallholder peasants have extreme difficulty in participating in this demand. Expensive and risky new techniques and inputs are required. More cash is needed to purchase inputs, and this requirement can be met only by seeking wage employment which, in turn, may conflict with home-farm employment needs. The process of commercialisation, by strengthening the needs of poorer peasants for cash in hand, may worsen the absolute position of the difficulties they face in increasing their volume of output.

Agricultural mechanisation and employment

In Latin America the extent of commercialisation is further advanced than elsewhere and the degree of dualism between the commercial, large farm sector and the smallholder, subsistence sector is extreme. However, there is scope for modernisation of the means of production to spread. A case study of the north-east of Brazil suggests that mechanisation and the increased use of tractors led to a fall in agricultural wage employment of 18 per cent over a ten-year period. Selective mechanisation can naturally extend the area under cultivation and, by reducing seasonality in labour demand, increase overall labour requirements and contribute to increased employment. It can furthermore permit double and multiple cropping. However,

15

premature mechanisation can easily result in displacing labour.

The question of mechanisation has been most often discussed from the standpoint of its implications for employment in the small farm – mainly rice growing – system in Asia. Mechanisation in this context covers the application of draught power to a number of farming operations in the fields, to threshing and to means of providing irrigation. Given the pressing need to raise levels of employment for the rural poor, in terms both of days worked and of wages paid, the impact of mechanisation can be crucial. In principle, the use of appropriate mechanised methods and of modern inputs such as fertilisers and pesticides can strengthen the differential edge which small farms generally enjoy over large farms in providing productive employment per unit of land. In addition, there is evidence that returns to scale in modernised wheat growing (in South Asia) are constant, and in paddy cultivation in fact decrease with holding size. However, it is larger rather than smaller farms which have benefited most from the introduction of modern and mechanised techniques. Larger farmers are not only more willing to take risks but generally have far easier access to credit. Furthermore, investment, for example, in a tubewell, which would require collective action by a number of smaller farmers, may well make sense for one larger farmer acting alone.

As a result, the benefits which modernisation and mechanisation could provide for employment have not materialised. Furthermore, inappropriate pricing policies for agricultural inputs, leading usually to underpricing, have encouraged the premature introduction of mechanised methods, which has complicated the problem. Asian countries today are signally failing to follow the experience of East Asian countries some 40 or 50 years ago, when labour used per hectare was much higher and output per hectare was also higher. Exactly why current Asian experience is so different is not clear. The greater availability of animal power (in South Asia) may be a part of the

answer, though climatic differences may also matter. In addition, the far greater range of techniques available today and probably a different form of government intervention in promoting agriculture both play a part.

The consequences of this failure to absorb labour productivity have been severe. In countries such as Indonesia and the Philippines the share of landless households has been steadily increasing as a result of demographic pressure on available land, land loss and technological displacement. Such households come to depend gradually on employment through labour hiring for farm operations. However, new techniques, including the use of chemicals and rotary weeders and, in Java, the shift from the knife to the sickle for harvesting, have affected their employment and incomes. In the Philippines the use of hired labour in total labour per hectare has increased but the share of the landless in net income has fallen since under the "Gama" system they undertake weeding in order to preseve their right to harvest the crop, keeping a one-sixth share.

In Indonesia the use of non-village contract labour has reduced work opportunities for the landless. This decline has affected female labour most severely and even the addition of a third crop to the annual cropping cycle has apparently not made up the employment loss. It would appear that meanwhile real wages have at best remained constant, though the possibility that they have actually dropped cannot be ruled out.

Temporary or seasonal employment

There is little information to show trends in temporary or seasonal employment over time. Scattered survey evidence, however, shows that the incidence of part-time wage employment is both high and probably increasing. In Bangladesh, Brazil, Ecuador, Egypt, the Ivory Coast, Mexico and Panama it seems that a growing proportion of the rural population, and in particular of the small farm population, is engaged in such work, some of

16

1.6

Declining small farm incomes and peasant migration: the Latin American experience

In many Latin American countries incomes from small-scale farming are falling. A growing number of smallholders find it increasingly difficult to meet household expenses and are obliged to look for alternative income sources. ILO research shows that in Ecuador, the Dominican Republic, Guatemala and Panama small farm earnings have decreased in real terms from 5 to over 30 per cent since the mid-1960s. There are many reasons for this decline. First, as noted earlier, the average size of small farms has decreased as population growth has resulted in a further subdivision of small farms. Another reason is that yields of many staple crops have been falling. Increasing soil erosion, partly the result of inefficient farm techniques, has been at fault. Another factor is a relative decline in producer prices for several staple crops intended to keep food prices and the urban cost of living low.

Many smallholders thus have to look for other opportunities elsewhere. A good proportion have left their farms to settle in urban areas. Very likely this has been one of the factors that has made the rate of rural-urban migration in Latin America the highest in the developing world. Others have kept their farms but sought temporary wage work in either urban or rural areas.

Indirect evidence indicates that the temporary migration of smallholders, particularly to large farms where seasonal variation in labour demand is substantial, is now important in many parts of Latin America. In Ecuador the share of small-scale farmers temporarily employed as agricultural wage workers has more than doubled since the mid-1960s. Temporary migration to urban areas can also be important, depending on distance and transport. Many workers on construction sites in Latin American cities are from rural areas, and a large proportion of these come from small farm households.

Temporary migration permits some small-scale farmers to increase total earnings, but it also has negative sides. The temporary migrant is poorly housed, exploited by middlemen and highly exposed to disease. Bolivian peasants from the highlands who migrate to the lowlands to pick cotton have a much higher incidence of climate-related disease than other workers in the cotton fields. The same susceptibility was noticed among Sierra peasants who migrated to the coastal city of Guayaquil (Ecuador) to work on construction sites. Moreover, an increasing reliance on wage income does not necessarily imply a higher standard of living. In Peru peasant farmers with a high proportion of wage income are considerably more undernourished than those relying more on farm revenues with a large element of subsistence production.

which may be provided by governments through public works schemes. Given the varied agrarian structure of these particular countries, it is certainly likely that the same applies elsewhere. However, it is doubtful that such casual employment has served to increase the incomes of these households, particularly if it follows a decline in the extent and profitability of small-scale farming. In Latin America it has been found that large farm owners have been using part-time employment as a substitute for full-time workers. It has also been found that incomes from temporary wage employment serve only to compensate for the dwindling income from small-scale farming (see box 1.6).

Rural employment crisis

The analysis can be summarised as follows. There is a widespread rural employment crisis in the developing world. Output growth rates have been constrained by institutional factors including unequal access to land and, in its turn, sluggish growth has often strengthened those very factors making for labour segmentation and social stratification. Growth alone cannot solve rural poverty. For growth to "trickle down" to poorer groups, certain preconditions are necessary. These were met in the past by such countries as the Republic of Korea and Japan. In most countries at present they are absent and there is a risk that growth will result in "marginalising" the mass of smallholders and labourers and benefit primarily the middle and larger commercial farmers. The transition in many parts of Africa from the customary land tenure system to commercial agriculture with large technological differences between the two seems to be having just this effect. Government policies favour the more progressive farmer; productivity in the smallholding sector declines, food production falls and labour migrates to urban areas or abroad in search of jobs.

When the supply of food increases too slowly in an economy characterised by unequal access to land, the forces of dualism are inevitably strengthened. Where demand exceeds supply, prices will rise and the effective demand for food of wage-earning and food-deficit farming households will fall. Furthermore, higher food prices favour the profitability of commercial farming and hence the consolidation of small into large holdings accompanied by tenant eviction. The supply of potential wage labour increases faster than the demand. In this context premature mechanisation may also reduce employment opportunities and earnings for the landless. Surplus producers, however, benefit directly from higher prices and indirectly from the inability of wage costs to keep up with output prices. Equilibrium is then achieved by a number of pressures working together to worsen the employment conditions and lower the food consumption of the poor. However, again in such an economy, higher food prices may be a necessary ingredient for stimulating output growth, which in turn should raise employment levels. The answer to the question whether the poor lose more from higher prices than they gain from increased employment may well vary. At all events, the beneficial effects of high food prices will be equitably shared throughout rural areas only if the critical variable, land, is more fairly distributed.

That the predominant socio-economic system in rural areas will aggravate the current rural employment crisis is evident. That it has not succeeded in achieving a fast rate of growth of agricultural output is also evident.

Processes in industrialisation

Manufacturing and employment

It has already been noted that industrialisation is rarely a major employment generator in the developing countries. Manufacturing, furthermore, which is the major component of the general industrial sector (along with mining and construc-

tion), accounts for about two-thirds of total employment in industry. The analysis here is concerned mainly with manufacturing. Within manufacturing the dominant form of employment is wage labour. This is not to overlook self-employment and the use of family workers. In India household-based industry in 1971 accounted for over half of rural manufacturing employment and nearly 20 per cent of urban manufacturing employment.

Not only may manufacturing itself often create little employment but a poorly conceived and implemented manufacturing policy may affect employment conditions adversely elsewhere in the economy. Any economic sector, if mishandled, can of course spoil employment opportunities elsewhere through, for example, the inadequate provision of transport or the creation of food scarcity. However, manufacturing has attracted considerable investment funds and mistakes may well be costly.

Despite the predominance of the wage mode of employment in manufacturing, workers' wage and income levels vary greatly. Human capital is often significant in determining income levels, with young, poorly educated women at one end of the scale and older, more experienced and better educated men at the other. In some countries vast wage differences between manual and white-collar occupations have survived from colonial days. In addition, the capital intensity of the manufacturing process (and hence the share of wages in total value added) often directly affects wage levels. Thus wages in food processing and textiles are generally far below those in chemical and petroleum industries or iron and steel. As industrialisation proceeds, the internal balance and structure of the manufacturing sector changes. Evidence from a number of countries shows that the highest rates of output growth have come in the production of capital and consumer durable goods, the lowest in consumer non-durable goods. Such growth rates respond, of course, to market demand: they by no means imply that the desire of the poor for consumer goods is satisfied. High rates of output growth frequently imply high rates of growth of productivity and their effects on employment may therefore be mitigated.

According to the World Bank estimates, employment in industry (and presumably also manufacturing employment) grew at about 4.8 per cent per annum for the period 1960-80 in the low-income developing countries and at a somewhat lower rate, 4.1 per cent, in the middle-income countries. In India, however, the rate was only 2.5 per cent. Industrial output in fact grew somewhat faster in the second group of countries, some 7 per cent per annum as against 4.3 per cent. The faster rate of employment growth in the poorer countries is no doubt a result of an expansion of output concentrated mainly in low-productivity consumer goods industries.

The share of manufacturing employment located in rural areas is often more than half the national total. It is estimated that 86 per cent of manufacturing employment is in rural areas in Sierra Leone, 70 per cent in Bangladesh, 63 per cent in Malaysia, 50 per cent in Pakistan, 57 per cent in India, 75 per cent in Sri Lanka and 87 per cent in Indonesia. Some rural manufacturing is of a simple handicraft nature, producing pots, baskets or sun-dried bricks for local demand. Such activities may well be at considerable risk from competition from larger enterprises with more standardised quality, and may survive solely because their clientele is too poor to afford competing products. Other activities are rural-based because they are more or less tied to the location of raw materials: food processing, including grain milling, and brick making are examples. These activities include so-called agro-based industries responding to the extent and diversity of crop production. Other activities again may include handlooms and similar production intended for nation-wide and foreign sale and organised through a network of inter-mediaries. Here low wages are frequent. Another set of activities corresponds to higher rural incomes, e.g. repair of agricultural machinery and

---

1.7

The putting-out system

There is a large workforce of women, men and children making products in their homes for outside markets. These workers are seldom organised, nor are conditions of work regulated. Where such workers are dependent on contractors working under the putting-out system for materials and markets, their employment conditions must be a subject of concern.

For example, rural women rolling beedies (cheap cigarettes) and crochetting lace in India, working a full day, receive a small fraction of the minimum wage. Yet the industry's exports and its profits are flourishing.

Not only traditional items but modern products as well, such as electronics, are produced under this system. Women work in their homes (in villages or urban slums) assembling radio components and Western garments. They are integrated into the export trade and into the world economy without any company or state benefits. Children, especially girls, are kept at home to work, adding a meagre but important supplement to the family income.

The idyllic image of independent women working at home, in control of their time and labour, is far from the reality, where the contractor and his employer control the regularity and remuneration of labour, and the worker is virtually without a choice. Sometimes workers' organisations have been formed and wage or piece rates raised, but more often attempts at organisation have led to a loss of even this unsatisfactory work, since other needy households can be found to take it on, in the next village, city or country.

---

manufacturing of tools, ploughs, carts, etc. Finally, there are modern activities, as in China, created perhaps by the deliberate decentralisation of the location of small or medium-scale fertiliser, chemical, cement and other plants.

Some of these rural manufacturing activities are well placed to survive competition from more modern industrial units. They may have a natural cost advantage through their location. Others survive through "product reservation", as in much of the South Asian handloom industry, where more mechanised units are by one means or another discouraged from expanding into the markets of handloom producers. In such a situation the employment conditions of the rural weavers can at best remain constant. In other cases,

19

1.8

Multinational enterprises

Direct investment by multinational enterprises in developing countries doubled during the 1960s, contributing to industriali-sation and employment. However, this development affected only about a dozen economically more advanced developing countries out of the 100 or so developing countries in the world. And it should not be forgotten that 75 per cent of all foreign direct investment remains in the industrialised market economy countries. The largest share of employment generated by the activities of multinational enterprises is found in developing countries with large potential markets or an export base, important natural resources and a pool of highly trainable manpower. As in the industrialised countries, multinational enterprises are concentrated in capital- and research-intensive manufacturing.

By 1980 direct employment provided by multinational enterprises in all developing countries reached about 4 million jobs (i.e. 0.5 per cent of their total labour force, excluding China), as against some 40 million jobs in the industrialised countries. However, there are great variations according to the country. The share of multinationals in manufacturing employment ranged from a low of 2 per cent in Thailand to a high of 70 per cent in Singapore, while accounting for between 20 and 30 per cent in such countries as Brazil, Kenya, the Republic of Korea and Mexico.

The figure of 4 million jobs tells only one part of the story. There is also a spin-off effect, which is hard to calculate but significant, in terms of indirect employment generated through economic links between multinationals and local firms, as well as through increased government revenue and incomes. At the same time, however, multinationals may in some situations displace employment in local enterprises.

final products are required, along with more intermediate and capital goods to make those final products. Different products determine their own production techniques to a large extent. However, there is often a range of techniques which can produce a given product, as well as a range of goods which can serve to meet the same felt needs of the consumer. Governments can intervene to support manufacturing growth by influencing both pro-ducts and techniques. Protecting the domestic market against foreign competition may increase sales of an unchanged locally produced market. Supplying cheap capital to large enterprises is likely to change the technique used to produce any given product.

Manufacturing is pre-eminently the sector that produces tradeable and non-perishable goods. The performance of developing countries in manufac-turing is thus highly affected by the plans and the policies of developed countries in this field and by direct foreign investment (see box 1.8). The influence of developed countries' policies has recently been apparent in the increased restrictions on developing countries' exports of manufactured goods to developed countries. But it is also apparent in the continuing reliance of developing countries on imports of capital and, to a lesser extent, of consumer goods from developed coun-tries. In the future the performance of developing countries in manufacturing may be affected more and more by South-South trade, particularly when trade barriers between developing countries, which at present are often higher than between North and South, are lowered.

In terms of world production, the locus of industrial activity has changed slightly. Between 1960 and 1980 there was perhaps a shift of five percentage points in the relative shares of developed and developing countries. UNIDO estimates that for heavy manufacturing the share of the developing countries in total world value added was less than 5 per cent in 1960 but over 6 per cent by the mid-1970s. Some "semi-indus-trialised" or "newly industrialised" developing

such as the putting-out system used for a consider-able part of garment production, employment conditions, above all wages, may be forced down in order to enable the industry to survive against competition from factories. Many forms of rural manufacturing have in fact been displaced in recent times; the manufacture of brass pots in Nepal is a well-known example.

Employment in manufacturing, like employ-ment in other economic sectors which are affected by the progress of manufacturing, depends consid-erably on forms of government intervention. Manufacturing includes both products and techni-ques. As incomes rise in any economy, different countries have expanded their exports of manufactured goods rapidly, to the extent that by 1979, 13 per cent of world exports of manufactured products came from developing countries (compared with 9 per cent in 1970).

Industrialisation and development

Industrialisation has always been assigned an important role in development. But while it was once viewed as the engine of economic growth that would transform underdeveloped societies, industrialisation became the cause of considerable disillusionment when the experience of the 1950s and 1960s showed that high rates of industrial growth were consistent with rural stagnation and urban poverty. More recent experience in the 1970s, particularly that of a handful of countries in Asia, has reaffirmed the crucial importance of industrialisation. But there is now a much deeper awareness of its limitations; it is also realised how decisive is the choice of an appropriate pattern of industrial growth.

In the 1950s and 1960s industrialisation was seen as holding the key to a better life. It was associated with modernisation and technological progress; it was a means of diversifying the economy and reducing dependence on foreign manufactures. True, it was known that there were constraints to be overcome, especially the size of the market, inadequate economic and social infrastructure and the low level of entrepreneurship, management and technical skills. But it was expected that if governments were prepared to offer fiscal and other incentives and to develop supporting institutions, industrial expansion would follow. Import substitution was thus an obvious strategy for favouring domestic manufacturing.

Import substitution was easy to initiate. A national market already existed for certain products, especially the consumer goods desired by an emerging middle class. By curtailing imports through tariffs and quantitative controls, domestic production from infant industries was encouraged and investment made profitable. Such a strategy usually proved successful at the outset, but unless incomes were growing quickly the first stage inevitably slowed down when the expansion of final consumer goods reached the limit of the domestic market. Governments then had to choose either *(a)* to shift import substitution to intermediate or capital goods production or *(b)* to persuade the recently established import substitution industries to shift to export markets.

The Republic of Korea and Singapore stand out as countries which successfully introduced export promotion policies after first pursuing some degree of import substitution in protected domestic markets. Singapore went through a brief import substitution phase in the mid-1960s but this was not allowed to distort the pattern of domestic production. The Republic of Korea, which earlier had radically transformed its agrarian structure, shifted away from import substitution around 1960 and then adopted policies offering broadly the same initiatives to production for both foreign and domestic markets. In both countries the effect on the volume of manufacturing employment was great.

Four Latin American countries – Argentina, Brazil, Colombia and Mexico – are representative of the second group which carried import substitution beyond its first stage. In Brazil the share of foreign capital goods in total investment fell from 16 per cent in 1960 to 8 per cent in 1977; in Colombia it fell from 29 to 21 per cent in the same period. When extended to capital-intensive industries requiring sophisticated technology and unable to utilise their production capacity fully, import substitution, given the limited size of domestic markets, becomes increasingly costly. (However, in recent years large parts of manufacturing industry in these countries have become internationally competitive. In 1977 Mexican manufactured exports amounted to 9 per cent of manufacturing output; in Colombia the corresponding figure was 12 per cent.)

Viewed in a larger perspective, import substitution failed to mitigate the overriding problems of unemployment and underemployment and mass poverty. In fact, the policies pursued had a number of adverse effects. Although consumer goods were cut, new industries became in fact more dependent on imported parts and materials. Frequently a country's response to balance-of-payments problems became one of increasing inflexibility while foreign exchange scarcity led to capacity underutilisation and lay-offs. In addition, sectoral imbalances were aggravated as resources were diverted away from agriculture into a manufacturing sector made artifically profitable through tariffs and controls.

When a country relies on a few large-scale enterprises, wage disparities and labour market segmentation tend to increase. Furthermore, competition is reduced so that prices of manufactures tend to rise. Lastly, fiscal incentives have frequently been given readily to companies and individuals already wealthy. At a relatively low level of development, the employment effects of industrialisation cannot be large and the net effects may be negative. Myrdal's examination of industrialisation in South Asia suggests that the "spread" or expansionary effects often expected of new industries have been exaggerated. Earlier proponents of industrial development had hoped for multiplier effects that would stimulate new, often complementary, investments in the production of parts and other inputs. But in Asia, and indeed in other developing regions, obstacles and bottlenecks reduced potential spread effects at an early stage. These problems included deficiency in the supply of technical and administrative personnel as well as skilled labour, inadequate transport and power systems and the continuing need to import materials and semi-manufactured goods.

As a result of the failure of rapid industrial growth to achieve broader development objectives and to benefit the poor, agriculture and rural development, which too often had been victimised by earlier industrial strategies, have become the centre-piece of the new development orthodoxy. However, it remains evident that in many developing countries the need for ordinary final goods in poor households is still immense and that industrialisation has a great role to play. The most modern or the most capital-intensive techniques will rarely be needed to meet this need. However, while it may be clear which goods are needed by poor households, it is not easy either to increase the purchasing power of these households or to determine how to take appropriate steps to restructure the pattern of industrial output.

The role of manufacturing industry would seem to be that of choosing techniques and aiming at producing goods that maximise the use of relatively unskilled labour (subject naturally to other efficiency constraints) while at the same time producing goods that efficiently meet the needs of the poor. Most products meet certain needs but wastefully "over-fill" others. Goods may be unnecessarily packaged or in other ways needlessly differentiated from competing products. Advertising and fashion play a role in attracting consumers away from the goods which may, in fact, provide the answer to their problems at the least cost. Futhermore, it can confidently be stated that many simpler and lower-cost products are also the end result of more labour-intensive processes. Thus there exists a "virtuous circle" by which shifts in demand patterns resulting from a changed distribution of income and shifts in tastes can raise employment levels and become self-reinforcing.

Governments' role in promoting this virtuous circle is mainly to ensure that small enterprises with simple techniques of production are not disadvantaged in relation to larger and more sophisticated enterprises. In fact, the opposite has usually been the case. Larger enterprises have generally had more immediate and privileged access to finance, to foreign exchange and to the organs of governments. Smaller enterprises may have sometimes gained in a rather negative fashion by being able to avoid the most onerous and unnecessary government controls, but they have rarely been helped to expand. Governments often run programmes of support for smaller firms, including the provision of supervised credit, but, since they rarely withdraw any support from the large-scale sector, the balance remains unfavourable for small enterprises.

This relative neglect of the small-scale industrial sector has been the more unfortunate because of the large share of employment it generates, particularly in rural areas. Employment in very small industrial enterprises has been estimated to range from about 50 to 90 per cent of total manufacturing employment (including part-time work) in a number of countries. Their corresponding share of output, however, has ranged from some 20 to 45 per cent. They thus commonly have a majority of employment but a minority of output.

Small- and large-scale sectors can well work hand in hand; in ideal situations, the manufacture of certain products can be shared between them. For example, a division can be made between ploughs and tractor attachments, on the one hand, and hand tools on the other. Moreover, bending the tariff structure and imposing excise taxes can be used to stimulate the small-scale sector and at least to prevent artificial encouragement of competition from larger enterprises. However, the small-scale sector often needs direct government support. The major constraints faced by small-scale enterprises include: *(a)* rudimentary worksheds and facilities; *(b)* inadequate supply of raw materials, in both quality and quantity; *(c)* limited market size and lack of organised marketing, including both the collection of orders and the sale of finished products; and *(d)* lack of finance to improve the quality and quantity of products. The major thrust of government policies would need to focus on market promotion. Market limitations have forced small enterprises to diversify their products and to combine repair and maintenance with manufacturing (e.g. of farm machinery) and they are unwilling to experiment with any new product.

1.9

Upgrading technology in Botswana

Research and development work by the Ministry of Agriculture resulted in the design of an animal-drawn plough-mounted planter, more efficient than the traditional broadcasting methods. After extensive field trials, prototypes were supplied to the Mochudi Welders Brigade to manufacture the planter locally. The Ministry then bought this equipment (and a cultivator for weeding) from the Brigade and, under the Government's Arid Land Development Programme, made them available to some 500 small farm households who benefited from an attractive subsidy and loan package. Under the same programme donkey draught power was introduced which, in turn, stimulated the use of an improved harness made locally by the Mochudi farmers from used tyres.

Government intervention at the enterprise level has often adopted a partial approach, seeking either to provide a single missing ingredient (e.g. a market outlet) or to remove a single bottleneck (e.g. raw material shortage). Very often such intervention amounts to a partial, disjointed and uncoordinated effort scattered over different parts of the country. To have a significant and lasting impact on production capability, the whole chain of activities, including research and development, development of product prototypes, market promotion and industrial extension of manufacturers, has to be integrated and designed as a comprehensive package. Implementation should be concentrated first in a limited area and later spread throughout the country. An example of this is given in box 1.9.

The choice of technology and of products largely determines who the beneficiaries of increased incomes and employment will be. The use of animal-powered and other inexpensive but well-designed and innovative farm equipment could make an important contribution to agricultural productivity, labour use and output in eastern and central southern Africa, for example, and to output and employment among rural-based manufacturing firms. But elsewhere new products

23

have adversely affected employment and incomes in traditional activities. This happened, for example, when corrugated iron roofing replaced thatching, processed sugar replaced honey and aluminium pots replaced pottery in Kenya.

Trade and industrial strategies and employment

The policy direction pursued by several Asian countries after an initial import substitution phase has already been contrasted with the industrial strategy of a number of larger Latin American countries. Export-led industrialisation became associated with very rapid growth and high rates of labour absorption from the mid-1960s onwards in Hong Kong, the Republic of Korea and Singapore. This increase in manufactured exports was instrumental in raising wages in those countries and generating full employment. Are these achievements replicable elsewhere in the Third World? What lessons can be drawn from their experience?

Most accounts begin by stressing the labour intensity and efficient resource use associated with the countries' export performance. In Singapore the ratio of the growth rate of employment to the growth rate of output rose from 0.29 in 1957-66 to 0.55 between 1970 and 1974. Clearly the openness of the economy resulted in a far more labour-absorbing growth path than hitherto. Simultaneously Singapore placed considerable emphasis on the expansion of primary and secondary education, followed by increasing attention to vocational, technical and professional training in the late 1960s. This paved the way for movement into industries relying less on cheap labour and more on a generalised level of skill. In Singapore and Hong Kong there was little rural hinterland to generate a constant stream of rural-urban migrants to provide cheap labour and hold down wages. In the Republic of Korea, where there was such a hinterland, radical agrarian policies had made sure that the worst rural poverty had already been eradicated.

The part played by foreign investment in stimulating manufactured exports varied considerably. In Singapore it was dominant. Between 1963 and 1976 the share of employment in both foreign-owned and joint venture firms in manufacturing rose from 32.8 to 68.7 per cent, while their share of output rose from 53.6 to 82.9 per cent and of export sales from 57.4 to 91.4 per cent. In the Republic of Korea and Hong Kong foreign firms had a much smaller part to play. Of course, in Korea an entreprenurial and managerial class had already emerged during the 1920s and 1930s, while Hong Kong benefited from an influx of entrepreneurs from China. This indicates that there is no set formula for acquiring investment capital and ensuring entrepreneurship. Furthermore, in the Republic of Korea exports have accounted for a much smaller share of domestic output (about 25 per cent) than in the other two countries.

The replicability of this experience should be viewed from the standpoint of desirability as well as feasibility. Labour discipline has tended to be at the expense of certain trade union rights. Moreover, the ultimate success of the newly industrialised countries must be judged in terms of their ability not only to achieve but to sustain industrial development. They are already experiencing competition from other developing countries which have begun to shift policies to favour labour-intensive manufactured exports; and the transition of the NICs to new capital-intensive and skill-intensive exports is proving more difficult.

Other criticisms have been made of export-oriented strategies. A common element of the strategy is often the creation of an export processing zone, whose materials are free from import or export duties. Enterprises are encouraged to settle by favourable tax provisions and, sometimes, by amendments to existing labour legislation. In a few cases, including Malaysia, a considerable volume of employment has been created. However, such enterprises may quickly leave for other countries if conditions change and may, in effect, play off one government against another. Furthermore, backward linkages into the rest of the economy may well be minor. Employment conditions within such zones may also be below the standard of the best employers elsewhere in the economy. Where an export processing zone is merely grafted on an otherwise inward-looking economy, the spread effects from an export-oriented strategy are likely to be few. However, in Singapore, for example, it seems that linkages in terms of subcontracting for supplies and parts for export products are being built up.

The test for the current NICs will come when competition from lower-wage countries steps up, at which stage they will need to shift in earnest to new capital- and skill-intensive products. However, the countries trying to follow the NICs will find themselves without the expected benefits if they have not fulfilled the apparent preconditions of successful agrarian reform and a high level of human resource development. Moreover, newcomers will find much more competition from within the Third World. Lastly, all contenders for export markets must face a much harsher international economic climate now than in the past.

While in many respects the prospects for the export of manufactures from the bulk of the developing world to developed countries may seem bleak, this should not be interpreted as further support for policies of import substitution. A consequence of the battery of controls which many developing countries have erected around their economy is the over-valuation of the exchange rate, which makes imports cheap and leads domestic producers to feel they are less competitive than they really are. New export lines are thus discouraged. Policies which are essentially neutral between the home and export markets would have a far greater effect on employment generation. This would entail the adoption of a more realistic exchange rate, thus increasing the profitability of new and existing exports, which might also be given initial support through tax and credit measures.

1.10

Definition of urban informal activities

Informal activities are generally defined negatively, as all economic activities which are not effectively subject to "formal" rules of contracts, licences, taxation, labour inspection, etc. "Formal", therefore, may refer strictly to government and public sector employment and to other enterprises offering similar conditions of employment. While a majority of the more educated labour force works under such conditions in formal activities, the larger part of the urban labour force works, in one way or another, under less formal conditions. A vast range of activities may thus be described as "informal". Such activities may include casual building labour, employed directly by a subcontractor working in turn for a government department; domestic service of one kind or another; a whole range of often illegal activities centring on drink and prostitution; hangers-on in the tourist industry; pavement hawkers, single-person food retailers and very small-scale commodity production recycling waste materials into building equipment or sandals.

Urban informal activities

The processes examined so far in rural areas and in industry have resulted in a considerable imbalance to which one response has been the growth of various urban "informal" activities (see box 1.10).

In studying the urban informal sector, attention has often been focused on the concept of a small-scale self-employed unit (which may none the less employ one or two other workers or apprentices). Such units may overlap at the edges with the small-scale manufacturing sector. As such, they can, in principle, be encouraged to expand by similar programmes of direct aid, through the provision of credit, help with product quality, marketing, etc. Outside the commodity producing sector, small-scale units in food retailing or in transport services may be assisted to form co-operatives, borrow money collectively, etc., and establish themselves on an independent, self-financing basis. The urban informal sector so defined is often reckoned to account for anything between one-

25

quarter and one-half of all urban employment. However, it must be stressed that such units account for only a part of all informal activities. If the whole range of urban informal activities were included, the share of employment would be considerably greater.

The logic of interest in urban informal activities is that such activities are seen to be partly interacting with those within the formal modern sector and partly independent of it. This raises both issues of economic dualism and the question of the role of such activities in the longer run.

High incomes and high spending are factors that encourage rural-urban migration. New migrants from rural areas are clearly an important labour source for various informal activities. But the relation of formal to informal activities is diverse. The informal sector may supply direct labour services to households with incomes from the formal sector, may be engaged in the repair and servicing of modern sector products, may collect and recycle modern sector products and may be engaged in subcontracted "putting-out" work for the modern sector. Some activities may be complementary to the modern sector as when bicycle rickshaws take passengers to the official bus route. Finally, informal activities may compete directly with the modern sector in retailing or in commodity production, including housing. In addition, informal activities may create and distribute goods and services aimed solely at the urban poor and people who have no connection with the formal sector.

Informal activities are thus by no means all "traditional" activities, although they may rely on traditional patterns of labour relations, contracts and obligations. Some of these obligations may be of an oppressive nature and amount to some form of debt bondage, enforced by violence. It is this traditional nature of informal activities that has seemed to constitute their "informality", particularly as regards ease of access to work. This informality has often been misunderstood and the existence of various forms of control has been disregarded, but it remains true that rural migrants usually can find some income through informal activities.

The levels of income provided by informal activities vary considerably. In particular, if the sector is to be able to enforce contracts and the fulfilment of obligations by its own members, it must itself be stratified economically and socially to an appreciable degree. And the hierarchy within the range of informal activities is no doubt perpetuated not only by the entry of poor rural-urban migrants at the bottom but also by the difficulty that any poor urban household has in accumulating savings, in finding opportunities for investment or in raising credit at reasonable terms and, increasingly, the difficulty that the children of poor urban households have in gaining acceptable educational credentials. But it must be stressed that informal activities are not simply "what the poor do", although it may be those activities which supply the needs of the poor. Informal activities support their own rich and poor, just as the formal sector includes a very large number of the poorly paid. It is clear in other respects that urban poverty and urban informal activities only partially overlap. Urban poverty is associated with poor housing conditions, undernourishment, school dropouts, poor water and sanitation facilities, etc. But the poor state and often insecure tenure of many squatter and slum areas is not reflected only in the primitive conditions of many informal sector workshops and other premises. In Jakarta, for example, it has been demonstrated that a quarter of the low income population consisted of formal sector workers. Similarly, an investigation in Davao, in the Philippines, put many informal sector workers into a higher income class than the low-income employees in the formal sector. Indeed, movement from a formal sector job to self-employment in an informal unit seems common and rational in many fast growing cities. There is thus no simple relationship between the formality or informality of employment and its income level.

The formal-informal relation gives rise to disagreement itself. Some observers point to the undeniable efficiency of many informal sector units in wringing a living from a small amount of capital and relatively low skills and to their effectiveness in recycling materials discarded by the modern sector and putting them to good use. Since credit is usually scarce and expensive for such units and quality control poor, cheaper finance and other assistance in training, marketing, product quality and upgrading equipment should go some way to creating income growth in many poor urban areas. This line of argument has pointed out that, far from being stimulated economically, most such units are often harassed by the authorities in the name of town planning or inappropriate building or hygiene codes, with negative effects on income growth.

However, this relatively optimistic approach is probably guilty of undue concentration on one part only of the whole range of urban informal activities. Another approach is to view the emergence of such activities as an unfortunate aberration: if structural change in rural areas could create an egalitarian growth path for agriculture and if small-scale enterprises were able to operate on the same terms as large-scale units, then most of the so-called informal activities might no longer exist. This view is hard to prove or disprove. Certainly if there were both less inducement to leave rural areas and a faster rate of creation of acceptable urban jobs, then no doubt some labour scarcity would be felt and the conditions of domestic service or casual building labour, for example, would improve. Of course, some flexibility, particularly in retail trading, is always necessary. In urban China it is reported that the number of new licences given to private individuals to run retail outlets, snack bars, barbershops, and shoe and bicycle repair, sewing and mending, transport and other services reached 810,000 in 1980. Furthermore, one-man enterprises are being promoted by interest-free loans. By 1985 it is estimated that around 10 million persons, i.e. about one-tenth of the total urban workforce, will be engaged in such activities.

However, the important question is whether urban informal activities can withstand competition from formal enterprises if it becomes privately worth while for the latter to intrude on the former and whether, therefore, in most economies informal activities can generate savings and create their own dynamic growth path. Most observers consider that informal activities are in nearly every way subordinated to formal activities and that in time the latter will expand and the former contract. Informal activities are denied access to certain inputs and to certain markets. Inputs are monopolised by the formal sector, which passes on only those which it does not want itself. A technological improvement for informally made products is almost impossible so that access to wealthier consumers insisting on stricter and higher quality is very restricted.

Many developing countries believed that economic development would sooner or later lead to the emergence of a modern sector (as regards both technology used and legal forms of ownership) sufficiently large to absorb additions to the labour force and in the process bring about full employment and higher incomes. Informal activities would then disappear and their participants would be absorbed into the formal sector. However, the formal sector is not capable of generating jobs as fast as it can generate output and many developing countries have begun to realise that these informal activities are no longer transitory. A few countries have even begun to consider which activities can be assisted, and how.

It is expected that the urban population of developing countries will double over the next two decades. In this context the role of informal activities in providing legal employment and incomes assumes considerable significance. Will it continue and under what conditions? Informal activities provide the main source of livelihood for most informal sector participants. Most of these, officially, are employees (as in domestic services), family helpers or self-employed. Hardly any would count as employers. In fact, of course, many of the so-called self-employed are highly dependent, for example, on wholesale suppliers of foodstuffs or on the owners of their rickshaws or taxis. The conventional categorisation of labour force groups is hardly sufficient to describe the informal sector. In Africa a majority of informal sector units have apprentices who learn skills on the job. With some exceptions in particular trades, the heads or owners of informal sector units are usually persons in their thirties, wage workers and apprentices tending to be younger. Though only half the increase in the urban population in developing countries is generally attributed to migration, informal activities appear to absorb a greater proportion. Migrants in this sector are younger and have a somewhat lower level of schooling than the rest.

In some cases attempts have been made to provide better operating conditions for small traders and commodity producers. In Indonesia, for example, informal trade activities have been relocated in clusters with support activities, and in Ghana space has been allocated for homogeneous clusters of activities (including vehicle repair and related services). However, such action may serve only to formalise a favoured section of the informal sector. In many other countries, however, the siting of informal activities is subject only to regulatory measures, usually of a negative and restrictive kind. One of the major concerns expressed by local authorities is that they might appear to be conferring legal status on "illegal" activities or illegal occupation of public land if these measures were to be liberalised. Two other problems thus arise: in the first place, the informal sector units are discouraged from investing in their premises owing to uncertainty of tenure; and secondly, they are often denied access to credit through formal institutions, as well as to other basic infrastructure amenities such as water and electricity.

While many countries have instituted special programmes to assist small enterprises, they have generally excluded informal activities. They have

tended rather to promote smaller-sized, formal sector units with a far superior level of capital, technology, skills and organisation. Considerations of equity have, however, prompted a few countries such as India to try to extend credit facilities to these units. However, a number of problems have been encountered. Banks have had difficulty in liberalising lending procedures, in identifying potential borrowers, since these are scattered in slums and other areas, and in recovering loans when locations are not permanent. The cost of processing small loans is not insignificant. Borrowers often cannot define their credit requirements precisely. Lastly, credit in itself may not suffice if complementary assistance in marketing, training, supply of machinery and raw materials and related facilities is not provided.

Similarly, in Ghana training courses for wayside fitters and mechanics have been offered and informal sector producers have been given advice and assistance in the production of prototypes (for example, of metal parts). But, in general, formal training and technology institutions have focused on support to the formal sector only. Only a few selected activities, such as handicrafts, have received attention because of their contribution to foreign exchange earnings, where some support has accompanied programmes of slum improvement on a self-help basis.

What, then, of the future of urban informal activities? Are they a mechanism for egalitarian urban development, or are they more likely to disappear gradually? Some informal sector units may eventually be absorbed into the formal sector at the same time as small-scale enterprises develop. Such a pattern of development is probably still far away and would, at all events, touch only a part of the range of informal activities. At the same time, existing informal activities may become formalised, if they continue to exist at all. Contracts would become clear and legally enforceable while conditions of work might gradually improve.

International and national responses to the employment crisis

The effects of various processes of development on labour and employment were described in the preceding pages. It is to be feared that they threaten the livelihood of much of the working poor. What can be done to arrest or reverse this tendency?

International policy measures

The first part of this chapter noted the deterioration in many developing countries' balance of payments because of slow export growth and adverse price movements. The increasing degree of indebtedness and the large burden imposed by interest and loan payments were also pointed out. In such circumstances, countries are forced to reduce the level of domestic activity and to make cuts in government spending. A State which is no longer able to meet its debt service payments must necessarily negotiate an agreement on debt rescheduling with its creditors, to which the International Monetary Fund is generally a party.

The terms of such an agreement may well involve a policy package, including cuts in subsidies, moving to a more realistic exchange rate (and liberalising import procedures as a condition for increased foreign assistance) and perhaps a reduction in government expenditure. In some situations where domestic economic management has been poor, such a package may be rational and beneficial. In other cases, it may lead to a fall in living standards for much of the workforce. Since the necessity for rescheduling will probably increase in the near future, the major creditor nations might consider a more selective policy package whereby, firstly, social programmes are preserved where possible, and, secondly, some countervailing steps, perhaps in the rural develop-ment field, are taken to preserve the welfare of the poor.

There are, of course, other long-term and structural means by which countries of the North can help. The most obvious is a reduction in protection. Agricultural protection in the North is still high, which is particularly disadvantageous for the poorer developing countries dependent on the export of raw materials. It is remarkable that in a world of decreasing trade barriers (but not non-tariff barriers) for manufactures, tariffs on agricultural products would seem to have risen. It has been estimated that agricultural protection in the European Economic Community rose from an average of 36 per cent in the late 1950s to 69 per cent in the early 1970s and that in the same period the level of protection doubled in Sweden and Norway.

The present world recession has made matters worse. Low economic activity has reduced the demand for commodities. Prices of most products are coming down and production is being cut. Stocks are high, awaiting a quick recovery of the world economy. But should this recovery take too long, prices will fall further, with disastrous effects on the export earnings of poorer countries.

One possibility for developing countries, particularly for tropical agricultural raw materials not competing with temperate products, would be greater domestic processing. Prices of processed raw materials tend to be higher and more stable and the domestic value added creates employment. ILO studies assessing the employment effects of first-stage processing of selected raw materials found that invariably these were considerable. However, the financial benefits from domestic processing rarely live up to expectations because of the structure of protection in industrialised countries. Tariffs on non-competing raw materials are often negligible, those on processed raw materials are not. Effective protection, i.e. the duty levied on the value added, can be high. An extreme example is vegetable oils where effective rates are 148 per cent, or eight times the nominal rates, making processing usually quite unprofitable.

In trade in manufactured products, non-tariff barriers in the North are increasing. To slow down imports of many manufactures and to allow domestic industry time to adapt, new import barriers have been erected. Thus, when tariff reductions agreed in the last round of multilateral trade negotiations (the Tokyo Round) are being implemented, non-tariff barriers (NTB) in selected product areas are increasing. The effects of these on total world trade are still limited, but this "new" protectionism is worrying, given its bias against imports from developing countries.

NTBs are often negotiated informally and bilaterally. As a result, the weaker partner is forced to concede. For example, since the early 1960s the world textiles trade has been subject to protective measures, affecting in particular imports from developing countries. The long-term arrangement on cotton textiles developed into the multi-fibre arrangement (MFA), which was signed in 1974 and renewed in 1977 and again in 1981. The first MFA allowed imports from developing countries to rise by at least 6 per cent a year. The first renewal reduced those rates and the second renewal hardly foresees growth in import quotas at all. This militates strongly against certain developing countries, but since most world textile exports still originate in OECD countries, it is doubtful whether these restrictions will provide much for the hard-pressed producers in the developed countries.

The "new" protectionism is sometimes defended as favouring new exporters in search of a market. But it is also a policy which limits exports from those who are producing and gives preference to those who are in no position to export. And it is a poor prospect for an incipient exporter to know that success may provoke import curbs.

There are therefore some very clear ways in which the North could assist the South. One

would be by no longer excluding agricultural products covered by the EEC's common agricultural policy from the provisions of the Lomé Convention. The same would apply to the widespread general system of preference which excludes processed agricultural products from developing countries as well as such manufactures as textiles, leather products and footwear. Further steps could include greater support for commodity agreements, an expansion of the STABEX facility operated by the EEC and an improvement and expansion of the compensatory financing facility of the International Monetary Fund.

National policies

But these international measures should be seen as no more than supplementing the developing countries' own efforts to control the process of development. In this respect a key issue must be the form to give to rural development in order to spread the benefits of growth to the rural poor and landless and to ensure a fast and appropriate pattern of output growth.

A higher growth rate of output against the background of unequal land distribution, increased tenancy and interlocked credit, land and labour markets may, in principle, both raise output (and increase the demand for labour) and lower the relative price of food (and thus raise real wages). In fact, there is little guarantee either that the investment resources needed to create growth on this scale would become available or that the pattern of growth would not result in a greater concentration of its benefits and that increased demand for wage labour might not just be confronted with an increased supply of landless and marginalised peasants.

The alternative is some form of land redistribution that would lower average holding size – and thus increase labour use and prevent premature and socially undesirable mechanisation – and remove the political and social forces which pre-empt the benefits of new technologies and local investment.

Above all, it would provide the basis for an output growth that is not achieved at the expense of rural poverty. There are naturally problems involved in any major structural change, but clearly the extent of the current rural employment problem demands a courageous remedy. It is also necessary to point out the risk that a redistribution of landholdings to individual peasants may be gradually reversed as such factors as indebtedness to neighbours and merchants cause the distribution of holdings once more to become concentrated. The risk could perhaps be averted by complete collectivisation of holdings, but this is likely to be unacceptable to most rural populations. Otherwise institutional changes are needed that will, firstly, prevent any process of land concentration and, secondly, ensure that new technologies are available and if possible used by all.

In addition to the need for far-reaching rural change, there is a need to redirect the process of modern sector development towards the promotion of more appropriate production units and of more appropriate production technology. A better balance of labour markets and a reduction in their differentiation would result from redistributive programmes carried out in rural areas. The pattern of government intervention in industry as regards pricing and taxation might also be reviewed. Although the nature of such changes, including the withdrawal of fiscal and other support from large-scale enterprises, is well known, policies and programmes are very rarely changed.

Lastly, striking a right balance in overall policies is of great importance. Too often a radical approach to rural development is accompanied by excessive claims for self-reliance within the world economy, leading to over-protection, industrial inefficiency and a low overall growth rate constrained by foreign exchange scarcity. Conversely, those countries which have succeeded in liberalising import procedures (no doubt with foreign assistance), achieving a realistic exchange rate and a healthy growth of exports, have too often ignored the necessity for domestic structural change and agrarian reform. These two lines of action are, in fact, often regarded as ideologically incompatible. One of them puts trust in market forces, the other calls for a redistribution of property. Furthermore, international support may appear to be forthcoming for one but not for the other.

The role of international support, however, seems clear. Liberalisation in the import structures of industrialised countries is an essential element. But active support, in the form of a promise of long-term programme aid to overcome the problems raised by initiatives towards structural change in rural areas, is also necessary.

Selected bibliography

Adelman, I. "Economic development and political change in developing countries", in *Social Research* (New York), Summer 1980.

Ahmed, I.; Kinsey, B. *Farm equipment innovations in eastern and central southern Africa* (Gower Publishing Company, Aldershot, Hampshire; forthcoming).

Allal, M.; Chuta, E. *Cottage industries and handicrafts: Some guidelines for employment promotion* (Geneva, ILO, 1982).

Balassa, Bela. *Development strategies in semi-industrial economies* (Baltimore, Johns Hopkins University Press, 1982).

Bardhan, P.; Rudra, A. "Interlinkage of land, labour and credit relations: An analysis of village survey data in East India", in *Economic and Political Weekly* (Bombay), Annual number, Feb. 1978.

Cortázar, R. *Necesidades básicas y extrema pobreza* (Santiago de Chile, ILO, PREALC, 1977).

FAO. *The fourth world food survey* (Rome, 1977).

Ghai, D.; Godfrey, M.; Lisk, F. *Planning for basic needs in Kenya: Performance, policies and prospects* (Geneva, ILO, 1979).
–; Lee, E.; Radwan, S. *Rural poverty in the Third World: Trends, causes and policy reorientations* (Geneva, ILO, 1979; World Employment Programme research working paper; restricted).
Gooneratne, W. (ed.). *Labour absorption in rice-based agriculture* (Bangkok, ILO, ARTEP, 1982).

ILO. *Employment effects of multinational enterprises in developing countries* (Geneva, 1981).

Kilby, P.; Bangasser, P. "Assessing technical co-operation: The case of rural industry", in *International Labour Review* (Geneva, ILO), May-June 1978.
Klein, E. *Notes on rural poverty in Latin America* (Santiago de Chile, ILO, PREALC, 1979; mimeographed).

Minhas, B. S. "Rural poverty, land redistribution and development strategy: Facts", in Sriniva-san, T. N. and Bardhan, P. K. (eds.): *Poverty and income distribution in India* (Calcutta, Statistical Publishing Society, 1974).
Myrdal, G. *Asian drama: An inquiry into the poverty of nations* (New York, Pantheon, 1968).

Paukert, F.; Skolka, J., Maton, J. *Income distribution, structure of economy and employment* (Croom Helm, London, 1981).

Sen, A. K. *Employment, technology and development* (Oxford, Clarendon Press, 1975).
Sethuraman, S. V. (ed.). *The urban informal sector in developing countries: Employment, poverty and environment* (Geneva, ILO, 1981).

UNIDO. *World industry since 1960: Progress and prospects* (New York, 1979).

World Bank. *World development report 1982* (Washington, DC, 1982).
–. *Accelerated development in sub-Saharan Africa* (Washington, DC, 1981).
–. *Brazil: Human resources special report* (Washington, DC, 1979).

Chapter 2

Employment in the industrialised market economies

Roughly 35 million unemployed by the end of 1983, i.e. about 10 per cent of their total labour force – this is the bleak prospect facing some of the most affluent nations of the world.[1] Is history repeating itself? Is the spectre of the 1930s, with its wake of social disasters, about to haunt the contemporary scene again?

This is the question anxiously being asked by the citizens of these countries and the major worry of their governments. It is also the irritating question being put to the doctors of the economy, who cannot agree on the diagnosis of the disease or its remedies.

This chapter reviews the main developments and, through an analytical examination of unemployment and employment in these countries, attempts to put them in perspective. The analysis is preceded by a brief look backwards, beginning precisely with the 1930s, and an examination of the factors that may have led to the present situation. The chapter concludes with a few comments on future prospects.

From 1930 to 1980: three contrasting periods

The half century from 1930 to 1980 may be broken down into three periods: at the outset, 15 years of slow growth beginning with the social disaster of unemployment during the Great Depression and ending with the Second World War; the 20- to 25-year post-war period of high growth, accompanied by virtually full employment in many countries; and lastly, beginning in 1973, the general fall in growth rates, together with rising unemployment which had reached high levels nearly everywhere by 1980.

□

In the 1930s unemployment reached unprecedented levels. Nearly 13 million persons in the United States were out of work, i.e. one worker out of four. In 1932 there were about 6 million unemployed persons in Germany, i.e. one worker out of three. In 1933 there were 2 million unemployed in France.

Most analysts agree that the Wall Street crash and its consequences elsewhere were not the real cause of the Depression of the 1930s, but only triggered it off. However, their agreement stops there. It is rather disheartening to note that, over 50 years after the event, they cannot agree completely on either the factors that ignited the explosion or even the place where the dynamite was stored (whereas the mechanisms and reasons of the crisis's spread are no doubt better known). In a television debate in 1969 between Milton Friedman and Paul Samuelson, two future Nobel Prize winners for economics, Friedman contended that the Depression originated in the United States and had a single cause, errors in the American monetary policy, while Samuelson maintained that the cause was to be found in the world economic system and was due to "a series of historical accidents"[2] (Kindleberger, 1973, p. 19). Whatever the case, the assessment of 1982 made by the secretariat of GATT (General Agreement on Tariffs and Trade) certainly applies to the 1930s: "There is no single, simple cause or explanation of the difficulty the world economy is experiencing . . . There are, instead, many factors and they interact in numerous – often circular and cumulative – causative chains" (*International trade 1981/82*, p. 10).

It is relevant to recall what the situation was in the United States on the eve of Black Thursday. There was a complete slump in agriculture and a decline in construction. The American industrial fabric was being completely overhauled: conventional consumer goods industries were depressed and absorbing a smaller share of capital and new techniques. The economy was dependent on purchases of luxury goods. From 1920 to 1929 capital (industrial and financial) incomes had risen by 45 per cent, while wage incomes had increased by only 13 per cent (Lorenzi, Pastré, Toledano, 1980, p. 8). The economic policy could not be relied upon to get the system out of possible trouble: the budgetary policy advocated a strict balance; the monetary policy was restrictive; the trade policy was protectionist; the financial policy towards the outside world was shortsighted (though it was the foremost creditor in the world, the United States did nothing to make the enormous international financial debt productive); and, lastly, the United States was – and this is a corollary of that attitude – opposed to international economic arrangements, and torpedoed the World Economic Conference of 1933 held on the initiative mainly of the ILO.[3]

The most striking of all the aspects of the Great Depression regardless of its causes or the place where it started were the absence of stabilising instruments at the international level and the refusal to establish world economic co-operation. C. P. Kindleberger, in his analysis of the many causes of the crisis, insists on this point: "The 1929 Depression was so wide, so deep and so long because the international economic system was rendered unstable by British inability and United

Table 2.1

Real gross domestic product per capita, annual growth rates (in percentage)

	1925-29[a] 1950-54	1950-54[a] 1963-67	1960-73	1973[b] 1980	1980[c] 1982
Australia	1.2	2.2	3.0	1.2	0.9
Belgium	0.6	3.0	4.5	2.2	−1.2
France	1.0	3.7	4.5	2.4	0.4
Germany (Fed. Rep. of)	1.2	5.0	3.7	2.4	−0.6
Italy	1.3	4.8	4.5	2.2	0.0
Japan	0.9	8.6	8.5	1.3	2.5
Netherlands	0.3	3.3	3.8	1.4	−1.8
Spain	..	..	6.0	1.4	0.0
Sweden	3.2	3.5	3.0	0.4	−0.2
United Kingdom	1.0	2.5	2.6	0.9	−0.8
United States	1.8	1.9	2.8	2.7	−0.7
OECD			3.9	1.7	−0.2

.. = not available.

[a] S. Kuznets: *Economic growth of nations* (Cambridge (Mass.), Harvard University Press, 1971), pp. 38-39. [b] *OECD economic outlook: Historical statistics 1960-1980* (Paris, 1982). [c] Estimated.

States unwillingness to assume responsibility for stabilising it in three particulars: *(a)* maintaining a relatively open market for distress goods; *(b)* providing counter-cyclical long-term lending; and *(c)* discounting in crisis. The shocks to the system from the overproduction of certain primary products such as wheat; from the 1927 reduction of interest rates in the United States . . .; from the halt of lending to Germany in 1928; or from the stock-market crash of 1929 were not so great . . . When every country turned to protect its national private interest, the world public interest went down the drain, and with it the private interests of all" (Kindleberger, 1973, pp. 291-292).[4]

The situation of Sweden in the 1930s is also worth noting. Though less important, it presents a certain interest since Sweden was the only country where the crisis had a milder impact and which succeeded in maintaining a respectable growth rate (see table 2.1). Here again, the analysts are unable to agree on the reasons for its success (apart from the modest size and specific features of the Swedish economy): some ascribe it to the application of Keynesian policies before they were announced (development of the domestic market owing in particular to the expansion of consumer goods industries, fiscal measures, employment promotion), while others stress the importance of the monetary policy which, under the influence of G. Cassel, maintained money supply at a stable level, thus avoiding a fall in prices and a serious deterioration of industrial production (Jonung, in Brunner, 1981, pp. 286-313). Whatever the case, the Swedish success may perhaps be attributed to an overall vision of economic machinery, a vision somewhat lacking among the authorities of other countries during the Great Depression.

□

The period from the end of the Second World War up to 1973-75 contrasted sharply with the preceding one. Large-scale unemployment gave way to virtually full employment, at least in the majority of countries. Most economies experienced a very high growth rate. On an average, the real gross domestic product doubled in the OECD countries. In Japan the increase was fivefold.

The commitment of countries to economic growth and full employment, at both the national and the international level, contributed greatly to this performance. After the terrible experience of the Great Depression and the war, governments, employers and trade unions were determined to sit down and discuss national economic policies and to observe the agreements concluded. Sweden and the Federal Republic of Germany are noteworthy examples of such a tripartite consensus.

Most governments were committed to employment. In its White Paper on Employment Policy, issued in 1944, the British Government officially recognised that the maintenance of a stable and high level of employment was a major

policy goal.[5] In April 1945 the Canadian Government followed suit. Even before the war, the Swedish social democratic Government had already pursued the target of full employment. In the Employment Act of 1946 the Government of the United States declared it to be "the continuing policy and responsibility of the Federal Government to . . . promote maximum employment, production, and purchasing power".

The ILO Employment Policy Convention, 1964 (No. 122), ratified by most of the industrialised countries, went even further, declaring that "each Member shall declare and pursue, as a major goal, an active policy to promote full, productive and freely chosen employment" and, in addition, providing that "the said policy shall aim at ensuring that: *(a)* there is work for all who are available for and seeking work; *(b)* such work is as productive as possible; *(c)* there is freedom of choice of employment and the fullest possible opportunity for each worker to qualify for, and to use his skills and endowments in, a job for which he is well suited, irrespective of race, colour, sex, religion, political opinion, national extraction or social origin".

All observers agreee that the phenomenal growth of consumption, linked to large-scale investments and decreasing prices for goods produced, was an essential factor in the success of what J. Fourastié has called the "30 glorious years". This "power horse of demand" was spurred first by post-war reconstruction activities and then by the growing consumption – mostly of durable goods – made possible by a regular increase in wages (through collective bargaining) and the effects of social security benefits, in particular pensions and health benefits.

The international economic scene also exerted a decisive influence. The establishment of a multilateral system for trade, currency and payments and of large economic communities provided a framework and rules for economic expansion and indeed led to expanding markets. The result was a

35

whole series of industrial innovations which raised labour productivity and led to substantial increases in income and profits. Lastly, energy prices were low. This interaction between consumption and investment was a concrete illustration of Keynes's argument that full employment can be guaranteed only by a high level of demand.

☐

Starting in 1973, the growth rates fell and then collapsed. The average annual growth of the real gross domestic product per capita, which was 3.9 per cent from 1960 to 1973 for the OECD countries, fell to 1.7 per cent from 1973 to 1980. Since 1980 we have had to speak of "negative growth" (about –0.2 per cent from 1980 to 1982 for the same countries).

Table 2.1, summarising the economic growth for the three periods described above, illustrates the severity of the phenomenon.

What has happened? Why?

If historians of the economy cannot agree on the reasons for the crisis of the 1930s, specialists today can hardly be expected to do better, and in fact the explanations they give of the current crisis do not agree either. Admittedly, it is extremely difficult, when caught up in the middle of the storm, to say what caused it, and we can merely note here the convergence of a certain number of phenomena that have brought the per capita growth rate in the OECD countries back down to the average historical pace since the nineteenth century, i.e. about 1.6 to 1.7 per cent.[6]

First of all, there were the two waves of oil price increases, in 1973 and 1979. While they do not explain the situation in themselves, they aggravated it, with the result that the gross domestic product in the OECD countries dropped by several points, inflation increased, investment decreased and interest and exchange rates became more unstable.[7]

Next, there was the phenomenal industrial development of Japan and the growing penetration of newly industrialised countries on the Western markets, affecting employment not only in the manufacturing sector but also in construction and the services largely dependent on it. The fact is that, while economic growth necessarily presupposes changes in the division – national or international – of production and therefore adjustment, the Western economies as a whole are adjusting poorly and too slowly to the new situation of economic trade.

In addition to these "exogenous" factors, there are developments peculiar to most of the economies in question: *(a)* the price of labour (wages plus payroll taxes and social security contributions) rises faster than productivity; *(b)* the labour force expands rapidly in the services sector where, while productivity usually increases more slowly,[8] wages follow those of the manufacturing sector; *(c)* public administration and social security expenditure absorbs a growing share of national income, which is anyway decreasing; *(d)* investment, and particularly investment in new industrial capacity, decreases; *(e)* the restrictive policies carried out by governments to combat inflation – spread throughout all the economies first by the methods of financing the Viet Nam war and then spurred further by the oil price increases and some of the distortions mentioned above – lead to a cumulative process of deflation, owing to their concomitance and the interdependence of these economies.

Few experts today would agree with the assessment of the MacCracken report, published in 1977, that "the most important feature was an unusual bunching of unfortunate events unlikely to be repeated on the same scale" (OECD, 1977, p. 103). Something fundamental happened, which seems to have gone largely unnoticed. The machinery that theoretically should have put the situation right was therefore started up. By 1980, however, though unemployment was growing, inflation showed little sign of abating. Furthermore, economic habits and social aspirations had not changed. People are reluctant to change their habits or accept less if the difficulties are felt to be passing ones. It is also felt necessary to persevere in the same path, for example as regards social security, when society as a whole considers that it has a duty to protect the growing numbers of persons affected by the recession and unemployment, and to maintain the level of protection provided.

At the centre of many analyses, however, is an important finding: the growing gap between the new reality and economic and social aspirations. It no longer seems possible to preserve and improve the economic system while continuing to demand from it in times of crisis what producers or consumers, public and private undertakings or trade unions, various interest groups or private citizens have derived from it, individually or collectively, in the recent past.

□

It is against this uncertain background that the tangible facts of unemployment and employment, dealt with in this chapter, must be seen.

We shall first analyse the nature and features of current unemployment (first section) and then those of employment (second section).

We shall then go on to describe the development of the labour-employment relationship: on the one hand, the trends of labour supply (third section) and, on the other, the trends of labour demand (fourth section). It will be seen how these two trends fail to meet. They form an arithmetic inequality, but in the wrong direction: instead of there being more jobs than workers, there are more workers than jobs.

Unemployment: trends, nature and characteristics

Volume of unemployment: around 10 per cent of the labour force in 1983

From 1960 to 1973 unemployment rates in North America varied between 4 and 7 per cent, while they were not higher than 2 to 3 per cent in Europe and Japan. This was the situation of virtually full employment of which the economists speak.

After the first oil crisis in 1973 unemployment rose quickly in most countries until the end of 1975 (see figure 2.1 and box 2.1 on unemployment). From 1976 to 1979 the unemployment rate in the OECD countries remained stable at about 5 per cent. In some countries, such as the United States and the Federal Republic of Germany, unemployment gradually diminished, while in others, such as France, Italy, Belgium and Spain, it continued to increase. In a few countries, such as Japan, Austria, Norway and Sweden, unemployment hardly changed during the 1970s. From 1980 onwards, unemployment rose very rapidly, particularly in Western Europe, and then, from mid-1981 on, in North America. In the United Kingdom the total number of unemployed is now more than 3 million and in France more than 2 million, while in the Federal Republic of Germany the 2 million mark was passed at the end of 1982. By that time, the unemployment rate exceeded 10 per cent in the United States – a status which it shares with Canada, the United Kingdom, Spain, Belgium and the Netherlands. At the same time about 30 million persons in the OECD countries were out of work, i.e. about 9 per cent of the total labour force.

Despite the fact that the United States economy has begun to pick up again in 1983, forecasts point to a continuing weakening of the labour market (except in North America). The rate of unemploy-

Figure 2.1
Standardised unemployment rates in 15 OECD countries (quarterly data, seasonally adjusted)

(a) Seven major countries

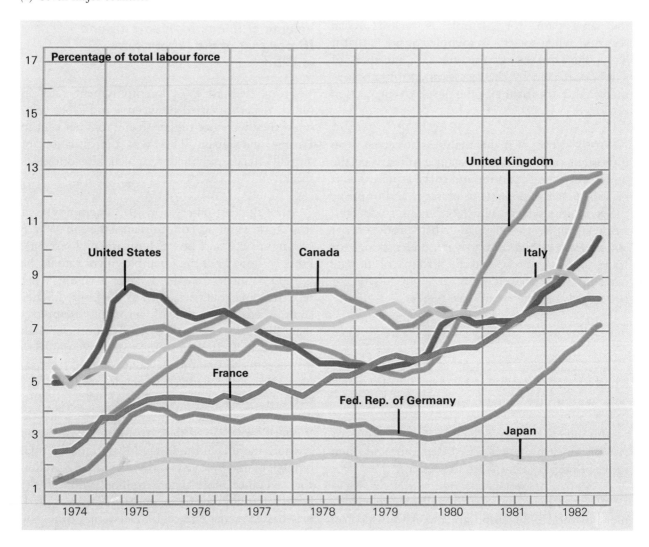

Source: OECD, Department of Economics and Statistics: *Quarterly Labour Force Statistics* (Paris, 1983), 1st quarter.

ment is expected to remain stable at slightly over 10 per cent, or 35 million unemployed, from the summer of 1983 on (OECD, July 1983) for all OECD countries. This overall rate would mean a slight drop in unemployment in the United States (down to 9.5 per cent by the end of 1984) on the one side and a rise in Japan (up to 3 per cent) and in Europe (up to 12 per cent) on the other.

The changing nature of unemployment

As the volume of unemployment increases, returning to rates that were frequent before the Second World War, its nature changes. Two facts are significant: the length of unemployment is increasing, and its volume does not necessarily reflect its true extent.

Figure 2.1 (continued)
Standardised unemployment rates in 15 OECD countries (quarterly data, seasonally adjusted)

(b) Other countries

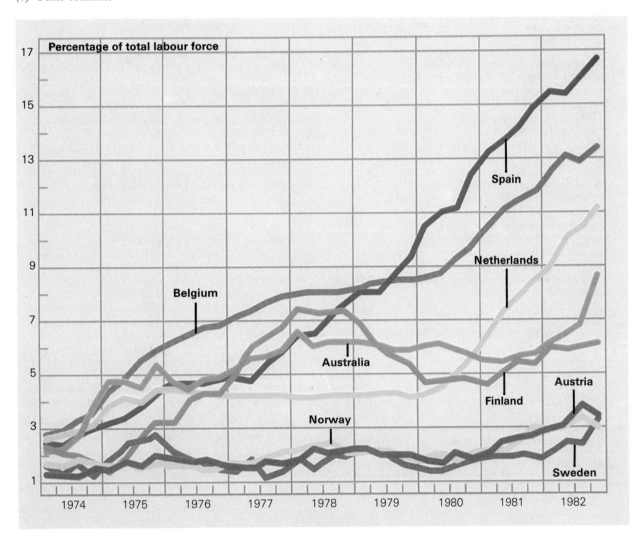

Source: OECD, Department of Economics and Statistics: *Quarterly Labour Force Statistics* (Paris, 1983), 1st quarter.

Growing duration of unemployment

Table 2.2 shows the number of long-term unemployed in the EEC countries.

The same trend emerges from the figures on unemployment duration for the United States. The percentage of persons who were unemployed for more than six months was 7.9 in 1973, 15.2 in 1975, 14.7 in 1977, 8.7 in 1979 and 14.0 in 1981. These figures are much lower than the European figures in table 2.2, mainly because in the United States people who are temporarily laid off are counted as unemployed, while this is not so in Europe. A large part of those laid off in the United States were rehired later on (Topel, 1982, pp. 769-787). Furthermore, mobility

---

2.1

Unemployment: definition and statistics

Definition of unemployment

In October 1982 the Thirteenth International Conference of Labour Statisticians adopted a resolution concerning statistics of the economically active population, employment, unemployment and underemployment. This resolution defines the unemployed as persons above a specified age who, during the reference period, were without work, were currently available for work and were seeking work.

This new ILO definition is very similar to the earlier one contained in the resolution concerning statistics of the labour force, employment and unemployment adopted by the Eighth International Conference of Labour Statisticians (ILO, Geneva, 1954). However, it includes certain amplifications and modifications for a more accurate measurement of unemployment.

It amplifies the criterion of seeking work by defining the steps involved.

It relaxes the condition of period required for seeking work by recognising that the search may have taken place at a recent date subsequent to the reference period.

It recommends that the application of the criterion of current availability for work should be based on appropriate tests developed to suit national circumstances.

It assimilates persons temporarily laid off with the unemployed, provided they have no formal job attachment and were currently available for work and seeking work. The notion of formal attachment is specified in the definition of employment given by the resolution.

It expressly includes among the unemployed students, homemakers and other persons mainly engaged in non-economic activities during the reference period who were at the same time seeking work or available for work.

In addition, it tempers the criterion of seeking work in certain situations, stressing availability for self-employment as well as paid employment. In this, the new definition is more in line with the situation in the developing countries.

Lastly, some new elements give it the flexibility needed to facilitate a comparison of unemployment statistics at the international level.

Statistical comparability

Most of the data published on unemployment are not comparable from one country to another since they are drawn from different sources or based on different definitions. Household and labour sample surveys tend to enlarge the above definition since they do not usually fix a minimum number of hours of work sought weekly or establish availability for work. Unemployment records, on the other hand, usually apply a stricter definition, covering only persons who are registered in the official employment offices and are seeking at least 20 hours of work a week.

Since the early 1960s the United States Bureau of Labor Statistics has brought out a series of unemployment statistics comparable internationally. (United States Department of Labor, Bureau of Labor Statistics: *International comparisons of unemployment*, Bulletin 1979 (Washington, DC), Aug. 1978.) It applies the official definition of unemployment, namely the total number of persons without work who are available for and actively seeking work. This definition is almost identical to the new ILO definition, except that it assimilates persons laid off or temporarily absent from their work with the unemployed.

The OECD now applies this adjustment procedure to most of its member countries (except Italy) and publishes the results in its series of labour statistics. (OECD, Department of Economics and Statistics: *Labour Force Statistics*, Quarterly supplement to the Yearbook (Paris, 1982), 3rd quarter.)

---

between employment and unemployment in the United States is substantially higher than in Europe, so that the American worker on an average is subject to more unemployment spells per year (but of shorter duration) than the European worker.

Is unemployment overestimated or underestimated?

Some analysts consider that unemployment is overestimated because of two phenomena: moonlighting and voluntary unemployment.

Though moonlighting or clandestine work undeniably exists, it is difficult to measure. This will be discussed at somewhat further length in the next section, when dealing with employment.

As for voluntary unemployment, i.e. persons unemployed because they do not wish to work at the going wage rates, some analysts consider that it has increased since the 1960s. In their view, the situation is further aggravated by existing unemployment insurance and social assistance programmes. It is true that the availability of

Table 2.2
Unemployed persons seeking employment for more than one year (as a percentage of total unemployment), European community

Country	1973	1975	1977	1979
Belgium	37.7	29.7	44.8	65.8
Denmark	..	9.4	37.8	38.8
France	21.7	16.4	26.6	33.5
Germany (Fed. Rep. of)	12.8	11.8	16.7	27.0
Italy	36.8	33.8	48.5	51.9
Netherlands	21.8	18.6	26.9	32.8
United Kingdom	30.4	14.8	27.5	21.8

.. = not available.
Source: Eurostat.

unemployment compensation relieves the unemployed somewhat of the necessity to accept any job at any wage. It allows them to search for suitable jobs at proper wages. In some countries the taxation of wages and the non-taxation of unemployment compensation, together with the existence of other unemployment-related benefits, have narrowed the difference between wages and compensation to such an extent that it has become unattractive for some persons to look for work (this is the so-called poverty trap). This will show statistically as an increase both in the total volume and in the average length of unemployment. As a result of the continuing recession, many countries have tightened the eligibility rules for unemployment insurance and social assistance and have reduced their benefits. This type of voluntary unemployment is therefore likely to be small.

On the other hand, various other phenomena suggest that unemployment is underestimated.

First, there is the phenomenon of discouraged workers. Some workers have given up looking for a job because they know from experience that jobs are not available. In the United States, where statistics on discouraged workers are collected regularly, it has been found that the number of discouraged workers increases in times of high unemployment. In other words, workers tend to be discouraged when jobs are not available, so that this type of unemployment cannot be regarded as freely chosen. In 1982 the number of discouraged workers in the United States was 1.5 million, i.e. about 1.5 per cent of the labour force. There is a high proportion of women and Blacks among discouraged workers: they account for 64 and 30 per cent of the total number, while they make up only 42 and 12 per cent of the labour force. Discouragement seems to be particularly widespread among older Black workers. Data on discouraged workers in Europe are not readily available, but estimates range between 1.5 and 3 million, or 1 to 2 per cent of the labour force, consisting mainly of women and people seeking part-time work.

Next, there is the phenomenon of involuntary part-time work. In 1983 there were more than 6.5 million non-agricultural workers involuntarily on part-time schedules in the United States, or about 6 per cent of the total labour force. Half of them were forced to work part time in their old jobs, while the other half were forced to accept a new part-time job. In Europe the number of workers in this situation is probably less since short time is applied less frequently.

In addition, many unemployed workers in Europe come under early retirement schemes and social security measures financed by the government. It is estimated that in the Netherlands in 1978 the volume of hidden unemployment among the beneficiaries of the Labour Incapacity Act amounted to about 140,000 work-years, or 3 per cent of the labour force (van den Bosch and Peterson, 1980). Lastly, it should be noted that the employment figures of some countries include persons who elsewhere would be regarded as unemployed. For example, the employment of many of the 170,000 beneficiaries of the active labour market policies in Sweden (4 per cent of the labour force in 1980) is directly subsidised by the Government for social reasons (Johannesson and Schmid, 1980).

41

2.2

Unemployment of minorities

Unemployment in the United States has been especially high among young Blacks (see table). It was 75 per cent higher than unemployment among young Whites in the early 1960s and 150 per cent higher in the early 1980s. The general rate of unemployment among Blacks (who accounted for 11 per cent of the total labour force in 1980) is nearly twice that of Whites. The rate of youth unemployment and general unemployment among the population of Hispanic origin is 50 per cent higher than the rate for Whites. In 1980 nearly two-fifths of Black youth were out of work as compared with one-quarter of White youth.

Other countries have experienced similar problems. In Western Europe, for example, the countries which admitted large numbers of foreign workers on a temporary basis when there was a shortage of labour in the 1960s, expecting that they would return home shortly, have found that many of them have settled there, married or brought their families to join them. The children have remained in the country of adoption where the economic situation has now become more difficult. Owing to their educational and social background, they find themselves at a disadvantage on the labour market in relation to the children of nationals. In Sweden, for example, the number of unemployed among children of foreign workers, many of whom have received little education and do not speak the language, is much higher than among Swedish youth. In the second quarter of 1979 the respective rates for adolescents were 12.1 and 7.5 per cent. For young adults, the corresponding rates were 6.4 and 3.1 per cent.

Youth unemployment rates by ethnic group in the United States

Age group	Ethnic group	Sex	1960	1973	1975	1980
16-19	White	Male	14.0	12.3	18.3	16.2
		Female	12.7	13.0	17.4	14.8
16-19	Black	Male	24.1	27.7	38.1	37.4
		Female	24.9	35.9	41.0	39.9
16-19	Hispanic origin	Male	..	19.0	27.6	21.7
		Female	..	20.7	27.9	23.7
20-24	White	Male	8.3	6.5	13.2	11.1
		Female	7.2	7.0	11.2	8.5
20-24	Black	Male	13.1	12.8	24.7	23.8
		Female	15.3	18.3	24.3	23.4
20-24	Hispanic origin	Male	..	8.2	16.3	12.2
		Female	..	9.0	17.2	11.9

.. = not available.

Source: United States Department of Labor: *Employment and training report of the President*, 1981.

Unemployment characteristics

The persons least exposed to unemployment are men between 25 and 54 years of age with a good education or good training. Many belong to what is called the primary segment of the labour market: they have full-time jobs, their incomes increase with age and they are able to make careers within large companies or the civil service. Others – semi-skilled or unskilled workers – are unlikely to be laid off during a recession because they are protected by various seniority rules in collective bargaining agreements. This leaves a large group of people who are more vulnerable to unemployment: women, youth, older workers and minorities (see box 2.2 on the unemployment of minorities).

Most of these people are unskilled or semi-skilled workers, which partly explains why employers prefer to hire men in the prime of life. This preference, however, also involves a non-economic element, which has led to some discrimination and segmentation of the labour market. In times of recession employers are able to choose. It would be too demanding and too costly to examine all new applicants. Some can thus be systematically eliminated. A study on the situation in the Federal Republic of Germany has shown that the occupational profile of the unemployed just after the dismissals of 1974-75 was the same as that of the employed. Since the gap between labour supply and demand continues to be large, employers have several times sifted the stock of unemployed and re-employed the best among them. The study identifies four handicaps: the fact of not having finished vocational training, of being older than 55, of having health problems and of looking

Table 2.3
Unemployment rates for men and women

Country	1973		1975		1977		1979		1981	
	Men	Women	Men	Women	Men	Women	Men	Women	Men	Women
Australia	1.4	2.8	3.5	6.2	4.5	7.5	5.0	8.0	4.7	7.4
Austria	0.6	1.8	1.4	2.3	1.2	2.3	1.5	3.1	1.9	3.6
Canada	5.8	5.1	6.2	8.1	7.2	9.4	6.6	8.7	6.9	8.4
France	1.7	2.7	2.7	6.1	..	..	4.0	8.9	..	..
Germany (Fed. Rep. of)	0.9	1.3	3.8	4.6	3.2	5.2	2.5	4.6	3.9	6.0
Italy	3.0	4.7	2.8	4.6	4.5	12.2	4.8	13.1	5.3	14.2
Japan	1.3	1.2	2.0	1.7	2.1	1.8	2.2	2.0	2.3	2.1
Norway	1.0	2.4	1.9	3.1	1.0	2.2	1.6	2.4	1.5	2.8
Spain	2.8	2.6	4.8	4.2	5.1	7.1	8.7	10.8	13.8	18.0
Sweden	2.3	2.8	1.3	2.0	1.5	2.2	1.9	2.3	2.3	2.7
United States	4.0	6.0	7.6	9.3	6.0	8.2	5.0	6.8	7.2	7.9

.. = not available.

Source: OECD: *Labour force statistics*, various editions.

for part-time work. The percentage of unemployed persons with at least two of these handicaps rose from 27 to 32 between 1975 and 1978, although the number of unemployed decreased during that period (Cramer, 1979, pp. 130-134). A study carried out in the Netherlands reached the same conclusion. Of the 220,000 unemployed persons registered in 1978, only 45,000 would be considered by employers for a permanent job. According to the authors, employers exclude women, young persons (under 25 years of age), workers over 55, migrant workers and workers living in "disreputable" areas (Valkenburg and Vissers, 1979, pp. 398-399).

Women are generally more likely to be unemployed than men (see table 2.3). Between 1973 and 1981 female employment rates were from 30 to 40 per cent higher than male rates in such countries as Canada, the Federal Republic of Germany, Sweden, Spain and the United States; between 40 and 90 per cent higher in such countries as Australia, Austria and Norway; and usually more than 100 per cent higher in such countries as France and Italy. In Japan, however, men face the same risk of unemployment as women.

Table 2.3 also shows that in six countries the number of unemployed women has grown faster than that of unemployed men, and that this trend is particularly strong in France, Italy and Spain. It would therefore seem that in these countries the recession has affected employment of women more than that of men. The opposite is true in Australia, Austria and the United States. It should be pointed out at this stage that the figures on unemployment do not fully reflect the labour underutilisation of women, since many of them are discouraged workers.

Another cause of great concern is the rapidly increasing rate of unemployment among youth. Since the end of the 1970s persons under 25 years of age who are available for and willing to work have at least twice as many chances of being underemployed as persons over 25 (see table 2.4). The Federal Republic of Germany is an exception to this rule, although even in this country unemployment among youth is higher than among adults. At the other end of the scale are such countries as France and particularly Italy, where youth unemployment is five times higher than adult unemployment. The table also shows that unemployment among youth under 20 years of age is usually more than 50 per cent higher than among those between 20 and 24, except in the Federal Republic of Germany.

Many factors have contributed to increasing youth unemployment. On the supply side, the youth labour force in the United States and Canada has increased rapidly since the early 1960s. The youth labour force in Europe, on the other hand, hardly increased at all until 1975, when the children born during the "baby boom" started to enter the labour market. In Japan the youth labour force increased slightly during the 1960s, but dropped by more than one-third during the 1970s. Between 1960 and 1980 the labour force participation rates of youth fell sharply in Japan and most European countries as a result of increased school attendance. In the United States, Canada and Australia increased school attendance has not had the same effect since many students combine school with work.

On the demand side of the youth labour market, there has been a decline in the number of unskilled jobs, in which many young persons find their first employment. There is, besides, a growing number of married women and immigrants (especially in the United States) competing for such jobs. The decline is also due to the shift out of agriculture and the decline of self-employment and small family businesses, which have greatly reduced family employment opportunities for youth.

The recession since 1973 has further contributed to increasing youth unemployment. In times of limited recruitment employers prefer to keep experienced adult workers rather than to hire young persons who are costly to train. This attitude is reinforced by provisions in collective agreements which prevent employers from laying off older workers in the event of recession.

It is difficult to say whether the position of unemployed youth is more precarious than that of

Table 2.4

Unemployment rates by age, adjusted to United States definitions

Country and date	Under 25		25 and over
	Under 20	From 20 to 24	
Australia			
1964	3.7	1.6	0.9
1970	3.8	1.8	1.3
1981	15.6	8.2	3.7
Canada			
1960	13.5	9.3	5.8
1970	13.9	7.5	4.2
1981	16.3	11.3	5.6
France			
March 1963	4.0	1.8	1.1
March 1970	7.0	3.7	2.0
March 1981	29.1	15.1	5.0
Germany (Fed. Rep. of)			
April 1963	0.3	0.4	0.3
April 1970	0.3	0.5	0.4
April 1980	3.5	3.5	2.4
Italy (unadjusted)			
1964	9.1	5.4	1.5
1970	12.3	8.8	1.5
1981	27.2	17.6	2.1
Japan			
1960	2.2	2.0	1.5
1970	2.0	2.0	0.9
1981	5.6	3.7	2.0
Sweden			
1962	3.3	2.0	1.2
1970	4.3	2.2	1.3
1981	9.6	4.9	1.8
United Kingdom			
April 1960	2.1	2.7	1.7
1971	..	..	3.4
1979	..	..	4.1
United States			
1960	14.7	8.7	4.4
1970	15.2	8.2	3.3
1981	19.6	12.3	5.4

.. = not available.

Source: United States Department of Labor, Bureau of Labor Statistics: "Youth unemployment: An international perspective", in *Monthly Labor Review* (Washington, DC), July 1981; and Bulletin 2098 and Supplement (Washington, DC, Aug. 1982; mimeographed).

Table 2.5
Structure of civilian employment; women and wage and salary earners (in percentage)

	Agriculture			Industry			Services			Women			Wage and salary earners		
	1960	1973	1981	1960	1973	1981	1960	1973	1981	1960	1973	1981	1960	1973	1980
Australia	10.3 [c]	7.4	6.5	39.9 [c]	35.5	30.6	49.8 [c]	57.1	62.8	..	33.6	36.3	83.5 [c]	86.4	84.1 [d]
Austria	24.6	16.2	10.3	40.3	40.6	40.1	35.1	43.2	50.0	..	38.4	38.2	..	75.4	82.9
Belgium	8.7	3.8	3.0 [d]	46.8	41.5	34.8 [d]	44.6	54.7	62.3 [d]	30.7	34.0	35.9 [d]	73.8	82.9	83.4
Canada	13.3	6.5	5.5	33.2	30.6	28.3	53.5	62.8	66.2	26.8	35.2	39.7	81.2	90.1	90.1
Denmark	18.2	9.5	8.3 [e]	36.9	33.8	30.0 [e]	44.8	56.7	61.7 [e]	31.8	41.1	43.6 [e]	76.4	81.5	83.9 [e]
Finland	36.4	17.1	11.1	31.9	35.7	34.8	31.7	47.1	54.1	44.8	46.1	47.6	63.7	80.8	86.3
France	22.4	11.4	8.6	37.8	39.7	35.2	39.8	48.9	56.2	35.2 [f]	36.0	38.0 [d]	69.5	80.7	82.9
Germany (Fed. Rep. of)	14.0	7.5	5.9	48.8	47.5	44.1	37.3	45.0	49.9	37.8	37.2	38.7	77.2	84.2	86.2
Greece	53.8 [c]	38.9 [h]	30.8 [e]	18.5 [g]	26.3 [h]	30.0 [e]	27.7 [g]	34.8 [h]	39.2 [e]	32.3 [g]	27.5 [h]	29.7 [e]	33.5 [g]	..	48.6 [e]
Ireland	37.3	24.8	19.2 [d]	23.7	30.9	32.4 [d]	39.0	44.2	48.4 [d]	26.6 [g]	26.6 [h]	28.5 [d]	61.4 [g]	70.6	74.3
Italy	32.8	18.3	13.4	36.9	39.2	37.5	30.2	42.5	49.2	30.1	28.7	32.3	58.4	69.4	71.5
Japan	30.2	13.4	10.0	28.5	37.2	35.3	41.3	49.3	54.7	40.7	38.5	38.7	53.4	68.7	71.7
Netherlands [a]	11.5	6.8	6.0 [d]	40.4	36.2	31.9 [d]	48.2	57.0	62.1 [d]	..	..	..	78.1	84.1	86.8
Norway	21.6	11.4	8.5	35.6	33.9	29.8	42.9	54.7	61.7	29.0	36.6	41.4	74.3	83.1	86.4
Portugal	42.8	34.8 [i]	28.5 [d]	29.5	34.5 [i]	36.0 [d]	27.7	30.7 [i]	35.5 [d]	18.7	40.0 [i]	38.8 [d]	74.3	65.9 [i]	66.7
Spain	42.3	24.3	18.2	32.0	36.7	35.2	25.7	39.0	46.6	..	28.0	28.6	61.0	67.2	69.6
Sweden	13.1 [j]	7.1	5.6	42.0 [j]	36.8	31.3	45.0 [j]	56.0	63.1	36.1 [j]	40.8	45.9	86.9 [k]	90.8	92.0
Switzerland	13.2	7.7	7.0	48.4	44.1	39.3	38.4	48.1	53.6	..	34.0	35.2	85.5	..	..
Turkey	81.1	64.5	60.4 [d]	8.6	15.1	16.3 [d]	10.2	20.4	23.3 [d]	45.2	..	..	13.6	29.7	34.2 [d]
United Kingdom	4.1	2.9	2.8	48.8	42.6	36.3	47.0	54.5	60.9	34.4	37.6	40.3	92.7	92.1	89.8
United States	8.3	4.2	3.5	33.6	33.2	30.1	58.1	62.6	66.4	33.3	38.5	42.8	83.9	90.3	90.6
OECD [b]	21.7	12.1	10.0 [b]	35.3	36.4	33.7 [b]	43.0	51.5	56.3 [b]	34.3	36.2	38.6 [b]	70.5	80.5	82.0

.. = not available.
[a] In work-years.   [b] Estimated.   [c] 1964.   [d] 1980.   [e] 1979.   [f] 1968.   [g] 1961.   [h] 1971.   [i] 1974.   [j] 1962.   [k] 1967.

Source: OECD: *Labour force statistics*, various editions.

other unemployed persons. There is no doubt that the transition from school to work is gradual and that the time taken has increased, regardless of the recession. Many young people, especially adolescents, are in no hurry to take up a trade and settle down. Consequently, young people frequently move between employment, unemployment and non-active status. Youth unemployment is however much more serious for those who must support a family or supplement a low family income. Moreover, prolonged unemployment of young adults (between 20 and 24 years of age) may have extremely negative long-term effects, such as discouragement and poor prospects for a career. In some countries, such as Japan and the Federal Republic of Germany, apprenticeship programmes for adolescents have been very successful, but it is doubtful whether they can be replicated in other countries with a different cultural background and during a recession when employers are trying to cut training costs. It should be further noted that the success of these programmes is also explained by the relatively low wages offered to the apprentices and by the employment security that is usually given in return.

□

What, in short, does this analysis of unemployment show?

Table 2.6   Annual percentage increase in civilian wage and salary employment by sector of activity in selected OECD

Sector of activity	Australia		Austria		Belgium		Denmark		France	
	1964-73	1973-80	1961-73	1973-80	1960-73	1973-79	1960-73	1973-79	1962-73	1973-80
Agriculture and mining	4.4	1.4	−7.0	−2.9	−7.6	−3.9	−8.3	1.0	−4.2	−5.1
Food, textiles, wood	1.3	−2.3	−2.2	0.2	−1.1	−4.5	0.6	−2.3	−0.1	−1.9
Chemicals and paper	−0.9	−0.5	−0.3	1.6	2.1	−1.1	1.4	−1.6	2.7	−0.6
Non-metallic minerals	−0.5	−0.2	−0.6	1.5	−0.9	−3.1	1.4	−3.0	1.0	−3.9
Metal trades	1.2	−1.9	1.2	0.9	2.3	−2.0	1.2	−1.1	2.2	0.0
Total manufacturing [a]	1.0	−1.7	−0.7	0.8	0.6	−3.3	0.3	−1.5	1.4	−1.0
Construction	3.2	−1.9	0.4	0.9	1.2	0.0	2.1	−0.2	2.6	−2.0
Trade, restaurants and hotels	5.4	0.6	1.5	2.9	4.2	0.7	2.6	−1.1	4.1	0.4
Transport and communications	2.5	0.7	1.6	−0.4	0.6	1.0	1.0	0.9	0.2	2.6
Financial and business services	11.0	1.6	4.4	3.3	8.7	2.4	6.4	3.5	6.8	4.4
Other services	5.0	3.5	0.8	3.6	2.5	3.1	5.0	3.8	3.1	2.9
Total services	5.4	2.0	1.4	2.7	3.0	2.2	3.9	2.4	3.3	2.4
Total employees [b]	3.7	0.7	0.0	1.6	1.5	0.1	1.8	1.3	2.1	0.6
Self-employed workers	0.7	4.8	−2.3	−4.8	−2.6	−0.4	−0.6	−1.5	−2.7	−1.5
Civilian employment	2.8	1.1	−0.6	0.3	0.6	0.0	1.3	0.8	0.9	0.2

[a] Including also other manufacturing.   [b] Figures refer to establishments employing at least 30 regular employees.   [c] Including public utilities.

First, in simplified figures: ten persons out of 100 are unemployed. Of these ten persons, five are young, and three of these are women.

Secondly, among the unemployed queueing up for unskilled jobs, the successful applicants will first be adult males (between 25 and 54 years of age), then women of the same age, followed by young persons; the last will be minorities and older workers.

Employment

In 1983 there is therefore a shortage of 34 or 35 million jobs to be made good in order to achieve full employment in these countries. But it should be pointed out that between 1960 and 1980 the economies of these same countries were able to provide their labour force with a net increase of some 65 million additional jobs. Persons in civilian employment (wage earners and the self-employed) rose from about 260 million in 1960 to about 325 million in 1980, i.e. an annual increase of 1.1 per cent. The average annual increase was roughly the same in 1973 to 1980 as in 1960 to 1973, owing to a large growth (2.2 per cent) in the United States. In a number of other countries, such as Austria, Italy, Norway and Portugal, civilian employment grew at a faster annual rate from 1973 to 1980 than from 1960 to 1973.

What are the characteristics of civilian employment at present? The labour force is made up almost entirely of wage and salary earners; women account for over one-third; and most of the jobs available are in the services sector.[9] This structure of employment already existed in the 1960s, but it has become more pronounced (see table 2.5).

Each of these aspects will now be examined in turn, and a trend towards another type of employment will then be described.

countries, 1960-73 and 1973-80

Germany (Fed. Rep.)		Italy		Japan		Norway		Portugal		United Kingdom		United States	
1962-73	1973-80	1962-73	1973-80	1961-73	1973-80	1960-73	1973-80	1960-73	1973-80	1960-73	1973-80	1960-73	1973-80
−2.9	−1.9	−3.6	−0.9	−6.9	1.2	−1.2	−0.8	−4.8	−7.6	−4.1	−1.5	−1.7	3.7
−3.0	−1.4	0.7	−0.4	1.6[b]	−2.1[b]	−0.7	0.9	1.5	−5.0	−2.0	−2.9	0.5	−1.3
4.5	−0.8	3.9	0.2	1.7[b]	−1.9[b]	1.0	−0.9	2.2	0.8	−0.2	−1.0	1.9	0.9
−4.5	−2.9	1.7	0.7	1.8[b]	−2.1[b]	2.7	−2.9	5.9	−5.2	−1.3	−3.3	0.6	−1.2
6.1	−0.4	1.6	0.9	4.3[b]	−1.4[b]	2.0	1.3	1.0	−2.5	−0.7	−1.6	2.1	1.0
−0.4	−1.0	0.7	−0.0	2.9	−0.8	0.9	0.2	2.0	2.8	−1.1	−2.0	1.4	0.1
0.8	−2.5	−1.3	0.7	4.4	2.2	1.3	0.2	2.3	2.6	−0.3	−1.2	2.7	1.0
1.0	−0.5	4.2	3.1	4.4	2.8	2.9	3.2	5.1	0.3	0.4	0.7	3.0	2.9
0.3	−0.4	1.0	2.7	3.3	0.5	−0.1	0.9	3.2	−1.6	−0.7	−0.2	1.4	1.3
4.2	1.0	2.6	5.4	1.6	3.0	7.3	7.6	10.2	−2.3	2.8	2.3	4.6	2.3
2.8	2.2	2.7	3.5	4.1	3.0	4.9	5.2	1.4	3.2	2.4	1.6	3.7	4.1
2.0	1.0	2.8	3.4	3.9	2.5	3.3	4.2	2.9	1.4	1.4	1.2	3.4	3.3
0.6	−0.2	0.6	1.5	3.2	1.4	2.2	2.7	0.7	0.5	0.1	−0.1	2.6	2.4
−2.8	−2.4	−3.2	−1.6	−1.7	−0.6	−1.9	−0.9	−0.3	7.8	0.8	−0.7	−1.9	1.9
−0.0	−0.5	−0.4	1.1	1.3	0.8	1.3	2.1	0.4	2.5	0.1	−0.1	2.0	2.2

Source: OECD: *Labour force statistics*, various editions.

Growth of wage and salary employment

For the OECD countries as a whole, wage and salary employment rose from 70.5 per cent in 1960 to 80.5 per cent in 1973 and 82 per cent in 1980. The sharp rise between 1960 and 1973 is due primarily to the drop in agricultural employment. In other words, family and self-employed workers in agriculture have taken up paid employment in industry or the services. Moreover, in many countries small outworking firms (clothing, leather, woodworking) and retail trades have not been able to withstand the competition from large enterprises, so that these craftsmen have become wage earners. Some countries, such as the United States, Canada, the United Kingdom and Sweden, seem to have reached the upper limit of 90 per cent. Others, such as Japan and the southern European countries, are still far from that limit.

Growing share of female employment

Another noteworthy long-term trend is the growing share of female employment. This trend, which was already evident between 1960 and 1970, became more pronounced between 1973 and 1980. The number of women in civil employment in the OECD countries rose from 34.3 per cent in 1960 to 36.2 per cent in 1973 and 38.6 per cent in 1980. In 1980 it was more than 40 per cent in the United States, the United Kingdom and the Nordic countries, but less than 30 per cent in most southern European countries and in Ireland.

Sharp decline in agricultural employment and slow overall reduction in industrial employment

The drop in agricultural employment in relation to total employment was particularly marked between 1960 and 1973, especially in such countries as Japan, Italy, Spain and Greece. In 1981 the share of agricultural employment was less than 4 per cent in the United States, the United Kingdom and Belgium, while the average share for all OECD countries amounted to 10 per cent.[10]

Industrial employment, for its part, has decreased slightly over the 20-year period for all OECD countries, dropping from 35.3 to 33.7 per cent of total employment. Exceptions are countries where agricultural employment accounted for more than 30 per cent of total employment in 1960: Japan, Italy, Finland, Greece, Ireland, Portugal, Spain and Turkey. In these countries industrial employment has increased, though its share in total employment has decreased since 1973 (see table 2.6).

In nearly all the countries industrial employment began to fall off in 1973, particularly in the consumer goods sector, including food processing, textiles, clothing, leather and wood products. This decline is due both to growing competition from newly industrialised countries in such sectors as clothing, leather and wood products and to a sharp increase in labour productivity, especially in food processing and textiles. The steady decline of employment in the minerals sector (including iron and steel) is due mainly to decreased demand for these products and high increases in productivity. Similarly, employment in the chemicals and paper sector, which had increased from 1960 to 1973 despite higher productivity, decreased from 1973 to 1980 as a result of lower world demand. Most industrial employment was created in the metal trades, a major sector including electronics, machinery and transport equipment. Employment here increased up to 1973; between 1973 and 1980 it continued to increase in the electronics sector because of the strong continuing demand for computers, office machines and video cassettes. Employment in the machinery sector has remained more or less stable because, despite high productivity increases, demand remains firm, particularly in the OPEC countries. Employment in the transport sector (motor cars and other vehicles) is decreasing because of slackening demand and higher productivity.

Employment in the construction sector depends on the state of the economy. Governments, private industry and private persons constructed less during the recession, so that employment grew at a lower annual rate (or even diminished) from 1973 to 1980 than from 1960 to 1973.

Growing importance of employment in the services sector

Employment in the services sector has been growing in all the OECD countries. Its share of total employment rose, on an average, from 43 per cent in 1960 to 63 per cent in 1981. It now accounts for two-thirds of total employment in the United States and Canada, though for less than 50 per cent in the countries of southern Europe and in Ireland. It grew at a faster annual rate from 1973 to 1980 than from 1960 to 1973.

This is the case in particular of the "other services" sector which, in 1980, accounted for between one-fourth and one-third of total employment. Employment in trade, restaurants and hotels, which accounted for about one-fifth of total employment in 1980, rapidly increased from 1960 to 1973 and continued to grow at a lower rate from 1973 to 1980. This lower growth rate is due to lower economic growth and high productivity increases in the wholesale and retail trade sectors. Employment in transport and communications accounted for between 5 and 8 per cent of total employment in 1980. It did not increase much from 1973 to 1980 because of higher productivity. Employment in the financial and business services, including banks, insurance companies and real estate companies, grew rapidly from 1960 to 1973 as a result of the boom and rapidly increasing personal incomes. Employment in banking and insurance rose with the rapid spread of branch offices. The growth, which continued up to 1980, is now slowing down because productivity is increasing with the wider use of electronic data processing. In 1980 the financial and business sector employed between 7 and 10 per cent of all wage and salary earners.

48

2.3

Public employment in the 1970s

General trends

According to the United Nations system of national accounts, the public service comprises the central administration, the provincial, state or regional administrations in federal and decentralised governments, the local authorities, social security bodies and government-run establishments. Although the demarcation line between government-run public enterprises and nationalised industries is sometimes blurred, the latter have been excluded from the definition.

In the OECD countries employment in the public services increased from 14.2 per cent of the total labour force in 1970 to nearly 18 per cent in 1979. The highest increases were recorded in Sweden and Denmark (from 20 to 29.8 per cent and from 16.8 to 25.5 per cent, respectively), and the other Nordic countries also recorded very rapid growth rates. In Australia, Japan, New Zealand and Switzerland, on the other hand, the share of public service employment appears to have remained stable throughout the period. In France, after a period of sharp growth from 1970 to 1975, public employment (state and local government) stagnated in 1976 and 1977 and from 1978 onwards increased only slowly, by 1.4 per cent annually. Its share of total employment rose from 15.9 per cent in 1970 to 17.3 per cent in 1981. In the United Kingdom, despite an 8 per cent increase in total general government employment (central government, national health service, local authorities) between 1974 and 1980, the share in total employment remained nearly constant, at around 20 per cent, from 1975 to 1979, when these trends were reversed. In the Federal Republic of Germany public employment increased by nearly 60 per cent between 1960 and 1980. The fastest growth was recorded during the 1960s, when the number of public employees rose by 3.7 per cent annually, as compared with an annual growth rate of only 0.4 per cent in the 1970s. With about 4.5 million public employees (3.8 million full-time and 0.7 million part-time employees) in the federal, Länder and local governments (including social security administration), the public service in 1981 accounted for more than 17 per cent of the total labour force. A similar development took place in Japan where, owing to the sharp expansion of administrative needs as a result of high economic growth, the number of national and local public employees increased significantly up to the first half of the 1960s.

In the late 1960s and in the 1970s, however, the number of national public employees showed virtually no increase, while local public employment (municipalities and prefectures) continued to expand, growing by 34.7 per cent between 1968 and 1980. The share of public employment in total employment nevertheless is by far the smallest of the major industrialised countries. In the United States the share of government employment (federal, state and local) in total employment increased from 17.7 per cent in 1970 to 19.1 per cent in 1975. Since then, however, its pattern of growth has been changing. Though it has showed modest growth rates at all levels, it has not kept pace with employment growth in the private sector of the economy. The federal share of total employment was relatively stable, dropping from 3.9 per cent in 1970 to 3.1 per cent during the first quarter of 1981, while the proportion of state and local government employment rose from 13.9 per cent in 1970 to 15.5 per cent in 1975, after which it also began to decline.

Rapid growth of regional and local government employment

Public employment has grown faster at the regional and local levels than in central government. This is due partly to heavy investments in education, health and social welfare, for which regional, provincial or local authorities are usually responsible. Moreover, many countries have made considerable efforts to decentralise decision-making. This process, which has led to a redistribution of public funds and personnel and to fresh recruitment at the regional and local levels, has been particularly marked in some Scandinavian and other European countries and, more recently, in Spain and France, but also in Australia and New Zealand.

Main government services

In virtually all countries the greatest growth in employment has taken place in the field of social services. It is in education, health and social welfare that the highest rates have been recorded, but public works and infrastructure, housing, transport and communications are close runners-up. New problem areas, such as energy and environment, have entailed new responsibilities. Changes in life style and shorter working hours have prompted the public sector to provide more recreational and leisure facilities. Owing to slower economic growth and a rise in unemployment, many governments have expanded activities in the field of employment promotion, vocational guidance, training and retraining. Police and security services have likewise increased in several countries.

The fields of education and health, taken together, account for more than half of total employment in some countries. Of the 1.4 million public employees in Sweden in 1979, 0.7 million were employed in health care and 0.3 million in education. In Italy, similarly, of the 3.4 million public employees at the central, regional and local levels, 0.9 million were employed in education and 0.6 million in the health services. In France the bulk of public servants employed by the State are to be found in the education services (+46.9 per cent). In the United Kingdom the national health service and the education services together employed more than 50 per cent of the total general government employees in 1980. In the Federal Republic of Germany more than 1 million full-time employees in the services and administrations of the Länder and local authorities were employed in the fields of health, sports, leisure, education, culture and science.

The large "other services" sector includes such community services as public administration, the postal service, public health and education, and such social and personal services as cleaning, beauty care, the film industry, car repairs, recreational facilities and medical, legal and educational services. Most community services financed by taxes are free – except the postal service and transport – while most social and all personal services are sold on the market. The government employs between 50 and 75 per cent of all persons working in the "other services" sector. This labour force continued to grow rapidly from 1973 to 1980, particularly in most European countries (see box 2.3). This growth was due partly to a greater need for public services, especially health services and local administration, but it was also due partly to a deliberate employment policy. Employment also rose very rapidly in private medical and educational services, legal services and entertainment, a development due mainly to increasing real incomes.

Towards another type of employment?

The large majority of employed persons have a full-time job and a labour contract without limit of time and are paid a wage or salary. This typical pattern of employment prevailed up to the early 1970s, but a new trend is now emerging.

The trend is already apparent in the number of people who work part time. Between 1971 and 1977 the number of part-time workers in France rose from 5.9 to 8.2 per cent. Since 1973 their number has slowly been increasing in such countries as Denmark, France, the Federal Republic of Germany, the United Kingdom and the United States and at a faster pace in Belgium and the Netherlands (see table 2.7). The only exception is Italy. Most part-time workers are women, and their share is increasing. Moreover, part-time work seems to have been more widespread during the recession in 1975, which tends to confirm that not everyone freely chooses this type of employment.

Table 2.7
Share of part-time employment in total employment and women in part-time employment (in percentage)

Country	Part-time employment				Of which: women			
	1973	1975	1977	1979	1973	1975	1977	1979
Belgium	3.8	4.9	6.1	6.0	82.3	85.1	87.0	89.3
Denmark	..	21.2	22.0	22.7	..	86.8	85.4	86.9
France	7.2	8.2	8.9	8.2	77.9	82.7	78.8	82.0
Germany (Fed. Rep. of)	10.1	11.2	11.7	11.4	89.0	89.6	90.5	91.5
Italy	6.4	6.0	5.9	5.3	58.3	58.7	61.3	61.4
Netherlands	4.7	9.5	9.7	11.2	80.2	81.3	81.1	82.5
United Kingdom	16.0	17.1	17.2	16.4	90.9	91.5	91.9	92.8
United States	16.7	18.7	18.2	17.8	64.4	63.0	64.3	66.0

.. = not available.

Source: Eurostat and United States Bureau of Labor Statistics.

Another trend is that more and more people are working for temporary work agencies, for subcontracting companies and on fixed-term labour contracts. In France about 1 per cent of the labour force work for temporary work agencies, while the number of subcontracting companies, particularly in services such as cleaning, maintenance, catering, etc., is increasing rapidly. In Japan industrial subcontracting has always been an important feature of the economy. Finally, private companies and the government itself are increasingly less willing to offer permanent contracts.

The development of part-time employment, often called "precarious" employment, is due to a large extent to the provisions of labour legislation with which many enterprises find it hard to comply in times of recession. Quite a few were able to carry out a flexible personnel policy in the 1960s because they could hire migrant workers. Since 1975 many large French firms, particularly in the automobile and aeronautical industries, have fired personnel with permanent contracts when orders were low, and then taken on personnel on fixed-

---

2.4

Clandestine employment

The growth in clandestine employment can be explained by various economic circumstances: *(a)* an increasing number of small enterprises tend to take on more clandestine workers than large enterprises; *(b)* it seems that illegal immigration has increased, even in a country like Italy which traditionally exported workers; and *(c)* the number of undeclared multiple jobholders is apparently increasing: these workers, who were limited in the past mainly to agriculture and building, are now to be found among all categories, and especially among teachers, firemen and policemen.

Estimates of the number of full-time or part-time clandestine workers vary considerably. The estimates from Italy range from about 2 million in 1974 to between 4 and 7 million in 1979, i.e. from 10 to 35 per cent of the labour force. In France, for the period 1979 to 1982, figures ranging from 800,000 to 1.5 million, i.e. from 3 to 6 per cent of the labour force, have been put forward. Other estimates mention 300,000 for Belgium, between 2 and 3 million for the Federal Republic of Germany, 750,000 for Sweden, between 2 and 3 million for the United Kingdom and even 25 million for the United States. In the Federal Republic of Germany it is estimated that 8 per cent of workers have an undeclared job in addition to their normal job, amounting to a total of 2 million moonlighters. One author estimates that at least one-quarter of the labour force in the United States and Canada comes within this category, while estimates in France, Sweden and Belgium range from 5 to 15 per cent (Crawford, 1978, p. 4).

Clandestine employment is the only job that many workers have. This includes the unemployed, migrant workers, pensioners, unregistered self-employed workers, housewives, houseworkers, temporary staff, students and children. Their number is difficult to estimate. Though some information is available from surveys, it is insufficient for extrapolations. According to a survey carried out by the Spanish Government, for example, half of the persons receiving unemployment benefits in the Seville region had a job. In France the employers' organisation in the Bouches-du-Rhône département estimated in 1976 that 80 per cent of the unemployed were working clandestinely. The number of clandestine immigrant workers in Europe at that time was estimated to be about 500,000. In the United States the estimate given by the Department of Justice was about 5 million. In Italy it was estimated that about 90 per cent of the 1 million houseworkers were engaged in clandestine employment. In 1974 nearly 10 per cent of old-age pensioners, housewives and holders of disability pensions were working in the Italian underground economy.

---

term contracts or from temporary work agencies when business picked up again.

Lastly, "clandestine" work is obviously increasing. Clandestine work may be defined as a principal or secondary gainful, non-casual occupation that is carried out on the fringes of the law or outside it altogether. It takes three main forms: undeclared employment of workers (especially in the clothing industry, building, agriculture, the hotel and catering trade, housework and domestic work); undeclared self-employment (finishing operations in construction, dressmaking, car repair, accounting, etc.); and undeclared multiple jobholding. Clandestine employment is only one part of the so-called underground economy, which also includes illegal cash transactions or barter and tax evasion (de Grazia, 1980, pp. 549-563). Authors like Feige claim that the underground economy is increasing and that it now accounts for nearly 20 per cent of national income in the United States. Others, like Dennison, deny this, but their arguments are based mainly on an analysis of wage incomes and clandestine employment and not on capital income.

Clandestine employment has always existed because both the employer and the employee benefit from it. The employer does not pay social security contributions or taxes so that the cost of labour is relatively low for him. The employee usually receives a higher take-home pay. For illegal immigrants, clandestine employment is the only way to have a job. Clandestine employment appears to have increased since the recession (see box 2.4) for several reasons. Faced with increased competition, many enterprises found it difficult to reduce labour costs and therefore resorted more often to clandestine employment. This was particularly the case with small enterprises. Faced with lower real wages, many workers tried to recover their losses by taking on a second, undeclared job or by working while receiving unemployment and other social benefits. Moreover, the increase in size of enterprises has made many jobs uninteresting and monotonous, with the result that many workers look for independent or autonomous work.

□

In short, these brief analyses show that the system of employment – which, as R. Salais has put it, operates like a "suction and force pump" – is singularly complicated. Along with the simple sequence of "inactivity prior to the age of employment – typical activity – inactivity after the age of retirement", there are now to and fro movements between typical employment, unemployment, atypical employment, early retirement. This is shown by the following figure.

The following two sections will describe how this system works, mentioning first the factors affecting labour supply and then some factors affecting labour demand.

Figure 2.2
The employment system

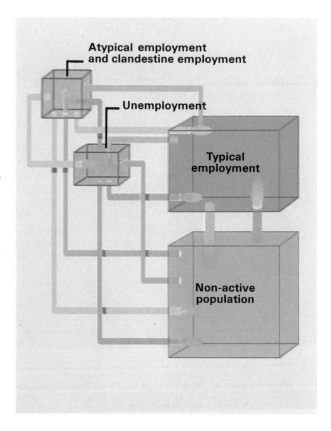

The labour force: dynamics of labour supply

Between 1960 and 1980 the labour force[11] of the OECD countries remained fairly stable at about 69 per cent of the population between 15 and 64 years of age. It grew at an average annual rate of 1.1 per cent, though slightly faster towards the end of the 1970s: from 1973 to 1980, it grew by 1.3 per cent, reaching the level of about 350 million persons in 1980. The increasing growth rates at the end of the 1970s (continuing in some countries in the 1980s) are due to a large extent to the so-called baby boom. The high birth rates after the Second World War declined steeply in North America around 1960 and about five to ten years later in European

countries such as Austria, the Federal Republic of Germany, Italy, the Netherlands and the United Kingdom. Consequently, the generation born of that boom entered the North American labour market in full force during the 1970s and will do so in most of the European countries in the years to come.

Between 1960 and 1980 labour participation rates among men, especially older men, decreased (see table 2.8). This is due to the long-term trend of increasing incomes and better pension provisions, which enable many men to retire earlier. In quite a few Western European countries labour force participation rates of men from 55 to 64 years have declined steeply since 1973 largely as a result of early retirement schemes intended to reduce the

Table 2.8
Male and female labour force participation rates (in percentage)

	1960			1973			1980		
	Total	Male	Female	Total	Male	Female	Total	Male	Female
Australia	67.2[b]	94.3[b]	38.9[b]	70.5	92.0	48.3	70.5	87.9	52.6
Austria	72.9	88.6[c]	50.4[c]	65.8	84.6	48.6	65.1	81.8	49.2
Belgium	62.2	88.5	36.4	63.6	84.7	42.5	64.2	80.2	48.0
Canada	62.3	91.9	32.0	66.7	86.1	47.2	71.8	86.4	57.3
Denmark	71.2	99.5	43.5	75.9	89.6	61.9	81.0	90.0[d]	70.8[d]
Finland	78.0	91.1	65.9	71.7	80.0	63.6	72.6	78.2	67.1
France	69.9	87.4[e]	46.1[e]	67.7	86.3	48.7	67.6	82.5	52.5
Germany (Fed. Rep. of)	70.5	94.9	49.3	68.3	88.9	48.7	65.4	81.7	49.3
Italy	64.1	93.3	36.7	58.9	84.9	33.9	60.9	82.9	39.8
Japan	75.8	92.2	60.1	71.7	90.1	54.0	71.8	89.1	54.9
Norway	64.3	97.2	36.3	67.8	84.7	50.6	75.5	87.5	63.2
Spain	60.5	99.8	23.6	62.7	92.9	33.4	56.4	81.3	31.9
Sweden	73.3[e]	93.1[e]	53.3[e]	75.5	88.1	62.6	81.0	87.8	74.1
United Kingdom	73.4	99.1	48.6	72.9	92.7	53.3	73.5	89.3	57.6
United States	68.6	91.7	42.6	68.4	86.2	51.1	72.4	85.4	59.7
OECD (except Turkey)	68.7[a]	93.7	44.7	67.9	88.3	48.0	69.7	85.5	52.1

[a] Estimated.   [b] 1964.   [c] 1968.   [d] 1979.   [e] 1962.

Source: OECD: *Labour force statistics*, various editions.

number of unemployed. Between 1970 and 1979 the participation rates of men aged 60 to 64 fell from 65 to 38 per cent in France, from 75 to 40 per cent in the Federal Republic of Germany and from 75 to 62 per cent in the United States. Significantly, the compulsory retirement age is moving in opposite directions in Western Europe on the one side and in the United States and Japan on the other. The tendency in Western Europe is to lower the age in order to release jobs for youth. In the United States recent legislation has removed any mandatory retirement age in the federal public service and has forbidden a mandatory retirement age below 70 in most other sectors. This policy seems to be inspired by a concern for the rights of older workers and the solvency of retirement funds. In Japan more and more firms are increasing the compulsory retirement age from 55 to 60 years. However, most Japanese workers wish to go on working because pension benefits are rather low. Many find a job in the same or another company (at much lower wages), but a large number of them become unemployed.

Between 1960 and 1980 the labour force participation rates of young people decreased drastically in Western Europe and Japan because of longer education, a trend that will continue in future, though to a smaller degree. In North America and Australia youth participation rates have been increasing because, though the number of youth attending school is growing, many of them tend increasingly to have a job at the same time.

The greatest change that has taken place in the past 20 years is the growing proportion of women (especially married women) in the labour force (see table 2.8). The proportion of women between 15 and 64 years of age has increased in all the OECD countries (except Turkey), rising from about 45 per cent in 1960 to 48 per cent in 1973 and to more

2.5

Labour force participation of women in Japan

In 1960 about one-third of the labour force, mostly women, worked in agriculture. As a result of the rapid growth of industry and services between 1960 and 1973, many women left self-employment in agriculture for paid employment in industry or the services. But, as the table shows, female labour force participation rates dropped considerably: from 54.5 to 50.6 per cent from 1960 to 1965 and from 49.9 to 45.7 per cent from 1970 to 1975. This was partly due to the fact that an increasing number of adolescents and young adults enrolled for secondary and higher education. The figure clearly shows that the percentage of young women entering the university rose very rapidly between 1960 and 1965 and between 1970 and 1975. It also shows that enrolment rates of young men and young women since 1970 have remained fairly constant, reaching the very high level of about 30 per cent in 1980. The same trend is found for enrolment in senior high school, with the rates of 95.4 per cent for girls and 93.1 per cent for boys in 1980.

Another interesting fact is that from 1960 to 1975 the labour force participation rates of women between 25 and 40 years of age declined, while they remained more or less constant for women over 40. The main reason for this is the declining importance of agricultural activities, which women can usually combine with household work and child-rearing. It is more difficult to combine household work with a job in industry or the services. Consequently, many women workers leave their jobs owing to marriage, childbirth and child-rearing. When women re-enter the labour force in their forties, many enterprises, especially the smaller ones, tend to hire them for temporary or part-time jobs. These women are not able to obtain the better paid, full-time jobs (in the larger enterprises) which, under the system of lifetime employment, are reserved almost exclusively for men. Under this system, which is based on seniority, the highest wages go to workers who have the longest period of service in the enterprise.

University entry rates by sex

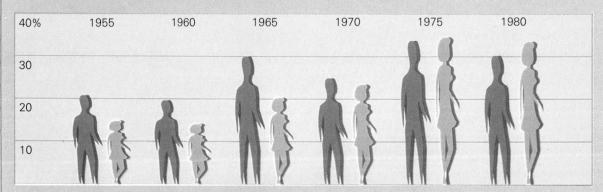

Source : Government of Japan Research and Statistics Division, Minister's Secretariat, Ministry of Education.

Labour force participation rates in Japan (%) = employed population + unemployed population/population aged 15 years and over

Age	1960	M	F	1965	M	F	1970	M	F	1975	M	F	1980	M	F
15-19		52.7	49.0		36.3	35.8		31.4	33.6		20.5	21.7		17.4	18.5
20-24		87.8	70.8		85.8	70.2		80.7	70.6		76.5	66.2		69.6	70.0
25-29		95.5	54.5		96.8	49.0		97.1	45.5		97.2	42.6		96.3	49.2
30-34		96.6	56.5		97.0	51.1		97.8	68.2		98.1	43.9		97.6	48.2
35-39		96.2	59.0		97.1	59.6		97.8	57.5		98.1	54.0		97.6	58.0
40-54		95.9	59.0		96.3	60.2		96.9	61.8		97.1	60.0		96.8	62.8
55-59		88.9	49.7		90.0	49.8		91.2	48.7		92.2	48.8		91.2	50.5
60-64		81.4	43.0		82.8	39.8		81.5	39.1		79.4	38.0		77.8	38.8
65 and over		56.9	25.6		56.3	21.6		49.4	17.9		44.4	15.3		41.0	15.5
Total		84.8	54.5		81.7	50.6		81.8	49.9		81.4	45.7		79.8	47.6

Source: Government of Japan, Statistics Bureau, Prime Minister's Office.

than 52 per cent in 1980. The most significant increases took place in Canada, the United States and the Nordic countries (Denmark, Norway, Sweden). It is interesting to note that, despite the recession, the increases between 1973 and 1980 were higher than those between 1960 and 1973. An exception is Japan, where there has been a decrease in the proportion of women due probably to the sharp drop in female family workers in agriculture and the preference given by employers to male workers (see box 2.5).

There are many reasons that prompt women to work outside their home. The main one is that they now receive better education and are on a more equal footing with men in this respect. Families have fewer children, and those they have are born closer together. In addition, divorce rates are growing and women who become household heads need a job. Changing attitudes about the equality of the sexes have also favoured the trend towards paid employment for women. Lastly, work is an important place for making social contacts (Paukert, 1982).

A number of powerful economic factors are also at work. Much of household work, such as cleaning and washing, is "mechanised"; the family needs a supplementary income in times of lower economic growth when the husband may earn less; some households activities, such as child care (nurseries, baby-sitters, etc.), have been "monetised"; and the rise in women's wages has increased the economic value of being a housewife. Moreover, the rapid development of the services sector, particularly the public sector, has increased the availability of part-time jobs and the demand for female labour.

A final factor that affects labour supply is the number of hours worked by persons with a job. In all countries this has tended to diminish for some time now. The working week is shorter, and leaves are longer. In addition, in times of severe recession, such as the periods 1974 to 1975 and 1980 to 1982, there tend to be sharp reductions in the average number of hours worked (especially in the manufacturing sector).

Japanese workers tend to work longer hours than workers in the industrialised West. In 1978 they worked 2,146 hours annually on an average, as compared with 1,957 hours in the United Kingdom, 1,934 in the United States, 1,799 in France and 1,728 in the Federal Republic of Germany. The difference is due primarily to the fact that in the West between 80 and 90 per cent of wage earners work a five-day week, as compared with 24 per cent in Japanese enterprises (especially the larger ones). Japanese workers also have shorter paid holidays, and often do not take them entirely. Lastly, they tend to work more overtime, though overtime rates are lower than in Europe and North America. It might be concluded that the benefits they derive from greater productivity are wage increases rather than shorter working hours.

Growth, productivity and employment: the dynamics of labour demand

The volume of employment depends primarily on the growth rates and patterns of the economy, i.e. the increase in the demand for goods and services and the change in its composition. The volume of employment also depends on productivity, which is largely the result of technology, work organisation and the quality of management. In the current situation, unemployment is due mainly to the slow-down or altered operation of economy, which does not supply or create enough jobs to meet demand.

Before discussing the phenomena mentioned at the end of the introduction to this chapter, which

Table 2.9
Vacancies (V) and registered unemployment (U) for selected years (annual averages in thousands).
Unemployment due to deficient demand ($U_{DD} = 100 \times \dfrac{U - V}{U}$) (in percentage)

Country	1960			1973			1981		
	U ('000s)	V ('000s)	U_{DD} (%)	U ('000s)	V ('000s)	U_{DD} (%)	U ('000s)	V ('000s)	U_{DD} (%)
Australia	63.3[a,b]	45.9[a]	27.5	108.0[b]	64.0	40.7	390.0[b]	35.0	91.0
Austria	83.0	30.0	63.9	41.0	66.0	(0.0)	69.0	25.0	63.8
Denmark	30.9	..	..	17.8	8.9	50.0	241.0	0.4	99.8
Finland	25.0[c]	8.9[c]	64.4	52.0	22.8	56.2	125.0	13.0	89.6
Germany (Fed. Rep. of)	271.0	465.0	(0.0)	274.0	572.0	(0.0)	1 272.0	208.0	83.6
Japan	750.0	399.0	46.8	670.0	687.0	(0.0)	1 260.0	372.0	70.5
Netherlands	30.1	92.3	(0.0)	110.0	67.1	39.0	385.0	21.0	94.5
New Zealand	0.6	6.8	(0.0)	2.3	3.5	(0.0)	48.3	3.4	93.0
Norway	17.1	4.0	76.6	12.8	8.2	35.9	28.4	6.5	77.1
Sweden	18.6[d]	37.3[d]	(0.0)	46.0	35.3	23.3	58.9	30.0	49.1
Switzerland	1.2	6.4	(0.0)	0.1	3.8	(0.0)	5.9	11.9	(0.0)
United Kingdom	377.0	315.0	16.4	619.0	403.0	34.9	2 566.0	97.0	96.2
Yugoslavia	191.3[d]	57.0[d]	70.2	382.0	54.0	85.9	809.0	77.0	90.5

.. = not available.
[a] 1964.   [b] Data from a labour force sample survey.   [c] 1961.   [d] 1962.
Source: OECD: *Main economic indicators*, various editions.

have contributed to lower growth and employment in recent years, a few words need to be said about the part of unemployment due to frictions or mismatches between labour supply and demand – what is often called frictional and structural unemployment. To put it simply, frictional unemployment occurs because it takes time for workers to change jobs. Structural unemployment occurs when the job offered is not located near the worker's home or he does not fulfil the qualifications required.[12]

The most common way of estimating structural and frictional unemployment is to compare vacancies and unemployment for each occupational group and each region, and separately for men and women.[13] In most countries such detailed data are not available, but only general data on vacancies and unemployment (see table 2.9). These data are usually based on the registers kept by official employment agencies, which cover only part of all vacancies and unemployment. This part probably increased over time because of stricter goverment regulations. Consequently, the figures for 1981 will probably be more reliable than those for 1960.

A comparison of vacancies and unemployment shows that in 1973, except in North America, unemployment due to deficient demand was either non-existent (with the number of vacancies exceeding the number of unemployed) or relatively low (less than half). This means that until 1973 such measures as training programmes, mobility incentives and better information on new jobs were able to play an important role in reducing unemployment. At the beginning of the 1980s mismatch problems on the labour market are still found only in Austria, Japan, Sweden and Switzerland. Elsewhere, demand-deficient unemployment accounts for over 90 per cent of total unemployment in OECD countries. In the United

Table 2.10
Structure of world exports by major regions (in percentage)

Sending countries or groups	Receiving countries or groups															
	United States		Japan		EEC		Other developed market economies		Developed centrally planned countries		OPEC		Non-OPEC developing countries		Total	
	1970	1980	1970	1980	1970	1980	1970	1980	1970	1980	1970	1980	1970	1980	1970	1980
United States	..	..	10.8	9.6	26.2	24.5	32.6	26.1	0.8	1.7	4.8	8.1	24.8	30.0	100.0	100.0
Japan	31.1	24.4	..	..	9.6	12.8	13.8	10.3	2.3	2.8	5.1	14.3	38.0	35.5	100.0	100.0
EEC	8.2	5.6	1.2	1.0	50.7	53.1	21.7	18.6	3.4	3.5	3.5	7.8	11.2	10.4	100.0	100.0
Other developed market economies	27.0	20.6	5.4	5.2	35.2	36.7	15.3	13.7	4.8	6.4	1.7	5.5	10.6	11.9	100.0	100.0
Developed centrally planned countries	0.7	0.9	1.5	1.1	12.4	18.2	8.4	11.3	60.3	51.1	2.2	3.1	14.4	31.2	100.0	100.0
OPEC	10.0	17.8	13.6	17.5	44.7	30.0	9.9	10.5	1.6	1.4	0.7	1.4	19.4	21.3	100.0	100.0
Non-OPEC developing countries	21.6	22.7	9.9	10.9	28.0	21.4	9.3	7.7	7.7	5.6	2.7	7.1	20.8	24.6	100.0	100.0
Total	12.6	12.0	5.0	6.2	35.3	34.7	18.1	15.0	9.2	7.3	3.1	6.5	16.6	18.2	100.0	100.0

.. = not available.

Taken from: United Nations: *Yearbook of International Trade Statistics*, 1980, Vol. I (New York, 1981), table C.

States estimates show that such unemployment, which amounted to about 60 per cent in the mid-1960s, climbed to 80 per cent in the late 1970s (Abraham, 1982).

International factors affecting employment

Any doubts that may have subsisted about the influence of international factors on growth and unemployment were quickly dispelled by the oil crises of 1973 and 1979. With the exception of net energy exporters, almost all countries experienced a deterioration in the terms of trade since the prices of imports increased faster than the prices of exports. Moreover, the price increases led to an almost chronic deficit in the current account position of some larger countries, such as France and Canada, and of most smaller OECD countries, except Switzerland and the Netherlands. The Federal Republic of Germany, Switzerland and Japan, and to some extent the United States, were able to retain a current account surplus because of their strong international competitive position,

while the United Kingdom benefited from North Sea oil and the Netherlands from natural gas.

International trade was further hampered by the instability of the currency market. Between 1974 and 1979 some US$115,000 million from OPEC countries was recycled, mainly through Western banks, into the industrialised market economies, the countries of Eastern Europe and the developing countries. The second wave of oil price increases generated about US$215,000 million in revenues during 1980 and 1981, which was used mainly to finance government deficits in the developed market economies and the increasing debts of some developing countries.

Despite slower and sometimes negative growth, most industrialised market economies have become more open. In the 1960s and the early 1970s this opening was due mainly to increased trade between European countries, especially members of the European Community, but since the first oil crisis it has also been due to the need for

Figure 2.3
Structure of the gross domestic product (in percentage)

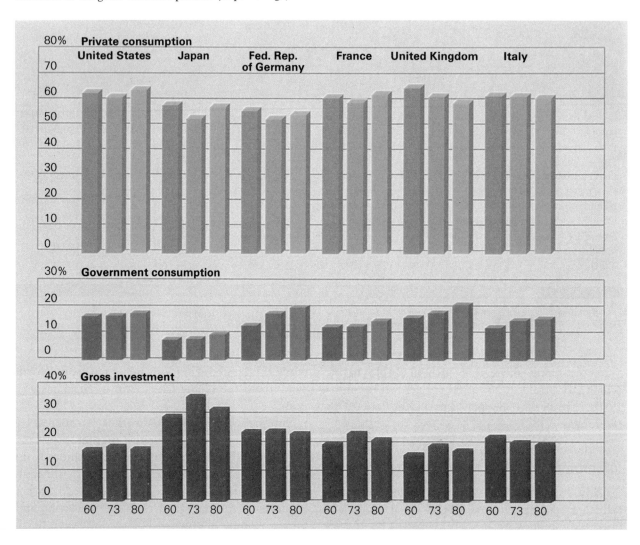

Note: The columns do not add up to 100 per cent since exports minus imports plus stock change are not included.

increased exports in order to pay the higher oil bill. Between 1973 and 1980 the value of exports, as a percentage of the gross domestic product, rose from 6.9 to 10.1 per cent in the United States, from 10 to 14 per cent in Japan, from 24.1 to 29.3 per cent in the European Community and from 31.6 to 35.8 per cent in the smaller OECD countries except Spain and Turkey, which have suffered most from the recession resulting from the oil crisis.

The oil crisis, increased competition among OECD countries and the emergence of the newly industrialised countries have upset international trade (see table 2.10). The most significant changes between 1970 and 1980, as shown by the table, are the increased oil exports from OPEC countries to the United States and Japan and also the growing OPEC market for exports from the OECD countries and the newly industrialised countries.

Figure 2.3 (continued)
Structure of the gross domestic product (in percentage)

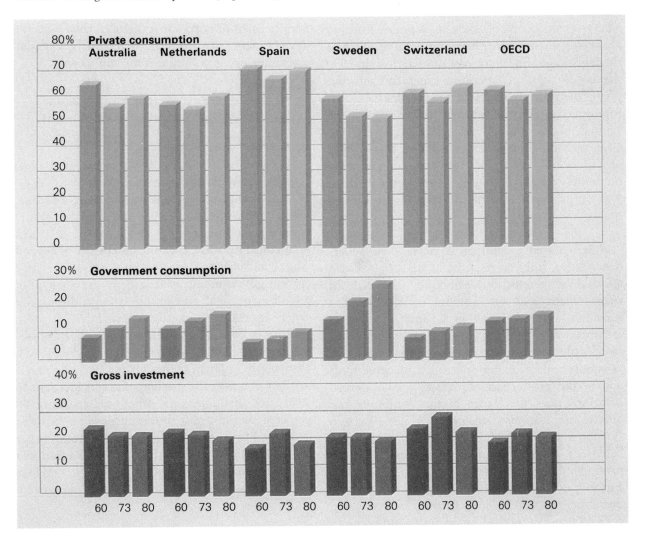

Note: The columns do not add up to 100 per cent since exports minus imports plus stock change are not included.

The table also shows that Japan exports much more to the other OECD countries than it imports. Other significant facts brought out by the table are the rapid increase in United States imports from and exports to the newly industrialised countries, which are the largest traders in the developing world, and the relative decline in trade among developed countries of the CMEA (Council for Mutual Economic Assistance).

As a result of low and sometimes negative growth, the OECD market has not expanded much since 1973. Nevertheless, Japan has succeeded in expanding its exports to the other OECD countries, to the detriment of both North America and Europe. The ensuing loss of jobs in sectors competing for imports has tended to reinforce protectionism. Examples are the dispute on iron and steel and agriculture between the United States and the European Community and the dispute on car sales between Japan and other OECD countries, such as the United States, France and Italy. Many countries, particularly in Western Europe, are trying to improve their competitive position through wage and labour cost moderation. In 1980 the hourly cost of labour in the manufacturing sector in most countries of the European Community was 10 to 30 per cent higher than in the United States, though in 1981, owing to the appreciation of the dollar, it was less than 10 per cent. It should be noted, however, that in 1980 the hourly labour cost in the same sector in Japan was only 56 per cent of the cost in the United States.[14]

International competitiveness, however, depends not only on the cost of labour. It is also affected by production techniques, the type of management and the amount of government subsidies. As mentioned in Chapter 7 on new information technology, Japan today is the recognised leader in the field of manufacturing tools such as robots and computer-controlled machine tools and in the production of "chips". The United States remains the leader in the computer and telecommunications market, while Western Europe is trailing behind. At the same time, Japan has been investing much more heavily in its production process than either the United States or Europe; in 1980 Japan spent 32 per cent of its gross domestic product on investments, as compared with 18 per cent by the United States and between 20 and 23 per cent by most countries in Western Europe.

Some analysts have recently started to question the attitudes of managers in the United States as compared with those of Japanese managers. According to these analysts, American and to some extent European managers have a preference for servicing existing markets rather than creating new ones and, owing to their concentration on short-term returns and "management by numbers", many of them have effectively forsworn long-term technology superiority as a competitive

weapon (Hayes and Abernathy, 1980, pp. 67-77). Another criticism made is that many managers are more preoccupied with financial control and the management of corporate portfolios than with the development of products that satisfy genuine consumer needs (Ohmae, 1982, pp. 46-55).

Domestic factors affecting employment

Growth of public expenditure

Between 1960 and 1980 government final consumption expenditure increased from 15 to 17.1 per cent and current government disbursements[15] from 25.5 to 35.6 per cent in all the OECD countries (see figures 2.3 and 2.4). Government final consumption expenditures consist mainly of wages and salaries paid to civil servants, while current government disbursements are the sum of government final consumption expenditure and other expenditure consisting mainly of social security payments. Current government disbursements have tended to increase faster since 1973, particularly in Japan (although at a fairly low level in 1980), France, the Netherlands and Sweden. In 1980 such disbursements amounted to about 40 per cent of the gross domestic product in most Western European countries and to about 30 per cent in North America and the Pacific. Particularly high percentages were found in the Netherlands and Sweden, which are prototypes of the welfare State.

This sharp rise in government expenditure is due to several factors. First, the number of persons receiving social security and social assistance benefits, especially unemployment benefits, has increased because of the recession. Secondly, the amount of these benefits and their coverage are increasing as a result of a broader social policy, a rapid rise in the cost of medical care and increasing expenditure on pension schemes (see Chapter 6). Thirdly, after the first oil crisis many governments expanded the number of jobs in the public sector to compensate for the loss of jobs in the private sector.

Figure 2.4
Current government disbursements as a percentage of GDP

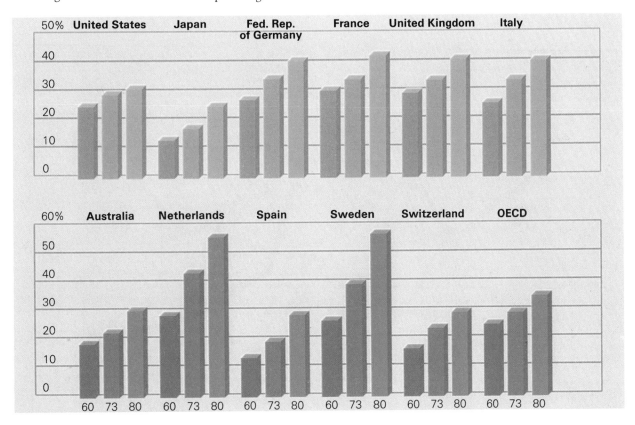

Source: OECD: *Historical statistics*, 1960–80.

Decline in investment

While the share of gross capital formation (private and public investments) in the gross domestic product increased between 1960 and 1973, with a corresponding fall in private final consumption expenditure, the opposite trend occurred between 1973 and 1980: the share of private consumption increased while the share of investment dropped. It is interesting to note that between 1960 and 1980 the share of gross investments in Japan accounted for more than 30 per cent of the gross domestic product, while it was less than 20 per cent in the United States and the United Kingdom.

The secretariat of GATT considers that the decline in investment, which became more pro-nounced after 1973, is due to two sets of factors: uncertainties that discourage enterprises from investing in technological innovations and what may be called tendencies towards the hardening of market relationships.

The main uncertainties concern *(a)* energy supplies and prices; *(b)* inflation, one of whose least studied aspects, "the increased variability of relative prices" (Blackhurst, Marian, Tumlir, Chapter II, 1978), makes international planning more difficult; *(c)* international economic relations which make exchange rates less predictable and tend to tighten access to markets; *(d)* the international financial system where a significant proportion of the world debt may be regarded as a "deadweight debt" because it is not accompanied

Figure 2.5
Annual percentage variation trends of real labour costs in relation to productivity in the manufacturing industry between 1961 and 1981 (cumulative distribution; national average = 100)

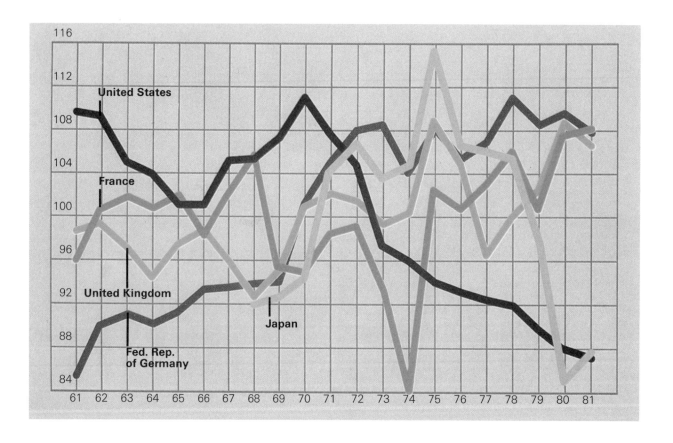

by any "additional production facilities from which to service it" (*International trade 1981/82*, p. 19).[16]

Added to these uncertainties, which are due primarily to the international economic environment (except non-imported inflation), are significant distortions resulting from national policies that, by affecting the composition of investment, create "bottlenecks in real capacity" (Blackhurst, Marian, Tumlir, 1978, p. 74) and are at the heart of the unemployment problem. The GATT analysts call in question here, explicitly or implicitly, certain industrial policies, on the part of both enterprises and trade unions. In the long run, in their opinion, the protection of threatened indus-

tries is never a paying proposition for either production or employment; besides, it tends to weaken export industries and thus jeopardises employment still further. Subsidies, including export subsidies, often impede the necessary adjustments and, above all, are self-defeating when coupled with protectionism. Lastly, cartellisation results in rising prices and lower productivity.

Increase of labour costs

At the same time, between 1960 and 1980, labour costs grew faster than the average productivity of the economy (see also Chapter 5 on incomes and wages). Labour costs include net

Figure 2.5 (continued)
Annual percentage variation trends of real labour costs in relation to productivity in the manufacturing industry between 1961 and 1981 (cumulative distribution; national average = 100)

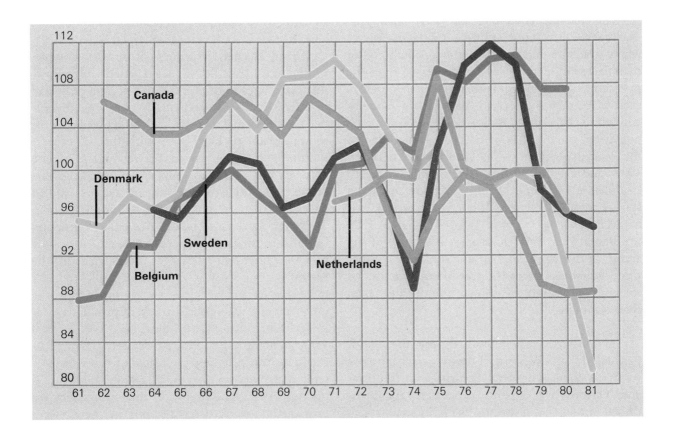

wages (take-home pay), payroll taxes and social security contributions by both employers and employees, as well as various fringe benefits such as private company pension schemes, free cars, expense accounts, etc., enjoyed by the better-paid employees in the private sector. Labour costs even tend to increase faster than labour productivity in manufacturing (see figure 2.5) where productivity however is higher than in the services. This is particularly true in the Federal Republic of Germany, the United Kingdom and Belgium, where employment in manufacturing decreased between 1960 and 1980 (see table 2.6). The trend is evident also in France and the Netherlands and, to a smaller degree, in Denmark and Sweden. Between 1968 and 1973 the cost of labour in the Japanese

manufacturing sector also grew faster than productivity, which increased by more than 10 per cent annually; the trend was reversed between 1973 and 1980. In the United States and Canada, where employment in manufacturing has increased since 1960, labour productivity has nevertheless been growing faster than labour costs. But it should be noted that in the United States it is particularly the services sector (see table 2.7) that has contributed to creating employment; between 1970 and 1980 most of the jobs created were in the relatively low-paying public and private professions. Wages and labour costs for unskilled work were relatively low because (see the first section) many young people, married women and immigrants were entering the labour market.

Moreover, there was a relative decline in the demand for unskilled labour in agriculture and small-scale industry.

When labour costs increase faster than productivity, the remuneration of capital is lower. Many statistics indicate that the profitability of manufacturing enterprises has decreased over the past ten years. Consequently, they either reduce their investments or do not increase their equity enough. Lower profitability however cannot be put down only to labour costs. It is also due to the over-investment which took place between 1967 and 1973, when governments tried to stimulate investment through tax allowances and special credits and when labour was scarce (Glyn, in Matthews, 1982, pp. 148-165). Since 1973 profitability has further decreased because of the slump in the world market and stronger competition which has kept producer prices low and led to underutilisation of capital goods and even their scrapping.

Labour costs rose rapidly during the 1970s, particularly in Western Europe, mainly as a result of increased social security contributions and various wage-fixing processes. As mentioned in the second section, the large majority of workers are employed in relatively stable jobs. Their wages and salaries are affected by fluctuations in the cost of living, pressures for a gradual increase in real wages, the relative movement of wages to one another and, of course, the state of the labour market (Zoeteweij, 1983). The role of collective bargaining and trade unions in wage trends is often stressed but, while collective agreements formalise wage adjustments, the general movement responds to considerations of fairness and reason. The employee and the employer have a strong common interest in maintaining a stable work relationship and avoiding the costs and bother that go with separation: finding a better job on the one side, and hiring and training new workers on the other. Such mutually beneficial relationships are maintained more easily when each party feels

that he gets a proper deal from the other: a reasonable work performance for a fair remuneration. However, this situation does not necessarily lead to price stability, full employment and adjustment to changing economic conditions.

At all events, in times of recession when productivity rises slowly, a systematic full adjustment of wages to rises in the cost of living can lead to inflation. This is particularly true when everyone considers that it is only right and proper for his remuneration to keep pace with that of others: within the same enterprise, between it and others, between major sectors (public and private sectors or services and goods producing sectors) and at times even between countries (airline pilots). These emulative effects lead not only to inflation but also at times to reduced employment opportunities. Increases in wages negotiated in the manufacturing sector are often followed by increases in the services sector (including the government) where the growth of productivity is lower. Since the share of the labour cost in total value added in this sector, particularly the government, is much higher, the prices of most services tend to grow faster than the prices of manufactured goods. As a result, more and more services previously provided by persons in the services sector or within the household are now provided by manufactured goods.

This transition towards the self-service economy can be noted in many spheres of life (Gershuny, 1978). Over the past 20 or 30 years spending on cinemas and theatres has given way to spending on television and video recorders, while household work, domestic help and laundry services have been replaced by domestic appliances. Expenditure on public transport services has grown much more slowly than expenditure on private cars. With the progress in technological developments, this shift from suppliers of services to domestic goods foreshadows the mechanisation of some services, provided mainly by the government, such as education and medical care.

What does this mean for employment in the services sector? If productivity in manufacturing continues to increase as fast as in the past 20 years and if an increasing part of private consumption will be satisfied by products rather than by services, then the 1980s may not show the increase in service employment that characterised the period between 1960 and 1980. This picture, however, may not be true for all services. Many of them – commerce, banking, business and some government services – are largely dependent on the manufacturing sector. Moreover, employment in such services as recreation and travel may expand if personal incomes continue to increase. However, it is unlikely that employment in the public sector and in personal and social services will increase. Since productivity increases in the government are low and labour costs grow at the same rate as in the private sector, the implicit price[17] of public services will rise more rapidly than that of goods and services produced in the private sector (Elliott and Fallick, 1981). It may well be that taxpayers will not be willing to pay such a price, particularly at a time when real personal incomes are decreasing.

Effects of policies to combat unemployment and inflation

The economic debate since the early 1970s has focused on the coexistence of inflation and unemployment, the so-called stagflation, two evils combined. Large-scale unemployment is unacceptable because it leads to frustration, a loss of income and social instability. Inflation, for its part, has undesirable redistributive effects, in particular for pensioners who depend on nominal benefits and persons holding deposit accounts and bonds; furthermore, it creates a climate of uncertainty which tends to inhibit and distort investment decisions, thus hampering economic growth and employment creation. For governments, the choice between inflation and employment became crucial after the first and second oil crises. Schematically, it may be said that after the first oil crisis countries tended to follow a policy of expansion, giving priority to employment,

whereas after the second priority has been given to combating inflation.

After the first crisis, most governments were able to finance their deficits by increasing their debts in the belief that the recession would be short-lived. Consequently they expanded their final consumption expenditures (not their investments) and payments on social security and social assistance.

When the second oil crisis occurred at the end of 1979, governments were in quite a different position than at the beginning of the first. The expansionary programmes adopted after the first oil crisis had increased government indebtedness and, more importantly, the rate of inflation. In the OECD countries the rate had climbed from 4.7 per cent in 1972 to 13.4 per cent in 1974; from 1976 to 1979 it remained stable at about 9 per cent, to climb again in 1980 to 12.9 per cent. Confronted with this situation, all the OECD countries, especially the United States and the United Kingdom, decided to concentrate on reducing the rate of inflation. How? By controlling the money supply and restricting credit. This dear money policy drove the long-term real interest rates up to the historically very high level of 5 per cent in the United States by the end of 1981 and to about 4 per cent in the United Kingdom. Since most countries had a balance-of-payments deficit in 1980-81 as a result of the second oil crisis, they had to follow that example. Otherwise they would have had to accept an even faster appreciating dollar and, as a consequence, increased inflation because of higher import prices. France alone embarked on an expansionary policy in May 1981. It was able to do so at the time because government indebtedness was still relatively low. In 1982, owing to large balance-of-payments deficits, the French Government switched to a more restrictive policy.

The strict monetary policy applied by these countries has been successful in bringing down the rate of inflation. From 1980 to 1982 it dropped from 10.4 to slightly more than 4 per cent in the

United States and from 12 to 6 per cent in the United Kingdom. This has been achieved at the cost of investment and employment. High mortgage rates have discouraged investments in housing, considerably reducing labour-intensive construction activities. High interest rates have made it more attractive to invest in high-yield bonds (particularly in the Eurodollar market), to the detriment of new investment.

Under the combined effect of higher interest rates and the economic recession, investment in the United States dropped by 6 per cent in 1982. In the United Kingdom it went down by 8.2 per cent in 1981, to rise again by about 1 per cent annually in 1982 and 1983. In the Federal Republic of Germany investment fell by 4 per cent in 1981 and 6 per cent in 1982, but may rise slightly in 1983. In Japan it rose by about 1.5 per cent annually from 1981 to 1983 and in France and Italy by about 2 per cent. Investment dropped much more in the smaller OECD countries, particularly in 1981: by 16 per cent in Belgium and Denmark and by 10 per cent in the Netherlands and Greece.

In the course of 1982 both the United States and the United Kingdom seemed to have forgone their strict monetary policy, with the result that interest rates are now going down, as in other OECD countries as well. Will the real interest rates follow suit? They have not at the time of writing this report.

Another feature of government policies since 1979 has been the slower growth of government expenditure and, in some countries such as the United States and the United Kingdom, a reduction in income taxes. This policy trend is inspired by the so-called supply economics, whose proponents maintain that excessive regulation and high taxes stifle entrepreneurial activity and investment. The main impetus, however, comes from fast-growing governmental indebtedness. In 1981 general government financing requirements amounted to 3.2 per cent of the gross national income in the United States, to 7.7 per cent in

Japan, to 13.2 per cent in Italy, to 16.3 per cent in Belgium and to 7.4 per cent in the Netherlands (BIS, 1982, p. 74). These requirements absorb about one-quarter of the domestic capital market[18] in the United States and about 65 per cent in Belgium and Italy, thereby contributing to higher interest rates and pushing out borrowers from the private sector. Governments are now in the uncomfortable position where expenditures, in particular unemployment and social assistance benefits, tend to increase rapidly while tax revenues tend to decrease as a result of the recession. Moreover, high interest rates make it very expensive to borrow and already absorb a large part of government budgets. The percentage of government expenditure devoted to investment is also declining. The changing composition and the slower growth of government expenditure weigh heavily on employment. The effect is already apparent in the United States and the United Kingdom, where government employment is hardly increasing; and the same is likely to happen in other countries. It may well be that the first increase of jobs in services and government which maintained full employment up to 1973 will not be produced again in the 1980s, to the detriment of employment.

Conclusions

At the time of writing this report, the signs of economic recovery visible in the United States since early 1983 seem confirmed. But it is hard to say whether the trend will continue and whether it will spread to the other OECD countries. It seems to have been triggered off primarily by an increase in private consumption and a revival of construction activity. The still high real interest rates and the indebtedness of developing countries could tend to curb investment in machinery and equipment and thus limit the extent of the recovery.

But even if growth rates pick up vigorously again in 1984, the OECD countries should try to avert a danger which they were not faced with overall between 1970 and 1975 but which is likely to be left them by the current crisis: the concomitance of high levels of economic growth and of unemployment. It is hardly conceivable that governments, the people affected and public opinion would resign themselves to such a situation.

There is something of a paradox, at least for the layman, in the fact that high levels of growth and unemployment should exist side by side since the economies in question are capable of remarkable dynamism (witness the 65 million additional jobs created between 1960 and 1980). Such a situation also aggravates the human dimension of the problem, for it leads to a waste of energy and social marginalisation. Such marginalisation – which is felt to be the case by most of the unemployed and the employed alike, regardless of their opinions about present employment – is all the more unacceptable as it involves a *de facto* discrimination: as we have seen, it is above all the young, women, unskilled workers and racial minorities who are most exposed to unemployment. The first and foremost social problem of these economies, therefore, is the composition of the unemployed labour force as much as the number of persons out of work. Moreover, while the compensation provided by society today makes unemployment less of a hardship than it was in the 1930s, it has not effaced the stigma attached to social marginalisation which is even more difficult to endure when society as a whole is prosperous.

Do the analyses miss the point?

It cannot be said that governments are unaware of the seriousness of the situation. Their principal objective is certainly to redress the situation and they have mustered an impressive array of means for the purpose. These, however, have proved to be ineffective and over-effective by turns: ineffective, because at the outset we had both inflation and unemployment; over-effective, because now that inflation has at last been brought under control in many countries, unemployment is rising at unacceptable rates.

One cannot help feeling that a systematic, in-depth analysis has not been made of the situation or, if it has, that it is based on an inadequate theoretical and conceptual framework. Is the ineffectiveness of the remedies due to mistakes in the diagnosis? Or are we faced with a new disease, a form of pernicious anaemia that causes producers, equipment and capital to languish? [19]

Towards an overall international analysis

Admittedly, the studies carried out over the past few years in the heat of the situation the results of which were summarised in the preceding sections are not without value. It is not certain, however, that they have brought to light all of the important factors that were already at work before the crisis or the profound changes that are taking place in the operation of the economy and the behaviour of individuals and social groups. It seems pertinent to ask why all the countries concerned do not carry out a joint analysis of the situation and try to reach some agreement, as suggested by the secretariat of GATT, on "the underlying causes of the problem" [20] with a view to identifying appropriate solutions. According to GATT, such solutions would have to involve a reform of trade policies, reviewing not only the macro-economic aspect – how to liberalise trade to a greater extent – but also the micro-economic aspects, i.e. how to restore the efficiency of a price system that has been thoroughly upset in the past decade or two.

Possible solutions to the problem can hardly be advanced until the underlying factors have been elucidated. But there is no reason why specialists of such organisations as the OECD, the EEC, the International Monetary Fund, GATT and the ILO – where economic and monetary policy-makers and the social forces are represented – should not urgently pool their efforts for the purpose of such an elucidation. The results, including suggestions about possible medium–term, concerted policies regarding growth, prices, capital flows and income, could be submitted to the various countries for consideration or even to an international economic and social conference.

It may of course seem presumptuous to think that government experts, international specialists and representatives of the social forces could reach an agreement on such complex questions. But such a joint consultation might at the very least be expected to produce a better understanding of the relative part played by various macro-economic factors and the behaviour of individuals and social groups in the cause and development of the situation, the nature of the changes that have taken place – for example, in resource-allocation and price-fixing machinery – and the transitional or permanent character of the phenomenon. Without such an analysis, the best-intentioned measures for absorbing unemployment may turn out to have harmful effects in the medium term. The economic rigour dictated by the short term may also turn out to be misleading, one that undermines the necessary conditions for recovery and leads to unjustified social rigour, in particular for the most underprivileged persons.

The "consensus": limits and conditions

It may also seem presumptuous to think that a common framework for discussion, even if there were a broad measure of agreement at the outset, could lead to a "consensus" at the international level or within each country. Such a consensus would be difficult for two reasons, one theoretical and the other political.

Theoretically, an important gap unfortunately exists concerning the role of institutions, ideologies, social groups and individual behaviour in economic life. Experts and politicians often give the impression that they think of the economy as a machine: it is enough to press the right buttons here and there and it will start working smoothly

again. Let us assume for a moment that everyone agrees on an apparently irrefutable economic analysis of the situation. Will all of us, individually and collectively, act in the light of that knowledge? It must be remembered that the historical battles for the distribution of national wealth were often fiercest in periods of low growth. Today, even if everyone were to agree that the time for sacrifice has come, it is most likely that both within and between countries, each would expect the sacrifices to come from the other and that no one would consent to them if he was not sure that everyone else would take an equal part in the effort.

This, then, is to place the debate on the political level as well and to stress the importance of institutions and machinery that allow a minimum platform of agreement to be achieved – which does not rule out clashes or conflicts. At the national level, some countries succeed in this better than others through an economic and social dialogue at the country level organised by formal machinery provided for in the political institutions or in collective bargaining arrangements or by informal, top-level consultation procedures between government and representatives of the social forces. At the international level, the existing arrangements worked better in times of growth than in times of crisis.

At all events, it is reasonable to think that the international analysis proposed here would facilitate the necessary economic and social dialogue and bring out the conditions for a minimum agreement within countries and between countries. It would show specifically, for example, how "every man for himself" may be harmful for all. It would reveal the conditions and advantages of a package of concerted international measures for the resumption of growth and the gradual advance towards full employment. The package could include proposals relating to the reduction of East-West tensions and the launching of a large-scale programme for the benefit of the developing countries.

2.6

Reduction of working time

There are many ways of reducing working time: fewer hours worked per week or per day, less overtime, longer holidays, early retirement, educational leave, lengthening of compulsory education, part-time work, job-sharing.

In assessing the long-term effects of these measures on employment, their impact on labour and capital costs, costs for the State, labour productivity and final demand must be evaluated.

The application of each individual criterion may lead to opposite conclusions. For example, there is disagreement about whether the reduction of the working week (or longer holidays) should take place with or without full wage compensation. If employers provide full wage compensation, the hourly labour cost will increase, but so will final demand. Too sharp an increase in the cost of labour may reduce the competitive position of enterprises in the long run, thereby reducing employment, while increased final demand may increase employment in the short term. A reduction in the working week may entail a lower degree of capital utilisation, leading to a higher capital cost per hour worked. But this cost could be reduced if workers accepted some form of shift work, which might increase the operation time of capital goods. In that case, employers would probably resort less frequently to overtime.

Many Western European countries have promoted early retirement, which has led to a reduction of surplus labour supply. Who in fact bears the cost of such measures? Those who contribute to social security or those who receive lower benefits? If employers' contributions increase, so do labour costs; if employees' contributions increase and their net income aspirations remain unchanged,

labour costs also increase; finally, if the State bears the burden, it will have fewer funds available for creating employment. These same trade-offs apply in the case of educational leave and the lengthening of compulsory education (though in these cases the assessment is more complicated because both measures are likely to increase labour productivity).

Part-time work and job-sharing (a full-time job carried out by two persons) seem to have fairly straightforward effects. They hardly affect final demand, do not increase the hourly labour cost and are unlikely to increase the capital cost. However, they make personnel management and collective bargaining more complicated. Moreover, part-time workers do not have the same rights as full-time workers.

A number of studies have been carried out to estimate the long-term employment effects of a gradual introduction of the 36/35-hour working week. Such an estimation requires a macro-economic model covering the whole economy. Under the most favourable assumptions, the effects on employment concern between 2 and 6 per cent of the labour force. But a study recently carried out in France (Marchand et al., 1983), to assess the impact of reducing the working week from 40 to 39 hours, arrives at a much lower estimate: according to this study, employment would increase by only 0.2 to 0.4 per cent. As a result of these studies, and a number of experiments made at the national level, as in Belgium and France, governments tend to prefer a reduction of working time negotiated at the enterprise or industry level. They can accelerate this process by implementing advantageous early retirement schemes.

69

A patchwork of solutions

All of this, however, is not to deny the value of various solutions now put forward for reducing unemployment: for example, the launching of special youth employment programmes; incentives for small and medium-sized enterprises; the development of new technologies in manufacturing and the services; the critical review of the influence of wage-fixing machinery on levels of employment and productivity; the various formal and informal measures to control prices and income; and the reduction of working hours in relation to job creation (see box 2.6). However, not all these factors make the same contribution to solving the problem as a whole, and their relative importance cannot be properly weighed without an overall framework for discussion and action.

Towards another type of employment?

This common framework, besides its intrinsic advantages, would serve as a form of exorcism, so to speak. For it is hardly conceivable that, once the underlying causes of the situation have been identified and the common medium-term objectives set, the countries concerned, which are among the most advanced economically and the most dynamic technologically, should not succeed in creating, despite the crisis, or perhaps because of it, the necessary conditions for renewed prosperity, even before the end of the present decade. The efforts made to adjust will then pay off, and the new trends observed in the field of employment – a new distribution between paid and unpaid work, the growing number of atypical jobs and activities where people can determine their own conditions of work – may develop. There is no reason why a higher level of prosperity should not permit a different distribution of work, reducing or varying its length and ensuring a suitable minimum income for all, including people outside the labour force. If this proves to be the case, the current employment crisis, rather than reflecting a passing storm, may well herald the dawn of another type of employment.

[1] There are 24 industrialised market economy countries, spanning the globe from North America to Australia and New Zealand and including western and southern Europe (except Yugoslavia) and Japan. They are members of the OECD (Organisation for Economic Co-operation and Development).

[2] A recent conference in the United States was no more conclusive. The discussion centred on two radically different scenarios, one stressing the monetary factor and the other the "real world". According to the first, the cause of the decline in real income and prices in the United States was the decrease of the money supply; an expansionist monetary policy could not only have prevented the slight economic recession that began to degenerate into Depression but would have prevented its spread to the rest of the world as well. According to the second, it was on the contrary the decline in one or the other of the factors constituting American national income – investment or consumption – that led to changes in the monetary flows and caused and then aggravated the Depression (Brunner, 1981).

[3] The proposal made by the ILO and Keynes to launch a large-scale public works programme financed by international credit was perhaps not the best, but it stressed the need for an international regulation of the crisis (besides a revival through demand). See W. Woytinsky: "International measures to create employment: A remedy for the Depression", in *International Labour Review* (Jan. 1932); resolution of the International Labour Conference, 16th Session, 1932, *Record of Proceedings*, p. 839. For an account of the failure of the World Economic Conference, see C. P. Kindleberger, 1973, pp. 199-231.

[4] This point is taken up by Jan Tumlir when summarising the view of most British economists in 1932 that "the world Depression was essentially a process of cumulative deflation which could be stopped by either a co-ordinated national or an agreed international provision of additional liquidity" (in Cairncross, 1981, pp. 165-166).

[5] However, it is often forgotten when citing the White Paper how limited the full employment objectives of the period were. This is highlighted by Professor J. Meade when he writes: "In the great Beveridge report on social security, all the figures were worked out on the basis of an average of 8 per cent unemployment. And the 1944 Employment Policy White Paper . . . also did the sums on the basis of average unemployment of 8 per cent. That was not ambitious enough. But to many people in the Treasury, it seemed like crying for the moon to start talking about an *average* of 8 per cent, when the minimum level of pre-war unemployment had been 10 per cent" (in Cairncross, 1981, pp. 260-261).

[6] W. Goldsmith has calculated this rate at 1.64 per cent for the United States between 1839 and 1959 (*Hearings on employment growth and price levels*, Joint Economic Commission, United States Congress (7 Apr. 1959), page 271). It should be noted that this percentage

corresponds to the arithmetic average calculated for 16 industrial countries from 1820 to 1979 (Maddison, 1982, table 3.1, p. 44).

[7] The oil shocks above all caused a loss in the terms of trade and a drop in domestic production due to an increase in world savings (S. Ostry, J. Llewellyn and L. Samuelson: "The cost of OPEC II", in *OECD Observer* (Paris), Mar. 1982, No. 115, pp. 37-39). A loss in terms of trade occurs when the price of imports (oil) increases faster than that of exports and requires a higher volume in exchange. For 1980 and 1981 the loss is estimated at about 1.75 per cent of the gross national product in the OECD countries. Since the surplus earnings of the OPEC countries could not be spent immediately, world savings increased. It is estimated that these extra savings reduced the gross national product of the OECD countries by nearly 3 per cent in 1980 and perhaps by as much as 4 per cent in 1981. Estimates are lacking for the first oil crisis, but the losses in both cases were probably about the same. It should also be noted that the massive transfer of funds to the OPEC countries had a great effect on trade and exchange rates. Exchange rates became more unforeseeable as a large part of the surplus "world savings" in the OPEC countries went into long-term deposits. Since rates of interest varied considerably according to the currency, many deposit holders switched from one currency to another, thus accentuating the movements under way. Consequently, investment became more risky and inflation was also pushed upwards.

[8] It should be noted, however, that the concept of productivity in the services is somewhat hazy owing to the heterogeneous nature of this sector, the difficulty of determining what contributes directly or not to production and statistical measurement problems.

[9] It is to the New Zealand and Australian economists, Fisher and Clark (1935 and 1940), that we owe the classification of the labour force into three sectors. The primary sector consists essentially of agriculture and mining, the secondary sector of industry and construction, and the tertiary sector of the "service industries", i.e transport and communications, business and finance, public administration and defence, professional and personal services, etc. In fact the services sector, which is now the largest, includes everything that is not included in the primary and secondary sectors. It is highly heterogeneous, covering truck drivers, insurance agents, nurses, computer specialists, teachers, etc. Revised classifications of the labour force have been suggested by the American economists, Parker and Porat, and the Australian economist, Jones, in particular. Parker and Porat propose four sectors: primary (extractive activities), secondary (industry and construction), tertiary (services not based on the transfer of information) and quaternary (information industry, including printing). For his part, B. Jones suggests five sectors, which he applies to the Australian economy: to the first two proposed by Parker and Porat, he adds a tertiary sector consisting of tangible economic services, a quaternary sector comprising data processing and a quinary sector covering unpaid work, homework where remuneration is secondary and professional services of a quasi-domestic nature.

[10] It should be noted, however, that there was an annual increase in employment in agriculture and mining in the United States, Australia and Denmark during the period 1973 to 1980.

[11] The labour force being defined, in simplified terms, as the sum of persons who are employed and persons who are unemployed.

[12] Addison and Siebert add that unemployment may also result from disagreement about wages; it is preferable, therefore, to put it down to insufficient demand. Moreover, conventional textbooks ascribe structural unemployment either to the lack of capital or to swift technological progress (Ackley, 1961, pp. 542-549). According to the classification devised by Addison and Siebert, this type of unemployment would come within the category due to the "growth deficit".

[13] As, for example, in the annual report on the labour market for 1979 published by the Ministry of Social Affairs in the Netherlands: *Jaarverslag Arbeidsmarkt, 1979* (The Hague, 1980).

[14] United States Department of Labor, Bureau of Labor Statistics: *International comparisons of manufacturing productivity and labor cost trends: Preliminary measures for 1981* (Washington, DC, June 1982).

[15] The figures for government disbursements somewhat exaggerate the State's influence on national income since a good part of social security contributions is taxed and is thus found again under the heading of "final government consumption expenditure". However, these disbursements do not include government investments.

[16] Jan Tumlir writes elsewhere that "the fundamental similarity between the 1920s and the 1970s lay in the fact that in neither period was international debt backed by productive assets . . . In the 1970s OPEC capital was . . . financing not new investments through which oil importing economies would adjust to the new situation but, in a large part, consumption, the postponement of adjustment" (in Cairncross, 1981, p. 193).

[17] It may be said that the same quantity of public services will absorb a growing part of national income.

[18] Loans on this market by the entire domestic non-financial sector.

[19] An old text of the French school of political economy may be relevant here: "The crisis, as the word clearly implies, is an abrupt disturbance in the economic balance. But it can be studied under two very different and even opposite aspects. Crises may appear as a sort of disease of the economic body: they present characteristics quite similar to those of countless diseases afflicting men. Some are of periodic nature, others are, on the contrary, irregular. Some are short and violent like a bout of fever, appearing with a sharp rise in temperature followed by an abrupt fall; others are slow like anaemia, as Mr. de Laveleye says. Some are localised in a given country, others are epidemic and go around the world, like cholera." (Charles Gide, *Cours d'économie politique*, Paris, 1931, Vol. I, p. 219).

[20] Press release GATT/1333, 11 Mar. 1983, p. 10.

Selected bibliography

Abraham, K. *Structural/frictional versus deficient demand unemployment: Some new evidence* (Cambridge (Mass.), National Bureau of Economic Research, Sep. 1982; mimeographed).

Ackley, G. *Macroeconomic theory* (New York Macmillan, 1961).

Addison, J. T.; Siebert, W. S. *The market for labour: An analytical treatment* (Santa Monica (California), Goodyear Publishing Company, 1979).

Aglietta, M. "Panorma sur les théories de l'emploi", in *Revue économique* (Paris), Jan. 1978.

Bank for International Settlements. *Fifty-second annual report* (Basle, June 1982).

Bartoli, H. (ed.). *Population, travail, chômage* (Paris, Economica, 1982).

Beveridge, W. H. *Full employment in a free society* (London, Allen and Unwin, 1944).

Blackhurst, R.; Marian, N.; Tumlir, J. *Adjustment, trade and growth in developed and developing countries* (Geneva, GATT, 1978).

van den Bosch, F. A. J.; Petersen, C. "De omvang van de verborgen werkloosheid in de WAO" (The volume of hidden unemployment under the WAO (Incapacity Insurance Act)), in *Economisch-Statistische Berichten* (Rotterdam), 16 Jan. 1980.

Brunner, K. (ed.). *The Great Depression revisited* (Boston, Kluwer-Nijhoff Publishing, 1981).

Cairncross, F. (ed.). *Changing perceptions of economic policy* (London and New York, Methuen, 1981).

Cramer, U. "Zur Messung struktureller Arbeitslosigkeit" (Towards a measurement of structural unemployment), in *Wirtschaftsdienst* (Hamburg, 1979), No. 3.

Dennison, E. "Is US growth understated because of the underground economy? Employment ratios suggest not", in *Review of Income and Wealth* (New Haven (Conn.)), Mar. 1981.

Elliott R. F.; Fallick, J. L. *Pay in the public sector* (London, Macmillan, 1981).

European Trade Union Institute. *The reduction of working hours in Western Europe* (Brussels, 1980).

Feige, E. "Macroeconomic malaise and the 'unobserved economy'", in *Economic Impact* (Washington, DC), No. 4, 1982.

Freedman, D. H. (ed.). *Employment: Outlook and insights* (Geneva, ILO, 1979).

GATT. *International trade 1981/82* (Geneva, 1982).

–. *International trade in 1982 and current prospects*, Press release No. 1333 (Geneva, 11 Mar. 1983).

Gershuny, J. *After industrial society? The emerging self-service economy* (London, Macmillan, 1978).

van Ginneken, W. *Unemployment in France, the Federal Republic of Germany and the Netherlands: A survey of trends and the causes and policy options* (Geneva, ILO, 1982).

Glyn, A. "The productivity slow-down: A Marxist view", in R. C. O. Matthews: *Slower growth in the Western world* (London, Heinemann, 1982).

Grazia, R. de. "Clandestine employment: A problem of our times", in *International Labour Review* (Geneva, ILO), Sep.-Oct. 1980.

Hayes, R. H.; Abernathy, W. J. "Managing our way to economic decline", in *Harvard Business Review* (Cambridge (Mass.)), July-Aug. 1980.

International Labour Office. *Growth, structural change and manpower policy: The challenge of the 1980s*, Report of the Director-General, Third European Regional Conference, Geneva, 1979.

Japan: Ministry of Labour. *Japan's labour economics, 1979 (A summary)* (Tokyo, Foreign Press Center, 1980).

Johannesson, J.; Schmid, G. "The development of labour market policy in Sweden and in Germany: Competing or convergent models to combat unemployment?", in *European Journal of Political Research* (Amsterdam), No. 8, 1980.

Jones, B. *Sleepers, wake! Technology and the future of work* (Brighton, Wheatsheaf Books, 1982).

Jonung, L. "The depression in Sweden and the United States", in K. Brunner, op. cit.

Keynes, J. M. *The general theory of employment, interest and money* (London, Macmillan, 1936).

Kindleberger, C. P. *The world in depression 1929-1939* (London, Allen Lane The Penguin Press, 1973).

Lorenzi, J.-H.; Pastré, O.; Toledano, J. *La crise du XXe siècle* (Paris, Economica, 1980).

Maddison, A. *Phases of capitalist development* (Oxford, Oxford University Press, 1982).

Magaziner, I. C.; Reich, R. B. *Minding America's business: The decline and rise of the American economy* (New York, Harbrace, 1981).

Malinvaud, E. *Théorie macro-économique*, Vol. I (Paris, Dunod, 1981).

Marchand, O.; Rault, D.; Turpin, E. "Des 40 heures aux 39 heures: processus et réactions des entreprises", in *Economie et statistique* (Paris, INSEE), No. 154, Aug. 1983.

Matthews, R. C. O. (ed.). *Slower growth in the Western world* (London, Heinemann, 1982).

Muhr, G. (ed.). *Beschäftigungspolitik in den achtziger Jahren* (Employment policy in the 1980s) (Cologne, Bund-Verlag, 1981).

National annual reports of ministries of labour, employment or social affairs (from 1979 onwards).

OECD. *Towards full employment and price stability* (McCracken Report) (Paris, 1977).

–. *Economic Outlook* (Paris), No. 32, Dec. 1982.

–. *Economic Outlook* (Paris), No. 33, July 1983.

–. *Labour supply, growth constraints and work sharing* (Paris, 1982).

–. *The challenge of unemployment: A report to Labour Ministers* (Paris, 1982).

72

Ohmae, K. "Foresighted management decision-making: See the options before planning strategy", in *Management Review* (New York), May 1982.

Osterman, P. *Getting started: The youth labor market* (Cambridge (Mass.), MIT Press, 1980).

Parent, J. *Le modèle suédois* (Paris, Seuil, 1970).

Paukert, L. "Personal preference, social change or economic necessity? Why women work", in *Labour and Society* (Geneva, ILO, International Institute for Labour Studies), Oct.-Dec. 1982.

Pommerehne, W.; Frey, B. S. "L'étendue de l'économie souterraine et son évolution: Méthode de mesure et estimations", in *Chroniques d'actualité de la SEDEIS* (Paris), 15 May 1982.

Puel, H. "L'éclatement du concept traditionnel d'emploi", in *Travail et emploi* (Paris, Ministry of Labour and Participation), Aug. 1980.

Salais, R. "Analyse des mécanismes de détermination du chômage", in *Economie et statistique* (Paris, INSEE), No. 93, Oct. 1977.

Scharpf, F. W. *The political economy of inflation and unemployment in Western Europe* (Berlin, International Institute of Management, 1981; mimeographed).

Standing, G. "The notion of voluntary unemployment", in *International Labour Review* (Geneva, ILO), Sep.-Oct. 1981.

Topel, R. H. "Inventories, layoffs and the short-run demand for labour", in *American Economic Review* (Nashville (Tenn.)) Sep. 1982.

Tumlir, J. "Evolution of the concept of international economic order 1914-80", in F. Cairncross (ed.), op. cit.

United States Department of Labor, Bureau of Labor Statistics. *International comparisons of manufacturing productivity and labor cost trends: Preliminary measures for 1981* (Washington, DC, June 1982).

Valkenburg, F. C.; Vissers, A. M. C. "De kloof tussen vraag en aanbod op de arbeidsmarkt" (The gap between supply and demand on the labour market), in *Economisch-Statistische Berichten* (Rotterdam), 25 Apr. 1979.

Zoeteweij, H. "Anti-inflation policies in the industrialised market economy countries", in *International Labour Review* (Geneva, ILO), Sep.-Oct. 1983 (Part I) and Nov.-Dec. 1983 (Part II).

73

Chapter 3

Employment in the planned economies of Eastern Europe[1]

The contrast between the employment situation in the Eastern European countries and that of the market economies discussed in the previous chapter is striking. Instead of unemployment, the problem is the increasingly severe shortage of manpower. Naturally, in any economy as vast and multifaceted as that of the USSR, for example, difficulties are bound to arise from time to time in equating the supply of labour with demand – the kind of problem which might come under the conventional heading of "frictional unemployment" and which is not immediately evident from the statistics. Be this as it may, the fact remains that the great majority of Eastern European countries enjoy full employment and apply in practice the principle of the right to work and of guaranteed work embodied in their constitutional texts.

This does not mean that they have no real difficulties to contend with. Indeed, there are serious problems which seem likely to become more acute in the years to come. In fact, for all the profound differences that separate the political, economic and social systems of Eastern Europe from those of the Western economies, one could argue that there is a feature which is common to both: the underutilisation of economic and human capacity. Just as the industrialised market economy countries have been seen to be suffering from a kind of anaemia, in spite of their high standards of living, a similar type of illness would seem to be affecting the otherwise totally different organisms of the Eastern European countries, where full employment does not mean that human resources are fully utilised and where output has often been below what would have been possible given the more efficient handling of physical resources and investment.

This chapter is concerned mainly with an analysis of the employment situation in these countries: its general trends, the tensions and constraints on the labour supply side, the sectoral distribution of employment. It also examines the problem of raising labour productivity, a prime objective not only in any full employment situation but also in the current demographic and economic circumstances of these countries.

Our analysis of the employment situation begins with a brief reminder of the general economic background. It concludes with a summary of prospects for the future.

Economic background: the declining economic growth of the late 1970s

Like most of the rest of the world, Eastern Europe is going through difficult economic times whose impact is being felt on living standards and on the level and structure of investment. Overall economic performance has deteriorated in particular over the past five years, but signs of forthcoming problems were already appearing at the beginning of the 1970s.

Table 3.1
Growth of net material product (average annual percentage change)

| Country | 1966-70 | | 1971-75 | | 1976-80 | | 1981-82 | | |
| | | | | | | | 1981-85 Plan | Actual growth | |
	Plan	Actual growth	Plan	Actual growth	Plan	Actual growth	1981-85 Plan	1981	1982
Bulgaria	8.5	8.7	7.7-8.5	7.8	7.7	6.1	3.7	5.0	4.0
Czechoslovakia	4.1-4.4	6.9	5.1	5.7	4.9	3.7	2.0-2.6	−0.4	0
German Dem. Rep.	5.4	5.2	4.9	5.4	5.0	4.1	5.1	4.8	3.0
Hungary	3.5-3.9	6.8	5.5-6.0	6.2	5.4-5.7	3.2	2.6-3.2	2.0	1.5-2.0
Poland	6.0	6.0	6.7-6.8	9.8	7.0-7.3	1.2	0.9	−12.1	−8.0
Romania	7.0	7.7	11-12	11.3	10-11	7.2	7.1	2.2	2.6
USSR	6.6-7.1[a]	7.8	6.5-7.0[a]	5.7	4.7[a]	4.2	3.4[a]	3.3	2.6[a]
Eastern Europe ex-cluding the USSR	5.6	6.5	6.7	7.8	6.6	3.9	3.9	−1.1	−0.1
Eastern Europe and the USSR	6.5	7.4	6.7	6.2	5.3	4.1	3.5	2.0	1.8

[a] NMP used.

Source: United Nations: *Economic survey of Europe in 1981* (New York, 1982; Sales No.: E.82.II.E.1), p. 133, and *Economic survey of Europe in 1982* (Sales No.: E.83.II.E.1), pp. 104-105.

The reasons for the present situation are both international and national. On the one hand, the world-wide economic recession naturally affects the Eastern European countries also, particularly the smaller ones more open to international trade. Moreover, the terms of trade have turned sharply against Eastern European countries other than the Soviet Union and have contributed to their difficulties.

On the other hand, there is a whole gamut of domestic factors involved. Since the Second World War the Eastern European countries have experienced what is now called "extensive growth", based on a growing labour force, shifts of labour from less productive to more productive sectors and high levels of investment. The general feeling is that this period of extensive growth is now over and that economic progress in future will have to take the form of "intensive growth", growth under conditions of diminishing increases in the labour force, more limited possibilities of investment and better utilisation of more and more scarce and expensive raw materials and energy.[2]

Despite signs of a decline in the rate of economic growth during the past ten to 15 years, the Eastern European economies continued to grow steadily, as can be seen from table 3.1, which traces annual percentage changes in national income (both planned and actually achieved) in terms of net material product (NMP).[3]

Although the rates of growth of national income differ from country to country, there are certain features which are common to them all.

First of all, the actual rates of growth in the period 1976 to 1980 were everywhere lower than those achieved between 1966 and 1975: the annual average rate of growth was 4.1 per cent as against 7.4 and 6.2 per cent respectively during the periods 1966 to 1970 and 1971 to 1975.

Secondly, the actual rate of growth for 1976-80 was lower than that envisaged by the national plans, while in the two previous periods the opposite was true in almost all cases.

Table 3.2
Changes in net material product used (annual percentage change)

Country and period	NMP used	Consumption			Net capital formation		
		Total	Personal	Social	Total	Net fixed capital formation	Changes in stocks
Bulgaria							
1976-80	2.8	4.0	4.2	..	0.1	2.4	5.3
1979	3.5	3.0	2.9	..	5.0	..	..
1980	5.1	3.6	4.0	22.2	9.5	−42.6	459.3
1981	7.7	5.3	4.9	7.1	4.8	..	..
1982	−2.0[a]	..	..	..	..	..	..
Czechoslovakia							
1976-1980	2.2	2.5	1.7	4.8	0.9	0.4	2.6
1979	1.1	0.9	−0.6	4.8	1.8	−8.5	101.7
1980	2.3	1.0	−0.1	3.7	8.2	1.1	39.3
1981	−4.5	2.2	1.7	3.5	−24.8	−13.3	−61.6
1982	−2.0[a]	..	..	..	..	..	..
German Dem. Rep.							
1976-80	3.7	3.8	3.9	3.1	3.1	3.4	−6.7
1979	1.6	3.3	4.1	0.6	−5.4	..	..
1980	4.9	3.0	3.4	−1.2	12.5	..	..
1981	1.5	2.6	2.7	2.8	−2.4	..	..
1982	1.0[a]	..	..	..	..		
Hungary							
1976-80	1.9	3.2	2.7	5.9	−2.3	−2.7	−9.8
1979	−5.5	2.9	2.4	5.8	−24.9	3.7	..
1980	−1.9	1.1	1.0	1.9	−11.3	−9.8	243.7
1981	0.1	2.4	2.2	3.6	−8.1	−24.6	160.9
1982	−2.0	..	1.0	..	−13.0	−(10-15)	..
Poland							
1976-80	−0.2	4.5	4.4	5.2	−11.8	−9.2	−29.0
1979	−3.7	3.1	3.2	2.4	−19.2	−15.4	−39.5
1980	−6.0	2.1	2.3	1.2	−29.5	−25.4	−61.3
1981	−12.3	0.0	0.5	−2.6	−60.4	−45.7	..
1982	−12.0	−13.0	−15.0	..	−2.0	..	..
USSR							
1976-80	3.8	4.5	..	..	1.6	..	..
1979	2.0	..	..	..	−3.3	..	..
1980	3.9	5.7	..	..	−1.6	..	..
1981	3.2	3.9	..	..	0.9	..	..
1982	2.6	..	..	..	..	..	..

.. = not available.

[a] ECE secretariat estimates at current prices.

Source: United Nations: *Economic survey of Europe in 1982*, op. cit., p. 120.

Thirdly, the planned rate of growth for the current five-year period is everywhere (except in the German Democratic Republic) lower, and sometimes very substantially lower, than for the previous period.

The deceleration of economic growth can thus be seen to fall primarily in the period since 1976 and is particularly pronounced in the years 1980-82. Table 3.2 shows in detail the impact of this deceleration on consumption and investment.[4]

These figures indicate a sharp drop in national income in Poland since 1976. In Hungary, too, the NMP used has declined since 1978, while the German Democratic Republic, Czechoslovakia and the Soviet Union have maintained a moderate rate of growth. In 1982 the NMP used fell in all countries with the exception of the German Democratic Republic and the USSR.

Table 3.2 shows that the burden of economic deceleration (and sometimes decline) was shifted mainly to capital formation, in order to safeguard both personal and social consumption. Throughout the period and in all countries, except for Poland in 1981 and 1982, there was some increase in total consumption even when the NMP used fell, but this was achieved at the cost of net fixed capital formation. Although the figures for total net capital formation are influenced by changes in stocks (for example, there were large increases in Czechoslovakia in 1979 and in Bulgaria and Hungary in 1980 and 1981), net fixed capital formation, which is decisive for labour productivity, dropped in all countries for which data are available (except for the German Democratic Republic up to 1981).

The maintenance of some growth of total consumption generally took the form of increases in social consumption (state expenditure on housing, health services, educational and cultural activities, etc.) rather than increases in personal consumption (again with the exception of the German Democratic Republic). This is also

Table 3.3
Real income and real wages (average annual percentage change)

Period	Real per capita income	Real wages per wage or salary earner	Real per capita income	Real wages per wage or salary earner	Real per capita income	Real wages per wage or salary earner
	Bulgaria		German Dem. Rep.		Romania	
1976-80	2.6	0.5	4.3	4.4	5.1	6.1
1979	2.9	1.5	3.4	4.8	3.3	3.9
1980	3.4	−0.3	3.1	3.7	2.4	3.0
1981	4.8	4.3	4.0	4.6	2.2	1.1
1982	2.7[a]	2.0[a]	3.3	3.0[a]	1.5[a]	1.0[a]
	Byelorussian SSR[b]		Hungary		Ukrainian SSR[b]	
1976-80	3.6	3.7	1.6	0.7	3.2	3.0
1979	4.0	2.1	0.1	−1.7	2.2	2.3
1980	2.8	3.8	0.4	−1.8	2.4	3.6
1981	3.2	2.0	2.2	1.5	3.0	2.0
1982	..	2.9	..	−0.5	..	..
	Czechoslovakia		Poland		USSR[b]	
1976-80	1.3	0.7	2.9	2.0	3.3	3.0
1979	−0.1	−0.6	2.4	2.1	3.0	2.1
1980	0.0	−1.0	0.6	3.4	3.5	3.4
1981	1.6	0.8	3.0[a]	1.5[a]	3.3	2.1
1982	..	−0.5[a]	−20.0[a]	−25.7	0.1	2.8

.. = not available.
[a] ECE secretariat estimates at current prices. [b] Average nominal wages.
Source: United Nations: *Economic survey of Europe in 1982*, op. cit., p. 191.

reflected in the statistics for net per capita income (which includes not only wages and other forms of income but also social consumption) and for real wages per wage or salary earner (see table 3.3). National plans for 1983 provide for a smaller increase in real per capita income and wages than in 1982.

The response of the Eastern European countries to their general economic difficulties is thus clear. The main burden of sacrifice is borne by fixed capital formation, followed by personal consumption and, only in the last instance, by social consumption. This is a policy of minimising social problems arising out of economic deceleration. However, cutting back in investments is bound to present difficult problems for the resumption of previous rates of economic growth.[5]

Employment situation and problems

Employment: a goal and major instrument of planning

The growth of production and full employment are among the principal objectives of the economic and social policy of Eastern European countries. Policy is defined and implemented through a general system of planning, and the planning of manpower is one of its essential mechanisms. Production targets are set according to the availability of labour and the expected growth of labour productivity (which in turn depends on a number of other factors). Economic difficulties may result in unsatisfactory growth of labour productivity, inappropriate structure of production, shortages of various types, balance-of-payments difficulties, but not in unemployment. In principle any surplus of labour supply over labour demand will be due to shortcomings in the planning mechanism, temporary and limited to a particular type of labour or to labour in a particular region. The preoccupation of Eastern European economists with labour mobility is a reflection of this concern with the full utilisation of labour.

National planning of manpower aims at providing full employment, at supplying the necessary labour for both the "productive" and the "non-productive" sectors of the economy, at facilitating better utilisation of the labour force and at regulating labour mobility. The plans also include indicators concerning average wages and the total wages fund, training needs and structure, and labour productivity. The last set of indicators constitutes the most important link with the overall plan, as it results in planned indicators of production.

The general planning system involves a number of levels, from the state planning commissions at the top to a complex network of regional authorities and broad economic sectors, and down further to enterprises. Although the enterprises play a role in the process, the existence of rather detailed production and labour plans naturally limits their freedom of action. During the 1960s, when most Eastern European countries gave enterprises greater authority in making decisions about the allocation of factors of production, including manpower, the number of planning indicators was reduced and, in some countries, direct planning of manpower was almost abolished. Since then these reforms have been abandoned and direct manpower planning has been reintroduced.

Principal employment trends

A backward glance at a number of major historical and political events is essential for an appreciation of the present situation.

At the end of the Second World War the countries of Eastern Europe found themselves at different levels of development: the German Democratic Republic and Czechoslovakia were already highly industrialised whereas in Bulgaria and Romania, for example, some three-quarters of the labour force was still employed in agriculture.

War-time experience also differed, with the German Democratic Republic, Poland and the USSR having suffered much heavier damage than Czechoslovakia and Hungary, where the damage was roughly of the order experienced by most Western European countries.

The end of the war also brought major changes of boundaries and a mass exodus of population, following great losses of life during the war.

Finally, the countries of Eastern Europe underwent a major political and institutional change which, along with a complete disruption of economic and social life, transformed the nature and structure of employment. Global nationalisation of industry was followed by nationalisation of other sectors of the economy and by the collectivisation of agriculture. Far-reaching though these changes were, some segments of the economy remained unaffected. In most Eastern European countries small, usually family-run enterprises remained, primarily in the services sector. State farms and co-operative farms existed side by side with private agricultural plots. In Poland a large part of agriculture remained in the hands of private farmers.

The early 1950s were marked by a great emphasis on industrialisation (with some exceptions, such as Bulgaria). As from this period, certain countries (Czechoslovakia and the German Democratic Republic, for example) started to experience labour shortages. As from the end of the 1950s total employment was determined by the growth of population, the age structure of the population, the labour force participation rates (boosted to the utmost, mainly by drawing more women into the labour force) and changes in the distribution of the labour force among economic sectors. Transfers between economic sectors could also influence a person's employment status, as when a collective farmer became a wage earner or when, in the USSR for example, a full-time worker on a private agricultural plot considered not as employed but rather as part of the "labour reserves" became a wage earner.

Table 3.4 shows the situation and trend of total employment, by sex. As can be seen, the number of economically active women increased much faster than that of men following the Second World War, with the result that the number of economically active men now only slightly exceeds that of women. In the German Democratic Republic and the USSR male and female employment are practically equal, though the USSR is an exception

Table 3.4

Active population by sex in Eastern European countries (according to censuses for years around 1950 to 1980) (in millions)

Country and period	Total	Men	Women
Bulgaria			
1956	4 150	2 405	1 745
1965	4 268	2 390	1 878
1975	4 448	2 366	2 082
Czechoslovakia			
1947	5 852	3 793	2 059
1961	6 483	3 823	2 660
1970	6 982	3 870	3 112
1980	7 849	4 185	3 664
German Dem. Rep.			
1950	8 477	5 090	3 387
1964	8 345	4 657	3 688
1971	8 214	4 413	3 801
1980 [a]	8 225	4 119	4 106
Hungary			
1949	4 154	2 950	1 204
1960	4 876	3 165	1 711
1970	4 989	2 933	2 055
1980	5 069	2 867	2 202
Poland			
1950	12 760	7 221	5 539
1960	14 264	8 091	6 173
1970	16 944	9 149	7 795
1978	17 962	9 806	8 156
Romania			
1956	10 466	5 727	4 739
1966	10 362	5 675	4 687
1977	10 794	5 867	4 927
USSR [b]			
1959	108 995	52 440	56 555
1970	117 027	57 990	59 037
1979	135 424	67 919	67 505

[a] Official estimates for 1980, excluding apprentices. [b] Including persons engaged exclusively in individual plot farming.

Source: ILO: *Year Book of Labour Statistics*, various editions; United Nations: *Economic survey of Europe in 1977*, Part II: *Labour supply in Europe: Demographic dimensions 1950-1975 and prospects* (New York, 1978: Sales No.: E.78.II.E.20); national statistics (for 1980).

80

Table 3.5
Population in Eastern European countries, by sex (thousands)

Country	Date	Total	Men	Women	Average annual percentage rate of change over previous census Total
Bulgaria	1946(31.12)C[a]	7 029	3 517	3 512	..
	1956(01.12)C	7 614	3 799	3 815	0.8
	1965(01.12)C	8 228	4 114	4 114	0.9
	1975(02.12)C	8 728	4 358	4 370	0.6
	1980(31.12)E[b]	8 877	4 422	4 455	(0.3)
Czechoslovakia	1947(22.05)C	12 164	5 910	6 254	..
	1950(01.03)C	12 339	5 997	6 342	0.5
	1961(01.03)C	13 746	6 705	7 041	1.0
	1970(01.12)C	14 345	6 989	7 356	0.4
	1980(01.11)C	15 283	7 441	7 842	0.6
German Democratic Republic	1950(31.08)C	18 388	8 161	10 277	..
	1964(31.12)C	17 004	7 748	9 256	−0.5
	1971(01.01)C	17 068	7 865	9 203	0.1
	1980(31.12)E	16 740	7 857	8 883	(−0.2)
Hungary	1949(01.01)C	9 205	4 424	4 781	..
	1960(01.01)C	9 961	4 804	5 157	0.7
	1970(01.01)C	10 322	5 004	5 318	0.4
	1980(01.01)C	10 709	5 189	5 521	0.4
Poland	1950(03.12)C	25 008	11 928	13 080	..
	1960(06.12)C	29 776	14 404	15 372	1.8
	1970(08.12)C	32 642	15 854	16 788	0.9
	1978(07.12)C	35 061	17 079	17 982	0.9
	1980(31.12)E	35 735	17 411	18 324	(0.9)
Romania	1948(25.01)C	15 873	7 672	8 201	..
	1956(21.02)C	17 489	8 503	8 986	1.2
	1966(15.03)C	19 103	9 351	9 752	0.9
	1977(05.01)C	21 560	10 626	10 934	1.1
	1980(01.07)E	22 201	10 953	11 248	(0.8)
USSR	1959(15.01)C	208 826	94 050	114 776	..
	1970(15.01)C	241 720	111 399	130 321	1.3
	1979(17.01)C	262 436	122 329	140 107	0.9
	1980(31.12)E	266 599	124 510	142 089	(0.8)

.. = not available.
C[a] = census.   E[b] = estimate.
Source: ILO: *Year Book of Labour Statistics*, various editions; United Nations: *Demographic Yearbook*, various editions; national statistics.

Table 3.6
Distribution of the population from 1950 to 1980, by age group and by sex (percentages, sex ratios [a] and dependency ratios [b])

	Men					Women					Sex ratios				
	1950	1960	1970	1975	1980	1950	1960	1970	1975	1980	1950	1960	1970	1975	1980
Eastern Europe (excluding USSR)															
All ages	100	100	100	100	100	100	100	100	100	100	111	108	107	106	106
0-14	28.5	29.7	26.0	24.3	24.9	25.0	26.3	23.3	21.9	22.5	97	96	96	95	95
15-59	1.7	59.3	60.4	61.6	62.9	63.0	59.3	59.1	59.5	60.0	113	108	104	102	101
60+	9.7	11.0	13.5	14.1	12.5	12.0	14.4	17.5	18.5	17.5	136	142	138	139	148
Dependency ratio	62	69	65	62	60	59	69	69	68	67	..	..	..	..	..
USSR															
All ages	100	100	100	100	100	100	100	100	100	100	128	121	117	115	..
0-14	37.7	34.6	31.7	28.3	..	26.4	27.5	26.0	23.6	..	97	96	96	96	..
15-59	58.6	58.1	59.9	62.5	..	62.7	60.2	59.0	59.4	..	137	125	115	109	..
60 +	6.6	7.3	8.4	9.2	..	10.9	12.4	15.0	17.0	..	210	206	210	213	..
Dependency ratio	70	72	67	60	..	59	66	68	..	..	..	..	..	..	..

.. = not available.

[a] Number of women per 100 men. [b] Number of persons below the age of 15 and aged 60 or over per 100 persons aged from 15 to 59.

Source: United Nations: *Economic survey for Europe in 1977*, Part II, op. cit.; national statistics (for 1980).

to the pattern just described in that, because of its much higher war-time losses of men, the first post-war census of 1959 established that the number of economically active women at the time exceeded that of men by 4 million.

Having established the general trend, we shall now examine in turn the principal factors influencing employment: *(a)* the demographic situation and population trends, which mainly determine the volume of potential employment; *(b)* labour force participation rates by sex and age, which determine real employment; *(c)* changes in the structure of the economy, which affect the distribution of employment by sector; and *(d)* labour productivity, which plays a crucial role both in economic growth and in the structure of employment.

Demographic factors

Population trends in Eastern European countries since the war are shown in table 3.5. It is immediately apparent that the proportion of women in the total population is almost invariably greater than that of men, particularly so – given the earlier demographic situation – in the German Democratic Republic, Poland and the USSR as a result of the war.

The most significant factor is the falling rate of population growth. This was due more than anything to the rapid decline in birth rates during the 1950s (when Western European birth rates were rising) and the 1960s. In the 1970s the birth rate began to increase in some countries (Czechoslovakia, Hungary), mainly as a result of vigorous policies in the form of child allowances, long paid maternity leave, etc. In most countries changes in abortion laws also affected the birth rates.

This demographic trend resulted in profound changes in the age and sex structure of the population. This, of course, is an element of major importance for employment, as it is the population between the ages of 15 and 60 which provides the bulk of the labour force. Table 3.6 shows the

Table 3.7
Birth rates, death rates and population growth rates in the Republics of the USSR (per thousand people)

	1940			1965			1970			1980		
	Crude birth rate	Crude death rate	Rate of natural increase	Crude birth rate	Crude death rate	Rate of natural increase	Crude birth rate	Crude death rate	Rate of natural increase	Crude birth rate	Crude death rate	Rate of natural increase
USSR	31.2	18.0	13.2	18.4	7.3	11.1	17.4	8.2	9.2	18.3	10.3	8.0
Russian SFSR	33.0	20.6	12.4	15.7	7.6	8.1	14.6	8.7	5.9	15.9	11.0	4.9
Ukrainian SSR	27.3	14.3	13.0	15.3	7.6	7.7	15.2	8.8	6.4	14.8	11.4	3.4
Byelorussian SSR	26.8	13.1	13.7	17.9	6.8	11.1	16.2	7.6	8.6	16.0	9.9	6.1
Uzbek SSR	33.8	13.2	20.6	34.7	5.9	28.8	33.6	5.5	28.1	33.8	7.4	26.4
Kazahk SSR	40.8	21.4	19.4	26.9	5.9	21.0	23.4	6.0	17.4	23.8	8.0	15.8
Georgian SSR	27.4	8.8	18.6	21.2	7.0	14.2	19.2	7.3	11.9	17.7	8.6	9.1
Azerbaidzheni SSR	29.4	14.7	14.7	36.6	6.4	30.2	29.2	6.7	22.5	25.2	7.0	18.2
Lithuanian SSR	23.0	13.0	10.0	18.1	7.9	10.2	17.6	8.9	8.7	15.1	10.5	4.6
Moldavian SSR	26.6	16.9	9.7	20.4	6.2	14.2	19.4	7.4	12.0	20.0	10.2	9.8
Latvian SSR	19.3	15.7	3.6	13.8	10.0	3.8	14.5	11.2	3.3	14.0	12.7	1.3
Kirghiz SSR	33.0	16.3	16.7	31.4	6.5	24.9	30.5	7.4	23.1	29.6	8.4	21.2
Tadzhik SSR	30.6	14.1	16.5	36.8	6.6	30.2	34.8	6.4	28.4	37.0	8.0	29.0
Armenian SSR	41.2	13.8	27.4	28.6	5.7	22.9	22.1	5.1	17.0	22.7	5.5	17.2
Turkmenian SSR	36.9	19.5	17.4	37.2	7.0	30.2	35.2	6.6	28.6	34.3	8.3	26.0
Estonian SSR	16.1	17.0	−0.9	14.6	10.5	4.1	15.8	11.1	4.7	15.0	12.3	2.7

Source: *Narodnoe khozyaistvo SSSR v 1980 gody* (Statistical Yearbook of the USSR in 1980), pp. 32-33.

changes in the age distribution of men and women between 1950 and 1980 for Eastern Europe excluding the USSR and for the USSR.

The important element in the table is the dependency ratio, that is to say, the ratio of the population aged less than 15 and 60 or over to the population between those ages (which represent most of a country's productive manpower). In Eastern European countries (other than the USSR) the male dependency ratio increased substantially between 1950 and 1960 but then started to decline until, in 1980, it was slightly below the 1950 level. This, however, was the net result of the falling percentage of males below the age of 15 compensating for an increasing percentage of men 60 or over. The female dependency ratio also increased sharply between 1950 and 1960 but, thereafter, declined only slightly. Over the whole period, the small fall in the percentage of females under the age

of 15 compensated only partially for the strong increase in the percentage of women 60 or over.

In the USSR the dependency ratio of women between 1950 and 1975 (the last date for which figures are available) followed a similar pattern, while the male dependency ratio declined over the same period as the war-depleted age cohorts gradually declined in relative importance. Because of this fact, the percentage of males below the age of 15 is abnormally high, but declining, just as the percentage of men 60 or over is abnormally low, but increasing.

As regards the sex composition of the labour force, the number of women per 100 men in the 15-59 age bracket declined in Eastern Europe (excluding the USSR) from 113 in 1950 to 101 in 1980 and, in the USSR, from 137 in 1950 to 109 in 1975.[6] This parallels, though at a higher level, the development in Western Europe where, during this same period, the small excess of women over men declined until women were in the minority.

It is interesting to consider how the population of working age will change in Eastern Europe between now and the end of the century.

Though at present the working-age population in Eastern Europe (excluding the USSR) is growing more slowly than that of Western Europe, the trend is expected to change during the decade. According to United Nations projections,[7] the working-age population (i.e. between the ages of 15 and 65) in Eastern Europe (excluding the USSR) will grow by only 2.21 per cent between 1985 and 1990 and by 4.9 per cent between 1990 and 2000. However, the picture will vary widely from country to country. The fastest growth is expected in Czechoslovakia with 2.7 per cent between now and 1990 and 6.7 per cent between 1990 and 2000, as a result of the pro-natalist policies of the 1970s, and in Romania and Poland which have always had birth rates above the average for the countries of Eastern European other than the USSR (3.6 and 3.2 per cent, respectively, between now and 1990 and 5.2 and 7.7 per cent between 1990 and 2000). Hungary's working-age population will grow at the very slow rate of 0.4 per cent between 1985 and 1990, rising to 1.4 per cent in 1990-2000. The situation will be similar in Bulgaria, with rates of 0.2 and 1.2 per cent for the same periods. The smallest increase will be in the German Democratic Republic, where the rate is projected to be 0.2 per cent between 1985 and 1990 and 0.7 per cent between 1990 and 2000, after which the working-age population is expected to decline.

In the USSR the working-age population will grow faster than in other Eastern European countries (3.6 per cent between 1985 and 1990 and 5.4 per cent between 1990 and 2000), though the increase will be slower among those between the ages of 15 and 60 which represent the bulk of the population. However, these average figures con-

Table 3.8
Labour force participation rates in Eastern Europe from 1950 to 1980 by sex[a]

Country and census years		1950	1960	1970	1980
Bulgaria					
1956, 1965, 1975	M	..	63.3	58.1	54.3
	F	..	45.7	45.7	47.6
Czechoslovakia					
1947, 1961, 1970, 1980	M	64.2	57.0	55.4	56.2
	F	32.9	37.8	42.3	46.7
German Dem. Rep.					
1950, 1964, 1971, 1980[b]	M	62.4	60.1	56.1	52.5
	F	33.1	39.8	41.3	46.2
Hungary					
1949, 1960, 1970, 1980	M	66.7	65.9	58.6	55.2
	F	25.2	33.2	38.6	39.9
Poland					
1950, 1960, 1970, 1978	M	60.7	56.2	57.7	57.4
	F	42.5	40.2	46.4	45.4
Romania					
1956, 1966, 1977	M	..	67.4	60.7	55.2
	F	..	52.7	48.1	45.1
USSR[c]					
1959, 1970, 1979	M	..	55.8	52.1	55.7
	F	..	49.3	45.3	48.1

.. = not available.
[a] Labour force as a percentage of total population. [b] Official estimates for 1980. [c] Including persons engaged exclusively in individual plot farming.
Source: ILO: *Year Book of Labour Statistics*, various editions; national statistics.

ceal an essential factor in the geographical distribution of employment, which is that birth rates in the European part of the USSR have been steadily falling while in the Asian part of the country they have remained at a very high level (see table 3.7).

This situation leaves the USSR with two options: *(a)* to transfer the surplus labour force of the Asian part of the country to the European part, though this has proved difficult in the past; *(b)* to increase investment in the Asian part of the country, which was the policy during the period of extensive growth – though it remains to be seen whether this would be feasible under the present "intensive growth" strategy when investment possibilities are more limited.

Table 3.9
Age-specific activity rates for men and women from 1950 to 1980 (per 100 men or women of specified age groups)

Country and period	Men 15-19	20-24	25-34	35-44	45-54	55-59	60-64	65+	Women 15-19	20-24	25-34	35-44	45-54	55-59	60-64	65+
Bulgaria																
1956	54	82	97	98	97	93	85	60	49	69	71	77	69	54	42	23
1965	35	78	97	98	95	84	55	23	33	72	85	88	74	35	18	6
1975	24	69	–	97	94	87	34	10	35	78	–	93	81	26	8	2
Czecho-slovakia[a]																
1951	50	74	89[b]	8[c]	96[d]	91[e]	–	37	65	63	48[b]	49[c]	53[d]	46[e]	–	18
1961	46	93	98[b]	98[c]	97[d]	89[e]	–	35	54	69	57[b]	62[c]	67[d]	51[e]	–	14
1970	35	91	99[b]	99[c]	97[d]	88[e]	–	22	42	79	79[b]	80[c]	79[d]	50[e]	–	9
1980	29	86	98[b]	–	98[f]	–	(88[e]) 84	46 (26) 14	30	83	91[b]	–	91[f]	–	(60[e]) 41	21 (9) 6
German Dem. Rep.																
1964	63	89	98	98	96	93	85	32	57	74	68	70	67	54	29	7
1971	27	87	98	98	97	92	83	27	29	75	79	80	77	62	31	8
Hungary																
1949	64	93	97	98	95	88	81	62	53	45	33	28	26	27	26	19
1960	57	95	99	99	97	93	70	57	48	55	49	51	48	31	26	21
1970	46	92	99	98	94	84	44	17	49	56	67	70	61	29	17	6
1980	45	92	98[b]	98[c]	94[d]	86[e] 72	13	4	41	60	70[b]	83[c]	80[d]	67[e] 19	9	3
Poland[g]																
1950	56	92	97	98	97	94	89	61	52	76	61	63	62	55	47	29
1960	47	88	97	97	96	91	82	60	41	68	63	68	67	60	49	32
1970	32	86	97	97	95	91	83	56	26	73	77	80	78	68	51	33
1978	29	83	97	97	90	81	62	35	21	68	77	82	75	58	37	19
Romania																
1956	88	95	98[b]	98[c]	98[d]	95[e]	–	78	77	78	74[b]	74[c]	75[d]	70[e]	–	46
1966	49	91	97[b]	98[c]	97[d]	92[e]	–	50	51	74	79[b]	79[c]	77[d]	65[e]	–	28
1977	37	97	94	96	91	79	45	15	32	76	83	83	74	52	25	10
USSR																
1959	63	93	90[b]	96[c]	94[d]	90[g]	83[h]	47[j]	63	86	74[b]	78[c]	75[d]	67[g]	49[h]	34
1970	42	85	96[b]	98[c]	96[d]	84	–	20	38	84	89[b]	93[c]	91[d]	48	–	7

[a] Excluding unpaid family workers. [b] 25-29. [c] 30-39. [d] 40-49. [e] 50-59. [f] 30-49. [g] Data adjusted to include the armed forces. [h] 50-54. [i] 60+. [j] 55-59.
Source: Poland 1960, 1970 and 1978: censuses; Romania 1977: census; Czechoslovakia and Hungary 1980: ILO, Bureau of Statistics; remainder: United Nations: *Economic survey of Europe in 1977*, Part II, op. cit.

Labour force participation rates

The size of the population of working age determines the bulk of potential employment but not the total, as the economically active population includes some men and women above the working age. Actual employment depends on labour force participation rates. The participation rates of the total labour force as a percentage of the total population, by sex, and the "age-specific" activity rates, again by sex, are illustrated in tables 3.8 and 3.9.

Table 3.8 shows that the labour force participation rates declined for men and rose for women between 1950 and 1980. Box 3.1 outlines the trend in individual countries.

As far as employment is concerned, however, it is the breakdown by age group which is significant. Table 3.9, which contains the principal data, highlights five important findings (the trends in individual countries are outlined in box 3.2):

1. Employment among adolescents of both sexes under the age of 20 fell, owing (as in Western Europe) to the development of education and training.

2. Between the ages of 20 and 55 the male activity rate was high, especially for men aged 25 or over.

3. Female employment increased rapidly for the entire 20-54 age group. Here, several factors are involved: higher levels of education, greater availability of time-saving goods and services (though less than in Western Europe), generally low wages of heads of households, egalitarian wage policies and higher minimum wages, and generous policies as regards social benefits and facilities (long maternity leave, provision of crèches and kindergartens, etc.).

4. Employment among older men, especially those aged 60 or over, declined, though the picture varied considerably from country to country.

5. The level of employment of women aged 55 or over remained high, with certain exceptions.

The declining employment of older men reflects the spreading of social security and the fall in the size of the active agricultural population. In countries where the latter was still large, the activity rate of this age group remained quite high.[8]

Variations in the activity rates for those aged 55 or over are mostly attributable to social security

---

3.1

Labour force participation rates by sex

Male participation rates

There was a particularly pronounced decline in the male participation rate in Czechoslovakia (from 1947 to 1961), in Poland (from 1950 to 1960), in Bulgaria (from 1956 to 1965) and in Romania (from 1956 to 1966). In the German Democratic Republic there was a steady decline between 1950 and 1980, from 62.4 per cent to 52.5 per cent. In the USSR the participation rate, which fell slightly between 1959 and 1970, increased again in 1980 practically to the 1959 level.

In the past decade the participation rate continued to decline in Romania (between 1966 and 1977), Hungary and Bulgaria. In Poland the male participation rate was stationary up to 1978 and in Czechoslovakia there was a slight increase.

Female participation rates

The female participation rate rose rapidly in Hungary, the German Democratic Republic and, above all, Czechoslovakia. Bulgaria and Poland already had high participation rates at the beginning of the period and the increase over time was thus relatively small. Romania's participation rate was extremely high in 1956 but thereafter declined more or less to the level of the other Eastern European countries. In these last three countries the high female participation rates already at the beginning of the post-war period were doubtless linked to the importance of agriculture in their economies.

The USSR, too, already had a high female participation rate in 1959 which remained basically unchanged, with a small drop between 1970 and 1979. The trend was attributable partly to the role of agriculture and partly to economic and social changes before the Second World War.

---

provisions. The high rate for the 60–64 age group in the German Democratic Republic undoubtedly reflects the fact that old-age pensioners can work and draw their pensions in full. This incentive was used to some extent in other countries, too, such as Czechoslovakia.

The Soviet Union is another example. In the USSR the 1956 National Pensions Act resulted in a substantial increase in the number of pensioners but, as the Act contained a provision for the suspension of pension payments to those who went on working, the employment of older persons dropped sharply. Whereas in 1956 there were 1,877,000 pensioners of whom 1,107,000 (59.0 per cent) worked, in 1957 the number of

3.2

Principal trends in the activity rates of individual countries, by age group and sex

Adolescents of both sexes under the age of 20

The biggest drop in the male activity rate was in Bulgaria (from 54 per cent in 1956 to 24 per cent in 1975) and in the German Democratic Republic (from 63 per cent in 1964 to 27 per cent in 1971). Even in Hungary, where the age-specific activity rate for this age group is the highest in Eastern Europe, there was a decline from 64 to 45 per cent between 1949 and 1980.

The decline in the female activity rate, which occurred everywhere, was particularly pronounced in Czechoslovakia, the German Democratic Republic and Poland.

Adult men between 20 and 55 years of age

Activity rates were very high, as much as 97 and 99 per cent for men aged 25 or over. In the 45-54 age group activity rates remained generally high, although there was a decline in Poland and Romania, to 90 and 91 per cent respectively.

Adult women between 20 and 55 years of age

The greatest change here was the rising employment of women between 25 and 55 years of age. The latest data show that 70 to 80 per cent of women in this category work, and there are some cases of activity rates over 90 per cent: Bulgaria (1975), 93 per cent of women between 25 and 44 years of age; Czechoslovakia (1980), 91 per cent of women between 25 and 49 years of age; USSR (1970), 93 per cent in the 30-39 age bracket and 91 per cent in the 40-49 age

bracket. The contrast with Western Europe is striking. The activity rate for women in this age bracket in France and the Federal Republic of Germany (1980) was around 50 to 60 per cent, and much lower in the Netherlands and in southern European countries. Only in the Scandinavian countries were female activity rates anywhere near those of Eastern Europe. However, part-time work is much more common among women in Western than in Eastern Europe.

Men aged 55 or over

There was a spectacular decline in activity rates among men in the 60-64 age group in Hungary (from 81 per cent in 1949 to 13 per cent in 1980) and Bulgaria (from 85 per cent in 1956 to 34 per cent in 1975), unlike the German Democratic Republic and Poland where the rate remained at a high level (83 per cent in 1971 and 62 per cent in 1978, respectively). Activity rates naturally vary according to the official retirement age.

Women aged 55 or over

Except in Bulgaria and Hungary, activity rates remained high. In countries with acute labour shortages (Czechoslovakia and the German Democratic Republic) participation rates for this age group rose; elsewhere, although there was a slight decline, the level was still high. Activity rates in Eastern Europe are everywhere higher than in Western Europe, with the exception of the Scandinavian countries.

---

pensioners increased to 2,711,000 of whom only 775,000 (28.6 per cent) worked; by 1960 there were 4,531,000 pensioners of whom a mere 532,000 (11.7 per cent) were still working (Smirnov, 1977). The percentage of working pensioners continued to decline until 1964, when only 10.1 per cent of 7,436,000 pensioners went on working and when concern with a falling labour force led the Soviet Government to revise the social security provisions. Most employed pensioners then became entitled to half their full pension; in the Urals, Siberia and the Far East, they were entitled to as much as 75 per cent, with a ceiling of 200 roubles a month for pensions and wages combined. In agriculture full pensions became payable for working pensioners.

The foregoing analysis suggests that labour force participation rates are strained to the limit,

and it seems most unlikely – at least in a number of these countries – that the share of women or pensioners in the labour force can rise much higher than current levels.

Structural changes in employment

Mention has already been made of the emphasis on industrialisation and extensive development after the Second World War. A high proportion of the national product was diverted into investment, particularly "productive" investment (i.e. investment contributing to the growth of the "material sphere" rather than the "social infrastructure"). By 1949-50 industrial production in all countries was above the pre-war level, though agricultural output generally had not yet caught up. During the 1950s large-scale collectivisation contributed to a rural exodus and a shift of the labour force to non-agricultural employment.

By 1960 industrial production formed a larger part of the net material product than agricultural production in all Eastern European countries, as shown in table 3.10.[9] The share of manufacturing in the NMP, which exceeded 60 per cent in Czechoslovakia and the German Democratic Republic, ranged between 42 and 52 per cent in all other countries, with the exception of Hungary, where it amounted to 37.6 per cent. The share of agriculture was 15.2 per cent in Czechoslovakia, 18.0 per cent in the German Democratic Republic and 20.7 per cent in the USSR, while in all other countries it was around 30 per cent. Between 1960 and 1980 there was a further reduction in the share of agriculture: in all countries except the USSR, the share had dropped by 1980 to roughly half the 1960 level. This reduction was mainly in the 1960s, while in the 1970s there was a slowing down of the trend and even a reversal in the past few years.

The structural changes in Eastern European economies are fully reflected in the changes in the structure of employment. Table 3.11 shows the distribution of the economically active population among the three major sectors of the economy.

The most striking change was the rapid decline in the agricultural share of total employment. In Bulgaria this dropped from 65 per cent in 1956 to 24 per cent in 1975 and, in Romania, from 56 per cent in 1950 to 30 per cent in 1978. Although detailed figures are not available for the years immediately after the war, one can safely generalise that in all Eastern European countries the share of agriculture in total employment was reduced by half between the end of the war and 1980 and by at least two-thirds in the traditionally agricultural countries such as Bulgaria and Romania.

The reduction in the agricultural labour force took place mainly during the 1950s and 1960s and resulted in a change of the sex and age composition of the agricultural labour force.

The situation up to 1970, when more women than men were employed in agriculture, is still true

Table 3.10
Structure of the net material product (as a percentage of the material sphere)

Country and period	Agri-culture	Industry	Construc-tion	Trans-port	Trade	Other
Bulgaria						
1960	32.3	47.3	7.0	4.2	9.0	0.2
1970	22.8	51.1	8.7	6.9	10.2	0.3
1975	22.1	52.1	8.8	8.2	8.4	0.4
1980	16.7	51.8	9.0	8.1	14.0	0.4
Czecho-slovakia						
1960	15.2	63.4	10.7	3.0	7.0	0.7
1970	10.5	62.1	11.3	3.8	11.3	1.0
1975	8.7	65.7	12.7	2.9	9.0	1.0
1980	7.3	64.8	10.7	4.3	12.4	0.5
German Dem. Rep.						
1960	18.0	62.6	5.2	4.4	13.4	2.3
1970	12.9	57.8	8.4	5.4	12.7	2.8
1975	11.1	59.1	7.4	5.0	14.6	2.8
1980	9.5	68.3	6.8	3.6	9.9	2.9
Hungary						
1960	29.8	37.6	11.6	5.6	14.1	1.3
1970	21.7	44.1	11.5	6.0	15.0	1.7
1975	17.9	46.2	11.1	5.8	17.3	1.7
1980	15.8	49.5	10.6	5.8	16.9	1.4
Poland						
1960	25.8	46.9	9.7	5.3	10.3	2.0
1970	17.3	54.6	9.8	6.7	9.9	1.7
1975	14.8	59.6	11.2	6.8	5.5	2.1
1980	15.3	54.7	9.3	7.4	10.7	2.6
Romania						
1960	34.9	42.1	8.9	5.2	6.2	2.7
1970	19.5	59.1	10.4	5.9	3.4	1.7
1975	16.6	57.1	8.4	5.6	10.6	1.7
1980	15.2	59.3	9.3	7.0	7.4	1.8
USSR						
1960	20.7	52.3	10.0	3.0	11.6	2.4
1970	22.0	51.1	10.4	3.8	10.9	1.8
1975	17.1	52.6	11.4	2.9	12.6	3.4
1980	15.2	50.9	10.5	4.3	17.7	1.4

Source: CMEA: *Statistical Yearbook – 1981* (Moscow, 1981).

Table 3.11
Active population by sex and major economic sector in Eastern European countries, between 1950 and 1980 (in percentage)

Country and year of census	Total				Men				Women			
	All sectors	Agricul-ture	Industry[a]	Services[b]	All sectors	Agricul-ture	Industry[a]	Services[b]	All sectors	Agricul-ture	Industry[a]	Services[b]
Bulgaria												
1956	100	65	19	17	100	55	25	20	100	78	10	12
1965	100	44	33	22	100	36	41	23	100	55	23	22
1975	100	24	43	33	100	21	48	31	100	26	37	37
Czechoslovakia												
1947	100	38[c]	37	25	100	30[c]	43	27	100	53[c]	27	20
1961	100	25	47	28	100	21	54	25	100	30	37	33
1970	100	17	48	35	100	17	55	28	100	16	40	43
1980	100	13	50	37	100	15	57	28	100	12	40	48
German Dem. Rep.												
1964	100	15	46	39	100	15	53	32	100	15	37	49
1971	100	12	49	40	100	12	57	31	100	11	39	49
1980[d]	100	11	48	41	100	12	59	29	100	9	38	53
Hungary												
1949	100	57	25	19	100	55	27	18	100	61	18	21
1960	100	40	36	24	100	39	40	21	100	42	29	29
1970	100	25	45	30	100	26	49	25	100	23	40	37
1980	100	19	44	37	100	21	48	31	100	15	39	46
Poland												
1950	100	56	22	22	100	46	29	25	100	68	14	18
1960	100	46	28	25	100	37	37	26	100	59	17	24
1970	100	39	34	27	100	32	44	24	100	46	24	30
1978	100	30	38	32	100	28	46	26	100	32	29	39
Romania												
1956	100	70	17	13	100	59	24	16	100	83	7	9
1966	100	57	25	18	100	45	35	20	100	72	12	16
1977	100	37	39	24	100	25	50	25	100	50	26	24
USSR												
1959	100	44	28	27	100	35	35	30	100	53	22	25
1970	100	26	38	36	100	25	45	30	100	27	31	42
1979[e]	100	21	39	40	100	..	..	..	100	..	..	..

.. = not available.
[a] Industry = mining and quarrying, manufacturing, electricity, gas and water and construction.   [b] Includes persons employed in the non-material sphere of the economy.   [c] Including quarrying.   [d] Official estimates for 1980.   [e] Official estimates.
Source: ILO: *Year Book of Labour Statistics*, various editions; United Nations: *Economic survey of Europe in 1977*, Part II, op. cit.; national statistics.

89

today, except in Czechoslovakia, the German Democratic Republic, Hungary and now even Poland. This is in sharp contrast with the situation in Western Europe, though there too a rapid decline in agricultural employment took place over the same period. In 1970, for every 100 men employed in agriculture, there were 23 women in England and Wales, 43 in France, 15 in the Netherlands, 22 in Belgium and 41 in Italy, as opposed to 110 women in the USSR (160 in 1959),

121 in Poland, 81 Czechoslovakia and the German Democratic Republic and 63 in Hungary.

There was also a change in the age composition of the agricultural labour force, with a growing proportion of older workers (26 per cent in Czechoslovakia in the early 1960s, for example).

During the 1970s agricultural employment continued to fall in all Eastern European countries,

Table 3.12
Changes in net material product and labour productivity (average annual percentage change)

Country	Five-year plan, 1976-80			Net material product, 1976-80			Labour productivity, 1976-80		
	Net material product (NMP) (1)	Labour productivity (LP) (2)	LP/NMP (3)	Five-year plan (FYP) (4)	Actual (5)	Actual/FYP (6)	Five-year plan (FYP) (7)	Actual (8)	Actual/FYP (9)
Bulgaria	7.7	7.7	1.00	7.7	6.1	0.79	7.7	6.1	0.79
Czechoslovakia	4.9	4.5	0.92	4.9	3.7	0.76	4.5	3.3	0.73
German Dem. Rep.	5.0	4.4	0.89	5.0	4.1	0.82	4.4	3.6	0.82
Hungary	5.4-5.7	5.4-5.7	1.00	5.4-5.7	3.2	0.58	5.4-5.7	3.7	0.67
Poland	7.0-7.3	5.9-6.1	0.84	7.0-7.3	1.2	0.17	5.9-6.1	1.7	0.28
Romania	10-11	9.4-10.4	0.94	10-11	7.2	0.69	9.4-10.4	6.6	0.67
USSR	4.7 [a]	3.5	0.75	4.7 [a]	4.2	0.89	3.5	3.2	0.91

[a] Net material product used.

Source: United Nations: *Economic survey of Europe in 1981*, op. cit., p. 137.

particularly in Romania and Bulgaria, where between 1971 and 1980 it was declining at an average annual rate of 4.7 and 3.3 per cent, respectively, and more moderately elsewhere (0.7 per cent annually in the USSR and between 1 and 2 per cent in the other countries).

The governments of some countries took measures to slow down this trend. In the past few years the number of young farm workers in Czechoslovakia and the German Democratic Republic increased and overall agricultural employment became stabilised. In Hungary the decline was stopped in 1978, since when there has been a small increase in the agricultural labour force.

Employment in industry and construction (including mining) was the main beneficiary of these transfers of the labour force, and very large increases in industrial employment were registered in all countries. Latest figures show Czechoslovakia with 50 per cent of the labour force in industry, the German Democratic Republic with 48 per cent and the other countries with between 38 and 44 per cent. Industry has also become an important employer of women, as in several countries almost 40 per cent of working women are active in this sector.

This great concentration on increasing industrial production was achieved at the expense of the relative neglect of the services sector. Eastern European countries today have a lower percentage of their labour force in services than Western European countries. While the percentage of employment has been increasing, it is typically in the range of 30 to 40 per cent of the labour force (a mere 24 per cent in Romania in 1977). On the other hand, Western European countries, where a shift from industry to services started earlier, have almost 50 per cent of the labour force in the services sector, and even more in such countries as France, the Netherlands, Sweden and the United Kingdom (see table 2.6 in the previous chapter). It can be expected that in future years the services sector will become the main recipient of employment increases in the Eastern European countries.

Labour productivity

To meet the targets laid down in the state plans, the Eastern European countries rely on the growth of employment and the growth of labour productivity. As the former has slowed down in recent years, labour productivity has acquired the utmost importance.[10] This was recognised in all the five-year plans for the period 1976 to 1980, as can be seen from table 3.12.

The first three columns show that, for 1976-80, Bulgaria and Hungary expected their growth to be 100 per cent dependent on the growth of labour productivity, while Romania and Czechoslovakia projected rates of 94 and 92 per cent, respectively. The USSR relied on a 25 per cent increase in employment and a 75 per cent increase in labour productivity, and the German Democratic Republic and Poland occupied an intermediate position.

During the period, however, none of these countries met their target. As can be seen from column 9, the planned increase of labour productivity was achieved only to the extent of 67 to 82 per cent, with two exceptions: 91 per cent in USSR and a bare 28 per cent in Poland.

The inevitable result was that the actual rate of growth of the net material product fell behind accordingly (see column 6). Czechoslovakia and Romania reduced the shortfall by a higher increase of employment in the material sphere than planned, while in Hungary, Poland and the USSR real employment in the material sphere grew less than had been planned and the real rate of growth of the NMP therefore lagged even further behind expectations. The most extreme example was Poland, whose NMP grew at only 17 per cent of the rate planned. The USSR achieved 89 per cent of the targeted NMP growth rate for 1976-80.

The situation did not improve in 1981 and 1982, when labour productivity in the material sphere declined by 12.2 and 4.2 per cent in Poland and by 0.6 and 0.2 per cent in Czechoslovakia. In all the other countries the growth rate in 1982 was lower than that of 1976-80.

As was pointed out by the United Nations Economic Commission for Europe, the decelerating trend of labour productivity in most Eastern European countries is not easy to explain. A number of commentators have put forward many explanations: rapid deterioration of terms of trade (except for the USSR), culmination of the negative effects of the extensive growth strategy, problems with agricultural production and with rail transport in the USSR, low level of mechanisation of manual work (particularly in auxiliary production), low productivity of manual labour due to a negative attitude towards unappealing jobs, "leisure fatigue" (fatigue which results from activities on days off and which carries over to the job), absenteeism and violation of labour discipline (Kostin, 1980).

These factors, together with shortcomings at various points of the systems of production and distribution to which the authorities have drawn attention in several of these countries, no doubt contributed to the slowing down of labour productivity growth but they cannot account fully for the sharp deceleration in recent years, particularly in 1981 and 1982. As the United Nations Economic Commission for Europe observes: "There are no grounds for supposing that either the quality of labour, the level of equipment and technology or of management declined in 1981. Hence the labour productivity movement . . . must have been due primarily to the effects of energy, fuel and raw material input shortages which brought about the deceleration of NMP growth rates, thus preventing a possible growth of labour productivity which might otherwise have taken place. This is probably the most logical explanation for all countries but Poland, in which the other factors . . . acted in the same direction" (*Economic survey of Europe in 1981*, pp. 167-168).

The problems of energy, fuel and raw material input do indeed seem to be the most prominent set of factors causing the difficulties in Eastern Europe. During the period of "extensive growth", when the aim was to increase industrial output at all costs and when energy and raw

3.3

Factors contributing to the deceleration in the growth rate of the Czechoslovak economy between 1975 and 1980: an econometric study

This study (I. Sujan: "An analysis of the factors contributing to the deceleration in the growth rate of the Czechoslovak economy in the period 1975-1980", in *Politicka Ekonomie* (Prague, Ceskoslovenska Akademie Ved.) No. 6, 1982) investigates the decline in the growth of net material product in the period 1975-80 as compared with the period 1965-75. The relevant data are shown in table A.

The study analyses ten factors which may have had an impact on the decline in the rate of growth and, with the help of a large econometric model, establishes their relative importance. The factors are listed in three groups: "objective" external factors, factors associated with the deterioration of the efficiency of the economy, and factors associated with the depletion of resources for extensive growth. The results are shown in table B.

The first five columns show the absolute amount by which the NMP was reduced, compared with the trend of 1965-75 because of the impact of each factor. Column 6 indicates the reduction in the rate of growth by comparison with the same period, in percentage points. The last two columns indicate the relative impact of individual factors on changes in the NMP in 1980 by comparison with 1965-75 (column 7) and on changes in the NMP growth rate (column 8). As the last two columns give more or less the same picture, we can analyse the factors from the standpoint of their impact on the reduction in the rate of growth (column 8).

Taken together, the ten factors account for almost 99 per cent of the deceleration in the rate of growth. The reduced rate of growth of employment in the material sphere is clearly an important factor, but less than one-quarter of the deceleration can be ascribed to it. The rest is due to other factors which can broadly be called labour productivity at the national level.

Some of these factors are external to the economy: factors 1, 2 and 3 together account for 26.14 per cent of the slow-down of NMP growth. More important still are factors 4 to 7, which reflect the declining efficiency of the economy. Most important of all are factors 8 to 10, which are associated with the depletion of resources for extensive growth and account for 41 per cent of the deceleration.

Certain factors acquired greater importance in the last two years of the period. Thus, the impact of world prices of raw materials and fuels greatly increased in 1979 and 1980, the reduction of domestic supplies of energy had a great impact in 1979, and declining investment and the deterioration of terms of trade with capitalist countries had an impact in 1980.

Table A
Changes in the rate of growth of selected macro-economic indicators

Indicators (at constant 1.1.1977 prices)	Average annual rates of growth			Change in the 1980 level resulting from the decline in the rate of growth (in thousand million Koruny)
	1965-75	1975-80	Change	
Net material product	6.39	3.83	−2.56	−65.2
Imports	6.41	2.58	−3.83	−31.0
Exports	6.32	7.55	+1.23	+9.3
Domestic use of NMP	6.41	2.36	−4.05	−105.5
of which:				
– personal consumption	5.14	1.66	−3.48	−42.5
– investment	7.67	3.47	−4.20	−33.1

Source: I. Sujan, op. cit., p. 597.

materials were relatively inexpensive, not enough attention was paid to the energy and raw material content of production. Eastern European specialists often point out that the unit of industrial output produced in the region requires higher energy and raw material inputs than a similar unit in Western Europe or North America. At the same time, Eastern European countries other than the USSR have to import large quantities of raw materials and fuel, which are now more difficult to obtain. Even in the USSR, which possesses abundant resources and exports some of its production, extraction is becoming more difficult as new deposits are usually located in relatively inaccessible and uninhabited regions.

This is confirmed by an econometric study made recently in Czechoslovakia, which is also

3.3 (continued)

Table B
Impact of selected factors on changes in the NMP

Factors	Changes in NMP in thousand million Koruny (at constant 1.1.1977 prices)					Annual percentage change in the rate of growth of the NMP	Share of factors	
	1976	1977	1978	1979	1980		In the change in the NMP in 1980	In the change in the rate of growth between 1975 and 1980
A. 1. Slow-down of rate of growth of world economic activity	−0.2	−0.8	−1.8	−2.9	−4.318	−0.161	6.62	6.28
2. Reduction of availability of raw materials and fuel on world market (non-price limitation)	−0.4	−0.9	−1.7	−2.5	−3.442	−0.130	5.28	5.07
3. Acceleration of rate of increase of world prices of raw materials and fuel	−2.3	−1.9	−3.5	−6.5	−9.969	−0.379	15.28	14.79
B. 4. Deterioration of terms of trade with capitalist countries (excluding prices of raw materials and fuels)	−0.6	−1.6	−1.5	−1.6	−5.043	−0.193	7.73	7.53
5. Relative (non-price) deterioration of export efficiency	−1.0	−2.2	−2.5	−1.4	−1.559	−0.061	2.39	2.38
6. Deterioration of raw material and energy requirements of production	0.0	−10.1	−15.1	−13.5	−13.084	−0.510	20.05	19.90
7. Slow down in starting production with new fixed capital	+1.2	+1.5	+0.9	+0.2	−1.151	−0.045	1.76	1.76
C. 8. Deceleration of increases in employment in the material sphere	3.6	−6.5	−8.3	−11.0	−15.598	−0.623	23.91	24.31
9. Deceleration of increases in energy supplies	+0.7	+0.5	+1.3	−5.1	−6.628	−0.270	10.16	10.53
10. Deceleration of investment increases	0.0	−0.5	−0.7	−1.2	−3.964	−0.162	6.07	6.32
Recapitulation								
A. External "objective factors"	−2.9	−3.6	−7.0	−11.9	−17.729	−0.670	27.18	26.14
B. Factors related to deterioration of trend of economic efficiency	−0.4	−12.4	−18.2	−16.3	−20.837	−0.890	31.93	31.57
C. Factors related to depletion of resources for extensive growth	−2.9	−6.5	−7.7	−17.3	−26.190	−1.055	40.14	41.16
Total A + B + C	−6.2	−22.5	−32.9	−45.5	−64.756	−2.534	99.25	98.85

Source: I. Sujan, op. cit., pp. 604-605.

probably valid for a number of other Eastern European countries (see box 3.3). Two conclusions can be drawn from this study.

First, it confirms the view of the United Nations about the importance of raw materials, energy and fuel in the deterioration of the economic situation. Increased prices, limited availability and increased requirements for these resources accounted for half of the reduction in Czechoslovakia's rate of growth.

Secondly, even though the depletion of resources for extensive development is a major contributory factor, so is the level of efficiency of the economy, undermined as it is by the excessively high requirements of Eastern European production for raw materials and energy.

Economic growth and employment: prospects in Eastern European countries

The five-year plans for the period 1981 to 1985 reflect the difficulties outlined in the first two sections of this chapter. As we have seen, national income has increased less than was projected by previous plans. The new plans recognise this situation and, everywhere except in the German Democratic Republic, set lower targets than before, sometimes even lower than the past rates actually achieved. In Bulgaria, Czechoslovakia and Poland the drop in the targeted rate of growth is quite sharp.

The most prominent feature of the strategy proposed is the emphasis on increasing the efficiency of the development process. This is a continuation and intensification of the intensive development strategy which aims at increasing efficiency and quality of production.

This policy is of course partly imposed on the countries by the difficulty of increasing employment, by the limits to investment, by growing problems with raw materials, energy and fuel and by the deteriorating foreign trade position (except in the USSR).

The policy has been defined by a Soviet economic journal [11] as follows: *(a)* the growth of labour productivity; *(b)* the rational use of productive potential, including increases in capital productivity through optimal exploitation of existing capacities; *(c)* the rational use of all material inputs with a view to decreasing material input per unit of output; *(d)* improving the quality of output.

Stagnation of employment is one of the factors leading to the adoption of the intensive development strategy. In the USSR employment is expected to grow at the rate of 1 per cent per annum, that is, at half the rate during the 1976-80

period. The increases will be mainly in the non-material sphere. Moreover, increases in the active population will be very unequally distributed geographically.

In the other countries employment increases will likewise be small, and in some cases there will be a decline; additional employment will be created mainly in the non-material sphere. In Hungary the plan will, if its targets are achieved, result in a reduction of about 120,000 jobs in industry and construction, though employment in the infrastructural sectors may increase by about 100,000 people in five years. In Czechoslovakia the increase in employment is expected to be about 1 per cent over the five-year period, as against 3.8 per cent between 1976 and 1980. There will be some reduction in employment in the primary sector, a stable situation in industry and a slight increase in the services sector, particularly in trade, education, medical care and science. In Bulgaria employment will increase in the non-material sphere and decline in the material sphere. In the German Democratic Republic employment in the material sphere will remain generally stable, and no shifts of labour between industrial sectors are envisaged. In Poland the government programme for overcoming the crisis and stabilising the economy offers only a broad outline of structural changes, but employment is expected to decline by about 100,000 people by 1985.

Coupled with other constraints, the somewhat bleak employment situation exerts a major influence on a number of planned measures. Because it is more limited, investment is intended to help to modernise and rationalise existing production rather than to create new production capacity. In Bulgaria, for example, 70 per cent of new fixed capital investment will go into modernisation and reconstruction and only 30 per cent into new projects. In the USSR the emphasis is on increased mechanisation of auxiliary production processes. The German Democratic Republic is planning to introduce some 45,000 industrial robots by 1985 in order to replace about 112,500 jobs. In all countries increased mechanisation is planned for agriculture in order to raise agricultural output with a declining or stable labour force.

In this climate of intensive development, better management and planning are crucial if the economies are to run more efficiently. Responsibility for plan fulfilment has already been shifted down the scale of organisational level and the cost-accounting principle *(khozraschet)* has been more widely introduced at every level. It is also intended to modify the indicators of economic performance, with a shift from gross physical and value indicators towards net value indicators, such as net output, income and profit. Finally, there is a tendency to establish a closer link between performance and remuneration, though the form this takes differs from country to country. While in Bulgaria the trend is towards a reduction of earning differentials, Hungary does not seem to fear growing disparities: "The real wages per capita of the economically active population", writes one economist, "will remain unchanged in the coming years. However, the financial situation of those who perform excellently will improve while for those who do not or only slightly improve their performance the continuation of their real wages cannot be guaranteed" (Havasi, 1981).

It is clear from the foregoing that the countries of Eastern Europe are facing a number of major, long-term economic problems, and it is not immediately apparent how they are going to overcome them.

Agricultural production is clearly one of these problems. It is not just a question of finding and developing the necessary physical and human resources; it is also a question of preventing wastage.[12] Raw materials, energy and fuel pose serious difficulties too, though these vary from country to country. In the Soviet Union their increase can be obtained only at a higher cost; moreover, part of these resources have to be exported in order to earn the foreign currency needed to import food and new technology. In the

rest of Eastern Europe declining imports of raw materials and fuel from the USSR will reduce the growth of trade within the CMEA, as well as the dynamism of domestic production. Furthermore, replacing imports from the USSR by imports from other countries entails stepping up exports towards them, and this these Eastern European countries have so far found very difficult. By and large, the terms of trade of Eastern European countries (other than the USSR) with the industrialised market economies and with the Soviet Union have been deteriorating – a tendency which can be expected to continue. Finally, any reorientation of production will come up against the problem of limited investment possibilities.

These countries, as we have seen, are therefore confronted by a number of limitations: limitations on the growth of employment, on the growth of investment, on the use of physical factors of production, on external trade. The numerous obstacles to intensive development and to improvements in the quality and efficiency of production seem difficult to overcome and, in some cases, present virtually insoluble contradictions. Compensating for shortages of manpower by mechanising or automating production processes requires massive investment; developing domestic production entails a greater use of raw materials and energy; and so on. At the same time, solutions involving more flexible day-to-day management and planning, offering undertakings greater incentives, and linking remuneration to efficiency may prove not to be compatible with the general principles governing the economic and social system of these countries. The countries of Eastern Europe therefore appear to stand at a crossroad. The decisions taken in the next few years will determine their economic development for a long time to come.

---

[1] Unless otherwise indicated, the term "Eastern Europe" is taken to include the USSR.

[2] The term "intensive growth" as used here does not refer to labour or capital intensiveness in the usual sense of a small volume of fixed capital associated with a highly intensive use of labour, or vice versa. Intensive development in Eastern Europe relates to the pursuit

of the best possible results by means of the optimum use of the limited resources available – energy, raw materials, fixed capital, labour. The term does not therefore imply any indication of the intensity of the various factors.

[3] This concept, which measures national income, is very different from the concept of gross national product or gross domestic product used elsewhere. To understand it properly, one must bear in mind the distinction made in the planned economies between the "material sphere" and the "non-material sphere". Activities in the material sphere include the production of goods and the provision of material services (i.e. services which contribute directly to production); material services include maintenance, transport and distribution of goods, telecommunications, mass media, printing, etc., but exclude such services as education and medical care. Only activities in the material sphere serve for the calculation of the NMP. Activities in the non-material sphere are considered as a redistribution of the values created in the material sphere and do *not* contribute to the NMP. The concept of net material product is therefore far more restricted than that of the gross national or domestic product. For a fuller description, see United Nations: *Comparisons of the system of national accounts and the system of balances of the national economy*, Part One: *Conceptual relationships* (New York, 1977; Sales No.: E.77.XVII.6).

[4] The national income concept used in table 3.2 is the net material product used, which shows how the NMP was used for consumption and net capital formation purposes. Rates of growth of NMP used in Eastern Europe since 1976 are considerably lower than rates of growth of NMP produced. In 1974 and 1975 the NMP used in most Eastern European countries increased more than the NMP produced, as imports greatly exceeded exports. However, in 1976 measures were introduced to reverse this trend in order to redress external imbalances. Since then the NMP used has been growing more slowly in all countries than the NMP produced.

[5] It could also make it more difficult to improve the quality of goods in so far as, for example, it impedes the development and dissemination of the necessary control instruments.

[6] The 1979 census data by age have not yet been published, but *Vestnik Statistiki*, No. 2, 1980, indicates that the ratio was about 100 for ages below 50.

[7] Medium variant projections made in 1980 by the Population Division of the United Nations Secretariat.

[8] In 1978 the activity rates in Poland for the 60-64 age group were 98.3 per cent in agriculture and 42.6 per cent outside agriculture, while for men aged 65 or over they were 86.4 per cent in agriculture and 7.9 per cent outside agriculture.

[9] The share of agriculture in the net material product tends to be undervalued for two main reasons: first, because of the freedom of the agricultural sector from turnover taxes and, second, because of the underpricing both of compulsory deliveries and of self-consumption. See "A note on some aspects of national accounting methodology in Eastern Europe and the Soviet Union", in United Nations: *Economic bulletin for Europe* (Geneva, 1959), Vol. 11, No. 3, pp. 64-65.

[10] Labour productivity measured at the national level usually grows faster than labour productivity measured at the sectoral level and this in turn grows faster than labour productivity at the industry and enterprise level. The reason is that, generally, the labour force moves from lower productivity to higher productivity industries and thus, even with no increase of labour productivity in any industry, it is possible to increase labour productivity at the national level. One factor influencing labour productivity at the national level is therefore the success of measures designed to move labour from low productivity to higher productivity industries. Many other factors determine the growth of labour productivity. Generally speaking, labour productivity is a rather synthetic indicator reflecting the performance of the economy as a whole (in this case, the material sphere of the economy).

[11] *Ekonomicheskaya Gazeta* (Moscow, 1981), No. 39, p. 3, quoted in United Nations: *Economic survey of Europe in 1981*, op. cit., p. 162.

[12] According to Soviet estimates, less than 55 to 60 per cent of potatoes grown are consumed, owing to losses incurred in the process of harvesting, transport and warehousing (V. I. Pavlov and A. N. Spektor: "Problems with respect to the efficient use of materials", in *Ekonomica i Organizatsiia Promyshlennogo Proizvodstva*, No. 4, 1981).

Selected bibliography

Aganbegian, A. G. *Changes in economic trends in the 1970s and some long-term implications: USSR and East European countries* (Geneva, United Nations Economic and Social Council, 1981, doc. EC.AD.(XVII)/AC.1/R.2; mimeographed; restricted).

CMEA. *Statistical Yearbook – 1981* (Moscow, 1981).

Havasi, F. "The sixth five-year plan of the Hungarian national economy (1981-1985)", in *Acta Oeconomica* (Budapest, Akadémiai Kiadó), Vol. 26, Nos. 1-2, 1981.

ILO. *Year Book of Labour Statistics*, various editions.

–. *Women at Work*, No. 2, 1979.

Kostin, L. A. "Labour productivity in the present stage", in *Ekonomika I Organizatsiia Promyshlennogo Proizvodoytva*, No. 12, 1980.

National economic plans, 1981-85.

National statistical yearbooks, various editions.

Smirnov, S. "The employment of old-age pensioners in the USSR", in *International Labour Review* (Geneva, ILO), July-Aug. 1977, pp. 87-94.

Sujan, I. "An analysis of the factors contributing to

the deceleration in the growth rate of the Czechoslovak economy in the period 1975-1980", in *Politicka Ekonomie* (Prague, Ceskoslovenská Akademie Ved.), No. 6, 1982.

Tikhonov, N. A. *Guidelines for the economic and social development of the USSR for 1981-1985 and for the period ending in 1990* (Moscow, Novosti Press Agency, 1981.

United Nations. "A note on some aspects of national accounting methodology in Eastern Europe and the Soviet Union", in *Economic bulletin for Europe* (Geneva, 1959), Vol. 11, No. 3, pp. 52-68.

—. *Economic survey of Europe in 1976*, Part II: *The five-year plans for 1976-1980 in Eastern Europe and the Soviet Union* (New York, 1977; Sales No. E.77.II.E.11).

—. *Economic survey of Europe in 1977*, Part II: *Labour supply and migration in Europe: Demographic dimensions 1950-1975 and prospects*; and *1980*, *1981* and *1982*.

—. *Economic bulletin for Europe: Comparative GDP levels* (New York, 1980; Sales No. E.80.II.E.3).

Chapter **4**

International migration for employment

Major regions and countries of migration

Mankind has witnessed migration since time immemorial. Wars, persecution, climatic changes and economic forces have been the principal movers of people. Migration in the properly international sense of the word is a comparatively recent phenomenon, dating back no more than 200 or 300 years. The mercantilists did not fail to realise the gains that could be had from the admission of skilled foreigners, or that the retention of unskilled nationals would keep wage levels down and thus help exports. The liberal thinkers following them favoured free trade in goods but were divided when it came to opening the borders to foreigners. Colonised populations were pressed into overseas mines, plantations, canal digging and wherever plentiful and cheap labour was needed. During this period, 60 to 70 million Europeans left for other continents and about 75 per cent stayed there, more than half of them in the United States. Industrialisation caused massive intra-European movements, as shown, for example, by the 960,000 foreigners employed in Germany in 1907.

Taking 1980 as a suitable benchmark, one might estimate the stock of economically active migrants in today's world as at least 19.7 to 21.7 million,[1] as will be detailed below. First, however, a few words need to be said on definitional and measurement problems.

Leaving aside refugees, tourists, pilgrims and nomads, the distinguishing characteristic of the migrants under consideration here is that they move to a country of which they are not nationals, for the purpose of employment. Nationality is an objective criterion. Whether the migrants subjectively intend to stay abroad or return, or whether the policies of the migrant-receiving or the migrant-sending country are designed to make them do either one or the other, is a different matter and frequently unclear or subject to change. Nationality is the only valid and reliable distinction, and migrants are therefore defined here as persons not possessing the citizenship of their country of employment.

Stock data lend themselves better than flow data to capturing the durable features of a rapidly evolving phenomenon such as migration. Stocks reflect inflows, remigration, naturalisations and natural population movements. Where lacking, they will be supplemented by flow statistics.

In absolute figures, the United States is the country where the largest number of economically active foreigners are present. Most of them are in an irregular situation as regards their admission, stay or employment. If one critically evaluates the recent spate of estimates, one might put the range of economically active foreigners in an irregular situation at between 2.5 and 4 million, with perhaps half coming from Mexico. As regards legal migrants, just over 5 million reported under the alien address programme in 1979 which, assuming labour force participation to average 50

Table 4.1
Selected Western European countries: recorded number of migrant workers in 1980 (in thousands)

Out-migration country	In-migration country									Total
	Austria	Belgium	France[a]	Germany (Fed. Rep.)	Luxem-bourg	Nether-lands	Sweden	Switzer-land	United Kingdom[b]	
Algeria	–	3.2	322.7	1.6	–	–	–	–	–	327.5
Finland	–	–	–	3.7	–	–	108.0	–	1.0	112.7
France	–	38.5	–	54.0	8.5	2.0	–	–	14.0	117.2
Greece	–	10.8	3.0	138.4	–	1.2	7.5	–	6.0	166.9
Italy	–	90.5	146.4	324.3	11.2	12.0	–	301.0	73.0	958.4
Morocco	–	37.3	116.1	16.6	–	33.7	–	–	–	203.7
Portugal	–	6.3	430.6	59.9	13.7	4.2	–	–	5.0	519.7
Spain	–	32.0	157.7	89.3	2.3	10.4	–	85.7	17.0	394.4
Tunisia	–	4.7	65.3	–	–	1.1	–	–	–	71.1
Turkey	28.2	23.0	20.6	623.9	–	53.2	–	20.1	4.0	773.0
Yugoslavia	115.2	3.1	32.2	367.0	0.6	6.6	24.0	62.5	5.0	616.2
Other	31.3	83.2	192.4	490.1	15.6	70.2	94.6	237.0	804.0	2 018.4
Total	174.7	332.6	1 487.0	2 168.8	51.9	194.6	234.1	706.3	929.0	6 279.0

– No migrants recorded or estimated, magnitude less than 500, or not applicable.

[a] October 1980, estimate by INSEE on the basis of its 1980 employment survey, which underestimates by several hundred thousand categories such as small-scale employers, home-based workers and workers living at construction sites. [b] May-June 1979, estimate by the Department of Employment on the basis of its 1979 labour force survey.

Source: National statistical yearbooks or monthly publications, and Commission of the European Communities.

Table 4.2
South American region: estimated number of migrant workers in 1974 (in thousands)[a]

Out-migration country	In-migration country									Venezuela (1981)	Total
	Argentina	Bolivia	Brazil	Chile	Colombia	Ecuador	Paraguay	Peru	Uruguay		
Argentina	–	–	–	3	–	–	18	–	25	20	66
Bolivia	500	–	45	70	4	4	–	60	–	10	693
Brazil	70	2	–	–	5	20	30	5	20	20	172
Chile	250	5	–	–	5	–	–	10	–	20	290
Colombia	–	–	–	7	–	50	–	5	–	605	667
Ecuador	–	–	–	8	60	–	–	20	–	20	108
Paraguay	470	–	70	–	–	–	–	–	–	–	540
Peru	–	35	–	40	4	5	–	–	–	20	104
Uruguay	80	–	3	–	–	–	–	–	–	–	83
Venezuela	–	–	–	5	33	–	–	–	–	–	38
Other	–	3	22	2	9	6	2	20	5	40[b]	109
Total	1 370	45	140	135	120	85	50	120	50	755	2 870

– Not applicable, no migrants of this nationality recorded or estimated, or magnitude less than 500.

[a] Excluding about 400,000 economically active border commuters and people of European origin. [b] Of which 30,000 from Trinidad and Tobago.

Source: ILO: *La condition des travailleurs migrants en Amérique du sud* (Geneva, 1974; mimeographed; General Conditions of Work Series, No. 31). These 1974 estimates have been taken over unchanged except for the number of Paraguayans in Argentina, which has dropped by 130,000.

per cent, would indicate the presence of 2.5 million migrant workers. Two-thirds are from developing countries. The combined stock, then, of active foreigners amounts to some 5 to 6.5 million people. In addition, about 200,000 active foreigners legally entered the United States as "non-immigrants", i.e. they were admitted temporarily. The other North American receiving country, Canada, admitted 63,000 foreign workers for settlement and 74,375 as non-immigrants (and it extended the authorisations of another 22,889 non-immigrant workers) in 1980, but the stock figure as defined here is not known.

Western Europe rivals North America in numbers of migrants. Table 4.1 shows a recorded number of 6.3 million active foreigners. Denmark, Greece, Italy, Norway and Spain also host migrant worker populations of the order of 50,000 each; and Italian authorities fear that as many as 0.5 million foreigners work illegally in this renowned emigration country. The number of dependants in Western Europe amounts to approximately double the number of recorded active foreigners.

South America represents the next largest group of migrant-receiving countries (see table 4.2). Although the estimates date back to 1974, their order of magnitude may safely be assumed to be still valid today, giving a total of perhaps 3.5 to 4 million migrant workers including commuters, Argentina and Venezuela having changed places as regards the total number of immigrants shown.

The Arab countries of the Middle East and North Africa employed 2.8 million foreigners in mid-1980 (see table 4.3). More than nine in ten came from developing countries. Many of these were not accompanied by the members of their families.

Figures in West Africa are difficult to pin down. Table 4.4 is somewhat out of date, but reports from the region do not speak of substantial changes. For the sake of simplicity, the 1975 total of 1.3 million is assumed to hold good for 1980.

South Africa registered a stock of 287,000 Black foreign workers in 1980, of whom 220,000 worked in mining and quarrying. Only an infinitesimal number of dependants were allowed to accompany them. During that year, 30,000 White foreigners were also admitted, 43 per cent being economically active.

In Oceania, Australia counted 90,000 settler arrivals (and numerous others) and New Zealand 42,000 in 1980. Here, too, the stocks of the foreign working populations are not known.

The total of 19.7 to 21.7 million active persons outside their country of nationality – which should be seen in conjunction with a similar number of dependants living with them – is a minimum estimate. It does not take account of *(a)* the stock of non-immigrant workers in the United States, *(b)* any of the active foreigners in Australia, Canada and New Zealand, *(c)* migrant workers who are in an irregular situation in Western Europe, and *(d)* the foreigners who can be found in smaller or greater numbers in every country of the world, in a regular or irregular situation, even though their presence is not documented in published statistics. Categories *(a)* to *(d)* doubtless add up to several millions; but whether the global stock of migrant workers is nearer 25 than 30 million must remain a matter of speculation.

While perhaps only moderately important at the global level, international migration is of great importance in many countries. Of the migrant-receiving countries, for example in the Gulf region, Kuwait and the United Arab Emirates stand out with, respectively, 69 to 85 per cent of non-nationals in their workforces in 1975 – proportions which are known to have risen since. In Switzerland foreigners account for more than one in five of the active population. Looking at the population as a whole, one might take Australia as an example where 58 per cent of the country's post-war growth is due to the inflow of foreigners. Of the migrant-sending countries, for example in the southern African region, Botswana and

Table 4.3
Arab region: estimated number of migrant workers in 1980 (actual figures)

Out-migration country	In-migration country										
	Bahrain	Jordan (excl. Palestine)	Iraq	Kuwait	Libyan Arab Jamahiriya	Oman	Qatar	Saudi Arabia	United Arab Emirates	Yemen	Total
Democratic Yemen	1 125	–	–	9 500	–	120	1 500	65 000	6 600	–	83 845
Egypt	2 800	68 500	100 000	85 000	250 000	6 300	5 750	155 100	18 200	4 000	695 650
India	12 300	500	2 000	45 000	32 000	35 600	11 850	29 700	109 500	2 000	280 450
Iraq	310	–	–	40 000	–	–	–	3 250	1 200	–	44 760
Jordan (incl. Palestine)	1 400	–	7 500	55 000	15 000	2 250	7 800	140 000	19 400	2 000	250 350
Lebanon	300	–	4 500	8 000	5 700	1 500	750	33 200	6 600	500	61 050
Oman	900	–	–	2 000	–	–	1 150	10 000	19 400	–	33 450
Pakistan	26 160	4 000	7 500	34 000	65 000	44 500	20 770	29 700	137 000	3 000	371 630
Somalia	–	–	–	500	5 000	400	–	8 300	5 000	500	19 700
Sudan	900	–	500	5 500	21 000	620	750	55 600	2 100	2 250	89 220
Syrian Arab Republic	150	–	–	35 000	15 000	600	1 000	24 600	5 800	1 000	83 150
Yemen	1 125	–	–	3 000	–	120	1 500	325 000	5 400	–	336 145
Other Arab	–	–	–	300	65 600	120	–	500	–	–	66 520
Other Asian	10 000	1 000	1 500	10 000	27 000	–	4 500	93 500	20 700	300	168 500
Other	10 250	2 000	2 000	45 900	44 200	4 670	22 930	49 800	54 100	1 450	237 300
Total	67 720	76 000	125 500	378 700	545 500	96 800	80 250	1 023 250	411 000	17 000	2 821 720

– No migrants recorded or estimated, magnitude less than 500, or not applicable.

Source: This table is based in large part on material collected as part of an earlier ILO study; seee J. S. Birks and C. A. Sinclair: *Internatonal migration and development in the Arab region* (Geneva, ILO, 1980); and by the same authors: *The socio-economic determinants of intra-regional migration* (United Nations doc. E/ECWA/POP/CONF.4/WP.29 of 1 May 1981), p. 18.
Note that this table neglects a small number of migrant workers about whom data are practically inexistent such as Sudanese in Egypt, Syrians in Lebanon, West Africans in the Sudan and Turks in Syria.

Lesotho stand out with, respectively, one-quarter and four-fifths of nationals employed in the modern sector being at work over the border. In Bolivia nationals who had migrated to other Latin American countries accounted for 13 per cent of the population and 40 per cent of the working population in the mid-1970s, while in Paraguay they accounted for 28 and 92 per cent, respectively.

International migration can have considerable economic importance for the countries concerned. A few illustrations will suffice. In 1978 the flow of migrant workers' savings (remittances) to major migrant-sending countries amounted to US$24,000 million. This provided a notable element of international financial flexibility and much-needed hard currency for many developing countries. On the part of migrant-receiving countries, for example, one in six cars made in the Federal Republic of Germany in 1980 can be attributed to the work of Mediterranean migrants, and the ratio would be higher if only production-line workers were counted. On the part of migrant-sending countries, for example, the inflow of remittances in the Yemen Arab Republic since the early 1970s has covered the country's growing trade gap, or – which amounts to the same thing – migrants' transfer payments have enabled the country to increase its imports corresponding-ly, amounting to about 600 times the level of exports at the end of the 1970s.

Refugees

Although refugees differ from migrants for employment in international law (and their num-bers are not included in the estimates of the preceding section), they cannot be overlooked today. In principle, refugees are persons who can claim "non-refoulement" (the right not to be returned) when they have to leave their own country for another because of a well-founded fear of persecution for reasons of race, religion, nationality, political association or social group-ing, as laid down in the United Nations Conven-tion and Protocol relating to the Status of Refugees of 1951 and 1966. In practice, problems of application and interpretation of these criteria abound, and thus of determining the size of the refugee population. The 1981 case load of the United Nations High Commissioner for Refugees (UNHCR) exceeded 8 million persons. About 5 million were under UNHCR protection in Africa, 2.5 million in Asia, 0.6 million in Western Europe and 0.3 million in South America. On the basis of the OAU's somewhat broader concept of refu-gees,[2] the United States Committee for Refugees estimated the 1981 global stock of refugees as 12.6 million, i.e. over 8 million political refugees plus nearly 4.6 million displaced persons, but not including persons "firmly resettled". Half of the 12.6 million had found asylum in Africa.

The OAU definition, and much current prac-tice, look beyond persecution to the horrors of war and its aftermath. But even this broader concept of refugees does not recognise explicitly economic factors such as famine, malnutrition and extreme poverty, which may compel people to uproot themselves with as much force as political or

Table 4.4
West African region: estimated number of migrant workers in 1975 (in thousands)

Out-migration country	In-migration country				
	Gambia	Ivory Coast	Liberia	Sierra Leone	Total
Ghana	–	24	2	3	39
Ivory Coast	–	–	8	–	8
Liberia	–	2	–	6	8
Mali	3	200	–	–	203
Senegal	15	11	–	–	26
Sierra Leone	–	1	3	–	4
Togo[a]	–	7	–	–	7
Upper Volta	–	418	4	–	422
Other	15	36[b]	18	35[c]	573[d]
Total	33	699	35	44	1 280

– No migrants recorded or estimated, magnitude less than 500, or not applicable.
[a] Togolese have in the main moved to Ghana, where the 1970 census enumerated 245,000 migrants of this nationality. [b] Probably an underestimate. It would appear that a greater number orginated from Guinea alone. [c] Mostly from Guinea.
[d] Includes about 224,000 economically active foreigners in Ghana (chiefly from Togo and the Upper Volta), 157,000 in Senegal (perhaps half coming from Guinea and Guinea-Bissau) and 50,000 in Togo (mainly from Ghana).
Source: The row totals are taken from a World Bank-supported research paper by K. C. Zachariah and J. Conde (1978) and relate to persons 15 years and older. The share of these totals in the whole of the in-migrant population has been estimated for the four countries shown as follows: Gambia, 62 per cent; the Ivory Coast, 49 per cent; Liberia, 64 per cent and Sierra Leone, 55 per cent. The arithmetic mean of these figures, 57.5 per cent, has been taken as the labour force participation rate of each of the eight nationalities shown in every in-migration country. The resulting figures can therefore be regarded as very rough approximations only.

religious persecution. The often invoked "economic refugee", while certainly existing in fact, is a non-existent category in international law.

Free migration

The most privileged migrants of all are those who benefit from free movement provisions, i.e. who have the right to enter certain other countries and take up jobs there.

For example, beginning in 1954 the Scandina-vian countries abolished labour market tests for the nationals of Denmark, Finland, Norway and Sweden. Iceland did not become a member of the Common Nordic Labour Market, as it is called, but its nationals are not subject to work permit requirement in Denmark and Sweden.

The European Communities are perhaps more widely known for their system of free movement. It has been fully in force since 1968 and now encompasses Belgium, Denmark, France, the Federal Republic of Germany, Ireland, Italy, Luxembourg, the Netherlands and the United Kingdom. Greece's incorporation is taking place in stages, and Portugal's and Spain's are under consideration. Persons from non-member countries desiring entry actually still have to grapple with the laws of individual States rather than a common jurisdiction; and once admitted they are not free to move among member States. The importance of the free movement provisions is clear from the fact that over one-quarter of the present stock of migrants in Western Europe benefit from them.

Two Arab countries, Iraq and the Syrian Arab Republic, unilaterally decided to exempt all citizens of other Arab States from the definition of "foreigner" for purposes of immigration and employment. The laws of some other Arab countries contain a few highly specific provisions distinguishing certain Arab citizens from foreigners. At the regional level the League of Arab States has, since 1957, agreed to recognise freedom of residence and employment between members. But the League's limited competence has not given rise to appropriate domestic legislation outside Iraq and the Syrian Arab Republic.

The Trans-Tasman Agreement between Australia and New Zealand eliminated, for Commonwealth citizens, the substantive control over the numbers or types of settlement or short-term movements.[3] The inhabitants of the South Pacific Islands of Niue, Tokelau and the Cook Islands possess the citizenship of New Zealand and need only passports, not permits, to work in that country. They are able to enter by right, without preconditions regarding jobs.[4]

Other regions of the world have also seen steps taken to remove border posts between labour markets. This is the case, for example, of the Economic Community of West African States established in 1975, and the Central African Customs and Economic Union established in 1964. However, it seems that practical implementation is still in the early stages.

The enthusiasm for free movement zones in the past several decades has recently been tempered by the realisation that the lifting of influx controls does not do away with the underlying economic and social forces determining migration and employment. While movements are unhindered when borders are open, they are still essentially influenced by the ups and downs of the economy. For example, the average stock of Italians in the Federal Republic of Germany was 267,000 and 274,000 during the two recession years of 1967 and 1976 respectively; it climbed to 412,000 during the boom year of 1973 and reached 305,000 during the relatively good year of 1980. The social dimension of free movement naturally includes a strict requirement of equality of opportunity and treatment, but by itself this does not remove socio-economic antecedents and realities, as table 4.5 shows. Allowing for different vocational training systems and categorisations, one cannot fail to note the relationship between the degree to which foreign workers in their home countries first obtained training and then skilled jobs, on the one hand, and the extent to which they filled skilled jobs abroad, whether immediately upon entry or later, on the other hand.[5] Free movement does not invalidate this relationship.

Official and business migration

This is one of the oldest forms of migration and at the same time contains several new elements which are manifestations of the increasingly diverse character of the international movements of economically active people. There are, in the first instance, official or religious movements, including diplomatic and assimilated personnel as well as persons coming to join religious bodies or perform pastoral duties. This heading also includes transport or media representatives and entertainers, i.e. foreign shipping or airline employees, journalists, writers, artists, entertainers and sportsmen. The final subgroup under this heading consists of entrepreneurs or representatives of foreign businesses plus the many foreigners occupying positions in multinational organisations – directors, general managers and administrative, legal or medical specialists of any kind, researchers, consultants and designers, as well as support personnel such as clerks, office machine operators, trainees and even secretaries.

Official and business migration may, despite the apparent disparity, be viewed as one type for two reasons. Firstly, most countries treat the people concerned distinctly better than other migrants in respect of admission, stay and employment. Secondly, much of it is associated with the transfer of knowledge and technology. Officials, journalists, investors and employers of multinational companies transmit knowledge among countries, frequently by intent. This can have important effects for the countries concerned.

The volume of this type of migration is rising on a secular upward trend. This is chiefly a reflection of the growing economic interdependence and of the closer personal, cultural and even sports linkages among countries. It is self-evident in the case of crews of ships or aircraft. It is visible in, for example, certain groups admitted temporarily to the United States (see table 4.6), in the

Table 4.5
Pre-migration and post-migration status of foreign workers benefiting from free movement provisions and others in the Federal Republic of Germany in 1976 (in percentage)

	Free movement	No free movement benefit			
	Italians	Greeks	Spa-niards	Turks	Yugo-slavs
Finished vocational training in country of origin	26	37	47	49	61
Employed as skilled worker before migration	29	17	35	30	47
Employed as skilled worker upon entry	13	12	16	18	30
Employed as skilled worker at time of survey	16	28	24	20	35

Source: Forschungsverbund: "Probleme der Ausländerbeschaftigung", in *Integrierter Endbericht* (Bonn, Federal Ministry for Research and Technology), July 1979, pp. 94, 97 and 117.

many thousands of Filipino entertainers in Japan and in the following comment of a knowledgeable Australian observer: "Many long-term visitors are de facto guest workers, often well-qualified persons, responding to advertisements by business or educational institutions and willing to work in Australia for a few years before moving on elsewhere. Others are professional and businessmen sent by their firms overseas to work awhile in an Australian branch office or factory – the increase of 'multi-national' activity in Australia has increased this flow considerably. Yet others are persons from developing countries who come for a few years for higher training and experience before returning home or going on to North America or Western Europe. These various visitor flows have by now reached a considerable total." (C. A. Price, 1981.)

Table 4.6
Selected groups of official and business migrants admitted temporarily to the United States, in various years

	1969	1970	1974	1975	1978	1979[a]
Foreign government officials	44 940	50 475	70 652	68 426	83 786	(64 200)
International representatives	19 956	23 766	34 385	32 624	44 042	(37 100)
Representatives of foreign information media	4 164	4 673	6 082	6 058	9 979	(10 500)
Temporary visitors for business	299 810	324 810	543 796	527 387	800 652	(883 500)
Treaty traders and investors	15 264	19 209	36 853	35 031	50 431	(49 300)
Intra-company transferees	..	3 618[b]	12 478	12 570	21 495	(21 900)

.. = not available.

[a] Data for 1979 are available only for the first nine months of the fiscal year, 1 October 1978 to 30 June 1979, and have been rounded upwards here on the assumption of regular distribution, hence the parentheses. [b] 1971 figures.

Source: United States Department of Justice, Immigration and Naturalization Service: *Annual Report* (various years) and *Statistical Yearbook* (1979).

Settlement migration

Policies aimed at settlement view suitable foreigners as future citizens and not as transients or an object of governmental discrimination. Humanitarian selection criteria are influential and can, as for example in the case of the United States, override economic criteria as regards both the relative number of admissions and the economic characteristics of persons qualifying on humanitarian grounds. The traditional immigration countries of North America and Oceania continue to admit each year up to 400,000 active foreigners plus a similar number of dependants.

However, while migrants have always appreciated the security of status accorded to settlers, they have by no means been as fixed on staying and becoming naturalised as is widely believed – contrary to the so-called temporary migrants in Western Europe, for example, who have turned out to be more settlement-minded than expected. The following figures illustrate that, despite the fact that the politico-legal distinction between settlement and temporary employment policies has important implications for the status of entrants, many migrants break the normative

strait-jackets into which they are pressed and follow their own instincts and preferences; and this happens apparently on an increasing scale. For example, in the United States 31 per cent of the 15.7 million immigrants between 1908 and 1957 remigrated (partly on account of the Depression of the 1930s) as did 18 per cent of the 3.4 million immigrants during 1960-70. The 1971 cohort of legal immigrants seems to have lost as many as half its members through remigration. In Australia 23 per cent of the 1960-70 settlers and 41 per cent of the 1971-80 settlers left again. This compares with a remigration rate of 68 per cent during 1961-76 in one of the European countries often identified with a temporary immigration system, the Federal Republic of Germany. As regards the granting of citizenship to foreigners, the United States naturalised 780,716 persons during 1975-79 or 0.36 per cent of the 216.7 million residents in the middle year of that period. The corresponding figures for France and the Federal Republic of Germany combined are 392,592 naturalisations or 0.34 per cent of the 114.6 million residents. Incidentally, rates of remigration and naturalisation differ significantly and fairly consistently among various migrant nationalities and largely account for either differences or similarities of average figures.

Table 4.7
Intake of brain drain categories from developing countries,[a] United States, 1972-79

	1972	1973	1974	1975	1976[b]	1977	1978	1979
Professional, technical and kindred workers admitted as immigrants	39 107	31 939	27 709	29 856	31 326	34 400	37 790	29 704
Workers of distinguished merit and ability admitted as temporary workers	4 997	6 151	6 590	6 193	5 294	5 047	5 110	5 962
Total	44 104	38 090	34 299	36 049	36 620	39 537	42 900	35 660

[a] From Asia, Africa, North America other than Canada, and South America. [b] Not including transition quarter (up to 1976 years end 30 June, from 1977 on years end 30 September).
Source: United States Department of Justice, Immigration and Naturalization Service: *Annual Report* (1972-77) and *Statistical Yearbook* (1978-79).

The settlement countries (and several Western European countries) have, rightly or not, become associated with the "brain drain". It is not always seen clearly, however, that the brain drain phenomenon is not necessarily a brain drain problem. The volume of movements from the developing to the developed countries appears to be declining slightly to judge by the statistics in table 4.7. The table shows gross inflows, i.e. figures which do not take account of the return factor just mentioned. (Return is supposed to be the norm for workers of "distinguished merit and ability".) More importantly, perhaps, it should be realised that the great majority of the "brains" from developing countries are admitted as relatives of previous immigrants, at least in the United States. Of the 381,281 people from developing countries admitted in 1979, the 29,704 professional, technical and kindred workers in table 4.7 constituted less than 8 per cent, and about nine in ten of these must have qualified as relatives under the humanitarian preferences, because only 3,414 professionals actually qualified on grounds of a prior job offer.[6]

Since the rise in oil prices, the brain drain has also assumed a South-South dimension. In the Libyan Arab Jamahiriya, for example, foreigners accounted for 58 per cent of all professional and managerial manpower in 1975, while other categories had considerably lower proportions.

World Bank experts estimate that, in the eight major Arab migrant-receiving countries, the 1975 stock of 278,700 professional and technical foreign workers will more than treble to 918,800 by 1985, compared with a mere doubling of the total stock of migrant workers. Among the least developed countries, Afghanistan, Bangladesh, Democratic Yemen, the Sudan and the Yemen Arab Republic supply brain drain categories to the Gulf countries.

Contract migration

In recent years contract migration has numerically overshadowed settlement migration, and the treatment of contract migrants in countries of employment has aroused a great deal more concern than the treatment of any other group of migrants. Foreigners admitted for the purpose of employment are rarely viewed as future nationals and are subjected to various forms of discrimination.

International contract migration occurs when a worker is officially granted permission to enter another country and take up employment in a given job and where a contract is concluded on his behalf or between him and the employer or enterprise for which he is to work. Contract migration itself takes several forms whose differences may have implications with regard to the treatment of the migrants involved.

Individual contract migrants are one distinguishable group. For the past hundred years or more, countries in the Americas, central Europe and southern Africa have called upon foreigners as contract migrants in a highly organised manner. Their annual numbers touched the million mark at the end of the 1960s. When admission began to dwindle in Western Europe as a result of the 1973 rise in oil prices, the number of contract migrants started to increase rapidly in the Middle East and Venezuela.

Another form of international contract migration came to prominence in the Middle East. This is the phenomenon of a certain number or group of foreign workers being admitted for the purpose of employment under a single authorisation or on behalf of a single employer. It has variously been referred to as block visa migration, collective contract migration or project-tied migration. None of the terms is entirely satisfactory in that none either covers the totality of this phenomenon or sharply delineates it from individual contract migration.

A block visa may be issued for, say, 25 domestic servants in the name of one head of a large family or service, or in the name of an agent who assigns the people to different employers. While the first case could equally be called collective contract migration, the second may well take place under a procedure where 25 individual contracts are covered by a joint entry and/or work permit.

Collective contract migration occurs where a gang of labourers moves with a small firm which provides labour-only subcontracting services or where a group of managers, foremen and workers of a large construction company enters the country to execute a contract won through competitive tender. But both a labour-only subcontractor and a principal employer might have recourse to individual contract migrants in the proper sense of the word, which blurs the distinction as far as their workforces are concerned.

Project-tied migration conjures up a picture of foreigners admitted to a migrant-receiving country for a period of time on the basis of a work contract with an enterprise or employer to carry out in that country specific projects that by their nature are limited in time. This definition would cover the main contractor who is responsible for a turnkey project and, by extension, a subsidiary contractor who executes merely a part of the whole and a labour-only subcontractor who contributes workers and perhaps hand-tools to its completion.[7] One problem with this definition is that it could be applied to ordinary individual contract migrants who are hired by a firm undertaking a specific construction or industrial project. Moreover, persons with special qualifications who go to a country to undertake specific short-term technical assignments[8] might at one time form part of a group of fixed-term workers recruited collectively while on another occasion they might be admitted as individual contract migrants, although their functions were essentially the same.

Project-tied or similar migration is a little-known form of labour migration between Western Europe and socialist countries. In the Federal Republic of Germany, for example, 11,335 Yugoslav, 6,914 Polish and 1,648 Hungarian project-tied migrants were employed at the end of January 1982. Conversely, 39 per cent of Finland's construction contracting exports were destined to the Soviet Union in 1981.

Where necessary, a distinction will be made here between individual contract migrants, on the one hand, and all contrasting groups, on the other, which will be referred to as "project-tied and similar migrants".

Marking off individual from other contract migrants can in fact be important because there may be legitimate differences in the treatment of the respective categories. The individual contract migrants are, as a rule, admitted for the purpose of employment that is not limited in time – which is quite different from being admitted for a fixed period of time or temporarily. For it is not the nature of the job occupied but the duration of the permit granted that is restricted, administratively, in time. Individual contract migrants admitted for a standard 12 months or some such period are mostly engaged on normal jobs of a permanent nature in so far as economic activities can be permanent, that is to say, the work is not finished after a predetermined standard period. Consequently, where individual foreigners are permitted to take up permanent jobs of this kind they should be treated, broadly speaking, in the same way as nationals who hold such jobs. This is undoubtedly the meaning of the non-discrimination tenet inherent in fundamental human rights, the ILO Constitution and international labour standards concerned with migrant workers.

"All human beings, irrespective of race, creed or sex, have the right to pursue both their material well-being and their spiritual development in conditions of freedom and dignity, of economic security and equal opportunity." (ILO Declaration of Philadelphia.) "Each Member for which the Convention is in force undertakes to declare and pursue a national policy designed to promote and guarantee, by methods appropriate to national conditions and practice, equality of opportunity and treatment in respect of employment and occupation, of social security, of trade union and cultural rights and of individual and collective freedoms for persons who as migrant workers or as members of their families are lawfully within its territory." (ILO Migrant Workers (Supplementary Provisions) Convention, 1975 (No. 143) Article 10.)

By contrast, project-tied and similar migrants are admitted for the purpose of employment that will be finished after a certain period of time – and here the receiving countries' restriction on their length of stay usually coincides with the antici-

pated duration of the project. It might be argued that such foreigners could be treated differently (in some respects deserving special assistance, in others not requiring the same privileges) from nationals holding comparable jobs in the migrant-receiving country.

It is not too difficult to give concrete meaning to equality in the case of individual contract migrants going to Western Europe or North America. More often than not, a standard of comparison is available in the form of a nation-wide, district-level or local collective agreement, law or regulation, court decision or arbitration award relating to an occupation, sector or employer. However, migrants in Arab OPEC countries sometimes find themselves in occupations or sectors without significant numbers of local workers and the kind of labour institutions or social legislation characteristic of advanced countries. Both individual and other contract migrants have on occasions performed jobs unknown to local workers or have worked in areas where, by reason of the sparseness of the population or the stage of development, no such jobs were hitherto performed. This, added to a situation where collective bargaining, government wage fixing or court ruling is the exception rather than the rule, means that contract migrants and the authorities protecting them are in the unenviable position of lacking points of reference for determining whether the wages and conditions are the same as or comparable to those of national workers. What constitutes discrimination or equality in this context is not clear.

The past few years have witnessed a certain disenchantment in Western Europe with the individual contract migration system. During a decade or two, tens of millions of people from ever more distant countries were actively recruited or gladly accepted. Policy-makers assumed that the stock of the migrant workforce could be regulated by the interplay of market forces and the intention of temporary expatriation attributed to the migrants (or actually written into the law of one major sending country – Yugoslavia). However, four

109

4.1

Social security for migrants

Migrants form a segment of society whose social security protection still leaves much to be desired. First of all, they may suffer from direct discrimination whereby non-nationals, especially those residing abroad, are excluded from certain benefits or, occasionally, denied any coverage at all. There is also discrimination which, though indirect, is no less a handicap and which, while not aimed specifically at foreigners, affects them most. Certain benefits, for example, are not paid to workers or members of their family who are resident or temporarily resident abroad. Entitlement to benefit may, too, be subject to the completion of a period of insurance, employment, occupational activity or residence – a difficult condition for migrants whose career takes them from one country to another. These are problems which face all migrants, regardless of their status, the type of migration involved or their motivations. Even workers on a temporary official mission or on business or who have an essentially itinerant activity (not to mention tourists) may have difficulty in obtaining treatment or compensation in the event of sickness or accident. In fact, it is not only migrants as defined in labour and employment regulations – i.e., persons who do not possess the nationality of the country in which they are employed – who have social security problems. Even those who are not or are no longer foreigners in the country where they apply for benefits – whether their country of origin or a host country of which they are naturalised citizens – may have difficulty in acquiring rights and in maintaining rights acquired in the country they have left.

Technically speaking, there is nowadays a solution to this problem. One possibility is to apply the ILO's standards which contain specific provisions regarding unequal treatment for nationals and non-nationals and the payment of pensions in the event of residence abroad. Alternatively, the more detailed bilateral and multilateral instruments concluded in accordance with ILO standards on the maintenance of the rights can be applied, frequently with the assistance of regional organisations for economic integration.

The fact remains, however, that the existing network of international arrangements of this kind, impressive though it may already be (ILO: *Liste des instruments internationaux en matière de sécurité sociale adoptés depuis 1946* (Geneva, 1974). A new up-to-date edition (in French only) is currently being prepared.) in no way corresponds to the variety and scale of migration. Workers are recruited from more and more distant countries and continents.

Once a certain level of development has been attained, some countries of emigration, particularly in southern Europe, become simultaneously countries of immigration. Others, where immigration has traditionally been for settlement purposes, now take on workers for fixed periods and specific jobs. New centres of immigration have grown up, especially in oil-producing countries. Meanwhile, social security has not always managed to keep up. Some of the oil-producing Arab countries in the Gulf area, for example, whose social security legislation is still highly discriminatory towards non-nationals, have not yet signed agreements with the countries of Asia, the Middle East and Africa from where the migrants come or ratified the ILO's basic Conventions on the subject. In Latin America and Africa, on the other hand, there has been a conscious effort to promote multilateral co-ordination among national systems. No solution has yet been found, however, either in the Caribbean or the Pacific.

Another drawback is that not all existing social security instruments have as wide a scope as the national legislation of the signatory States or provide for complete co-ordination to fit different circumstances. The United States has decided to replace simple agreements confined to equality of treatment by more comprehensive arrangements. In other countries one of the principal shortcomings of existing instruments is that they do not make sufficient allowance for "non-contributory" benefits guaranteeing a minimum income that are not subject to a qualifying period of contributions or occupational activity but only to residence and, sometimes, means of existence.

In relations between industrialised and developing countries reciprocity agreements, if too strict, may mean that the social security instruments do not extend to branches or benefits for which there is no provision in the legislation of the less developed of the contracting parties. For example, the legislation of the migrants' country of origin may not include family and unemployment benefits; a way should therefore be found of offering equitable compensation for the loss of rights which migrants and members of their family may suffer if they return to or are resident in that country. In more general terms, migrants should be protected against the possible negative repercussion of the current economic crisis, by ensuring that the benefits to which they are entitled are not reduced or stopped if they return to their country of origin.

---

factors changed the situation. In the first instance, with few exceptions the policies pursued did not go so far as administratively to force out the foreign workers who had come to the end of their contracts or who were unemployed.[9] Secondly, one central but initially inoperative element of Western European policies was what one might call a progressive adjustment system which gradually lifts the restrictions placed on new entrants in respect of economic and social rights.[10] Regular employment of one year in Sweden, three years in Belgium and the Netherlands, four years in France and the United Kingdom, five years in the Federal Republic of Germany, eight years in Austria and five to ten years in Switzerland (depending on the migrant's nationality) puts the foreigner on a par with nationals as regards access to jobs and practically assures him of the right to stay indefinitely, barring some grave political misconduct. The thresholds are much lower or inexistent as regards family reunification. Thirdly, for many years policy-makers assumed that the migrants' intention corresponded to those they wished them to have, i.e. the intention to stay for a short time and to return home afterwards. Later research revealed that this was far from being the case. Fourthly, although there was a remarkable degree of return, as already mentioned in the earlier comparison with settlement migration, the numbers admitted were simply so large that the relatively small proportion of stayers accumulated continuously and, over time, substantially. As a result of these mutually reinforcing factors, there were as many migrant workers in Western Europe at the end of the 1970s as at the beginning, despite the fact that the influx of first-time workers was reduced to a trickle after 1973. Many of them were dependants who had joined the breadwinner or children born in the migrant-receiving country. Suddenly, the economic and social costs ascribed to foreign minorities filled the front pages of the newspapers.

While some migrants worked their way up the hierarchy to positions in line with their former or newly acquired skills, the bulk remained something of a substratum to the local working class. They were disproportionately hit by the recession of the mid-1970s and the early 1980s, being especially vulnerable on account of their lower qualifications, the higher sensitivity of many industries in which they were employed (construction, car, steel, textile, etc.) and their lack of seniority.

In 1980 in the in-migration countries other than the United Kingdom listed in table 4.1, there were over 4.5 million people under 25 years of age of foreign nationality, usually (if somewhat inaccurately) denoted as second-generation migrants.

Table 4.8
Socio-economic status of foreign manual workers in Belgium and France: father and son compared (in percentage)

	Belgium (Italians)		France I		France II	
	Father	Son	Father	Son	Father	Son
Unskilled	91[a]	52[a]	46	32	32	50
Semi-skilled	9[b]	25[b]	28	42	42	31
Skilled	..	15	26	26	26	12

.. = not available.
[a] Unskilled workers and minors.　[b] Low and middle range of qualifications.
Source: Belgium = F. Dasseto et A. Bastenir: *Un prolétariat non fixé. La deuxième génération d'immigrés italiens en Belgique* (Louvain-la-Neuve, Groupe d'étude des migrations, 1981), p. 172.; France I = Secrétariat d'Etat aux travailleurs immigrés: *La nouvelle politique d'immigration* (Paris, 1977), Ch. XI.; France II = *Revue française des affaires sociales*, Special issue: "Les migrations externes", Vol. 32 (Apr.-June 1978), p. 117.

Approximately 1.5 million were economically active. An attempt to determine whether they are leaving the lower working class positions of their parents reveals only contradictory evidence to date. The three surveys on Belgium and France reported in table 4.8 do not provide final representative answers since they measure the skill level of sons early in their working life.

While second-generation migrants who were born in the migrant-receiving country or who entered it prior to compulsory school age come up to the standard of locals in their educational and vocational achievements, those who entered school at a later age – and a great many of them did or will do so in the coming years – experience enormous difficulties, largely on account of their failure to master the local language. Special programmes have been designed to help them overcome their handicaps, but implementation in times of social austerity is not what it might be in better times.

Worse still, second-generation migrants have been disproportionally hit by the unemployment affecting Western Europe, of which the young people generally are the chief victims. In France, for example, of all wholly unemployed foreign jobseekers, 26.8 per cent were less than 25 years old in 1980, or twice the proportion of young foreigners in the total migrant labour force, 13.4 per cent. In Sweden the unemployment rate of second-generation migrants was 6.9 per cent compared with 3.4 per cent of local youth. "A sociological time bomb . . . may be nearing flashpoint in several countries of Western Europe." [11]

The Arab countries of the Middle East and North Africa have promoted project-tied and similar migration, mainly in order to prevent the occurrence of social and cultural problems. Although there are some signs of settlement, primarily among Arab migrant populations, general satisfaction with the system prevails on the part of both the migrant-receiving and the migrant-sending countries. In its most extreme form of enclave development or work camps, an agricultural, industrial or service project is situated away from the population centres; foreign contractors and workforces are engaged to put up the buildings and infrastructure; they return home upon completion of their contract and are replaced by operations and maintenance teams; the workers have little contact with the locals and few opportunities to be spendthrift; large-scale flows of homeward-bound savings are a source of satisfaction to the families left behind and the governments of migrant-sending countries.

Project-tied and similar migration also has its questionable sides. To name but the most striking, it occasionally drains skills currently in short supply in migrant-sending countries and generally disrupts family life. It is afflicted by abuses at the stage of recruitment and the start of work. In the commercially most successful model of all, that of the Republic of Korea, virtually every aspect of the migrant workers' daily life is under the protection and control of their employers. They are forbidden to form unions while in the Middle East; the individual contracts provide the only means of bargaining and settling disputes. Government-determined minimum requirements for accom-

modation in the camps – standards of living space, sanitary and recreation facilities as well as medical care – are not always met nor strictly enforced. Work-related deaths and injuries are high and rising; the workmen's compensation system is unsatisfactory. And there are the unresolved issues of equality of opportunity and treatment mentioned earlier.

Project-tied and similar migration is another manifestation of the increasing diversity and complexity of contemporary international labour movements. Although overseas construction contracts netted by firms from the Republic of Korea in 1981 reached a huge US$13,000 million (mostly in Saudi Arabia and other Middle Eastern countries), these firms were earning only about 30 per cent of the contract amount, with the rest going to Western European suppliers of equipment and materials. The migrant-sending country itself benefits mostly only from the wages of its construction workers.

The complexity of international contracting may be illustrated by the example of Riyadh University in Saudi Arabia. The project is entrusted to the Bouygues-Blount joint venture, dominated by the French construction and contracting firm Bouygues. Most of the work is subcontracted. At the start of 1982, Bouygues-Blount had 250 managers and executives onsite, while the number of subcontract staff was more than 2,000. The figure will reach 10,000 when the project is at its height. A consortium of companies from the Republic of Korea is engaged on general construction. An Italian group has the electricity contract. A French group and an Italian-British group are installing plumbing and air-conditioning. Firms from Sweden supply the telephone system, the Federal Republic of Germany supplies the control networks, and France provides the audio-visual services.

Project-tied and similar migration is likely to be an enduring and, perhaps, a growing form of international migration in the future. There are a number of pointers in that direction. Firms from the Republic of Korea are expanding into Africa and Asia. In Nigeria a first contract was negotiated for a US$170 million hotel and housing contract with the Sokoto State Government. In non-Arab Asian countries, Korean contractors won more than US$1,000 million in new contracts in 1981, compared with less than US$300 million in 1980.

Irregular migration

Free or settlement migration, official or business migration, individual or project-tied and similar migration are all forms of regular migration, but they do not cover the totality of present-day movements. Irregular migration is a distinct, additional and sizeable phenomenon.[12] It is widespread in both North and South America and can be found in West Africa, the Middle East, Western Europe and Oceania too, i.e. in all major regions of regular migration. It is a complex and insufficiently researched subject. Its depth and breadth are not revealed by such popular images as the surreptitious border crosser in Hong Kong or the sly "coyote" in California. Some light can be thrown on the matter by differentiating among four kinds of irregular migration.

Firstly, a number of irregular flows are due to administrative inefficiency or convenience, with regularisation taking place at a later stage. France is one of the countries convinced that it is neither desirable nor possible to seal all borders and to subject every entrant – tourist, businessman, worker, etc. – to draconian control and verification. Successive Governments have felt obliged to tolerate a margin of regularisation, i.e. to legalise *ex post facto* the residence of foreign workers and their dependants who had not entered through the cumbersome official machinery but whose entry would in all likelihood have been approved had it been processed as it should have been in the first instance. Irregular migrants whose presence is judged not to correspond to this assumption are excluded or deported. Similarly, for years Saudi Arabia has drawn on the labour resources of the neighbouring Yemen without institutionalised introduction or screening of entrants at the border. Workers have usually been registered after they found employment, sometimes months or years later.

Lack of explicit policies or administrative capacity naturally gives rise to irregular migration. Most South American countries would fall into this category, even Venezuela until the second half of the 1970s. Another example of irregular immigration due to lack of governmental measures is the flow of Bengali Muslims into the Indian State of Assam since the Second World War.

The third major category of irregular immigration can be attributed to porous laws or incompatible laws. The United States is a good example. It is illegal to enter the country outside the procedures provided for by the Immigration and Nationality Act of 1952. But a group of politically powerful growers succeeded in making the law self-contradictory through an amendment providing that it is not illegal to employ irregular migrants. People who cross the border without being spotted, or who comply with the entry procedures but then contravene the restrictions of time or status placed upon them, have found many employers welcoming them with open arms.

The fourth major kind of irregular migration is the one most often imagined in the context of illegal migration, i.e. foreigners who knowingly circumvent unequivocal immigration or employment laws or employers who disregard such laws. This actually happens in most countries suffering from irregular migration, such as Australia, but it is worth while to separate out this form of irregularity from the others described. Again, the diversity of the phenomenon is striking and worrying, for there is no simple solution to this global problem.

113

The potential number of international migrants is rising in the poor countries of Africa, the Americas and Asia at a time when the opportunities for regular admission and employment seem to be dwindling. Population growth will add masses of people to the developing countries for the foreseeable future. Conventional development instils more rising expectations – at school, through the media, etc. – than can be satisfied in the short run. Consumption standards become worldwide and normative. The imbalance between expectations and the means to attain them domestically will create a certain emigration pressure. The youthfulness of developing countries' populations will facilitate mobility as will the availability and cheapness of means of mass transport across continents and oceans. The developed market economy countries appear all more or less disposed to cut back on the intake of foreigners for social or economic reasons or both. In resource-rich developing countries one senses a similar trend. The interactions of rising emigration pressure from poor developing countries and decreasing opportunities for regular in-migration might well lead to more irregular migration.

New Zealand citizenship, and approving it only for about 20,000 Samoans living in New Zealand". *The Times* (London), 23 Aug. 1982.

[5] The average of the first two percentages for each nationality in table 4.5, divided by two, is a reasonably accurate indicator of the extent of skilled employment immediately after entry. The figures would be 14 for Italians and Greeks, 21 for Spaniards, 20 for Turks and 27 for Yugoslavs. This means that about one in two skilled migrants starts off in a lower position than his qualifications would suggest. In the course of time, some of this setback is made good.

[6] Still, for developing emigration countries it makes no difference whether they lose brains owing to humanitarian rather than economic determinants of immigration policies.

[7] Labour-only subcontracting takes place when there is a written or oral contract between an employer (the principal contractor) and an intermediary having as the major or even exclusive object the supply of labour on a site for a certain job. The prime contractor or the labour-only subcontractor may be either foreign or domestic in the eyes of the law of the migrant-receiving country. Whenever the workers of the labour-only subcontractor are foreign, one can speak of international labour-only subcontracting.

[8] Who are defined in the ILO Migrant Workers (Supplementary Provisions) Convention, 1975 (No. 143), as "employees of organisations or undertakings operating within the territory of a country who have been admitted temporarily to that country at the request of their employer to undertake specific duties or assignments, for a limited and defined period of time, and who are required to leave that country on the completion of their duties or assignments" (Article 11(2)*(e)*), and who are by that fact exempted from the provisions of Part II of the Convention relating to equality of opportunity and treatment for migrant workers.

[9] Unfortunately this happened also, sometimes in contradiction of the law and, on the part of the migrants, sometimes in ignorance of the law. By and large, returns took place on economic grounds or because of a certain sense of insecurity and hostility or personal and family problems rather than through administrative action.

[10] It is worth noting in passing that non-nationals have even been accorded certain civil and political rights, such as voting in municipal elections, in Sweden and several cantons of Switzerland.

[11] *ILO Information* (Geneva), No. 1, Feb. 1982, p. 1.

[12] Migrants in an irregular situation may be considered as all those who *(a)* in respect of admission and stay, are within the territory of a country of which they are not nationals and have not complied with the formalities or obtained the authorisations required for admission to and stay in the country concerned or cease to fulfil the conditions to which their admission and stay are subject, or *(b)* in respect of the exercise of economic activity, work in a country of which they are not nationals and have not complied with the formalities or obtained the authorisations required to exercise an economic activity or exercise one for which the said formalities and the authorisations obtained are not or are no longer valid.

[1] Which is some 50 per cent higher than the 14 million figure given by the United Nations Department of International Economic and Social Affairs in: *Review and appraisal of the World Population Plan of Action*, Population Studies, No. 71 (New York, 1979, Sales No. E.79.XIII.7), p. 30.

[2] The OAU Convention on Refugees of 1969 added people fleeing external aggression, foreign domination or events seriously disturbing public order to the flight-from-persecution basis of the United Nations.

[3] Passports are required for identification since July 1981 for people entering Australia from New Zealand.

[4] "New Zealand and Western Samoa have signed an accord depriving nearly 100,000 Western Samoans of the right to automatic

Selected bibliography

Ahmad, M. *Emigration of scarce skills in Pakistan* (Geneva, ILO, 1982; mimeographed International Migration for Employment working paper; restricted).

Bhagwati, J. "The brain drain", in *Tripartite World Conference on Employment, Income Distribution and Social Progress and the International Division of Labour*, Background papers, Vol. II: *International strategies for employment* (Geneva, ILO, 1976).

Birks, J. S.; Sinclair, C. A. *International migration and development in the Arab region* (Geneva, ILO, 1980).

–; –. "Demographic settling amongst migrant workers", in International Union for the Scientific Study of Population (IUSSP) (ed.): *International Population Conference* (Manila, 1981), Solicited papers (Liège, Derouaux, 1981), Vol. 2.

Böhning, W. R. *Guest worker employment, with special reference to the Federal Republic of Germany, France and Switzerland – Lessons for the United States?* (Geneva, ILO, 1980; mimeographed World Employment Programme Research working paper; restricted).

–. *International contract migration in the light of ILO instruments, with special reference to Asian migrant-sending countries* (Geneva, ILO, 1982; mimeographed International Migration for Employment working paper; restricted).

Böhning, W. R. (ed.). *Black migration to South Africa* (Geneva, ILO, 1981).

Fergany, N. *The affluent years are over – Emigration and development in the Yemen Arab Republic* (Geneva, ILO, 1980; mimeographed World Employment Programme Research working paper; restricted).

Garson, J.-P.; Moulier, Y. *Clandestine immigrants and their regularisation in France, 1981-1982* (Geneva, ILO, 1982; mimeographed International Migration for Employment working paper; restricted).

ILO. *La condition des travailleurs migrants en Amérique du Sud* (Geneva, 1974; mimeographed; General Conditions of Work Series, No. 31).

ILO/ARPLA. *Emigration for employment*, Report on ARPLA Symposium on Overseas Recruitment Procedures for Senior Officials of South Asian Countries, Islamabad, May 1981 (Bangkok, 1981).

Jasso, G.; Rosenzweig, M. R. "Estimating the emigration rates of legal immigrants using administrative and survey data: The 1971 cohort of immigrants to the United States", in *Demography* (Washington, DC, Population Association of America), Aug. 1982.

Kim, S. *Contract migration in the Republic of Korea* (Geneva, ILO, 1982; mimeographed International Migration for Employment working paper; restricted).

Lazo, L. S.; Teodosio, V. A.; Sto. Tomas, P. A. *Contract migration policies in the Philippines* (Geneva, ILO, 1982; mimeographed International Migration for Employment working paper; restricted).

Price, C. A. *Long-term emigration and immigration: A new force in Australian international movements*, Paper prepared for the General Conference of the IUSSP, Manila, Philippines, December 1981.

Price, C. A. (ed.). *Australian immigration: A bibliography and digest*, Supplement No. 4 (Canberra, Australian National University, 1981).

Report of the United Nations High Commissioner for Refugees to the United Nations Economic and Social Council (doc. E/1982/29, 14 May 1982; mimeographed).

Storer, D. (with the assistance of Faulkner, A.). *Out of the shadows: A review of the 1980 Regularisation of Status Programme in Australia* (Geneva, ILO, 1982; mimeographed Interna-

115

tional Migration for Employment working paper; restricted).

Swamy, G. *International migrant workers' remittances: Issues and prospects* (Washington, DC, World Bank, 1981; World Bank staff working paper, No. 481).

United States Department of Justice, Immigration and Naturalization Service. *1979 Statistical Yearbook of the Immigration and Naturalization Service* (Washington, DC (n.d.)).

Warren, R.; Peck, J. M. "Foreign-born emigration from the United States: 1960-1970", in *Demography* (Washington, DC, Population Association of America), 1980.

Chapter 5

Wages in the world: trends and problems

Growth of national incomes

Gross national product per capita

The most common measure of the progress made by countries over a period of time is income. Similarly, average income is the concept most often used for comparing levels of development.

Income is not the only measure of development. Since the early 1960s governments, international organisations and economists have stressed the importance of other objectives of development (employment in the ILO's case) and of other ways of measuring progress. The acceptance of other objectives and other measures does not, however, diminish the importance of the concept of income for taking stock of what has happened in the world over the past two decades.

Income is a concept, or rather a set of concepts, which summarises what society has produced and what its members have earned. Different definitions are used for this "summary" (national income) and for the constituent parts of the major component of national income (household incomes). These definitions serve different purposes. For a world-wide survey such as we shall attempt in this chapter, we face the inevitable problem of statistics, in spite of the great progress made in this field in the past 20 years.

We shall start by tracing the global trend of incomes in the world, in the light of the rate of growth of national income in different countries.

We shall then comment on the way income is distributed within countries and on the policies by which countries redistribute income. This is a field in which information is particularly scarce, despite the large amount of work undertaken during the past decade, particularly by the ILO and the World Bank. Finally, we shall examine a number of problems associated with one particular type of income – wages.

The relative prosperity of a country can be gauged by comparing some concepts of national income (usually gross national product (GNP) or gross domestic product (GDP)) per capita. The progress made over the period of time can be measured by comparing annual rates of growth of per capita national income. This is done in table 5.1.

The comparison of per capita GNP, expressed in one currency (United States dollars) is not without its dangers. The difference between the "richest" and the "poorest" countries in this table appears much larger than it actually is, since the use of official exchange rates to convert national currencies to United States dollars does not accurately measure the relative purchasing power. For this reason the United Nations International Comparison Project has developed reliable measures of real GNP on an internationally comparable scale. Although data have been calculated so far for only a limited number of countries and there is a time lag in the preparation of these figures, it is clear that the range of disparities between countries is considerably reduced. Thus, for 1975, if we take United States per capita GNP as 100, conversion at

Table 5.1
Gross national product per capita

Countries	Per capita GNP US dollars (1980)	Per capita GNP Average annual growth, 1960–80 (percentage)	Countries	Per capita GNP US dollars (1980)	Per capita GNP Average annual growth, 1960–80 (percentage)	Countries	Per capita GNP US dollars (1980)	Per capita GNP Average annual growth, 1960–80 (percentage)
Low income economies			El Salvador	660	1.6	*High-income oil-exporting countries*		
Bhutan	80	−0.1	United Republic of Cameroon	670	2.6	Libyan Arab		
Chad	120	−1.8	Thailand	670	4.7	Jamahiriya	8 640	5.2
Ethiopia	140	1.4	Philippines	690	2.8	Saudi Arabia	11 260	8.1 [a]
Nepal	140	0.2	Nicaragua	740	0.9	Kuwait	19 830	−1.1 [a]
Burma	170	1.2	Papua New Guinea	780	2.8	United Arab Emirates	26 850	4.3 [a]
Mali	190	1.4	Morocco	900	2.5			
Burundi	200	2.5	Congo	900	0.8	*Industrial market economies*		
Rwanda	200	1.5	Peru	930	1.1			
Upper Volta	210	0.1	Nigeria	1 010	4.1	Ireland	4 880	3.1
Zaire	220	0.2	Jamaica	1 040	0.6	Spain	5 400	4.5
Malawi	230	2.9	Guatemala	1 080	2.8	Italy	6 480	3.6
Mozambique	230	−0.1	Ivory Coast	1 150	2.5	New Zealand	7 090	1.8
India	240	1.4	Dominican Republic	1 160	3.4	United Kingdom	7 920	2.2
Haiti	270	0.5	Colombia	1 180	3.0	Finland	9 720	4.0
Sri Lanka	270	2.4	Ecuador	1 270	4.5 [a]	Australia	9 820	2.7
Tanzania	280	1.9	Paraguay	1 300	3.2	Japan	9 890	7.1
Guinea	290	0.3	Tunisia	1 310	4.8 [a]	Canada	10 130	3.3
Uganda	300	−0.7	Syrian Arab Republic	1 340	3.7	Austria	10 230	4.1
Pakistan	300	2.8	Jordan	1 420	5.7 [a]	United States	11 360	2.3
Central African Republic	300	0.9	Turkey	1 470	3.6	Netherlands	11 470	3.2
Benin	310	0.4	Republic of Korea	1 520	7.0	France	11 730	3.9
Niger	330	−1.6	Malaysia	1 620	4.3	Belgium	12 180	3.8
Madagascar	350	−0.5	Costa Rica	1 730	3.2	Norway	12 650	3.5
Sudan	410	−0.2	Panama	1 730	3.3	Denmark	12 950	3.3
Togo	410	3.0	Algeria	1 870	3.2	Sweden	13 520	2.3
Middle-income economies			Brazil	2 050	5.1	Germany (Fed. Rep.)	13 590	3.3
			Mexico	2 090	2.6	Switzerland	16 440	1.9
Ghana	420	−1.0	Chile	2 150	1.6			
Kenya	420	2.7	South Africa	2 300	2.3	*Non-market industrial economies*		
Lesotho	420	6.1	Romania	2 340	8.6 [a]			
Democratic Yemen	420	12.1 [a]	Portugal	2 370	5.0	Poland	3 900	5.3 [a]
Indonesia	430	4.0	Argentina	2 390	2.2	Bulgaria	4 150	5.6 [a]
Yemen	430	4.5 [a]	Yugoslavia	2 620	5.4	Hungary	4 180	4.5 [a]
Mauritania	440	1.6	Uruguay	2 810	1.4	USSR	4 550	4.0 [a]
Senegal	450	−0.3	Iraq	3 020	5.3	Czechoslovakia	5 820	4.0 [a]
Angola	470	−2.3	Venezuela	3 630	2.6	German Dem. Rep.	7 180	4.7 [a]
Liberia	530	1.5	Hong Kong	4 240	6.8			
Honduras	560	1.1	Trinidad and Tobago	4 370	3.0			
Zambia	560	0.2	Greece	4 380	5.8			
Bolivia	570	2.1	Singapore	4 430	7.5			
Egypt	580	3.4	Israel	4 500	3.8			
Zimbabwe	630	0.7						

[a] Rates calculated for a somewhat shorter period than 1960–80.

Source: World Bank: *World development report 1982*.

Table 5.2
Growth rate of per capita GNP, by group of countries and by population, 1960-80

Average annual growth rate	Number of countries	Population in 1980 (in millions)
−2.3-0	11	89.1
0.1-0.9	12	84.7
1.0-1.9	15	820.9
2.0-2.9	20	672.9
3.0-3.9	21	391.1
4.0-4.9	15	666.5
5.0-5.9	9	224.5
6.0-6.9	2	6.4
7.0-7.9	3	157.4
8.0-8.9	2	31.2
− −		
12.0-12.9	1	1.9
	111	3 146.6

Source: Calculated from data in table 5.1.

the official exchange rate shows India's per capita GNP as 2, whereas converting at purchasing-power parity exchange rates gives a figure of 6.6. Per capita national income in the United States was thus 15 times (and not 50 times) higher than in India.

Table 5.1 contains information on 1980 per capita GNP and on average annual growth of per capita GNP between 1960 and 1980 for 111 countries. What picture can we derive from this information?

The first observation is that in 11 out of the 111 countries listed, per capita GNP has actually decreased during the past two decades. In six countries (Bhutan, Mozambique, Uganda, Madagascar, Sudan, Senegal) there was a slight drop, with average annual rates of decline between 0.1 and 0.7 per cent; in four countries (Chad, Niger, Ghana, Kuwait) the decline was much larger, ranging from 1.0 to 1.8 per cent. The largest decline was that of Angola, with an average annual negative rate of growth of 2.3 per cent.

Table 5.2 presents these data in ascending order of average annual growth rate, with the number of countries and population for each level. It shows that, while the per capita GNP declined in 11 countries, there was economic growth in 100 other countries. In some instances this growth was spectacular and in most cases quite reasonable. Roughly half of the countries (56) for which data are available (China being the notable exception) had an average growth rate of 2.5 per cent per annum, 17 countries a rate above 5 per cent and 27 countries rates ranging from 0.1 to 1.9 per cent. There was thus a substantial – probably unprecedented – increase in income throughout the world, but it was a quite uneven growth.

The performance of individual countries is even more impressive if we take into account the size of the country. Leaving aside China and a few other countries (with a combined 1980 population of 1,227 million inhabitants) for which the GNP growth data are unfortunately not available, the following picture emerges. Per capita income declined in 11 countries with a 1980 population of 89.1 million, but increased in 100 countries with a 1980 population of 3,057.5 million. The bulk of this population (2,775.9 million in 1980) lived in 80 countries where per capita income grew at rates between 1 and 6 per cent per year. Taking together all countries for which data are available (whether they registered growth or decline in per capita income), the typical annual growth rate is 2.8 per cent. This is the median growth rate showing the line separating the 50 per cent of the 1980 population living in countries with a higher per capita income growth from the 50 per cent of the population living in countries which grew at the slower, and in some cases negative, rate. This rate of growth represents an increase in per capita income over the 20-year period of 65 per cent. Rarely, if ever, did any country in history achieve such growth over such a short period as that which has been achieved during these 20 years by the whole world.

Of course, the rate of increase differed from country to country. World Bank data for individual countries are grouped by the level of income in 1980 and by other characteristics and show, for each group of countries, the following average per capita income and average rate of growth (in both cases weighted by population):

	US$	%
Low-income economies	260	1.2
Middle-income economies	1 400	3.8
High-income oil exporting countries	12 630	6.3
Industrial market economies	10 320	3.6
Non-market industrial economies	4 640	4.2

These figures give some indication of the pattern of income growth between 1960 and 1980, a pattern which differed from one group to the next. The high-income oil-exporting countries experienced the highest growth rate. The non-market industrial economies (i.e. the planned economies of Eastern Europe) grew at a fast rate in the 1960s but registered a decline in the 1970s, as we saw in Chapter 5.[1] The industrial market economies grew at 3.6 per cent, and the middle-income economies at a slightly higher rate. The low-income economies – 25 countries with a 1980 GNP of up to US$410 – grew at the slowest rate of 1.2 per cent per annum.

Although the picture presented here is probably reasonably accurate, the grouping is open to serious reservations. The "middle-income economies" group is a mixed bag including some Western European countries (Portugal, Greece), an Eastern European planned economy (Romania), some newly industrialising countries (Republic of Korea, Singapore, Hong Kong, Brazil), some genuinely middle-income countries (mostly in South America) and a number of low-income countries included in the middle-income category only because their 1980 income was 10 or 20 dollars higher than the arbitrarily fixed ceiling.

A more serious reservation has to be made regarding the conclusion that, because the "indus-

trial market economies" and the "middle-income economies" grew three times faster than the "low-income economies", the gap between the low-income countries and the others was rapidly increasing over the 20-year period. As Singer and Mahmood have shown,[2] this polarisation hypothesis, although often repeated, is based on a statistical delusion. When countries are grouped according to per capita GNP at the end of the period, it is natural that there should be a strong correlation between the level of income and the rate of income growth over some previous period. Over a very long period the relation becomes tautological. In order to estimate whether "the rich are getting richer while the poor are getting poorer" or, in other words, whether the economic gap between the richer and the poorer countries is constantly widening, one would have to group countries at the beginning of the period over which the rates of growth are measured. Singer and Mahmood have found that, over the period 1970 to 1978, gross national product in absolute terms increased at a rate of 4.3 per cent in industrialised countries and of 5.7 per cent in developing countries. If differential population growth rates are taken into account, the rates of per capita GNP growth become very similar: 3.4 per cent per annum in industrialised countries and 3.3 per cent in developing countries.

The findings of Singer and Mahmood are also interesting as regards the dispersion of per capita GNP in particular groups. Thus, in the industrialised countries group, growth in the lower income countries (between 1960 and 1978) was somewhat faster and the relative differences between industrialised countries were reduced. The same is true of the low-income countries. In the middle-income countries group, however, the countries which were richer in 1960 continued to grow faster than the poorer countries and the dispersion in this group accordingly became wider. Taking both developed and developing countries together, there was indeed a widening of the relative gap between countries' income, although the relation between the level of income

Table 5.3
Rates of growth of per capita national disposable income and GDP (average annual rates of growth at constant prices)

Country	National disposable income		Gross domestic product, 1960-80	Country	National disposable income		Gross domestic product, 1960-80
	1960-70	1970-78			1960-70	1970-78	
Argentina	1.76	2.37 [a]	2.2	Italy	5.31	2.10 [b]	3.6
Australia	4.04	2.41 [b]	2.7	Jamaica	2.45	3.66 [d]	2.8
Austria	4.19	3.92 [a]	4.1	Japan	8.62	2.78 [c]	7.1
Belgium	4.75	3.15	3.8	Republic of Korea	8.11	11.91	7.0
Canada	3.78	3.95	3.3	Mexico	4.32	2.13	2.6
Costa Rica	2.53	6.90	3.2	New Zealand	2.05	1.93	1.8
Dominican Republic	2.71	2.25	3.4	Norway	4.21	2.51	3.5
Ecuador	2.29	5.68	4.5	Panama	5.20	0.88	3.3
El Salvador	1.61	2.14	1.6	Paraguay	1.33	5.11	3.2
Finland	4.91	2.58 [b]	4.0	South Africa	2.86	1.32	2.3
France	5.36	3.10	3.9	Spain	6.29	3.25	4.5
Germany (Fed. Rep.)	4.05	2.73	3.3	Sweden	4.11	1.06	2.3
Greece	8.11	4.31	5.8	Thailand	3.58	4.08	4.7
Honduras	1.20	−0.54 [b]	1.1	Tunisia	2.69	7.55	4.8
India	1.36	1.41 [b]	1.4	United Kingdom	2.32	1.39	2.2
Ireland	4.20	2.08 [c]	3.1	United States	2.78	2.22	2.3
Israel	5.19	2.96	3.8	Uruguay	2.90	0.43	1.4

[a] 1970-75.   [b] 1970-77.   [c] 1970-76.   [d] 1970-74.

Source: Calculated from data in United Nations: *Yearbook of National Accounts Statistics* (various years); and ILO: *Year Book of Labour Statistics* (various years). Column 3 is taken from table 5.1.

of a country and its rate of growth was not statistically significant (although it is if we ignore the "statistical delusion" and compare the rate of growth of the countries and their level of income at the end of the period).

Our conclusion can thus be: *(a)* that income (as measured by per capita GNP) grew at a quite substantial rate over the past 20 years but fell in 10 per cent of the countries; *(b)* that the rate of growth was of the same order in developed and developing countries, but in the developing countries group the middle-income countries did better than the low-income countries; *(c)* that in the industrialised countries and in the low-income countries there was a convergence, while in the middle-income countries there was a divergence, in the course of

development; and *(d)* that the relative gap between countries has widened.

Other indicators of income growth

National disposable income

The growth of income has so far been described in terms of growth rates of per capita gross national product (GNP). However, since the concept includes elements such as consumption of fixed capital, a more limited concept of income could be used, such as the "national disposable income". This is defined as "the net receipts of residents from employment, entrepreneurship and property and from unrequited transfers, including net current transfers from the rest of the world".[3] Data for this concept are less easily

Table 5.4 Changes in social indicators between 1960 and 1980

	Life expectancy at birth (years)		Infant mortality rate (per thousand) (aged 0-1)		Population per physician			Population per nurse			Per capita commercial energy consumption (kg of coal equivalent)		
	1960	1980	1960	1980	1960	1977	1960-77 ratio	1960	1977	1960-77 ratio	1960	1979	1960-79 ratio
Low-income countries	42	57	165	94	8 960	5 810	154	6 650	4 840	137	331	421	127
Middle-income countries	51	60	125	80	16 920	5 840	290	3 440	2 510	137	418	965	230
High-income oil-exporting countries	45	57	173	99	13 310	1 380	964	4 500	3 010	149	1 015	2 609	257
Industrial market economies	70	74	30	11	820	620	132	470	250	188	4 257	7 293	171
Planned industrial economies	68	71	36	25	660	340	194	350	200	175	2 913	5 822	200

	Number enrolled in primary school as percentage of age group		Number enrolled in secondary school as percentage of age group		Number enrolled in higher education as percentage of population aged 20-24		Adult literacy rate (percentages)	
	1960	1979	1960	1979	1960	1978	1960	1977
Low-income countries	76	94	15	49	2	3	26	50
Middle-income countries	76	94	15	39	4	11	49	65
High-income oil-exporting countries	28	81	5	44	7	9	25	
Industrial market economies	114	102	64	88	17	37	99	
Planned industrial economies	101	100	48	93	11	20	98	100

Source: World Bank: *World development report 1982.*

obtainable and are not as up to date as per capita GNP. It is interesting, however, to verify whether the conclusions reached with the more limited data bear out our findings regarding per capita GNP. This information is presented in table 5.3 for two separate periods (1960-70 and 1970-78), together with rates of growth of per capita GDP between 1960 and 1980.

It is clear from these figures that the conclusion about GNP also applies to national disposable income, even if the period covered is somewhat different. In four cases, per capita national disposable income (at constant prices) grew faster than per capita GDP (Canada, El Salvador, Republic of Korea, New Zealand), and in two cases (Dominican Republic, Thailand) more slowly. But in all other cases the rates of growth were of the same order.

Quality of life

The growth of income in a country is reflected in progress in the standard of living. It is therefore useful to compare the progress during the past two decades in a number of indicators of the quality of life for the broad groups of countries. This is done in table 5.4.

The indicators show generally great progress in all groups of countries. Life expectancy increased sharply not only in the group of low-income countries (except in one or two cases where there was a decline) but also in the high-income oil-exporting countries and middle-income countries, as well as in the developed countries (both market and planned economies), where it rose by three or four years. The difference between developed and low-income countries in life expectancy, as with the other social indicators, is very large. Infant mortality has been reduced by more than half in almost all developed countries but only in a few developing countries. All countries, however, reported a reduction in infant mortality.

Similarly, almost all countries reported an improvement in the population-doctor and population-nurse ratio. In some cases the improvement was quite dramatic, with the number of doctors in certain countries increasing by several hundred per cent. In a few countries (Sri Lanka, Madagascar, Morocco), the population-doctor ratio deteriorated but these are countries which have had generally better ratios than other developing countries.

Progress in education over the past 20 years has also been very great. Whereas 20 years ago only 75 per cent of children were enrolled in primary schools in low-income and middle-income countries, over 90 per cent are enrolled now. Perhaps even greater progress has been achieved in secondary education, for which the enrolment ratio more than tripled in low-income countries and in developed countries about 90 per cent of children were enrolled. In higher education enrolment ratios doubled or more than doubled in all groups, with the exception of the low-income countries. Relative progress was particularly noticeable in a number of Latin American middle-income countries (Venezuela, Mexico, Costa Rica, Ecuador, Peru and others), where higher education enrolment ratios increased by four times or more.

The changes in social indicators generally confirm the information provided by GNP and national disposable income data. The 1960s and 1970s were a period of quite rapid growth, probably unprecedented on a world-wide scale, but a growth which was far from uniform, with some countries lagging far behind.

However, even though 100 countries experienced growth in per capita national income, this does not mean that the income and standard of living of all the people in these countries has improved. While in a number of cases economic growth over the past two decades was accompanied by an improvement in the distribution of income, elsewhere distribution was highly unequal and, in some instances, even deteriorated. The reasons for this are manifold and complicated.

The economic structure of the country, its level of development and the distribution of income-generating assets are among the factors which, together with economic and social policies, influence the distribution of income within a country. It is a major problem which we shall discuss now.

The distribution of household income

We shall first explain the nature of the distribution of income among households and, secondly, consider the effects of a number of government policies which deliberately and directly attempt to change the pattern of household income distribution.

Distribution of income

As has already been noted, the growth of per capita income within each country has not been uniform. For some people income has increased more than the national average rate, for others it has increased less, and for others it has declined. Unfortunately, precise data on the subject are difficult to come by. The work done by international organisations (particularly the World Bank and the ILO) and by national authorities and scholars has resulted in some progress, but a great deal remains to be done. The difficulties caused by the dearth of statistics are accentuated by concep-

123

tual problems which further complicate international and intertemporal comparisons.

Some of the problems can be mentioned here. Although most incomes flow to households, a few do not, such as profits from state-owned enterprises or non-distributed corporate profits. When measuring what counts as income, some observers put an annual value on the occupation of a privately owned house; others do not. What household-based activities should be included as income? How should they be measured? Many countries attribute a value to firewood collected and vegetables grown by the household but not for grain milling undertaken at home. There is, too, the problem of establishing what constitutes a household, and whether to include members temporarily absent. What criteria should be used?[4]

Once the above problems have been resolved, information is collected, generally through a random household survey, to provide a statistical measure of household income distribution. Various other problems then arise, of which the most serious is the extent of under-reporting of incomes. This can be roughly corrected, although sometimes only by means of another set of doubtful statistics.

On the basis of the information collected, households can be ranked in terms of their position on the income scale – that is to say, whether they are among the richest or poorest 10, 20 or 5 per cent – and in terms of their share of total income. Such data can be presented in a simple graphic form (the so-called "Lorenz curve") or so as to yield a summary measure (the Gini coefficient). Without going into technical details, the Gini coefficient (which is the measure used in this chapter) can be said to range from 0 to 1. The closer the coefficient is to 0, the greater the equality of incomes; the closer to 1, the greater the inequality.[5]

One further complication should be mentioned here. The distribution of income by household often reveals that larger households, with more

---

5.1

Rural-income gaps in sub-Saharan Africa

The ILO has investigated the size of the average rural-urban income gap in 14 countries of sub-Saharan Africa. The analysis proceeded in three stages. In the first stage, broad indicators of revenue were assembled based simply on prevailing prices. In the second stage an allowance was made, wherever possible, for different urban and rural price levels. In the third stage an attempt was made to compare the earnings in rural and urban areas of workers with a common skill level.

The results of the first stage showed an average rural-urban gap with values of from 1:2 to 1:3.3 for the poorest of three groups of countries (including a value of 1:3 in the Upper Volta). For the middle group values were much higher, ranging from 1:4 (Benin) to 1:8 (Lesotho). For the final and wealthiest group, values fell again, mostly to around 1:2 (including a value of 1:2.4 in the Ivory Coast). This pattern of change follows both the increasing degree of urbanisation and the growth of rural non-farm activities. In the second stage, estimates were made of the difference in rural-urban prices. These showed a price gap ranging from 10 to 40 per cent between town and country. The result was naturally to reduce the average rural-urban income gap but not, by and large, to change the observed cross-national pattern.

Finally, a range of national data was reviewed in order to place the income and expenditure level of the average agricultural worker (whether employed or self-employed) within the hierarchy of urban occupational earnings. For French-speaking countries the results can be summarised as showing that average agricultural incomes were similar to those of urban informal sector employees or unskilled modern sector workers paid around the minimum wage. In Kenya the agricultural-urban wage gap was found to be still significant at 1:2.9; in Nigeria and Tanzania, however, the ratio approached unity.

---

earning and non-earning members, have larger incomes in absolute terms. They cannot, however, necessarily be said to be better off. The ILO has therefore made a joint effort with the World Bank to recast income distribution statistics on the basis not of whole households but of individuals. The result generally is to make the distribution of incomes somewhat more equal.

The final measure of income distribution calculated is a mixture of a number of factors. One such factor is the change in personal income levels throughout an individual's lifetime, the life-cycle effect. Workers may well have a peak earning

Table 5.5
Inequality of household and per capita income distribution (national coverage) after taxes and transfers (Gini coefficient)

Country	Year	Household	Per capita	Notes	Country	Year	Household	Per capita	Notes
South and Central America					*Asia and the Pacific*				
					Bangladesh	1973/74	0.36	0.28	unadjusted
Argentina	1970	0.44	..	unadjusted	Fiji	1977	0.47	0.46	adjusted
Brazil	1972	0.61	..	unadjusted	India	1975/76	0.42	0.38	unadjusted
Chile	1968	0.45	..	unadjusted	Indonesia	1976	0.44	..	unadjusted
Costa Rica	1971	0.49	..	unadjusted	Islamic Republic of Iran	1973/74	0.52	0.47	adjusted
Dominican Republic	1976/77	0.47	0.47	unadjusted	Republic of Korea	1976	0.38	..	unadjusted
El Salvador	1976/77	0.47	0.47	unadjusted	Nepal	1976/77	0.53	..	unadjusted
Honduras	1967	0.61	..	unadjusted	Philippines	1970/71	0.47	..	unadjusted
Mexico	1968	0.56	0.58	adjusted	Sri Lanka	1968/69	0.35	..	unadjusted
Panama	1976	0.57	..	unadjusted	Thailand	1971/73	0.51	..	unadjusted
Peru	1972	0.57	..	unadjusted					
Trinidad and Tobago	1975/76	0.45	..	unadjusted	*Western Europe*				
Venezuela	1970	0.51	..	unadjusted	Denmark	1976	0.30	0.27	adjusted
					France	1975	0.39	0.35	adjusted
Africa					Germany (Fed. Rep.)	1974	0.36	0.32	adjusted
Egypt	1974/75	0.40	0.38	adjusted	Ireland	1973	0.32	0.29	adjusted
Kenya	1976	0.59	0.59	adjusted	Spain	1973/74	0.37	0.34	adjusted
Malawi	1968/69	0.39	..	unadjusted	Sweden	1979	0.30	0.22	adjusted
Tanzania	1969	0.42	..	unadjusted	United Kingdom	1979	0.31	0.27	adjusted
Zambia	1976	0.56	..	adjusted					

.. = not available.

Source: Estimates prepared under a joint ILO–World Bank project (to be published).

power in their thirties or forties, so that a different demographic structure will affect income distribution. Another factor is the propensity of young people to set up their own households, something which may slow down in a recession. Finally, at least for developing countries, inequality measures are generally calculated separately for urban and rural areas. However, the national coefficient is not an average of the two sectoral coefficients and may well be higher than either, because of the income gap between rural and urban areas (see box 5.1). This gap makes an independent contribution to the value of the income distribution measure. In most developing countries inequality is higher in urban than in rural areas, although there are some exceptions to this rule – for example, in Latin America, where rural inequality is often extreme.

Table 5.5 presents data on inequality of income for a broad range of countries. The data refer to household and, where possible, to per capita income. Some of the coefficients have been adjusted to bring their data base in line with the aggregate figures of the country's national income accounts, but not all. The data relate to income after taxes and transfers.

The factors influencing distribution of income in a country are manifold. Many of them are linked to the level of employment and to the employment structure. The difference in the productivity level in particular sectors and the nature of employment (wage earners, self-employed workers, tenant farmers, etc.) are major forces determining the income distribution structure, as has already been seen in Chapter 1, particularly with regard to agriculture.

The classic hypothesis on the behaviour of measures of income distribution over time is that, with economic development, income distribution first becomes more unequal and later more equal. In other words, development starts by accentuating inequalities and subsequently reduces them – the well-known Simon Kuznets hypothesis, or curve.[6] This would seem to be borne out by the fact that, generally speaking, inequality is less in developed than developing countries. Theoretically, it was assumed that the advent and increasing strength of profitable "modern" sector activities in traditional developing countries would distort the existing distribution towards greater inequality and that, with the virtual disappearance of traditional activities and increased scarcity of labour as a factor of production, the distribution would subsequently become more equal.

However, this is only a general tendency to which there are many exceptions. Faster growth may stimulate inequality under certain conditions of asset ownership and economic structure. Government policies – not only redistributive policies but all economic policies – may influence the degree of equality. The experience of individual countries is thus highly variable.

Table 5.5 shows the wide range of values of Gini coefficients measuring inequality, from 0.30 in Sweden (for households) to 0.61 in Honduras. However, two general remarks are in order. The coefficients for per capita income tend to be somewhat lower than those for household income, which means that the latter may exaggerate inequality. Moreover (although this is not shown in the table), the process of adjustment generally raises the value of the coefficient by a slight amount, so that some of the unadjusted coeffi-

cients certainly understate the extent of the inequality.

As can be seen, the inequality in Western European countries is relatively low and its measures fall within a fairly narrow range. The same cannot be said of the three other regions covered by the table, where the range of values of inequality is quite high. On the average, inequality is probably highest in Latin America and lowest in Asia and the Pacific but the number of examples quoted is really too small to support any generalisation. Of the poorest among the countries listed – namely, Bangladesh, India, Nepal, Malawi, Tanzania and Sri Lanka – only Nepal displays a high inequality. Moreover, South-East Asia has higher inequality than South Asia, perhaps because of the faster growth it has experienced, while the Republic of Korea is a well-known exception. The high inequality in many Latin American countries is probably caused both by the dualistic pattern of rural landholding and by the large extent of urban poverty. Finally, it is commonly believed that in China income is fairly equally distributed. However, no survey data in any way comparable to that produced for other developing countries exist and scattered evidence points to rather large differences between regions and between urban areas and their immediate countryside, on the one hand, and remote areas, on the other (Vermeer, 1982).

We have noted that during the past 20 years the average income in most countries has grown, often at a very impressive rate. Looking at this picture of distribution of income we have just presented, we might ask what changes in the distribution have occurred over this period.

The point should be made from the outset that concrete evidence is scanty, as few countries have comparable data available for other periods. Having said this, we can now attempt a provisional generalisation.

In a number of countries income distribution improved during the period. In Sri Lanka, for example, the share of the poorest 60 per cent of households increased from 27.4 per cent of income in 1963 to 35.4 per cent in 1973, in Costa Rica from 23.7 per cent in 1961 to 28.4 per cent in 1971, in Turkey from 20.8 per cent in 1963 to 24 per cent in 1973, and in Colombia, where income is very unequally distributed, from 19 per cent in 1964 to 21.2 per cent in 1974.

Many countries registered little change in the distribution of income. Between 1961 and 1971 the income share of the poorest 60 per cent of households in the Philippines and in Peru remained practically unchanged. India and Bangladesh have also had more or less the same distribution throughout the past two decades.

Income distribution has worsened in several countries. In Brazil the share of the poorest 60 per cent of households declined from 24.8 per cent in 1960 to 20.6 per cent in 1970, and in Mexico from 21.7 per cent in 1963 to 19.7 per cent in 1975. But this deterioration does not mean that the poorest households were worse off in absolute terms at the end of the period than at the beginning; it means that their income increased at a slower rate than total household income. During the stated period, the total household income in Brazil grew at an average rate of 3.1 per cent per annum, while the income of the bottom 60 per cent grew at only 1.2 per cent. In Mexico the rate of growth of total income was 3.2 per cent, but that of the bottom 60 per cent of households only 2.4 per cent (Chenery, 1980).

In these cases, the growth effect was stronger than the worsening income distribution effect, and even the lower income classes shared to some extent in the benefits of economic growth, although their relative position within society deteriorated. However, it is likely (although no data are available) that, if we focus attention on the poorest 10 or 20 per cent of the population (rather than on the poorest 60 per cent), the absolute level of income in some countries with a low growth rate, coupled with a worsening income distribution, declined in absolute terms.

Policies with respect to the transfer of income and wealth

The overall distribution of income is determined by the structure of the economy and of employment, by the pattern of income-producing asset ownership and by economic and social policies (and also by the interplay of these factors). Some policies have a very direct bearing on the distribution of income. Four different sets of such policies will be examined below: *(a)* policies that set out to transfer wealth (or, in many agrarian economies, control over land) between households; *(b)* policies that transfer income through taxation and the distribution of cash benefits; *(c)* policies that give benefits in kind to all households in relation to certain needs, such as education or health care; and *(d)* policies that adopt a target-group approach by favouring the economic position of poorer households, generally by directly increasing their employment situation by special credit and work programmes.

The transfer of wealth

The pattern of wealth distribution among households gives a powerful, although incomplete, explanation of the inter-household distribution of incomes. Assets are certainly more concentrated in their distribution than is income since some households, after all, have none. Thus in Sri Lanka in the late 1950s, the richest 10 per cent of agricultural households held 56 per cent of all agricultural assets. The poorest 40 per cent held 4 per cent. A transfer of assets from wealthier to wealthless families will, so long as the latter can retain the particular assets involved, improve the distribution of income. The most effective means of redistributing asset ownership so as to lower income inequality will of course depend on the characteristics of the poor and on the sectors in which they work. Generally, the poor are the rural landless or land-poor and urban chronically underemployed and marginal workers, not those regularly employed.

The process of asset redistribution from families higher in the income scale to families

127

lower in the scale may not always give a completely unequivocal shift towards a reduction in income inequality. This can be for two reasons. Firstly, the employment position of groups further down the income scale may be adversely affected. For example, a programme of land distribution to those with hitherto marginal landholdings may reduce employment for the completely landless previously working for the larger farmers. Secondly, the poor may be affected not through a change in their asset holdings or in their employment opportunities but through a change in output prices and, unmistakably, by any change in the efficiency with which the transferred assets are managed.

Within urban areas, asset redistribution among households has always played a minor role in any income distribution strategy. Productive industrial assets have frequently been removed from private hands, but such enterprises have hardly ever been subsequently presented to a group of workers as personal property. In certain socialist countries and in scattered examples elsewhere, productive enterprises are co-operatively owned so that an element of profit-sharing is possible. In many developing countries, however, the conversion of privately owned enterprises into co-operative ownership by existing workers will not directly benefit the poorest of the poor. Taking enterprises into government hands with all other conditions – of employment and profitability – unchanged will effect a partial redistribution, inasmuch as the wealth and income levels of certain households, perhaps resident abroad, will be reduced. Previous profit flows should become available for general government pruposes, but the effect on households in the lower income ranges will be minor.

The scope for the transfer of productive assets in the agricultural sector is clearly wider than in urban areas. Nevertheless, it must be recalled that agriculture is by no means necessarily the major employment sector in a rural area; various forms of industry and construction are also significant. The major distributive land reforms of the late 1940s and early 1950s in Asia would probably not have the same impact on income distribution if carried out today and would in any event be more complex to implement, given the present greater integration of agriculture and rural industry. Nevertheless, there is no doubt still scope for straightforward redistributive land reform in many areas of the world by which either average operational holding sizes are reduced or tenants are given ownership rights, or both. The former process is associated with greater labour intensity per unit of land as well as greater land productivity. The production and employment effects of the latter may not be significant, and may even be negative if the previous landlord in effect directed the farming operations of the tenant. However, an asset transfer will have taken place and the patterns of income will reflect this as well as the extent of compensation paid.

A distributive land reform may be shortlived. Small peasants with no resources but their land are very dependent on suppliers and merchants. Forms of debt relationship can easily arise which allow effective control over land to pass from their hands. Furthermore, farm households are almost certain to adopt different farm technologies, which benefit some more than others. Finally, there will always be a tendency for larger farm households to rent land from those with fewer able-bodied members, and this process could also contribute to a return to land concentration.

A distributive approach to land reform is not always practicable. In many instances, larger and well-established farms have been expropriated which, for various reasons, could not be subdivided and which already supported a permanent labour force. This was the pattern of land reform in Chile begun after 1965, which bypassed the smallholding sector and, after a transitional period, set out to confer ownership of large farms on the workforce involved. After five years it was found that wages and employment had risen faster on the expropriated farms than elsewhere and that the major beneficiaries were the previous permanent workers earning a wage around three times the legal minimum. However, in the first round of land reform in Sri Lanka in 1972, for example, when many medium-sized holdings passed into a form of co-operative ownership, a major effort was made to recruit unemployed youth and associate them with the permanent labour force.

Taxation and cash transfers

Alongside government expenditure, taxation has great potential significance in changing the distribution of income. The desirability of a "progressive" tax structure is generally accepted, on the grounds that a one-unit reduction of consumption will cause far less loss to the welfare of the rich than it will cause to the welfare of the poor. In developing countries, moreover, the tax base is almost always monetary income or expenditure, so that the very poor must be to a certain extent exempt. Conversely, there is sometimes an apparent unwillingness or inability to tax richer individuals or companies heavily, a similar distaste for taxing land and a corresponding preference for raising indirect tax rates, which can be less easily "finely tuned" towards progressivity.

ILO studies show that, in developing countries, the incidence of indirect taxes on the incomes of the poor is frequently higher than on the incomes of the rich. In the Philippines in the early 1970s, the poorest 10 per cent of households paid the equivalent of 26 per cent of their incomes as indirect taxes, compared with 11 per cent for the richest 10 per cent (Tan, 1975). When measured against consumption (which for the poor will on average exceed income and for the rich fall short of income), however, indirect taxation usually shows a slight degree of progression, rising in Chile from 10 per cent for the poorest 10 per cent of households to 18 per cent for the richest 5 per cent (Foxley et al., 1979). But, of course, the savings of the rich go untaxed. However, the possibility of high indirect taxes on luxury goods does serve to show that indirect taxation has a role as a redistributive instrument.

It is more difficult to measure the incidence of direct taxation because of the difficulty of assigning the burden of this form of taxation to any particular income group. Corporate taxation may well in effect be passed on in the form of higher prices, while salaries may be adjusted to absorb higher levels of income tax. A further problem concerns the taxation of agricultural, primary exports. Here, the export tax may be paid either by the foreign consumer or by the domestic producer (who often earns a relatively low income), depending on the strength of demand for primary exports in foreign markets. The taxation of exports of rice from Thailand seems to have had the latter effect (Holtsberg, 1982). However, even bearing all these complications in mind, the usual picture is that direct taxation in developing countries does impinge far more on the richest 5 and possibly 10 per cent of the population than on the rest. ILO studies show that direct taxes paid by the richest 5 per cent of households exceed that of the average household by anything from 40 to 300 per cent (Lecaillon et al., 1983). However, direct taxation distinguishes badly between the very poor and the less poor, since effective rates of tax incidence are fairly stable up to the higher income brackets.

The complete picture for developing countries is that taxation does reduce the degree of inequality in the distribution of income, but usually to a quite small extent. It may come as a surprise that in a number of Western industrialised countries the converse applies and taxation worsens the distribution of income, again by a relatively insignificant amount. Average tax rates scarcely vary between income groups but are often extremely high for the poorest 10 or 20 per cent of the population. The reason is that the primary income of these groups, against which the tax burden is measured, is extremely low and, of course, their disposable income is largely made up of transfers.

Table 5.6 gives information on the impact of direct and indirect taxation on the distribution of income in a number of countries.

Table 5.6
Taxes as a share of primary income of households

Income group (percentage)	United Kingdom (1975)	United States (1970)	Hong Kong (1971)	Philippines (1971)	Sri Lanka (1973)	Islamic Republic of Iran (1971)	Chile (1969)	Colombia (1970)	Panama (1970)
0–20	180	52	8	37	12	9	18	15	9
21–40	43	40	7	23	15	7	17	10	11
41–60	39	34	7	19	15	7	16	10	14
61–80	38	31	7	18	17	7	17	11	15
81–90	38	29	7	19	19	8	16	11	16
91–95	40	29	9	22	19	9	18	12	17
96–100	41	38	30	29	29	9	24	25	23
Gini coefficient									
Before tax	0.423	0.444	0.496	0.496	0.239	0.554	0.456	0.555	0.591
After tax	0.442	0.456	0.403	0.494	0.201	0.553	0.448	0.540	0.571

Source: J. Lecaillon, F. Paukert, C. Morrisson and D. Germidis: *Income distribution and economic development: An analytical survey* (Geneva, ILO, 1983).

In Western industrialised countries the impact of cash transfers on household incomes is very considerable. In the United Kingdom in the mid-1970s, among households composed of two adults and one or more children, the poorest 10 per cent received a cash transfer equal to some 50 per cent of their original income. For older households, more especially pensioners, the vast majority received on an average cash transfers equal to 14 times their original income. It has been estimated that the inequality of income in the United Kingdom in the late 1960s was reduced by 25 per cent through the operation of cash transfers, in Australia by 13 per cent and in the United States by 10 per cent. According to the Royal Commission on Income and Wealth (Background paper No. 4, 1977), "in all instances direct transfer benefits play a more important role in the redistributive mechanism than direct taxes". The result is that the distribution of incomes net of taxes and transfers is more equal than that of the original incomes. In Sweden, in the early 1970s, for example, the result was a drop in the Gini coefficient from 0.48 to 0.30, a fall of nearly 40 per cent.

In developing countries the extent of cash transfers is naturally far more limited. Apart from

minor charitable programmes, cash transfers usually take place within the context of a social security or provident fund scheme, necessarily restricted to the households of certain classes of workers (and almost always excluding the self-employed). As a result, considerable sections of the poor cannot benefit from such transfers, an exclusion which is clearly far greater in Africa, for example, than in Latin America. Within the coverage of such schemes, however, particularly social security schemes, some redistribution towards poorer members does take place. Provident funds, which provide a lump-sum payment on retirement built up by proportional contributions from wages, have no such progressive impact. In some cases, social security schemes may lead to redistribution from the poor towards the middle-income classes.

In developed countries cash transfers have proved relatively successful in abolishing poverty. An ILO study on the effectiveness of income maintenance payments in alleviating poverty in four Western industrialised countries in the early 1970s came to the following conclusions. About 30 per cent of the population would have been below the poverty line if there had been no income maintenance payments; the existence of such payments reduced the share of the population below the poverty line to 10 per cent. The poverty gap (that is, the total amount by which the incomes of the poor fall below the level needed to bring them up to the poverty line) was some 4 or 5 per cent of GDP before cash transfers. After benefits the poverty gap was less than 1 per cent. In terms of national poverty lines, the poverty gap was reduced to negligible proportions; in other words, for national purposes anti-poverty income maintenance programmes more or less succeeded in what they had set out to achieve (Beckerman et al., 1979).[7]

Pensioner households formed an overwhelming share of poor households in two of these countries (Belgium and the United Kingdom) and from 40 to 50 per cent of poor households in the other two (Australia and Norway). Single adults (with and without children) made up over 40 per cent of poor households in Australia and nearly 25 per cent in Norway. Viewed in another perspective, between 70 and 90 per cent of single pensioners were below the poverty line (before benefits), using the international poverty line, as were from 15 to 40 per cent of single person households but only 5 to 15 per cent of couples with children. After benefits, again using the international poverty line, these rates were considerably reduced. Among married couples generally, only 2 or 3 per cent remained in poverty, although around one-third of pensioner households was still below the poverty line.

Social services expenditures

The contribution of government expenditures in such major social fields as health and education to the redistribution of income can be viewed in three ways: *(a)* the use made of services provided, by income class of beneficiaries, valued at cost price; *(b)* the later and dynamic effects of better health and higher levels of education on relative levels of earnings; and *(c)* the extent to which services provided are appropriate to the needs of the intended beneficiary groups.

Under the first method, information is generally collected through a household income and expenditure survey and data are compiled on such matters as the number of visits a household member makes to a government health centre or the school enrolment of the household's children. This "access" to official facilities is then given a value set by the unit cost of these activities. This value can be treated in two ways: it can be compared with the income of the benefiting household, for each income class, or it can be viewed as a share of total government expenditure benefiting an income group compared with the share of households in that income group (so as to be able to state, for example, that 10 per cent of households receive 10 per cent of expenditure).

The first approach usually shows that the additional "income" given by the use of health or education services can be a relatively significant share of income for the poorest groups – up to 18, 20 or even 30 per cent – falling to a small share for the wealthiest groups – 2 or 3 per cent or less. A very similar range appears to prevail in certain industrialised countries such as the United Kingdom. In this way the distribution of government expenditure on these services goes some way towards compensating for the distribution of private expenditure, which follows private income. Calculations of Gini coefficients including the value of services received must necessarily yield a lower measure of income inequality. The reduction can be substantial: some 10 per cent and often considerably more in developing countries, and up to 30 per cent in developed countries, especially those where private health and education expenditures are minor (Lecaillon et al., 1983). Table 5.7 contains data on the imputed value of specific government services by household income group for the same countries as table 5.6.

The alternative approach, that of comparing the share of benefits received with the share of households in the relevant income class, gives a very different picture and raises other issues. In general, the poorest group of households receives

131

Table 5.7
Specific government expenditure benefits[a] as a share of household income

Income group (percentage)	United Kingdom (1975)	United States (1970)	Hong Kong (1971)	Philippines (1971)	Sri Lanka (1973)	Islamic Republic of Iran (1971)	Chile (1969)	Colombia (1970)	Panama (1970)
0–20	1 100	180	27	32	20	15	73	40	54
21–40	70	60	24	14	17	8	60	17	36
41–60	27	26	21	11	17	8	46	13	16
61–80	17	19	13	9	15	5	34	11	11
81–90	15	16	7	9	12	5	29	13	7
91–95	12	14	5	6	12	5	26	17	6
96–100	8	10	2	4 5	3	22	8	6	
Gini coefficient									
Before benefits from government expenditure	0.423	0.444	0.443	0.479	0.234	0.570	0.456	0.580	0.590
After benefits from government expenditure	0.304	0.376	0.403	0.461	0.210	0.559	0.405	0.566	0.559

[a] Including social security.

Source: J. Lecaillon, F. Paukert, C. Morrisson and D. Germidis: *Income distribution and economic development: An analytical survey*, op. cit.

a proportionate amount of health benefits and of primary education services: that is to say, the poorest 20 per cent of households receive 20 per cent of benefits and services (or, in the case of the Islamic Republic of Iran, up to 30 per cent). Mounting the education ladder, however, the picture changes. In higher education the rich have far more and the poor far less than their share; for example, the richest 5 per cent of households had 50 per cent of tertiary education in the Islamic Republic of Iran, 18 per cent in Hong Kong and 17 per cent in Sri Lanka. Clearly, government-provided primary education and general health services may be treated as of lower quality by the rich, and private services used in their place.

So far we have discussed only health and education services. These are the major government services and the most likely to display a pro-poor pattern of distribution. But transport services, for example, are apt to be subsidised on a pro rata basis, so that the greater the personal expendi-

ture the larger the absolute amount of subsidy. Thus, in Sri Lanka the poorest 20 per cent of households received less than 5 per cent of transport benefits. Housing services are often a means of effectively subsidising savings, in which case they help the rich rather than the poor. However, certain countries, of which Singapore and Hong Kong are major examples, have constructed a considerable volume of housing for rent, an approach which is certainly far more likely to benefit the poor.

The second method of calculating the incidence of government social expenditure on income redistribution is to measure the effect on earnings of providing universal and reasonable levels of health care and education. Will such provision not help to equalise precisely those elements of human capital to which earnings seem statistically related? If a geographical region is neglected as regards health and education, some effect on income levels would be expected. Does not the same apply to a social class?

It has frequently been argued that the "redistribution of human capital" (meaning higher average levels of school enrolment and greater equality of educational opportunity) is a sufficient condition for incomes to be "redistributed" within a later generation of workers, and this in a fairly painless way. This is far from certain, however, and it does not seem very likely that social programmes alone can achieve either greater equality of opportunity within the labour market or a reduction in the gap in inter-occupational earnings. Developing countries with high levels of past and present school enrolment do not display a greater equality of income distribution than the rest. Furthermore, the main predictor of educational levels is not the distribution of income but the level of income.

It is impossible for in-school activities to compensate wholly for an underprivileged household environment. Children from poor households just do not perform as well in tests of mathematics and thinking ability as children from wealthier backgrounds (Richards and Leonor, 1981). Schooling alone cannot provide equality of opportunity in the search for a job. Linked to this is the high drop-out rate among the children of the poor, even when educational facilities are at hand. Next, the whole phenomenon of unemployment among the educated points to the distortions in labour markets which prevent the extra educational input from being put to good use. Finally, there is no evidence at all that higher levels of education for unskilled workers at the bottom of the occupational ladder do anything to put them in a more favourable relative income position. Relative earnings are apparently most strongly linked to occupations, whatever the educational content of the occupation. It is therefore doubtful whether social programmes alone can lead to greater income equality in a succeeding generation.

The last way of gauging the effect of government social programmes on the redistribution of income is to ascertain whether the services provided are appropriate to the needs of the beneficiary groups. In the health field in particular, there has been considerable controversy around this issue, and new forms of primary health care have been proposed which are considered economically and culturally more acceptable to the poor (see WHO research since 1979, and Richards, 1982). The question of health needs is tricky. Far more people have clinically diagnosable diseases than ever either perceive symptoms or act on that perception. Broadly, furthermore, the rich are more likely both to perceive symptoms and to seek treatment. Yet the poor generally have a greater need for treatment. Rarely do programmes take this into account, however, and the sources of health care used by the poor are usually of a lower quality than average.

The same is true of education. The quality of educational facilities open to the children of the poor is almost everywhere below average national levels. Yet again, their need for good education is higher than average, simply because of the absence of compensating home backgrounds.

The target group approach

The target group approach is designed to make up for the very slow process of the "trickle-down" of the benefits of economic growth. Target group programmes direct investment, funds, credit and work opportunities to persons or to geographical areas known to be in poverty. Bureaucratic supervision of such programmes is intended to ensure that their benefits are not "hijacked" by more prosperous groups. Thus, the target group approach is intended, within a generally market-oriented economy, to bypass the working of the market. It tends to demand very considerable inputs of administrative talent and certainly risks encouraging dependence on government support and discouraging self-reliance.

India has experimented with a large number of target group programmes which have been centrally funded but executed in as decentralised a manner as possible. They have had mixed success.

Some have succeeded in providing work, and therefore an income, for previously underemployed members of poor rural households; they have created efficient and productive assets, even though the assets developed did not provide longer-term employment for all. Others have failed, as for example when large farmers have managed to benefit from the subsidies provided by splitting up their holdings and registering them under different names.

☐

We can now summarise the conclusions that can be drawn about these various policies. First, taxation and government expenditures can help to alleviate poverty, provided they avoid the disincentive effects of excess taxation. Second, cash transfers are the simplest and most direct form of income redistribution but, because of the possibility of abuse, their overall cost of implementation is quite significant; moreover, they are usually beyond the reach of developing countries. Third, asset redistribution has been used relatively rarely as an instrument of income distribution, although collectivisation has been practised in many socialist countries; its scope for most countries, even for most agrarian countries, is nevertheless limited. Fourth, the target group approach can be very beneficial, provided of course that bureaucratic supervision is both efficient and manageable.

The overall conclusion of our survey of income development over the past two decades is, to the possible surprise of many observers, rather optimistic. Growth of average income has been achieved in most countries in which the overwhelming majority of the world's population are concentrated. The record as regards the distribution of income is less clear: in a certain number of countries income distribution has improved, while inequality has widened in others. But, once again, the great bulk of the population of the world has experienced an increase in income, even if it has been smaller than would have been warranted by the growth performance of their countries. There

is obviously much room for improvement in the field of redistributive measures, particularly in the developing countries. It cannot be denied, however, that here too there has been an improvement in the past decade, particularly in the provision of government services in education and health. Without an extension of these services to broad layers of society, it would not have been possible to achieve the dramatic improvement in such social indicators as life expectancy and adult literacy that we have witnessed in the past two decades.

With these broad observations on the growth of incomes in general, we can turn now to one type of income which is of specific interest to the world of labour: wages.

Wages[8]

In industrialised market economies the bulk of household incomes derives from wage employment. Wage decisions have an important bearing on the overall distribution of income, the functioning of the labour market and the performance of the economy as a whole. In large measure, they determine the allocation of expenditure between consumption and investment, the extent of inequalities among various categories of workers, the number, location and character of the jobs that are created, the levels of productivity achieved by the workers on those jobs and the degree of overt or hidden conflict surrounding terms of employment. Even though in developing countries the proportion of wages in national income is smaller, many wage earners work in strategic sectors of the economy, and the maintenance of an appropriate balance between wages and other forms of income is widely recognised as playing a critical role in the development policy. Moreover, in both developed and developing countries, wages cannot be viewed as simply the product of ineluctable market forces. They are affected by the policy decisions of employers, trade unionists and governments.

Real wage trends

Table 5.8 presents the available data on real wage changes during the 1970s and contrasts these with rates of growth of gross per capita national product. Several limitations to these statistics need to be pointed out. To begin with, the table covers only a portion of the developing world. Many of the smaller, least developed countries, particularly in the Caribbean, Africa and the Middle East, do not publish statistics on wage trends. Another limitation is that the data are indicative mainly of wage movements in the larger non-agricultural establishments of the formal sector and may not reflect at all closely the trends in the informal sector or in rural areas. Moreover, the trends in real wages have been estimated in a rather crude fashion. Broad-based averages of earnings or wage rates have been "deflated" by dividing them by consumer price indexes in order to arrive at a constant price measure of wages. No attempt has been made to take into account disposable as opposed to gross wages or other influences on living standards. Nor have corrections been made for technical weaknesses in the underlying wage and price statistics or to allow for changes in consumer expenditure patterns under inflationary conditions or for shifts in the sectoral distribution or occupational composition of the labour force. The result is that the data can be considered only as giving a rough indication of changes in purchasing power of wages during the period covered.

Despite their weaknesses, these data do serve to shed some light on how wages have adapted to the context of the accelerating inflation and more restrained growth of the 1970s. The most striking feature is the difference in the experience of the developed and developing countries. In the former, real wages have continued to rise. The only apparent exception is the United States, but if allowance had been made for the rapid expansion of women and young workers that occurred in the labour force, a small improvement in real earnings would be shown for this country as well (Flaim,

1982). Although the rates of growth of real wages have generally not matched those of the prior decade and have tended to slow down or even to turn negative at the end of the 1970s, still the longer-term pattern has been one of continuous improvement. Moreover, with only few exceptions, national rates of growth of real wages have not deviated substantially from the rates of growth in national productivity as reflected in changes in real per capita GNP.

The situation is altogether different in the developing countries. Not only have there been large differences from country to country but also real wages have frequently fallen, sometimes substantially. To some extent, these variations among developing countries appear to be accounted for by large differences in the rates of economic growth. Thus, in some of the countries where growth has been unusually rapid, real wages have improved substantially (Botswana, Egypt, Hong Kong, Republic of Korea and Ecuador, for example). Where the economies have been stagnant or in regression, real wages have generally suffered (Sierra Leone, Zambia, Nicaragua). But the relation between economic growth and increases in real wages has been far from close. Improvements in real wages have often been either well ahead or behind trends in national economic growth. In this respect, as well as in the marked fluctuations from year to year in real wage levels, the pattern of wage movements in developing countries has been highly unstable, and undoubtedly quite disruptive. All this would suggest that the existing wage determination mechanisms have not always adapted well to the changed economic environment of the 1970s and that often much might have been gained by achieving a more orderly evolution of incomes in the wage-earning sector.

Another striking difference concerns the size of the increases in real wages. In industrial market economies the increases, with only relatively few exceptions, have been somewhat higher than the rates of economic growth. To some extent this

Table 5.8
Annual rates of growth as a percentage of real wages and of per capita GNP in the 1970s

Developing countries						Industrial economies		
	Wages	GNP		Wages	GNP		Wages	GNP
Africa			*Latin America –*			*Market economies*		
Algeria	−0.6	2.8	*Caribbean*			Australia	3.1	1.4
Botswana	4.1	12.0	Bolivia	−1.8	2.3	Austria	3.3	3.5
Burundi	−2.5	1.5	Colombia	0.7	3.7	Belgium	4.6	2.9
Egypt	2.3	5.3	Costa Rica	3.7	3.2	Canada	1.4	2.9
Kenya	−2.1	2.6	Dominican Republic	0.3	3.7	Denmark	2.7	2.1
Malawi	−2.4	3.0	Ecuador	4.6	5.4	Finland	2.4	2.2
Mauritius	4.6	6.4	El Salvador	−1.8	1.4	France	4.2	3.0
Nigeria	2.4	5.3	Guyana	1.5	0.0	Germany		
Sierra Leone	−4.8	−1.2	Honduras	2.6	0.5	(Fed. Rep.)	2.9	2.6
Zambia	−3.2	−1.9	Mexico	2.2	1.9	Ireland	4.4	2.3
			Nicaragua	−2.6	−1.6	Italy	5.6	2.3
Asia			Panama	−0.3	1.3	Japan	3.8	3.9
Brunei	0.0	4.6	Peru	−2.8	−0.2	Luxembourg	4.0	3.5
Burma	−8.4	2.0	Puerto Rico	1.5	−0.3	Netherlands	3.4	2.2
Fiji	5.2	3.0	Uruguay	−5.3	2.9	New Zealand	1.8	0.5
Hong kong	3.0	6.5	Venezuela	−0.5	2.7	Norway	3.4	3.7
India	1.6	1.6				Spain	8.0	3.0
Israel	2.4	1.6	*Europe*			Sweden	2.2	1.1
Jordan	0.2	6.1	Greece	6.0	4.1	Switzerland	0.9	1.1
Republic of Korea	9.8	8.1	Portugal	7.2	1.1	United Kingdom	2.0	1.9
Pakistan	3.8	1.5	Turkey	2.8	3.5	United States	−0.4	2.2
Philippines	−4.1	3.9	Yugoslavia	1.8	5.4			
Singapore	2.0	6.7				*Non-market economies*		
Sri Lanka	5.2	2.5				Bulgaria	2.0	5.6
Syrian Arab						Czechoslovakia	2.1	4.1
Republic	−0.7	4.6				German Dem. Rep.	3.9	4.7
						Hungary	2.2	4.8
						Poland	4.9	5.2
						USSR	3.0	4.1

Note: Real wages have been calculated from data on non-agricultural wages and consumer price indexes. Where data on wages in non-agricultural activities as a whole were not available, manufacturing wages were used. For descriptions of the basic data, see ILO: *Year Book of Labour Statistics*, 1981, and *Technical guide 1980: Descriptions of general series published in both the Bulletin and the Year Book of Labour Statistics*, Vol. I, Consumer prices, and Vol. II, Employment – unemployment – hours of work – wages (Geneva, 1980). Growth rates for wages, where possible, were calculated with data covering the period 1970-80. Frequently, information covering shorter periods had to be used in making the estimates. Rates of growth of per capita GNP (real) cover the period 1970-79. For limitations on these data, see Technical Note in the *1981 World Bank atlas* (Washington, DC, 1982). Growth rates have been computed by the least-squares method which involves fitting trend lines to the logarithmic values for each year of the time period. With this method, all available observations within the relevant time period are considered and the growth rates obtained are less influenced by cyclical or irregular factors at the beginning or end of the period.

Sources: Calculated mainly from data appearing in ILO: *Year Book of Labour Statistics*, 1980 and 1981, and World Bank: *1981 World Bank atlas*, op. cit. Supplementary sources used for Botswana and the Philippines.

may reflect the priority given to protecting the position of wage earners under increasingly difficult economic conditions. In developing countries the prevailing pattern has been just the opposite. Real wage improvements have often trailed well behind the GNP. This tendency, which contrasts sharply with that observed during the 1950s and up to the mid-1960s (Smith, 1969), reflects the policies of wage restraint that have been introduced by many of these countries. Increasingly, governments have placed the highest priority on expanding employment opportunities, rectifying rural-urban income inequalities and dampening rural-urban migration flows. Consequently, it has been considered important to ensure that a major part of the growth "dividend" is reflected in an increase in the number of jobs in the more productive sectors of the economy and not absorbed by improvements in the well-being of those already fortunate enough to be fully employed. For this reason, efforts have been made to keep real wages from rising as rapidly as national productivity in the initial stages of the development process until such time as the bulk of the labour surplus has been absorbed.

It may be asked, however, whether in many cases the degree of wage restraint applied, either accidentally or by design, has not been excessive. As table 5.8 shows, in about a third of the developing countries covered, wage restraint has been so stringent that long-term declines in purchasing power have been produced. Moreover, judging from fragmentary information on those countries where regular wage and price statistics are not published (often the least developed countries), it seems quite likely that the number of countries in which wage movements have not kept pace with rising prices is considerably larger than indicated in the table. This is a matter of some concern since for many good reasons it has traditionally been thought that wage policies should seek, except during crises or periods of generally falling incomes, at least to preserve the purchasing power of the lower-paid categories of workers. Apart from considerations of equity, there is the fact that to do otherwise runs the risk of undermining the motivation of the workers concerned and of generating conflict. Where it is considered necessary to alter the relative income levels of various categories of workers, this can be achieved through differential rates of growth in nominal incomes without eroding existing living standards.

5.2

Real wages in OECD countries since 1975

In the 1950s and 1960s wage earners in developed market economies generally enjoyed substantial and virtually continuous improvements in their purchasing power. Wage determination could safely proceed from the presumption that increases in consumer prices would be wholly offset. Negotiations could focus on the scope that existed for augmenting "real" wages. However, as shown in the table, by the mid-1970s this pattern was broken. In almost half of the 20 OECD countries covered, the selected indicator of real wage trends shows hardly any change between 1975 and 1981. Either nominal wages just managed to keep pace with prices or periods of real wage improvement were followed by periods of decline. Moreover, even among those countries that registered some improvement in purchasing power, the overall rates of increase were noticeably slower than those recorded previously and frequently interrupted by years of stagnation or decline. The period since 1979 has been been particularly problematic. The rate of growth of the weighted average real wage index for all the countries has gradually slowed down to the point where no significant improvements were apparent after 1979.

Index numbers of real earnings in the manufacturing sector in OECD countries (1975 = 100)

	1975	1976	1977	1978	1979	1980	1981	1982
Australia	100	101	100	99	98	99	99	–
Austria	100	102	105	107	109	110	110	110[a]
Belgium	100	102	104	107	110	112	115	112
Canada	100	106	109	107	106	107	106	106[a]
Denmark	100	104	105	108	112	113	113	114
Finland	100	101	98	97	101	102	102	–
France	100	104	107	111	113	115	116	119[a]
Federal Republic of Germany	100	102	106	108	110	110	110	109
Greece	100	114	123	135	136	139	142	–
Ireland	100	99	101	107	110	112	108	–
Italy	100	104	111	115	118	119	124	125
Japan	100	103	103	105	108	108	109	111
Netherlands	100	100	101	102	102	100	97	97[a]
New Zealand	100	96	95	96	98	99	102	98
Norway	100	107	108	108	106	105	102	102[a]
Spain	100	111	109	122	130	134	140	140
Sweden	100	107	103	101	101	97	97	95
Switzerland	100	100	100	103	101	102	101	102
United Kingdom	100	101	96	101	103	102	103	106
United States	100	102	105	106	103	99	98	98
Weighted average	100	103	105	107	108	108	108	–

– Not available.

[a] Estimates based on data for the second and third quarters.

Source : Calculated from series on wages and consumer prices appearing in OECD : *Main Economic Indicators*, various issues. The earnings series used are those available from national sources which most closely correspond to average earnings paid per employed wage earner per hour, including overtime pay and regularly recurring cash supplements.

Adapting to inflation

With the worsening of stagflation over the past ten to 15 years, most governments have come under increasing pressure to take direct action with a view to reconciling individual wage- and price-fixing decisions with national economic objectives. Although the origins of the inflation of the 1970s have frequently been linked to a complex set of factors, the persistence of inflation and its growing insensitivity to the usual array of fiscal and monetary policies have frequently been attributed to the gradual entrenchment of inflationary expectations and to the institutional arrangements for wage and price fixing. Such a diagnosis has prompted governments to try to influence the wage decisions of workers and employers. The effectiveness or not of the various measures taken has dominated wage policy debates over the past two decades.

In many cases these attempts have been limited to general exhortations. Official government declarations have urged restraint or specific courses of action, well-publicised guide-lines for wage and price adjustments have been elaborated and procedures have been put in place for investigating and publicising "inflationary" behaviour or practices. The assumption underlying these actions has been that, once "socially responsible" behaviour has been defined, those taking the wage and price decisions will feel compelled by their sense of public duty to act accordingly even though this may be in conflict with their obligations to the specific interests they represent.

Whether incomes policies based on mere exhortations have ever had an appreciable effect on behaviour remains a matter of some doubt. However, what has become clear is that repeated exposure to them and the consequent increasing awareness of their limited effectiveness have severely eroded their credibility. Thus, in the United States the programme of voluntary guide-lines operated by the Council of Wage and Price Stability in 1979 and 1980 appears to have been much less effective than the similar programme operated in the early 1960s. Moreover, some observers have even argued that voluntary guide-lines programmes have been counter-productive in that the proposed maxima have actually served as minima in negotiations and that, by encouraging the public to believe that there was an easy way out, they may have delayed the taking of the painful steps necessary to control inflation.

Various ways have been tried to add credibility to government pleas for wage restraint. One has been to back them up with vague threats or specific sanctions such as a refusal to grant government contracts to firms that violate the established norms. However, such action has often been criticised as too arbitrary, limited and haphazard in its effects. Another approach has been for the government to apply the restraint on wage increases first to its own employees. But attempts to do so have often been the source of labour disputes, as public sector trade unions naturally see themselves as the victims of discriminatory treatment. Another approach has been to promote greater centralisation in bargaining on wage adjustments. Efforts at persuasion have been considered more likely to succeed when the number of individuals to be influenced is reduced; they can see more clearly the relationship between their decisions and the effects on the economy as a whole and they can safely assume that whatever settlements are reached will not be undermined by subsequent "leapfrog" negotiations. But in practice bargaining structures have not proved to be subject to easy manipulation, since such action risks creating an untenable gap between the views of the trade union leadership and those of the rank and file membership.

This being so, governments have had to consider, usually quite reluctantly, the alternative of mandatory wage and price controls. These have varied in scope: short-term pay pauses or freezes, temporary modifications to wage indexation arrangements, comprehensive systems of control over wages and prices extending over several years. However, their repeated use has generated increasingly cautious, if not sceptical, attitudes. Many observers, particularly in industrial market economies, believe that mandatory controls, especially where they have been maintained in place for some time, are of limited effectiveness and even dangerous because of their legacy of suppressed inflation, relative wage and price distortions and real or imagined wage inequities. Inflation has often not been slowed down as much as hoped, and subsequent price and wage explosions have effaced many if not all of the results achieved. Moreover, except as a short-term emergency measure, it is difficult for the social partners to tolerate the inequities and restrictions that statutory incomes policies impose.

Disappointment with the results of incomes policies in either their mandatory or their voluntary forms has generated two types of response in industrial market economies. The first has been an increased wariness of any form of explicit intervention and a shift of attention towards what are viewed as the basic causes of the inflationary process rather than just its "symptoms". The second has been for governments to try to make the parties to collective bargaining more responsive to their own goals of stability, growth and social equality, and vice versa. In other words, a patient policy of tripartite consensus-building has been pursued. This has been attempted in various ways, such as the institution of informal or formal consultative arrangements at the national level, where the major issues of national economic policy can be considered, or the negotiation of national agreements with which the government is directly or indirectly associated. The latter form has been of particular interest, since these agreements have linked pay settlements to such measures as the introduction of guarantees of real income, the modification of various tax and price policies, changes in wage structure in favour of the lower paid, various non-pecuniary gains such as industrial relations reforms or increased participation,

and the achievement of specific employment promotion targets.

This has not been an easy policy to institute and it has not always been successful. In recent years, a number of national tripartite bargaining arrangements have broken down because of shifting economic and political conditions and the difficulty of maintaining a single approach to incomes policy over long periods (in Ireland and Norway, for example). Still, the general trend seems to have been towards some form of continuing co-ordination whereby, at the very least, the points of view of all concerned are brought into the open and compared and, at the most, a broad consensus can be reached along the lines of the anti-inflation programmes.

With the acceleration of inflation during the 1970s, wage indexation provisions have become a significant element of pay determination in industrial market economies. Yet attitudes towards wage indexation vary greatly. In some countries (Austria, Federal Republic of Germany, Japan) it continues to be avoided for fear of the possible inflationary consequences and of an undue narrowing of the scope of negotiations. In other countries where wage indexation provisions have traditionally covered only a portion of the workforce (Canada, France, Switzerland, United States), reliance upon it has recently increased. In still other countries (Belgium, Denmark, Italy, Luxembourg, Netherlands), comprehensive wage indexation systems have been a long-standing practice but have become of critical importance in the inflationary environment of recent years. In addition to protecting purchasing power, they have been viewed as an important means of promoting industrial peace by narrowing the scope of disagreement over wage issues. However, although still cherished by trade unionists, these comprehensive systems have come under increasing attack from employers and governments as being too inflexible in the prevailing economic environment. Proposals to limit the frequency or extent of compensation provided through indexation arrangements have been a source of protracted disputes, for example in Italy. Such limitations have actually been introduced in some situations by government incomes policies (in Belgium, Finland, Netherlands and Norway, for example). Interestingly enough, however, in other contexts various forms of indexation have been introduced as a pay determination mechanism in the hope that, with purchasing power being protected in this way, overall wage demands would be more moderate (Australia, Greece, Ireland, Sweden, United Kingdom). This reflects the conviction that the principle of indexation itself cannot be characterised as inflationary but that its effects will greatly depend on the extent of compensation for price increases provided through the system and the precise manner in which it is integrated with other pay determination decisions.

Although the responses to the wage determination problems created by the accelerating inflation of the 1970s have in many respects been similar in both developed and developing market economies, there have been a number of important differences, which in the event reflect different approaches to incomes policy measures.

The first difference is that developing countries tend to prefer indirect means of influencing wage decisions. It is true that in recent years several countries have adopted incomes policies: national tripartite agreements regulating wage adjustments (Philippines, Tunisia), guide-lines for wage adjustments elaborated by tripartite bodies (Fiji, Singapore), mandatory controls (Brazil, Kenya, Jamaica, Nigeria). None the less, developing countries still appear generally more ready to pursue their wage policy objectives by less direct means, such as exercising close control over the machinery for statutory minimum wage fixing, promoting or requiring the use of arbitration in the settlement of wage disputes and seeking to persuade the parties to collective bargaining to align their action with national economic policies. Moreover, where public enterprises account for a large part of the non-agricultural economy, it has been possible for the government to exercise substantial control over wage determination decisions through the adoption of uniform policies for the public sector (Algeria, Bangladesh, Egypt, India, Tanzania).

Another important difference is that governments carry much more weight in developing countries, even when the tendency is towards policies based on a "tripartite national consensus".

A third major difference is that, whereas wage policies in industrial market economies have been focused primarily on the adaptation to inflation, in developing countries just as much emphasis has often been given to rectifying the structural imbalances to which these economies are subject. There has frequently been much concern with reducing the gaps in income between the formal and informal sectors in both urban and rural areas so as to expand employment opportunities and improve the overall distribution of income. These objectives have complicated the preparation of wage policies and have sometimes resulted in quite erratic movements of wage incomes and dramatic declines in purchasing power for many categories of wage earners.

A final difference is that in some developing countries governments, rather than being preoccupied with restraining wages, have been concerned about the failure of wages to follow general movements in prices and incomes. The fact is that the existing wage determination machinery is often poorly adapted to the new inflationary environment. Moreover, with the notable exception of those economies where hyper-inflation conditions have existed for a number of years, wage indexation has not been widely practised in these countries. As a consequence, a number of governments have at various times decreed special cost-of-living allowances or wage increases aimed at protecting the purchasing power of wage earners. While often being effective for this

5.3

Incomes policies based on tripartite consensus

Here are three examples of countries that have successfully implemented incomes policies based on tripartite consensus.

In the 1960s gloomy employment prospects in *Singapore* prompted the adoption of a vigorous industrialisation programme including a stringent policy of wage restraint. By the end of the decade, however, economic conditions had improved markedly and the maintenance of this wage policy no longer appeared feasible or desirable. The objective shifted towards the achievement of an orderly and steady increase in wages. To foster this, the National Wages Council (NWC) was established in 1972, composed of a chairman appointed by the Government and three members each from workers', employers' and government organisations. The NWC is an advisory body with the following terms of reference: to assist in the formulation of general guide-lines on wage policy; to recommend necessary adjustments in the wage structure, with a view to developing a coherent wage system consistent with long-term economic development; to advise on desirable incentive systems for the promotion of operational efficiency and productivity in various enterprises.

The most important decisions taken by the NWC have been annual recommendations for wage increases. These recommendations, arrived at by consensus, have no obligatory force but have generally been accepted by employers and workers as the basis for negotiations. Flexibility in implementation is encouraged. In the event of disagreement, disputes are referred to the Ministry of Labour for conciliation and, failing this, to the tripartite Industrial Arbitration Court for settlement. In practice, the recommendations of the NWC have had an important impact on wage movements throughout the economy. In 1979 the NWC shifted to a "higher" wage policy intended to help restructure the national economy towards more skill-intensive and higher valued industries and services. Part of the recommended increases in wage costs has been allocated to the Skills Development Fund, which is used to promote the upgrading and retraining of workers. The Fund also ensures that the cash mobilised by the higher wage costs will benefit all the employers who take the initiative to invest in the skills of their employees.

In *Fiji*, after a period of considerable instability in economic and industrial relations, a Tripartite Forum was established in 1977, under the chairmanship of the Prime Minister, with a view to bringing about some common understanding among employers, employees and the Government on important matters of national interest, such as wages, prices, job creation and security, industrial relations and general economic and social development. Although the Forum has no statutory authority, the parties have voluntarily agreed to abide by the decisions reached. Annual remuneration adjustment guide-lines have been agreed, fixing maximum increases which unions and employers are free to negotiate, as well as the special treatment to be given to lower-paid employees, workers with scarce skills, pay anomalies and lump-sum payments. The annual agreements have also sought to promote the adoption of sound industrial relations practices and established special procedures for handling disputes over dismissals and other forms of conflict, investigating employers' claims of inability to pay and reviewing price increases for essential goods. Employer and employee contributions to the National Provident Fund have also been raised with a view to increasing the availability of local investment capital on reasonable terms for creating new employment opportunities in specified areas.

In 1977 the central organisations of employers and workers of *Tunisia* concluded a five-year "social pact" with a view to harmonising wage movements with the objectives of the Fifth Development Plan (1977-81). During this period, the parties undertook to maintain industrial peace, to increase production and to improve the purchasing power and living and working conditions of wage earners. Various government measures to further these aims were announced at the same time, such as the introduction of a system of incentives to small and medium-scale farmers in order to increase agricultural production and increase subsidies for basic foodstuffs to offset rises in prices resulting from higher wages. Wages in the private sector were to be reviewed annually at the national level on the basis of changes in the cost of living and productivity. In effect, the annual rounds of wage negotiations have been largely carried out within the framework of the tripartite National Minimum Wage Commission. In addition, a safeguard clause stipulated that wages would also be raised whenever prices increased by over 5 per cent and remained at this level for six months. In return, it was agreed that collective agreements due to terminate during the period of the social pact were not to be amended in such a manner as to lay additional financial burdens on the undertaking.

purpose, they have on occasion had some unfortunate side-effects, such as the introduction of distortions into enterprise-level wage structures and systems or the creation of confusion as to who bears the main responsibility for making regular wage adjustments: the government or the employers' and workers' organisations through the mechanism of collective bargaining.

Lastly, brief mention must be made of the countries of Eastern Europe. As a result of their centralised systems of controls on prices and wages, they have for the most part been reasonably successful in avoiding rapid rises in consumer prices. However, there has been growing recognition that these systems of control, while quite effective in limiting inflation, may hamper efforts to ensure that the goods and services produced are those most needed and that labour is used efficiently. Difficulties of price and wage fund regulation have frequently been associated with certain problems encountered by these countries: labour hoarding and shortages, the use of inefficient work or production methods, failure to co-operate in the setting of meaningful production targets, the production of poor quality goods, the accumulation of unsaleable inventories and inadequate supplies of consumer goods or poor adaptation to consumer needs. It has become clear that, in the design of wage regulation systems, there is some conflict between the objective of maintaining control over the overall growth of wages in line with planned wage targets and the objective of achieving high levels of economic performance. Responses to this dilemma over the past ten to 20 years have varied. In some of these countries (for example, Czechoslovakia, German Democratic Republic, USSR), a high degree of centralisation has been maintained in the system of wage regulation but efforts have been made to incorporate more effective incentives for good performance: for example, instead of having the wage bill based just on the gross value of output, various links have been introduced with sales, profits, material utilisation, productivity, etc., and the fixed portion of remuneration has been raised so as to limit problems of "wage drift". Elsewhere, the system of general economic management has become more decentralised, with enterprises being given more economic and financial autonomy and wage regulation becoming less direct. It is, however, in those Eastern European countries that have moved furthest in the direction of decentralisation that difficulties of "open" inflation have become the most troublesome (for example, in Hungary and Poland).

Reducing inequalities

In most industrial market economies priority has been given to improving the relative position of the lowest paid categories of workers. This has been done in various ways and to different degrees through wage adjustments that give proportionally more to the lower paid, restrictions on the pay increases of those earning above specified amounts or relatively rapid increases in statutory minimum wages.

However, the scope for compressing the wage structure has remained a matter for some debate. There have been fears that if the process is carried too far, attempts by the higher paid to re-establish their relative position would rekindle inflationary pressures. There has also been concern that if the position of the lower paid were improved too rapidly, the motivation of the skilled categories would be diminished and the lowest productivity workers could find themselves priced out of the labour market. With respect to this latter point, a parallel has been drawn between the acute unemployment among young workers and the level of their wages (OECD, 1980). It is of interest to note that in the United States, where this issue has been extensively debated, a major study of statutory minimum wages concluded that their effects on teenage unemployment had been smaller than suggested by prior research and advised against the introduction of a special lower rate for young workers (Report of the Minimum Wage Study Commission, 1981). A study of the French experience also failed to show that statutory minimum wages significantly worsened the employment prospects of the young (OECD, 1982).

Analyses of changes in wage structures during the 1970s have not been common, but one such study for selected EEC countries has revealed a number of developments suggesting that the attempts to bring about greater equality have had some discernible effects (Saunders and Marsden, 1981). Although wage structures were found to be quite stable during the 1970s, there was some evidence of a slight narrowing of the overall dispersion of pay in the United Kingdom and France. In the United Kingdom this appeared to be associated with the egalitarian provisions of some of the pay policies of the period, whereas in France it appeared to be the product of the minimum wage. In Italy a reduction in inter-industry differentials was attributed to a deliberate union policy. Moreover, in the four countries studied (France, Federal Republic of Germany, Italy, United Kingdom), the pay differential of the managerial and higher-paid non-manual occupations declined, as did the differential between skilled and manual workers. To what extent these reductions reflected the influence of accelerated inflation or egalitarian pay policies, as opposed to longer-term trends towards greater equality brought about by shifting supply and demand conditions on the labour market, remained a matter of some doubt.

The most prominent target over the past 15 years in industrial market economies for the reduction of inequalities has been the gap between male and female earnings. Many of these countries have adopted equal pay legislation making sex discrimination in pay illegal, and the principle of equal pay has received substantial support in collective bargaining agreements, government administrative orders and judicial decisions. As a result, much progress has been made towards eliminating the more blatant forms of pay discrimination such as separate pay scales for men and women. None the less, the gap between male and female earnings, although in a few countries narrowing somewhat in the wake of legislative efforts, has generally remained distressingly large, even for workers with roughly similar qualifications. It is now evident that this gap is due mainly to the concentration of women in the lower-paying occupations and industries rather than to men and women being paid differently in the same or similar jobs.

What is being done to remedy the situation?

Attention is increasingly being focused on two aspects of the problem. On the one hand, there is the widely recognised need to desegregate jobs so as to ensure that women have access to the higher-paying occupations. On the other hand, it is recognised that steps are needed to right the fact that jobs where women predominate may be poorly paid simply because they are seen as "women's work" and not because of any productivity or work-related attributes. Job evaluation or other means should be able to ensure that equal pay is applied not only for jobs that are the same or similar but also for jobs that are of "comparable worth" or, as prescribed by ILO Convention No. 100, of "equal value". A significant step in this direction was taken in 1975 when the Council of the European Communities issued a directive indicating that the principle of equal pay set out in Article 119 of the Treaty of Rome means equal pay "for the same work or for work to which equal value is attributed". The directive also indicates that, where a job classification system is used for determining pay, it must be based on the same criteria for both men and women and so drawn up as to exclude any discrimination on grounds of sex. The directive has given rise to considerable legislative activity to ensure conformity with the broadened concept of equality. So far, however, the full impact of this change and parallel changes outside the EEC is yet to be felt (Bellace, 1980).

In developing countries the attack on wage inequalities has been focused on raising what are often desperately low wages. The main instrument used has been statutory minimum wages, and over the past ten to 20 years their use has expanded considerably. Now, virtually all developing countries have minimum wage laws whose scope has been expanded to cover more and more workers. The Minimum Wage-Fixing Machinery Convention, 1928 (No. 26), had, as of January 1982, been ratified by 95 countries, making it one of the most widely adopted international instruments of the ILO. At the same time there has been a general move away from highly selective and variegated approaches to minimum wage fixing (different rates for specified types of economic activity, categories of workers and regions) and towards greater reliance on uniform structures of general minimum wages of broad coverage that not only simplify the processes of rate fixing and enforcement but also enable protection to be extended to all workers. Despite innumerable problems of practical implementation in developing countries, the principle of minimum wage fixing for all wage earners has achieved widespread acceptance in view of the need to provide some protection against the many abuses that may arise in the employment relationship in labour surplus economies and the limited scope of alternative forms of wage regulation.

Frequently, the introduction of minimum wage fixing in developing countries has been accompanied by rather ambitious expectations. In addition to bringing about major improvements in low wages, governments have sought to use minimum wage fixing as a means of controlling the general level and structure of wages prevailing throughout the economy, in line with their macro-economic policy objectives. Unlike the pattern apparent in industrial market economies, the wages actually received by many workers have often been either directly or indirectly affected by the minimum rates fixed.

With the passage of time, there has been growing recognition of the danger of trying to exercise close control over wages in the labour market or attempting to bring about major changes in the distribution of income by altering the wage structure. In particular it has been found that, if minimum wages are fixed too high, the basic objective of a reduction in poverty is unlikely to be achieved. Although poverty is likely to be reduced when minimum wages are used to raise excessively low wages to levels in line with prevailing wages, if rates are fixed so high that most wages rise significantly and the gap between the earnings of wage earners and the self-employed in both urban and rural areas is widened, then there may be a serious risk of adverse effects on employment and the distribution of income. For these reasons, there has been a growing reluctance in developing countries to use minimum wage fixing as an instrument of macro-economic policy

and a tendency to confine its role, as in the case of industrial market economies, to providing "safety-net" protection (Starr, 1981 (a)). Considerable caution was exercised during the 1970s as regards of both the size and the frequency of minimum wage adjustments, which have generally been limited to preserving purchasing power. In sharp contrast with the experience of the 1950s and the 1960s, minimum wages in most developing countries increased less rapidly than average wages or per capita national income (see table 5.9). Unfortunately, caution in the adjustment of minimum wages has on occasion been carried to the point where they have suffered substantial declines in their real value and lost all relevance, even as a device for providing limited safety-net protection (Starr, 1981 (b); ILO-PREALC, 1980; Watanabe, 1976).

Reforming wage systems and structures

Many of the principles and practices of wage administration followed in industrial economies were introduced in the period during and immediately following the Second World War. While since then the process of refining techniques and improving methods of application has continued, little in the way of entirely new conceptions or approaches seems to have gained a major foothold. During the 1970s there were none the less some indications of a number of noteworthy developments in at least a few of these countries.

To begin with, there appears to have been some movement away from traditional forms of payment by results, under which earnings are linked in an incremental fashion with measures of individual output. In part, this has reflected changes in technology and production arrangements that have made it more difficult to measure the contribution to output of individual workers and more essential to encourage co-operative, flexible, innovative and predictable behaviour. Moreover, there have been growing doubts about the motivational effectiveness of the traditional schemes and the willingness of workers to tolerate fluctuations

144

Table 5.9
Indexes of minimum wages, average wages and per capita national product at constant prices in developing countries
(average 1966-67 = 100)

Country	Minimum wage (average, 1976-77)	Average wage (average, 1976-77)	Gross per capita domestic product (average, 1976-77)	Country	Minimum wage (average, 1976-77)	Average wage (average, 1976-77)	Gross per capita domestic product (average, 1976-77)
Latin America				*Africa*			
Argentina	44	79 [a]	127	Algeria	109	..	141
Brazil	94	141 [a]	191	United Republic of Cameroon	95 [c]	..	134
Colombia	90	99	141	Central African Republic	78		111
Costa Rica	97	144	142	Chad	86		94
Ecuador	105 [b]	148	152	Congo	112	..	116
El Salvador	110	92	114	Egypt	96	99 [d]	142
Guatemala	64	69	136	Ghana	54	..	91
Mexico	140	132	123	Ivory Coast	124	..	121
Panama	84	106	123	Kenya	104	..	125
Peru	91	106	117	Libyan Arab Jamahiriya	248	..	111
Asia				Mauritania	127	..	104
Nepal	72	..	100	Morocco	94	..	143
Papua New Guinea	225	..	135	Niger	91	..	86
Philippines	54	63	133	Rwanda	81	..	138
Sri Lanka	126	128	120	Senegal	113	..	99
Turkey	143	111	150	Tanzania	110	..	124
				Togo	88	..	124
				Tunisia	130	..	175
				Zaire	40	..	99
				Zambia	73	..	98

.. = not available.
[a] 1974-75. [b] Per capita, 1968-69. [c] 1976 only. [d] 1975 only.

Source: Gerald Starr: *Minimum wage fixing: An international review of practices and problems* (Geneva, ILO, 1981), p. 194.

145

in earnings for reasons beyond their control, as well as concern about their propensity to give rise to safety and health risks and industrial conflict. The shift has been towards either time payment schemes (with or without some form of merit rating and explicit performance standards) or to payment-by-results schemes based partly at least on non-output related measures of performance or on group or enterprise indicators of performance. Where individual payment-by-results schemes have been retained, the variable portion of the pay packet has tended to be reduced.

Another development has been that, owing to changing social attitudes and equal pay or other legislation, employers have rationalised their payment practices and followed more open policies about pay. They have adapted their pay structures to make them both equitable internally and competitive externally. Particularly for non-manual workers, there has been increasing recourse to various formal job evaluation procedures, and those directly affected have been given an increasing say in the development of the new pay structures.

Another practice has been to harmonise the treatment of all categories of employees (production workers, clerical workers, etc.). Staff status arrangements have involved uniform or broadly similar sick pay and pension schemes, leave entitlements, access to canteen and other facilities, wage pay scales and methods of pay calculation.

Finally, the 1970s were marked by a growing interest in the concept of employee financial participation. In a number of countries (France, Federal Republic of Germany, Japan, Netherlands, United Kingdom, United States) various forms of individual worker profit-sharing, stock-ownership or saving schemes have been introduced. In most cases the schemes are voluntary, with or without financial incentives provided by the government, although in France and the Federal Republic of Germany financial participation has been introduced primarily on the initiative of the public authorities. Although the main goal of most of the schemes is to improve worker motivation, they are also viewed as a means of ensuring a wider distribution of wealth, reducing the antagonisms in employer-employee relations and promoting greater savings and investment (Remus, 1983). In a number of countries (especially Denmark, the Netherlands and Sweden) there have been extensive debates on the possibility of establishing large-scale capital funds that would be collectively owned by wage earners and financed through profit-sharing and payroll levies. These schemes are seen not only as vehicles for substantially augmenting savings and investment and redistributing wealth but also as a way of encouraging wage restraint and of providing workers with a more meaningful participation in enterprise-level decisions. These proposals have been strongly resisted by employers.[9]

In the planned economies of Eastern Europe[10] efforts were made to adapt the highly centralised system of wage regulation to the changing labour market and production conditions of the 1970s. The systems of basic wage rate tariffs have been modified with a view to achieving greater inter-

branch uniformity and providing appropriate incentives for workers to acquire higher skills. Moreover, increased pay is being given to workers willing to take on the more difficult work, to put up with unfavourable working conditions or to do more tasks or jobs. The widely applied payment-by-results schemes have also been modified so as to encourage not just higher levels of output but also better quality, more efficiency in the use of resources, improved labour productivity and more innovations. As in industrial market economies, changes in technology and the need to improve co-operative behaviour have resulted in more of the schemes being based on group or enterprise-level performance. The systems applied for allocating funds to enterprises for the payment of wages have been modified as well so as to take into account, in addition to indicators of the volume of production, broader measures of performance such as the productive efficiency of the enterprise and the quality of production. Incentives have also been established for the acceptance of more demanding production targets. An interesting development in this direction in the USSR has been the increasing application of the Sheyokino method, which involves the establishment of a stable, planned remuneration fund for several years. Savings in wages resulting from the use of a smaller labour force are used to finance the payment of additional wages for increases in the volume of individual production, job enlargement for workers acquiring additional skills or the payment of one-time bonuses for any suggestions aimed at raising labour productivity that are taken up. Another major innovation has been team contract work. Under this scheme a team of workers enters into a contract, on the basis of existing norms, to complete a specified project for a fixed sum of money. The team is given flexibility to organise the work in the way it sees fit and savings in the wage bill are made available for the distribution of bonuses to the team members.

In the past, wage structures in many developing countries have been plagued by large inequalities

146

that do not seem to have their origin in economic or social necessity. This has been particularly evident in Africa and Asia, where the differences in pay between the highest and lowest categories of workers inherited with independence were generally very wide. Gradually efforts have been made to introduce more egalitarian pay structures. With the rapid expansion of education in many of these countries, the justification of high pay differentials on the grounds of scarcity of workers with suitable qualifications was no longer as valid. In addition, for many of the categories in short supply, the problem was not the absence of a financial incentive to enter the occupation but rather the lack of sufficient educational or training facilities.

However, the pay structures that have emerged, while generally more egalitarian, have often suffered from serious defects. One of the more prominent of these is the close linkage that has been established in the public sector between relative pay and the general level of formal education rather than the relative labour scarcities for particular types of jobs. Too many people have been attracted to general administration and clerical work and too few into specific technical or skilled manual jobs (Hansen-Radwan, 1982). Another frequent form of imbalance is found in the pay of the top categories of civil servants. The wage restraint measures that have been applied to them have sometimes been so stringent that their pay has fallen dramatically in purchasing power and well below the levels that could be earned in the private sector or in some public enterprises. Talented officials have left the civil service and others have had their work motivation severely blunted. In some cases this has prompted governments to take steps to harmonise pay in the public service, public enterprises and the private sector. Yet another form of distortion has arisen from the proliferation of various special allowances, bonus payments and fringe benefits. Although at one time serving quite legitimate functions, many elements of total remuneration may, with the passage of time, lose their original rationale. Their retention may simply serve to complicate pay

calculations unduly, provide inappropriate incentives, give rise to disputes over unfair treatment and make the relationship between what people do and what they get paid more remote.

Finally, in view of the desperate need to improve productivity levels in many developing countries, efforts have been made to establish closer links between pay and performance. The scope for bringing about improvements in this way has been considered large, since existing levels of individual worker performance have been much below their potential, the workers generally place a high value on financial rewards and job control is mainly in their hands. However, the introduction of effective individual payment-by-results schemes has often been made quite difficult by the problems involved in fixing "accurate" production norms in the absence of trained staff and the presence of severe deficiencies in work organisation. Moreover, the operation of the schemes has sometimes been compromised by a lack of trust in the fairness of their administration or by frequent reductions in bonus earnings caused by disruptions to production for reasons beyond the worker's control. More attention has been focused on simpler approaches based on departmental, plant or enterprise-level measures of performance. In a number of countries (Bangladesh and India, for example), schemes of this type have been adopted on a wide scale. However, given the remoteness of the link between what workers do on a day-to-day basis and the measures of performance relied upon, their motivation effectiveness has sometimes appeared questionable (Khan, 1981).

The formulation of appropriate wage policies is, under the best circumstances, a very difficult process which necessarily involves striking a delicate balance between numerous conflicting goals and interests. The deteriorating economic climate has not made the task facing wage policy-makers any easier. Two main lessons appear to have emerged from recent experience. The first is the need to maintain existing wage determination mechanisms under constant critical review in order to ensure that they are capable of generating the quick responses required by rapidly changing economic conditions. There is no guarantee that approaches which operated reasonably well under conditions of ensured growth and stable prices will continue to function satisfactorily in the present economic climate. The second lesson is that various aspects of wage determination at both the enterprise and the national level will have to be reconsidered in the light of what can be expected to be a much more competitive and demanding economic environment. Practices with respect to wage levels, structures, systems and components will have to be more closely scrutinised than in the past to assess whether they are compatible with what will undoubtedly be an increased emphasis on the goal of higher productivity in the years to come.

[1] The figures for GNP and its growth in Eastern Europe are very rough estimates by the World Bank and differ from data on the net material product and its growth given in Chapter 3.

[2] H. W. Singer and R. H. Mahmood: "Is there a poverty trap for developing countries? Polarisation: Reality or myth?", in *World Development* (Washington, DC, World Bank), Vol. 10, No. 1, 1982. The existence of this delusion has been pointed out earlier, for example by D. Morawetz: *Twenty-five years of economic development, 1950-1975* (World Bank, Washington, DC, 1977), but only Singer and Mahmood have proved it statistically.

[3] Net current transfers from the rest of the world are not included in the gross domestic product.

[4] The United Nations and the ILO have a body of recommendations on these and many other factors that have a bearing on statistics.

[5] A Gini coefficient of 1 would mean that a single household was the recipient of all income; a coefficient of 0 would indicate that all households had the same income.

[6] There is a wealth of literature on the so-called "Kuznets curve". See F. Paukert, 1973.

[7] The poverty line used here has been based on the minimum income levels established by governments in national assistance programmes. The international poverty line refers to a standard uniform percentage of whatever the average personal disposable income is in each country.

[8] The term "wages" is used here in its broadest sense to cover both wages and salaries and direct and indirect forms of payment.

[9] For two conflicting views on the Swedish proposals, see R. Meidner: "Collective asset formation through wage-earner funds", and H. G. Myrdal: "Collective wage-earner funds in Sweden: A road to socialism and the end of freedom of association", both in *International Labour Review* (Geneva, ILO), May-June 1981, pp. 303-317 and 319-334.

[10] This account is based largely on unpublished monographs prepared for the ILO by D. Karpukhin, Y. Ananceva and Y. Kokin of the USSR and M. Kabaj of Poland.

Selected bibliography

Alailima, P. *Fiscal incidence in Sri Lanka* (Geneva, ILO, 1978; mimeographed World Employment Programme research working paper; restricted).

Beckerman, W. in collaboration with van Ginneken, W., Szal, R. and Garzuel, M. *Poverty and the impact of income maintenance programmes* (Geneva, ILO, 1979).

Bellace, Janice R. "A foreign perspective", in E. R. Livernash (ed.): *Comparable worth: Issues and alternatives* (Washington, DC, Equal Employment Advisory Council, 1980).

Chenery, H. *Structural change and development policy* (Washington, DC, World Bank, 1980).

Flaim, P. O. "The spendable earnings series: Has it outlived its usefulness?", in *Monthly Labor Review* (Washington, DC, United States Department of Labor), Jan. 1982.

Foxley, A.; Aninat, E.; Arellano, J.-P. *Redistributive effects of government programmes: An ILO study* (Oxford, Pergamon Press, 1979).

Hansen, B.; Radwan, S. *Employment opportunities and equity in Egypt* (Geneva, ILO, 1982).

Holtsberg, C. "Rice pricing policy" in P. Richards (ed.): *Basic needs and government policies in Thailand* (Singapore, Maruzen Asia, 1982).

Hsia, R.; Chau, L. *Industrialisation, employment and income distribution: A case study of Hong Kong* (London, Croom Helm, 1978).

ILO. *Collective bargaining in industrialised countries: Recent trends and problems*, Labour Management Relations Series, No. 56 (Geneva, 1978).

–. *L'indexation des salaires dans les pays industrialisés à economie de marché* (Geneva, 1978).

–/PREALC. *Asalariados de bajos ingresos y salarios mínimos en América latina*, Investigaciones sobre Empleo No. 18 (Santiago, Chile, 1980).

India, Ministry of Agriculture and Irrigation. *Report of the Review Committee on Pilot Intensive Rural Employment Project (PIREP)* (New Delhi, 1977).

Khan, M. A. *Incentive schemes in industries of Bangladesh* (Dacca, UNDP/ILO National Management Development Programme, 1981), Vol. 1.

Kuznets, S. "Economic growth and income inequality", in *American Economic Review* (Menasha, Wisconsin), Mar. 1955.

–. "Quantitative aspects of the economic growth of nations: VIII. Distribution of income by size", in *Economic Development and Cultural Change* (Chicago), Jan. 1963.

Lecaillon, J.; Paukert, F.; Morrisson, C.; Germidis, D. *Income distribution and economic development: An analytical survey* (Geneva, ILO, 1983).

Lee, E. "Changing approaches to rural development", in *International Labour Review* (Geneva, ILO), Jan.-Feb. 1980.

Mehran, F. *Distribution of benefits from public consumption expenditures among households in Iran* (Geneva, ILO, 1977; mimeographed World Employment Programme research working paper; restricted).

Morawetz, D. *Twenty-five years of economic development 1950 to 1975* (Washington, DC, World Bank, 1977).

Mouton, P. *Social security in Africa: Trends, problems and prospects* (Geneva, ILO, 1975).

OECD. *Youth unemployment: The causes and consequences* (Paris, 1980).

–. "The impact of minimum wages on young people's jobs: The French experience", in *OECD Observer* (Paris), No. 118, Sep. 1982.

Paukert, F. "Income distribution at different levels of development: A survey of evidence", in *International Labour Review* (Geneva, ILO), Aug.-Sep. 1973.

Remus, J. "Financial participation of employees: An attempted classification and major trends", in *International Labour Review* (Geneva, ILO), Jan.-Feb. 1983.

Richards, P.; Gooneratne, W. *Basic needs, poverty and government policies in Sri Lanka* (Geneva, ILO, 1980).

–; Leonor, M. *Education and income distribution in Asia* (London, Croom Helm, 1981).

Richards, R. "Meeting basic health care needs", in P. Richards and M. Leonor (eds.): *Target setting for basic needs* (Geneva, ILO, 1982).

Royal Commission on the Distribution of Income and Wealth: *Report No. 4: Second report on the standing reference* (London, HMSO, 1976).

–. *Background paper No. 4: The distribution of income in eight countries* (London, HMSO, 1977).

Saunders, C.; Marsden, D. *Pay inequalities in the European Communities* (London, Butterworths, 1981).

Smith, A. D. *Les problèmes de la politique des salaires dans le développement économique*, Cahiers de l'Institut international d'études sociales, Cahier No. 9, Vol. I (Paris, Librairie sociale et économique, 1969).

Starr, G. "Minimum wage fixing: International experience with alternative roles", in *International Labour Review* (Geneva, ILO), Sep.-Oct. 1981 (a).

–. *Minimum wage fixing* (Geneva, ILO, 1981 (b)).

Tan, E. *Taxation, government spending and income distribution in the Philippines* (Geneva, ILO, 1975; mimeographed World Employment Programme research working paper; restricted).

United States. *Report of the Minimum Wage Study Commission*, Vol. 1 (Washington, DC, 1981).

Vermeer, E. B. "Income differentials in rural China", in *China Quarterly* (London), Mar. 1982.

Watanabe, S. "Minimum wages in developing countries: Myth and reality", in *International Labour Review* (Geneva, ILO), May-June 1976.

Zoeteweij, H. "Anti-inflation policies in the industrial market economies", in *International Labour Review* (Geneva, ILO), Sep.-Oct. and Nov.-Dec. 1983.

Chapter 6

Social security in the highly industrialised countries

Crisis of the Welfare State . . . Challenge to social security . . . End of the all-powerful State . . . That headlines such as these should in many countries provoke fierce controversy attests, were it still necessary, how important a role social protection plays in all industrialised societies. Those who take a firm stand on the issue, however, are not always as fully informed as they should be. Basic facts are sometimes overlooked and discussion becomes obscured by learned considerations or distorted by ideological convictions.

This chapter attempts to put those facts before the reader so as to place the debate in a more objective and dispassionate context and clarify the issues involved. Beginning with a description of social security systems as they stand more than 35 years after the Second World War, it shows the breadth – and the shortcomings – of the protective network which all these societies have developed in their struggle against social insecurity. The chapter goes on to examine the factors contributing to the current difficulties and the shock to most of these systems caused by the economic crisis. It concludes with a brief look at some of the proposals that have been advanced in an effort to respond constructively to the principal questions posed by the crisis.

The role of social security in highly industrialised countries

Over the past 35 years the industrialised countries have been profoundly influenced by their social welfare systems. The objective of these systems has been, first and foremost, to give individuals and families a sense of security, to reassure them that the vagaries of social, economic and human affairs need not cause any significant decline in their standards of living. They correspond to a deep-rooted preoccupation of modern society. Social security was recognised as one of the rights of man in the Universal Declaration of Human Rights adopted by the United Nations General Assembly in 1948.

Influenced by concepts formulated in the course of the Second World War (the Beveridge report in 1942 and Recommendations Nos. 67 and 69 adopted by the International Labour Conference in 1944), social security as an expression of organised collective solidarity came to associate the idea of prevention and rehabilitation with that of compensation. Various means were employed and those used today are still based essentially on social insurance, on the one hand, originally entailing the exercise of an occupational activity, and social welfare, on the other, which includes the provision of public services for the protection of the national community as a whole.

After the Second World War social security developed quickly, either through the systematic revamping of earlier schemes, as in the United Kingdom, or through the progressive adaptation and improvement of existing institutions as in the Federal Republic of Germany. Progress was rapid and in several directions: the range of people covered and of "contingencies" provided for was extended; the efficiency of the whole system was improved. It is indeed remarkable, at least in the case of certain countries, that progress should have been maintained right up to today in spite of the unfavourable economic climate of recent years.

Broadening the scope of social security

Many countries' social security schemes, which with few exceptions concerned only a segment of wage earners in 1945, now cover the bulk of the population. The personal scope of these schemes has thus been enlarged, sometimes by extending them to the entire national or resident population from the outset, sometimes by gradually generalising the coverage afforded by existing occupational schemes.

The establishment of universal schemes – whether public service schemes or national insurance schemes – has had a radical effect, for it has meant immediate coverage for the whole population irrespective of any income-related considerations, at least in those branches (medical care, pensions, family benefits) for which universal protection is considered most justified.

As regards medical care, several countries – most recently Denmark and Italy – have followed the example of the USSR, New Zealand and the United Kingdom and instituted a national health service; others (Finland, Norway and Sweden, for example) have introduced a universal health care scheme in the form of national insurance. For pensions, the countries of the British Commonwealth, the Nordic countries and others such as Switzerland have likewise set up universal schemes. It is, however, in the field of family

benefits that such schemes are most common, France being the latest to join the majority of industrialised countries that have adopted them. In addition to the above, the Netherlands has a universal disability scheme and New Zealand a universal accident compensation scheme.

Those countries, such as Belgium, France, the Federal Republic of Germany, Italy and others, especially in continental Europe, which have retained the occupational system for all branches or for certain branches only, have all embarked upon a process of general coverage by stages.

Initially, coverage was extended to those categories of wage earners and salaried employees who were still outside the system; in a number of countries this was the case, for example, of agricultural workers, domestic employees, workers employed by small undertakings and highly paid employees. In most of these countries, the social security system now applies to all paid employees – with the notable exception of the Netherlands, which has a ceiling for coverage under its health insurance scheme, Canada and the United States, where agricultural and domestic employees are not covered for certain branches (or in certain states).

Many countries have extended the protection afforded by the system beyond paid employment to include all or part of the self-employed. The United States, for example, incorporated most of the latter in its 1955 pensions scheme. Other countries, such as France, have created special schemes for them. In some Eastern European countries social protection, which already existed for members of agricultural co-operatives, has been extended in recent years to self-employed workers in the agricultural sector. Several countries have social security arrangements for artists, ministers of the Church, members of religious congregations and communities, etc. A further step has been taken by granting self-employed workers benefits which seemed hitherto necessarily restricted to wage earners and salaried employees, such as daily sickness compensation in Luxembourg and Norway, benefits in respect of employment injuries and occupational disease in Sweden and unemployment benefits in Denmark.

Finally, a number of countries have taken steps to extend coverage to all those who tend to slip between the gaps in a social protection network based on socio-occupational criteria (mainly non-active persons). Some categories (students, for instance) have been assimilated to workers engaged in an occupational activity. In order to fill any last gaps in their system and so cover the entire population, some countries (Austria in 1977 and France in 1978) have introduced a form of personal insurance whereby anybody not already compulsorily covered is entitled to join on a voluntary basis.

Others, such as Belgium, have guaranteed a minimum social income to all members of the national community without sufficient resources. In Japan national pension and medical insurance schemes have been instituted for all residents not already covered by an occupational scheme.

Though the result has often proved highly complex, this process of gradual extension has enabled a significant number of industrial countries committed to an occupation-linked concept of social security, both in Eastern and Western Europe, to offer medical insurance, pensions and family benefits to most if not all of their population.

The link between an occupational activity and the right to social security, done away with under universal coverage, is also obviously affected by this process of generalisation. However, workers (at any rate, paid employees) continue to receive preferential treatment since they are usually covered for a larger number of contingencies and in many countries non-workers are not yet entitled to quite the same benefits, though the trend is often towards greater parity.

If we look at the material scope of these schemes, we find the same tendency towards wider coverage. Whereas the range of contingencies catered for in 1945 was still limited in many countries, the vast majority of social security schemes nowadays cover the nine internationally recognised branches listed in ILO Convention No. 102,[1] which constitutes the standard framework for such schemes. Notable exceptions include many Eastern European countries, which have no system of unemployment benefit (the right to employment being normally guaranteed), Switzerland, where insurance is only partly compulsory (though well over 90 per cent of the population belongs to a medical insurance fund), and the United States, where family benefits do not exist and state medical insurance is available only to a very small segment of the population (old people and indigents).

Although the United States has no general system of medical insurance, much of the population is privately insured. However, in the case of an insurance contracted by an undertaking, which would seem to be the usual case, losing one's job automatically entails the loss of entitlement to health care benefits. It is estimated that, because of increasing unemployment, during the past few years over 60 million United States citizens (workers and members of their family) lost the contractual medical coverage to which they were previously entitled.

Isolated instances are found of a tendency to innovate and to create new branches of social security. Several European countries, for example, have evolved collective housing or training schemes, though this is generally outside the traditional framework of social security.

More effective protection

Equally significant progress had been made since the Second World War in providing more effective protection. This has taken various forms.

153

An initial improvement was guaranteed earnings. First, many of the countries which adopted a system of uniform cash benefits have established a link – at least in the case of long-term replacement benefits – with previous earnings, whereby one can to a certain extent maintain one's earlier standard of living and thus benefit from greater security. Various methods are used, the most common (in Canada, the United Kingdom and the Nordic countries, for example) being to combine the uniform cash benefits (which became basic benefits) with complementary benefits varying according to a worker's income. Countries with only a uniform cash benefits system – mainly for short-term contingencies – have often raised the level of benefits substantially (in the Netherlands, up to the minimum wage) so as to afford genuine security, at least for the most underprivileged categories.

Secondly, and especially in the case of long-term contingencies, cash benefits have been geared to the cost of living or level of wages to compensate for inflation. While a few countries have opted for ad hoc adjustments, many others have introduced more or less automatic indexation arrangements. At least during periods of growth, a system that takes into account rising standards of living, particularly as reflected in average wages (for example in France, the Federal Republic of Germany and the Netherlands), is more advantageous, than one that makes allowance only for the price-indexed cost-of-living increases as in Sweden and the United States. Indexation can take other forms and be based on the minimum wage, as in Greece, or on the kind of mean wages-cum-price index that Finland has been using since 1977. Accelerated adjustments, as practised in Canada where cash benefits are reviewed on a quarterly rather than an annual basis, are likewise conducive to more effective protection.

Thirdly, compensatory benefits have been raised to a level more on a par with earnings, especially for short-term contingencies. In 1952 Convention No. 102 laid down minimum percentages for the various periodical payments to standard beneficiaries; though for the most part fairly modest (ranging from 40 to 50 per cent of earnings according to the branch concerned), they were comparable to those practised at the time in several industrialised countries. Today, an appreciable number of countries pay up to 100 per cent of earnings for maternity benefits and for temporary disability benefits in the event of employment injuries and occupational disease.

In the case of maternity, 16 Eastern and Western European countries now offer compensation amounting to 90 or 100 per cent of earnings. The same is true of 11 European countries in respect of employment injuries and occupational disease. The percentage in these two branches is at least 60 per cent in the bulk of the other industrialised countries with a proportional benefits system. Sickness benefits have also progressed, though at a lower level; in Luxembourg, Norway, Austria and, under certain conditions of length of employment, in several Eastern European countries, they have already reached 100 per cent.

Though not insignificant, progress has been less impressive in the case of benefits paid to persons who are no longer active. In the typical case of an average wage, the replacement rate of 40 per cent established for old-age pensions in Convention No. 102, which was still applied in the great majority of countries in the mid-1950s, is now exceeded in many instances.

Another improvement is that many countries which instituted a system of proportional benefits from the start have introduced minimum benefits, specifically in the case of persons who have ceased all activity. This means that, just as in countries with basic pensions, every person covered by the scheme is guaranteed a minimum security benefit regardless of his or her previous career. Moreover, in some cases, the law governing the payment of benefits takes into account a person's general lack of resources as well as the existence of a contingency involving a loss or reduction of a person's means of existence. The core of Australia's social security system, for instance, is a minimum guaranteed income scheme for persons who cannot work, are prevented from working or are unable to find work. Other countries have combined a contingency protection system with a similar form of general protection: this is true of the United Kingdom with its Supplementary Benefits Act and Family Income Supplements Act, of Belgium which has instituted a right to minimum means of existence, and of Israel which recently adopted a law on guaranteed income.

Another method of improving the effectiveness of social protection has been to increase the maximum period during which benefits are payable. In respect of maternity, for example, the duration of benefits, which in the 1950s was generally speaking 12 weeks, has been raised to 35 weeks in Finland, 31 weeks in Italy, six months in the Federal Republic of Germany, the Democratic Republic of Germany and Sweden, 20 weeks in Hungary and 18 weeks in Norway. Unemployment benefits have followed suit, and the maximum period, which tended to be 26 weeks, has in a number of countries been extended to one year or more (two years in the Netherlands), though the level of benefits is usually reduced after a specified period (in Belgium there is no time-limit on unemployment benefits). As for medical care benefits, the restrictions on duration which were the rule prior to the Second World War have almost everywhere been lifted. Except in a few social security schemes, such as in Portugal and Turkey, medical care is available for as long as necessary.

Protection has also been improved by diversifying benefits. Health care benefits, for example, have been broadened to include dental care, eye care and certain preventive treatment. Under the family benefits branch, several countries have added new benefits to the traditional child allowances. These are mainly benefits payable in the event of a birth and, here and there, various other benefits for orphans, disabled persons, etc. France has a particularly wide range of family benefits; the general family maintenance benefit (regular and supplementary family allowances) may be combined with pre- and post-natal maternity benefits and such special benefits as housing allowances, special education allowances and allowances payable at the beginning of each school year.

Several countries have followed Hungary's example of introducing benefits for mothers (and sometimes fathers) who have to give up work to look after a sick child. Sweden recently instituted a special benefit enabling either parent to interrupt work for 90 days during the first eight years of a child's life. In another direction, unemployment benefit schemes have been both refined and extended, for example to include young people and older workers.

It is impossible to detail here all the ways in which protection has been reinforced. One should perhaps mention, however, that a deliberate effort has been made to adapt protection to the requirements of elderly persons and the handicapped and that many countries have broadened their definition of employment injury, occupational disease and disability.

Social security as an essential component of national policies

Social protection schemes on such a scale leave a profound imprint on industrial societies, where they have frequently become an essential component of various aspects of the country's social policy – health, family, old age and even employment and housing. They play an important part in the day-to-day life of workers and their families and in the national economy.

For workers the compensatory and supplementary income available under a social security scheme and the facilities it affords for obtaining medical care are an enormous social achievement. This indirect income not only accounts for a large proportion of household incomes (34.5 per cent in France in 1982) but offers workers an assurance that they can rise above the poverty that their parents or grandparents may have had to endure. Any threat to this social achievement is therefore bound to affect them profoundly. Just how deeply they are attached to it has been shown in various opinion polls and is reflected in the particular sensitivity of trade unions to any policy liable to reduce existing guarantees.

Given the developments described in the two previous sections, it is hardly surprising that, in financial terms, social security should play a more and more significant role in the national economy.

Between 1953 and 1977 the budget earmarked for social security expenditure multiplied by 3.3 in the United Kingdom, by 4.9 in the United States, by 6 in France and by 7.9 in Sweden (discounting the effect of inflation and of changes in the size of the population). In the OECD countries social security receipts in the strict sense (social insurance and assimilated schemes, including family benefits programmes) ranged in 1960 between 3 and 12 per cent of the domestic product. By 1977 the figure had risen to between 7 and 23 per cent. In the Eastern European planned-economy countries it stood at this time at between 7.5 and 16 per cent of the net material product. Since 1977, because of rapidly declining economic growth rates, the cost of social security as a percentage of national resources has tended to rise even more quickly. Using the definition adopted by the European Economic Community for its social protection accounts (considerably broader than that used by the ILO in its survey of the cost of social security), expenditure under this heading in 1980 in the Community at large represented 26 per cent of the gross national product as opposed to 19 per cent in 1970, with individual percentages ranging from 21.4 in the United Kingdom to 30.7 in the Netherlands.

Because of the volume of expenditure involved, these transfers have a considerable effect on the economy. In the post-war decades they have played a significant role in the prosperity of the industrial economies.

In general terms, social security programmes have helped to maintain a climate of security and stability. "Satisfactory social protection increases the individual's sense of security. It facilitates social relations, contributes to industrial peace and helps to avert disputes. The social system must not be looked upon as part of the inevitable socialisation which the productive sector is obliged to accept under a liberal regime. There is a beneficial – though inconspicuous – link between social welfare and economic profitability" (report of the Committee on Social Protection and the Family for the preparation of France's Eighth Plan).

Social security is conducive to the development of a country's productive forces. A well-cared for workforce is more productive, and therefore more profitable. By replacing lost earnings or raising an inadequate income, social security makes for a more diffuse purchasing power and increases the outlets for consumer goods. It has accordingly been a major factor of sustained economic growth. By making it possible to satisfy the demand for certain (e.g. health) goods and services whose cost is beyond the means of most households and by redistributing income (e.g. from the healthy to the sick), it encourages the development of sectors of the economy (such as the health sector and the leading industries associated with it).

In times of crisis, it has a steadying effect. Social transfers act as "buffers" at both the national and the local level, where they can prevent a process of contraction overtaking the most sorely affected regions. Particularly in respect of unemployment, moreover, certain benefits tend to facilitate the indispensable restructuring of the system of production. They can, in this regard, be thought of as the tribute which society is prepared to pay to progress.

There is, however, the other side of the coin: the apparently irresistible increase in social expenditure, a source of genuine concern which the current economic crisis has done nothing to mitigate.

Social security systems and the economic crisis

Social protection has come up against the full force of the economic crisis which descended on the world in the 1970s. Already towards the end of the 1960s serious difficulties were beginning to appear, precisely because of the extent and speed of its expansion which available resources were insufficient to finance. In many countries social security had for a long time been in a state of endemic financial crisis. The widening of the scope and raising of the level of protection were not alone to blame for this state of affairs. A number of autonomous factors contributed to the rise in costs. Though it is hardly possible here to describe them all, two of these factors are salient enough to call for a few remarks: the increasing cost of medical care and the ageing of populations.

Rising costs

The problem of containing expenditure on health

In the years following the Second World War it was generally believed that a comprehensive health care programme would reduce morbidity and that, as consumption of health services became stabilised, the overall proportion of the gross national product devoted to such expenditure would not vary significantly over time. This has not proved to be the case. Over the past 15 to 20 years the cost of health care provided under social security schemes has soared, leaving the economic indicators behind. Between 1960 and 1977 the cost of medical care benefits at constant prices multiplied by at least five times in many countries, including Canada, Finland, France, Japan and the

United States. Moreover, as a proportion of the gross domestic product, expenditure under this heading rose, for example, from 2.7 per cent in 1960 to 5.7 per cent in 1974 in the Federal Republic of Germany, from 2.3 per cent in 1959 to 7.1 per cent in 1970 in Canada, from 1.7 per cent in 1960 to 5.1 per cent in 1974 in the Netherlands and from 2.2 per cent in 1960 to 7.3 per cent in 1974 in Sweden.

The trend is obviously attributable in part to the expansion of social security programmes that have made medical care available to far more people than before. But above all it is the reflection of a general phenomenon encountered in all industrialised countries: the increasingly rapid progression of the share of the health sector in economic and social activity in general. To a large extent, this progression is independent of the socialisation of the cost of health care. As a proportion of the gross domestic product, for example, the pattern has been much the same in the United States and in France between 1950 and 1975 rising from 3.8 per cent to 8 per cent in the former and from 3 per cent to 7.3 per cent in the latter – even though, unlike France, the United States has no comprehensive social security medical care programme. This rapid progression must be seen against the changing patterns of consumption as the cost of living rises: the consumption of health care has risen faster than that of traditional products such as food and clothing but less rapidly than the consumption of durable goods and insurance.

There are many reasons for this. Technical progress has opened up enormous possibilities as regards the effectiveness of health care, but the cost involved can be astronomical, especially as the larger the number of illnesses than can be cured the larger the number of potential patients; the behaviour pattern of both patient and doctor is becoming geared to a higher level of consumption. The supply of health care has expanded rapidly: medical personnel in particular have increased enormously in number (in the United States alone the increase is expected to be 50 per cent between

1980 and 1990) and the relative earnings of paramedical personnel are in many cases rising. The population of the industrialised countries is ageing and elderly people require more frequent, longer and more costly medical care. Higher standards of living and education likewise encourage a more frequent use of medical care. The evolution of society, too, contributes to the rising consumption of health care, partly because the "right to health" has become a basic right and partly because industrial society is more and more pathogenic: it produces sick people and fosters diseases, and this again leads to an increasing use of medication. Finally, there are those who consider that the booming cost of health in certain countries can be ascribed to the fact that the prevailing social security system operates within the framework of the liberal organisation of the medical profession.

Whatever the forces causing the volume, quality and price of health care to increase may be, their impact on the expanding cost of social security is a source of great concern to the public authorities, which are torn between the two irreconcilable objectives of containing the increase in social security contributions and guaranteeing equal access for all to the best available health care. No definitive answer has yet been found to this problem, which the economic crisis has done a great deal to aggravate. Some countries have taken or are planning to take measures aimed at restricting demand. Benefits looked upon as superfluous have been cut or done away with altogether, such as thermal cures in the Federal Republic of Germany and Italy and "placebos" in France; above all, patients are sometimes required to make a greater financial contribution, as is the case in several European countries. Another way of curbing expenditure on health has been not so much to manipulate social security legislation as to rationalise the supply of health care (investment in hospitals, management of medical institutions, medical demography, the pharmaceuticals market), by concentrating on the price structure of medical goods and services, on the remuneration of medical practitioners and the exercise of their profession, etc., and by trying to combat the pathogenic characteristics of society more effectively.

But the effectiveness of these measures may be very much restricted by a variety of constraints of a historical, political, psychological and economic nature. Thus, it may be difficult to develop prevention in times of crisis, because of the high costs involved. The success of efforts to link prevention with the method of financing – for example, by taxing products such as tobacco and alcohol that are health hazards – has so far been only limited. Attempts to contain expenditure may also conflict with the objectives of unemployment policy: for example, a country may wish to create new jobs in the health sector when prospects elsewhere are bleak (Austria, France, Sweden), but this raises the issue of the financial cost to the sector.

Some countries have, in recent years, nevertheless managed to curb the annual rate of growth of expenditure on health care benefits (from 18.1 per cent in 1974-75 to 8.6 per cent in 1978-79 in the Netherlands, for example); yet it still outpaces economic growth. Given the very gloomy economic prospects, containing expenditure on medical care is therefore more than ever on the agenda. What is needed are lasting solutions, particularly since it has been found that, more than in other branches, major savings can be made without undermining the rights of the persons protected. Keeping expenditure within bounds, one might add, would seem to be easier in countries whose social security objectives are the responsibility of a national health service, such as the planned economies of Europe, the United Kingdom and Italy, although this may be at the cost of severe constraints on supply.

One possibility is to influence the demand for health care by modifying the ratio between public and private expenditure; but this runs the risk of reducing access to such care for the most under-

Table 6.1
Persons aged 65 or more as a percentage of the total population

Country	1970	1980	2000
Bulgaria	9.6	12.0	15.0
Canada	7.9	8.8	9.8
Finland	9.2	12.1	13.9
Greece	11.1	15.9	17.6
Hungary	11.5	13.7	15.0
Italy	10.7	12.9	14.7
Japan	7.1	8.6	13.2
Luxembourg	12.7	14.8	15.9
Poland	8.3	10.0	12.5
Romania	8.6	10.2	12.5
Spain	9.8	11.4	13.6
Switzerland	11.4	12.2	13.5
USSR	7.8	10.1	12.2
United States	9.8	10.7	10.9

Source: ILO: *Labour force estimates and projections, 1950-2000* (Geneva, 1977).

privileged. More could be done to influence supply in such a way as to eliminate wastage, particularly as regards hospitalisation (for example, by imposing restrictive budgets). This is an area in which a primary care strategy could be effective. Longer term solutions whose importance this strategy has revealed are also envisaged, such as bringing an education factor into play with a view to modifying the patterns of behaviour of medical practitioners and the public.

The consequences of an ageing population

The ageing of the population is a general trend in most industrialised countries. Partly as a result of declining birth rates and partly because of higher life expectancy, the share of elderly people in the total population has risen sharply over the past 30 years. Though several countries (Austria, Ireland and the Federal Republic of Germany, for instance) are currently experiencing a reversal of the trend, the proportion is expected to continue increasing in certain other countries, particularly those where the phenomenon has hitherto been less marked. This is illustrated in table 6.1.

Within the group of elderly persons, the oldest segment of the population is steadily increasing in size. Already, persons aged 75 and over account for 4 to 5 per cent of the total population and 30 to 38 per cent of the population over the age of 65.

The phenomenon has a direct bearing on the increased cost of social security. As we have seen, an ageing population entails a greater use of health care facilities. Obviously, moreover, the impact is bound to be greatest for the branch concerned with old-age benefits. Combined with the extension and maturing of old-age benefits schemes, with improved benefits and with the lowering of the retirement age, the relative increase in the number of older people leads to a steady and unavoidable increase in expenditure on this particular branch. Benefits paid under pensions schemes (old-age, invalidity, survivors) are more and more often the biggest item of expenditure of social security systems. In many countries (Austria, Federal Republic of Germany, Italy, Netherlands, USSR) over half the expenditure on social security already goes into pensions; in several cases, the rising cost of pensions is expected to continue and even to accelerate after 1985. Elsewhere, on the other hand, there are signs that the percentage of the population over the age of retirement is declining slightly.

The population structure is especially important because of the general tendency to lower the age of entitlement to pension, as a result either of workers' demands or of official action to take some of the pressure off the employment market. Advancing the age of retirement obviously increases the number of old-age pensioners. For many industrialised countries, lowering the retirement age from 65 to 60 would have the effect of increasing their number by 30 to 50 per cent, which would mean a considerable extra financial burden on the active population.

In so far as the ageing of the population is partly attributable to a declining birth rate, one might expect the rising cost of pensions to be offset by a lowering of family benefits. In certain countries this does indeed seem to be the case. In Luxembourg the share of pensions in total social security expenditure between 1960 and 1977 rose from 43.7 to 52.9 per cent whereas that of family benefits dropped from 19.9 to 10.7 per cent. In several countries, such as France and Italy, the decrease in the share of family benefits was actually much greater than the increase in the share of pensions, mainly owing to a sharp decline in the purchasing power of the former. In other countries such as Austria and the United Kingdom, however, the trend was quite different. In practice, the social security cost of an extra pensioner is only marginally offset by the saving on one less dependent child. Besides, the recent tendency of certain countries to improve family benefits as part of their family and demographic policy inevitably further reduces this kind of compensatory effect.

The rising cost of old age therefore continues to pose serious problems, and notably that of its financing. Under pay-as-you-go schemes, a steadily decreasing number of active persons are called upon to bear the cost of an increasing population of older people. In some countries at least, this raises the question of just how far solidarity among generations is prepared to go.

As far as long-term solutions are concerned, the first step must be to counteract the ageing process – both the ageing of the population as a whole (by raising the birth rate) and the ageing of the individual. A more immediate solution is to reorganise pension schemes so as to cut costs by making them more rational and, at the same time, more equitable, though this may well come up against fierce opposition, particularly at the psychological level. Reversing the current trend towards a lower retirement age would have the same effect, but this is only possible if the employment situation is improved. An interesting case in point is the USSR where, although retirement at 60 is an established social gain, the labour market situation is such that pensioners are encouraged to carry on working. Over 30 per cent

of old persons on invalidity and old-age pensions actually do so. By limiting the possibility of combining a wage with an old-age pension (though the permissible limit is in fact quite high), the cost of pensions is prevented from becoming excessive even though the proportion of older people in the Soviet population is rising.

The economic crisis and its repercussions on social security

Even before the economic reversal of 1973-74, it was obvious that social security costs in industrialised countries were increasing. So long as national income maintained a steady, rapid growth and unemployment remained at an acceptable level, the situation was manageable, at least for a time; and social progress could thus be maintained. Inflation, though not unknown, was if anything an advantage as far as social expenditure was concerned since it was the receipts that were the first to rise.

This state of equilibrium was completely upset by the economic crisis. Simultaneously, there was a drop in receipts, whether based on the payroll, on total income or on output, and an increase in financial commitments caused by the growing volume of certain items of expenditure (unemployment benefits, early retirement pensions, etc.). In other words, whereas social protection had hitherto benefited from relatively favourable economic conditions, the situation after 1973 changed radically, leaving the social security systems torn between opposing forces.

Costs increase all the more as economic performance declines. At the same time, some items of expenditure seem to be irreducible, especially if they are linked to the structure of the population. Yet the system is also expected to cushion the crisis by ensuring that certain consequences of the malfunctioning of the economy are socially tolerable. Moreover, just as social expenditure begins to appear excessive, the economic crisis (and the transformation of society) highlights the inadequacy and shortcomings of social

Table 6.2
Unemployment benefits as a percentage of total social security benefits and of the gross domestic product

Country	1971		1980	
	As a percent-age of total social security benefits	As a percent-age of the GDP	As a percent-age of total social security benefits	As a percent-age of the GDP
Belgium	4.4	0.8	10.4	2.7
Denmark	4.1	0.8	11.9	3.2
Germany (Fed. Rep.)	0.6	0.1	3.7	1.0
France	1.1	0.2	6.5	1.6
Ireland	5.4.	0.7	8.3	1.7
Italy	1.2	0.2	1.9	0.4
Luxembourg	0.0	0.0	2.1	0.5
Netherlands	3.1	0.6	6.3	1.9
United Kingdom	5.6	0.9	8.6	1.8

Source: Eurostat (Statistical Office of the European Communities): *Social accounts – Accounts of social protection in the EEC 1970-1975*, and *Social Protection*, Statistical Bulletin, 1-1982; United Nations: *Yearbook of National Accounts Statistics 1979*.

protection and the need to cater to unsatisfied requirements. It is a vicious circle that is hard to break.

Social security as a cushion against the crisis: the cost of unemployment

Unquestionably at the root of the current difficulties encountered by social security systems in market-economy industrial countries is the steady rise of unemployment, whose disruptive effects were analysed in Chapter 2. Its impact on social security takes various forms.

In systems financed by contributions, the deteriorating employment situation has a direct impact on receipts as the number of contributors declines. At the same time, it has become a major factor in rising cost, as can be seen from table 6.2 showing the proportion of unemployment benefits (including early retirement benefits) in total social security benefits and in the gross domestic product in the countries of the European Economic Community.

By way of example, unemployment benefits in France rose in absolute terms from 722 million francs in 1970 to 21,000 million francs in 1979 and, in the Federal Republic of Germany, from DM.722 million in 1970 to 15,048 million in 1981.

Moreover, unemployment benefits – or the social welfare payments that may take over from unemployment benefits [2] – are not the only items of social security expenditure generated by unemployment. Other branches that are not included in these figures are also affected: old-age pensions, invalidity pensions, sometimes socio-occupational rehabilitation benefits for victims of unemployment, and even family benefits when they are designed to encourage women not to seek or continue in employment.

As we have seen, the higher cost of old-age pensions is due in part to the lowering of the actual age of retirement and this, to a considerable degree, is bound up with the employment situation. In the case of invalidity pensions, the concept of an invalidity carrying an entitlement to benefit broadened during the 1970s to allow for the additional difficulty for persons suffering from an infirmity of finding work in times of mass unemployment. In the Netherlands the rapid increase in the number of persons receiving invalidity pensions has been found to be linked to the worsening economic situation. In Italy, too, where the number of beneficiaries of invalidity pensions (over 5 million) is slightly greater than that of old-age pensioners, the increase is in good measure attributable to underemployment, numerous beneficiaries being concentrated in the least developed parts of the country. In addition, there is the cost of maintaining certain social benefits for the unemployed (health care, the counting of periods of unemployment for old-age insurance purposes, etc.) for which there are no corresponding receipts in payroll systems.

In practice, social security is not only used to compensate for the prejudice caused by a malfunctioning economic system; it also plays an impor-

Table 6.3
Social security receipts[a] as a percentage of the gross domestic product or net material product

Country	1960	1970	1977
Austria	10.75	13.93	16.19
Belgium	10.61	14.13	10.08
Canada	4.69	8.73	11.33
Finland	4.81	7.59	12.83
France	9.24	–	18.83
German Dem. Rep.	–	13.15	16.16
Germany (Fed. Rep.)	11.25	13.02	17.75
Hungary	8.75	10.95	15.13
Italy	9.81	13.27	16.72
Luxembourg	11.81	13.92	21.78
Netherlands	9.91	17.60	23.25
Switzerland	5.86	7.84	12.26
Sweden	6.77	14.10	20.35
USSR	6.84	7.87	9.42
United States	3.44	5.58	7.06

– Figure not known.

[a] Not including complementary schemes, which in some countries represent a significant factor.

Source: ILO surveys.

tant role in employment policy, by exempting certain categories of workers such as young persons from contributing to the scheme (as in Belgium, France and Italy), by taking older workers and sometimes women off the labour market, and so on. This tendency to use certain social security mechanisms in what may well be a vain attempt to combat unemployment further undermines the systems' financial equilibrium.

Is the cost of social security too high? Restricting the volume of social transfers and financing

Because it has to carry the added burden of high unemployment, social security often finds itself in the dock. It is accused of being partly to blame for the current situation and of preventing any satisfactory solution. There are two reasons for this: the so-called "drift" of social transfers which are already said to play too large a role in the economy and are continuing to increase, and the excessive level of social security contributions payable by undertakings. This raises the whole question of the method of financing.

Limiting social transfers

The point has already been made that in a number of countries social security expenditure began to accelerate from 1970 onwards. Moreover, as economic growth declined, the share of such expenditure in domestic production increased rapidly through the 1970s. This is illustrated in table 6.3 showing the trend of receipts as a percentage of the gross domestic product or net material product (NMP).[3] The table is based on ILO surveys of the cost of social security and comprises both social insurance and assimilated schemes and family benefits schemes, i.e. the bulk of national social security systems.[4]

One question which is raised more and more frequently is whether there is a point beyond which public social security contributions become intolerable and whether the volume of social transfers should therefore be limited.

Setting a limit on social security contributions means assessing society's capacity to bear the cost of social protection. This, however, is an extremely difficult undertaking and entails a fair degree of subjective judgement. There are two aspects to be considered, the economic aspect and the psychological aspect.

Economically speaking, the more highly developed social security systems have a number of effects, both positive and negative.

On the negative side, there is above all social security's impact on investment and on the cost of labour.

By and large, the existing systems are in effect a means of redistributing the income of the rich towards the poor. As the tendency to save is generally greater among the rich, this redistribution reduces their savings capacity and thus limits the resources available for investment.

As to the cost of labour, it must be borne in mind that, along with wages, social security contributions are part and parcel of total remuneration. Unless it corresponds to an increase in production, a rapid increase in this total remuneration adds to the financial strain. It has an inflationary effect and may run counter to a country's employment policy. Given a situation where, in the interests of the economy, the total wage bill has to be kept down, there are bound to be repercussions on the wages themselves and on both the employers' and the workers' social security contributions. Where, then, should the emphasis be placed? On wages and salaries or on social security contributions? It is of course for each society, and especially the working population, to decide for itself. One can, however, observe that societies that have reached a fairly high level of prosperity tend to give precedence to income security and to such matters as health.

On the positive side, there is first and foremost the fact that social security systems contribute to solving the social problems caused by a depression. This contribution has already been outlined above, and it is fair to say that, so far at least, the bulk of the unemployed have not on the whole joined the marginal population of society. From the social standpoint, the major difference between the current economic crisis and the Depression of the 1930s is precisely the existence of powerful social security systems.

These systems are not just a kind of social buffer. They also act as an economic buffer. If social security did not help to stimulate demand by transferring resources to the unemployed, the present crisis would be more severe. People who harp on the excessive cost of labour or the need to encourage savings for investment purposes tend to overlook the fact that the economic process is the result of the interplay of supply and demand. Even with large-scale saving, investment would serve

no purpose if the resulting products found no buyers. In the same way, even if the cost of labour is low, employment generated by the domestic market will not grow as long as there is no effective demand for the goods and services produced. Here again, one can argue that current social security systems have done much more to stimulate demand than in the 1930s, when they were more rudimentary. Be that as it may, the fact remains that, though social security is a system of redistribution that can absorb shocks in the short and medium term, its long-term existence can only be guaranteed by a strong economy in which there is a correlation between the advantages it is supposed to provide and productivity.

From the psychological standpoint, the question is whether, as social security contributions increase, there comes a point where they can no longer be tolerated because they discourage the beneficiaries from working and the undertakings from continuing to operate.[5] The level of tolerance may vary from country to country, and particularly according to the way the burden on society is shared. Generally speaking, however, although a rapid increase in income makes it more easy to bear the extra financial burden, in times of economic stagnation any attempt to raise the level of contributions quickly becomes less and less readily accepted. It is therefore essentially the psychological as well as the ideological and political impact that determines the limit on social security contribution, but it is a limit that there is no way of calculating.

Though it is generally agreed that there must be an absolute limit to the growth of social benefits, the fact remains that it is quite impossible to pinpoint and that it varies with time. There would therefore seem to be little future in trying to devise a "golden rule" for fixing the share of national income to be set aside for such benefits. At least in certain countries and in the present economic situation, however, there are those who contend that social security budgets should not be allowed to grow faster than the gross domestic product.

Changing the method of financing

In the face of the rising cost of social protection, more and more official attention is being given to the question of funding. Second thoughts have been expressed about the value of traditional methods of financing which are proving less and less able to meet rising costs and in any case are not suited to the development of social security and the broadening of its functions. A rationalisation of the financing of social security systems therefore seems increasingly called for.

The method of financing varies from scheme to scheme. For the most part it relies on contributions from employers and/or workers based on wages in the case of schemes run along social insurance lines and on taxes in the case of those that have evolved out of social welfare schemes. Though the structure of financing has changed a great deal over the years, there are still sharp contrasts from one industrialised country to another, as we can see from table 6.4.

These differences apart, payroll contributions are the predominant method of financing in most industrial countries. In the European Economic Community 68.9 per cent of expenditure in 1980 was funded by contributions; of these the share borne by the employer has, with a few rare exceptions such as the Netherlands, become much greater than that borne by the worker. The most frequent method of keeping receipts in step with rapidly rising costs has been to raise the level of contributions from undertakings, which is already close to 40 per cent of direct remuneration in several countries such as France, Italy and Sweden. Table 6.4 shows that in certain countries employers' contributions account for nearly two-thirds of the total resources of the social security system.

Table 6.5 illustrates how widely the share of social security contributions in total labour costs can vary from country to country.

In Italy the share is over 30 per cent of the total cost, whereas in Denmark it is less than 5 per cent.

Table 6.4

Percentage distribution of social security revenue according to origin, 1977

Country	Persons insured	Em- ployers	Public auth- orities	Capital return	Other receipts
Belgium	20.8	43.1	32.7	2.7	0.7
Canada	9.1	15.0	70.9	4.9	0.1
Denmark	2.6	3.4	90.9	3.1	–
Finland	17.5	63.8	10.9	7.8	–
France	23.9	65.4	8.7	1.2	0.8
German Dem. Rep.	23.5	26.0	50.4	–	0.1
Germany (Fed. Rep.)	38.3	39.6	19.8	1.6	0.7
Hungary	16.2	46.7	36.5	–	0.6
Italy	15.8	65.3	14.4	3.0	1.5
Japan	30.6	30.1	22.2	8.7	8.4
Netherlands	44.1	36.3	14.6	4.5	0.5
Switzerland	48.2	24.5	21.8	4.8	0.7
Sweden	2.0	65.1	20.5	12.4	–
United States	38.8	52.0	6.2	3.0	–

– Magnitude nil or negligible.

Source: ILO: *The cost of social security: Tenth international inquiry, 1975-1977* (Geneva, 1981).

Yet in spite of the fact that the Danish social security scheme is financed almost entirely by taxes, the cost of labour in the country has increased. It is therefore difficult to maintain that the increased cost of labour can be put down to social security contributions. Many other factors are involved, including the net wage and the general level of taxation. However, when all the factors making up the total cost of labour grow faster than productivity, then in the long term one can expect a slower rate of employment creation and a higher rate of inflation, or both.

Many people nevertheless hold that employment would benefit from a method of financing that was more neutral vis-à-vis the various factors of production, and specifically if labour-intensive undertakings were relieved of some of the financial burden. Various reforms along this line have already been suggested and, in some cases,

Table 6.5

Social security contributions as a percentage of the total cost of industrial manpower, 1978

Country	Percentage
Belgium	22.3
Denmark	4.2
France	25.8
Germany (Fed. Rep.)	20.1
Italy	32.1
Luxembourg	14.4
Netherlands	24.1
United Kingdom	15.1

Source: Eurostat (1981): *Wages and income*, Rapid information 1-1981, and *Social indicators, 1960-1978*.

implemented, such as substituting the value added for wages as the basis for calculating contributions (though the positive impact of this method on employment is contested) or introducing a bias in favour of undertakings employing more labour (Finland has three levels of contributions that are inversely proportional to labour intensiveness). A less controversial arrangement is to remove the ceiling on contributions in countries where it still exists (France and the Federal Republic of Germany, for example), as such ceilings would seem to be prejudicial to employment creation.

In countries where funding is mainly based on payroll contributions, it has been suggested that greater reliance on taxation could help the employment situation in so far as the higher taxes did not unduly penalise the undertakings. A component of this kind would also serve to adapt the financing mechanism to the particular nature of the benefits (benefits independent of a person's income would be financed out of general taxation) and to share the cost more equitably. It is felt that a reform along these lines, entailing a reassessment of the entire structure of compulsory taxation and social security contributions, would enable financing to be diversified and thereby contribute to a more balanced budget. Funding would thus be less at the mercy of the ups and downs of the economic

situation; efficiency, too, could benefit from an optimum distribution of the cost of social protection. By contrast, countries such as Denmark, where most of the receipts come out of public funds, and the United States, where opposition against what is seen as high taxation is strong, are talking of raising the share of contributions, in the first instance, and maintaining a strictly contributory system of financing, in the second. In the USSR the contributions of undertakings were recently raised substantially so as to reduce the share borne by the State, to finance improved benefits and to use manpower more rationally.

Is expenditure on social security too low? Gaps in social protection

While on the one hand there is pressure to restrict social security rights so as to cut back, or at least contain, a level of expenditure considered to be overloading the economy, at the same time attention is being drawn to gaps in current social protection systems and to their inability to cope effectively with all the repercussions of the crisis. Above all, a great deal is made of the fact that pockets of "poverty", which before the crisis still existed in all industrialised countries, are tending in the present situation to grow. Poverty, however, is a complex phenomenon which derives above all from an accumulation of handicaps for which social security legislation is only a partially effective remedy.

That specific problems of protection exist for several categories of unremunerated or particularly vulnerable persons is undeniable. The protection of women in the home, for example, depends on the benefits to which the husband is entitled; yet in most countries women carry very little insurance if they are widowed or disabled or abandoned by their husband. Many women's careers are interrupted because of the need to devote time to bringing up their children; consequently, the old-age benefits they receive are very meagre. Some categories of migrant workers are still badly covered, too, especially those from Third World countries; the network of international agreements on the subject is quite inadequate, and some agreements are in any case incomplete. Moreover, in many countries that have based their social security system on occupational schemes, handicapped persons who became disabled before ever being employed form a category which is still not covered by social security.

The level of certain benefits, such as survivors' benefits, continues to be too low. Furthermore, unless the adjustment of long-term benefits is guaranteed, they tend to be eaten away by inflation. The right to benefit of young school-leavers and of married women entering the labour market is generally limited. The inadequacy of certain benefits is demonstrated by the growth of social welfare. In the United Kingdom in 1978, 20 per cent of pensioners and widows over the age of 60 were receiving welfare benefits. In the same country the number of beneficiaries of social welfare has increased steadily since 1948. Studies conducted in several countries indicate that older people account for a substantial proportion of those living below or close to the poverty line. Without social security benefits, the proportion would be much greater.

Although many countries have introduced legislation extending the period during which benefits are payable, unemployment benefits currently pose severe problems in this respect. As we have seen, the average period of unemployment is tending to lengthen. Consequently, many of the unemployed have now reached the end of their period of entitlement and have only welfare to turn to. Social welfare – which is an integral part of social security – is supposed to come into play essentially in cases of indigence, whereas "regular" benefits (such as social insurance benefits, etc.) are not necessarily restricted to the most under-privileged. A more global approach is, however, possible: in Belgium, for example, a 1974 Act established a right to minimum means of survival for any person in a situation such that neither his work nor his personal income nor his social security allowances can provide him with suffi-

cient resources. Sweden on the other hand, in a recently proposed reform, chose not to recognise the concept of an unconditionally guaranteed minimum income for all for fear of encouraging unjustified transfers in favour of non-priority categories.

Given the structure of most contributory schemes, it is also apparent that current systems do not necessarily reduce social inequalities. What is known as vertical redistribution (from higher income to lower income categories) varies in fact from country to country, according to the system of benefits and, above all, of contributions. While quite effective in certain cases, especially in countries where social welfare arrangements play a more important role – such as the Scandinavian countries and the Netherlands and under the pension scheme of the United States – this redistributive effect is less marked in countries such as Belgium and France. On the other hand, horizontal redistribution – from the active to the non-active population, for instance – is generally quite substantial. Both contributions and benefits may also suffer from a kind of distortion whereby the more well-to-do groups may acquire a relatively larger share of the benefits (known as the "Matthew effect").[6]

These few examples show that much still remains to be done to make social security schemes more effective and to share the financial burden as equitably as possible. For any progress to be made in this direction, it is widely felt that socio-economic policies must be more consistent, particularly as regards the necessary links between taxation and social security, on the one hand, and between social security and an unemployment policy that is not just a set of ad hoc measures, on the other.

A more streamlined social security system and a more consistent social policy are reforms for which a number of countries have felt a need for some years now. Unfortunately, an unfavourable economic climate and the resulting distortions have made it more difficult, though no less necessary, to adopt corrective measures that take account of all available resources.

The debate today

This being the situation, governments are in a great quandary. Because of the constraints imposed by an economic crisis which seems to be more structural than transitory, they find it impossible to allow social security to continue developing as it has been but are at a loss to decide what kind of reforms are indispensable.

Obviously, there is no miracle solution. Ever since the 1970s governments have been producing a series of reports on the social security outlook; for the most part, their recommendations are still being studied. From time to time measures have been adopted aimed at adjusting, restructuring or curbing expenditure by cutting down on social benefits, but this would seem to have been more often under the pressure of circumstances (some of the measures being in fact only temporary) than part of a deliberate policy.

Let us look at the proposals that have been widely aired in public. Liberal circles tend to question and to challenge the very concept of the protective role of the State. Those who are somewhat cursorily qualified as "supply economists" consider that compulsory payroll deductions, if too high, undermine economic growth by penalising the supply of labour and investment. They also believe that too much security saps a society's dynamism. Social protection systems, they often claim, have gone too far in relieving the family and the individual of their responsibility to face up to social contingencies; the individual should "manage his own social progress". Their proposal, therefore, is to reduce public expenditure, especially social expenditure, and to put the accent on individual responsibility. It is openly

admitted that this would entail a partial dismantling of social security; more emphasis would be placed on direct income than on social benefits, and social protection would pass partly into "private" hands. Social security would be restricted to the provision of minimal protection for the have-nots (either through a welfare system or by means of a negative tax). Proposals such as these reflect a current of opinion which does not seem to be endorsed by the majority and, though they have elicited a response in a few countries, they appear to have little appeal elsewhere. The feeling is that they undermine the general level of acquired rights to social benefits, and they invariably provoke very strong reactions, especially from the workers.

There have been other suggested means of restricting the protective role of the State. One such proposal is for "selective" action, whereby social benefits would be granted on a less indiscriminate basis and would focus on carefully chosen target segments of the population. This would mean that far more benefits would be subject to a means test. Other suggestions – though not always very clearly defined – imply the existence of a dual labour market, in which a highly productive sector closely integrated with the world market would co-exist with a more loosely knit sector corresponding to what one might call a more "convivial" society. The workers in the former sector would retain a high degree of social security while in the latter they would be encouraged to assume responsibility for social contingencies themselves. In this way social protection would be more autonomous and more decentralised.

Critics of this and similar proposals readily point to the difficulties they would involve. It is argued that they could stretch the social fabric dangerously and jeopardise the rights acquired by vast categories of the population. Moreover, they are said to run counter to the internatonal commitments (including ratified ILO Conventions) of a number of countries. By and large they tend to be resisted by people who consider that the fight against insecurity and poverty is one of the responsibilities of the State. Because they go against the most widespread aspirations, they have not on the whole found much favour with governments.

What, then, is the alternative? At present, governments are mainly concerned with rationalising and, if necessary, restructuring their social security systems.

Broadly speaking, increased thought is being given to the interplay of the economic and social spheres. Let us take, for example, the kind of injuries that workers may sustain because of various production processes, regardless of any corrective action that may be taken. There is a suggestion that the production sector could perhaps "internalise" these damages to a certain extent, adopt as it were a more preventive approach by improving physical planning, work schedules, working conditions and public transport and stepping up both anti-noise and anti-pollution campaigns instead of passing the burden on to the community as a whole through social security. Although this would undoubtedly increase the immediate costs of production, it might reduce them in the long run if the overall burden for society, and thus for the productive sector, could be alleviated.

A more practical approach could be the adoption of concrete measures to adapt the social security resources better to the objectives sought – in other words, to trim and streamline the whole institution so as to make it more efficient. The types of measures proposed vary according to the branch of social protection. Quite obviously, because circumstances differ so widely from country to country, particularly as regards the nature and scope of existing social security systems, they cannot be the same in every case, and those who advocate such an approach consider that it should not in any way entail reducing the personal scope of social security.

As far as medical care is concerned, the main objective is to control rising costs without restricting access to health care, in other words, to improve the cost-efficiency ratio in the use of available resources. We have already seen that this is more easily done in countries that have a national health service. Elsewhere, all kinds of measures are necessary to eliminate superfluous and exorbitant expenditure. In order to adapt resources better to real requirements, the first target tends to be hospitalisation: avoiding hospitalisation altogether if patients can be cared for just as efficiently by less costly means, monitoring hospital planning closely so that there is no superabundance of hospital beds, and improving management (for example, by means of fixed budgets). Some countries feel that more could be done in the way of controlling medical demography in its various aspects (number and distribution of doctors), reviewing the method of remuneration of medical practitioners and the way they practise their profession, cutting down where necessary on the range of drugs and controlling prices.

A similar approach would be to make better use in each case of the appropriate level of personnel and technology, in accordance with the principles of the primary health strategy.[7] This strategy combines preventive care and treatment and, at an initial stage, involves an (upgraded) general practitioner working in conjunction with a multidisciplinary support team. This primary care team as a whole is given great priority. It incorporates a system for channelling patients towards specialised or hospital treatment and operates as far as possible with the participation of the population for which it is responsible.

The point has been made that containing expenditure on health requires an intense effort of education – in other words, education of the medical staff about the economic and social aspects of health and education of the public about the advantages and disadvantages of the various medical acts.

As regards pensions, it is generally thought that costs will continue to rise as the population ages and pension schemes mature. However, because they account for such a large part of social security, many countries are looking for ways of rationalising and, if necessary, restructuring existing schemes while maintaining the current general level of protection for as much of the population as possible.

What exactly is behind these big words "rationalisation" and "restructuring"?

The first task is to eliminate wastage or standardise the benefits, in the broad sense of the term, afforded by the schemes which, specifically, would mean in future cutting down on the relative privileges enjoyed without legitimate reason by certain socio-economic groups under a multiplicity of occupational schemes.

For identical benefits the contributory effort demanded from each category, too, must be standardised (this applies particularly to self-employed workers).

Stricter rules are needed as regards both combining pensions with earnings or replacement incomes and taking pensions into account for income tax purposes.

In order to reduce the strain on pension schemes significantly, old-age insurance and disability insurance must no longer be used as ad hoc policy instruments for attenuating the effects of the crisis (for example, lowering the pensionable age for economic reasons and granting disability pensions too freely). In other words, the long-term requirements of pension schemes (i.e. their future financial equilibrium) should prevail over short-term preoccupations in areas other than social protection.

Finally, certain countries need to reconsider the balance between cash benefits and social services for the aged.

For the economy as a whole, family benefits are, as we have seen, a far smaller financial burden than medical care benefits and pensions; their relative cost has declined sharply over the past 20 years. Whether or not this is desirable is often questioned, and further thought may need to be given to the place allotted in social security schemes to family policy, given its demographic dimension (the issue of family and demographic policy was raised at the European Population Conference held in Strasbourg from 21 to 24 September 1982). If families are to be helped rationally, the major requirement is that the fiscal component should be co-ordinated with the social security component within the framework of a family policy so as to meet the families' real requirements and, especially, those of the most underprivileged.

In the field of unemployment, in which existing benefits play a vital role in the survival of millions of unemployed workers, rationalisation would mean better co-ordination of the various forms of assistance, more money for training and retraining, benefits that are better suited to the needs of the unemployed – especially the most destitute among them – and would help to discourage beneficiaries from drifting away from the labour market.

As regards cash benefits in general, whether in the form of pensions or short-term benefits, it would often seem that they could be reorganised in such a way as to give priority to the most underprivileged categories, such as the disabled and single-parent families.

As to the social welfare system as a whole, here again an effort must be made to reduce wastage and management expenses, to combat the hypertrophy and red tape that make the institution unmanageable. This means a great deal of streamlining and, as far as possible, decentralisation, as well as wider participation by bodies other than government agencies' associations, for example. Social security funding arrangements are also generally thought in many countries to be in need of reform so as to make them clearer and more straightforward. It is suggested in some quarters, for example, that benefits linked to earnings could be financed by contributions and universal benefits out of taxation. There are also plans to make benefits more equitable so that the effort demanded from the various categories of the population is at least proportional to their contributory capability (by doing away with the ceiling on contributions, for instance) and better geared to the requirements of the economy.

□

This, then, is the general, though highly incomplete picture, of the kind of measures that are being contemplated in order to adapt social security better to its constraints. We might note in conclusion that, in so far as the majority of the population remains attached to what it looks upon as an inalienable social conquest, governments are sure to do everything – narrow though their margin of manoeuvre may be – to retain at least its essential features. Indeed, the constraints imposed in times of crisis may help the systems to develop. The main problem is how to make an accurate assessment of just what decisions have to be taken during the crisis which will not jeopardise the institution after the crisis.

Short term versus long term: economists are familiar with this dilemma and, though politicians may find it less congenial, it may give them the chance they need. After all, learning today how to adapt the growth of social security to that of the economy is not just an indication that we are determined to preserve the essentials but a commitment to broaden social protection further once the growth curve starts to climb again.

[1] Social Security (Minimum Standards) Convention, 1952 (No. 102). The nine branches are as follows: medical care, sickness benefits, unemployment benefits, old-age benefits, employment injury benefits, family benefits, maternity benefits, invalidity benefits and survivors' benefits.

[2] More and more people tend to be unemployed for longer than the maximum period of unemployment benefits. In the United Kingdom in February 1982, 53 per cent of the unemployed depended totally or partially on social welfare granted on the basis of income and 430,000 received no benefits at all.

[3] The net material product (NMP) applies to planned economy countries. As defined (see Chapter 3, note 3), aggregate figures for the NMP are lower than those for the gross domestic product used by market economy countries.

[4] The proportion of social security contributions in the gross domestic product has become a key indicator. As noted in Chapter 2 (note 1), its value should not be exaggerated. In Sweden, according to Gösta Rehn, whereas social transfers accounted for 28 per cent of the gross national product, the net figure was probably around 20 per cent. (A. Hautefeuille: "Le modéle suédois sur la défensive", in *Futuribles*, July-Aug. 1981, p. 46).

[5] See also Chapter 2, pp. 40-41.

[6] "For whosoever hath, to him shall be given, and he shall have more abundance; but whosoever hath not, from him shall be taken away even that he hath" (Gospel according to St. Matthew, Romans 13:12); see H. Deleeck: "L'effet Matthieu", in *Droit social* (Paris, Librairie Sociale et économique), Nov. 1979.

[7] Principles laid down at the UNICEF/WHO conference held in Alma-Ata in 1978 and recognised by all the highly industrialised countries at the World Health Assembly in 1980.

Selected bibliography

ILO

Euzéby A. and C.; Mouton, P.; Perrin G. *Sécurité sociale: Quelle méthode de financement?* (Geneva, 1983).

Meeting of Experts on the Rising Cost of Medical Care under Social Security (Geneva, 17-20 May 1977):

Cost trends, causes and possible cost containment measures (Geneva; doc. RCMC/1977/D.2; mimeographed).

Report (Geneva; doc. RCMC/1977/D.12 (Rev.); mimeographed).

Meeting of Experts on Occupational Accident Prevention and Compensation (Geneva, 29 January-2 February 1979): *Report* (Geneva; doc. OAPC/1979/D.18 (Rev.); mimeographed).

Pensions and inflation: An international discussion (Geneva, 1977).

Rjanitsina, L. "Public consumption funds in the USSR", in *International Labour Review* (Geneva), Dec. 1973.

"Social security at the crossroads", in *International Labour Review* (Geneva), Mar.-Apr. 1980.

Social security for the unemployed (Geneva, 1976).

Tamburi, G. "Escalation of state pension costs: The reasons and the issues", in *International Labour Review* (Geneva), May-June 1983.

Veldkamp, G. M. J. "The coherence of social security policy", in *International Labour Review* (Geneva), Nov. 1973.

Woodhouse, Sir Owen. "Personal injury legislation in New Zealand", in *International Labour Review* (Geneva), May-June 1980.

ISSA

Beattie, R. A. "Financial disequilibrium due to the evolution of employment and unemployment", in *International Social Security Review* (Geneva), No. 2, 1982.

Fisher, P. "The social security crisis: An international dilemma", in *International Social Security Review* (Geneva), No. 4, 1978.

Improving cost-effectiveness in health care, Studies and research No. 19 (Geneva, 1983).

Methods of financing social security: Their economic and social effects, Studies and research No. 15 (Geneva, 1979).

Questiaux, N. "Social protection and the crisis", in *International Social Security Review* (Geneva), No. 3, 1982.

Official reports

Commission of the European Communities. *Social security problems – Points for consideration*, Communication from the Commission to the Council (Brussels; doc. COM(82)716 final; mimeographed), 17 Nov. 1982.

European Centre for Social Welfare Training and Research. Regional Expert Meeting on the Consequences of the Economic Crisis for the Present and Future Development of Social Welfare, *Eurosocial Reports*, No. 17 (Vienna, 1982).

France. *Rapport de la Commission: Protection sociale et famille*, Preparation of the Eighth Plan (Paris, La Documentation française, 1980).

OECD. *Unemployment compensation and related employment policy measures: General report and country studies* (Paris, 1979).

–. *The Welfare State in crisis* (Paris, 1981).

–. *Proceedings* of the OECD Meeting on Unemployment Insurance Issues and Alternative Uses of Unemployment Benefits Funds (Nuremberg, 8-9 November 1982).

United States Congress. *Social security in Europe: The impact of an aging population*, Information paper prepared for use by the Special Committee on Aging, United States Senate (Washington, DC, United States Government Printing Office, 1981).

United States National Commission on Social Security Reform. "Report", in *Social Security Bulletin*, Feb. 1983.

Studies

Aaron, H. J. *Economic effects of social security*, Studies of Government Finance (Washington, DC, Brookings Institution, 1982).

Abel-Smith, B. *Value for money in health services: A comparative study* (London, Heinemann, 1976).

Blaustein, S. J.; Craig, I. *An international review of unemployment insurance schemes* (Kalamazoo (Michigan), W. E. Upjohn Institute for Employment Research, 1977).

European Institute for Social Security: EISS Yearbook 1978-80, Part II: *Social security reforms in Europe* (Deventer (Netherlands), Kluwer, 1980).

Flora, P.; Heidenheimer, A. J. *The development of Welfare States in Europe and America* (New Brunswick, Transaction Books, 1981).

Fournier J.; Questiaux N. *Le pouvoir du social* (Paris, PUF, 1979).

Gough, I. *The political economy of the Welfare State* (London, Macmillan, 1979).

Greffe, X. *L'impôt des pauvres, nouvelle stratégie de la politique sociale* (Paris, Dunod, 1978).

Guéguen-Baslé, J.; Baslé, M. *La politique sociale: Histoire, enjeu et crise* (Paris, Hatier (collection Profil), 1981).

Higgins, J. *States of welfare: Comparative analysis in social policy* (Oxford, B. Blackwell and M. Robertson, 1981).

Max Planck Institut für ausländisches und internationales Sozialrecht. *The evolution of social insurance, 1881-1981: Studies of Germany, France, Great Britain, Austria and Switzerland*, edited by Peter A. Köhler and Hans F. Zacher in collaboration with Martin Partington (London, Frances Pinter, 1982, and New York, St. Martin's Press, 1982).

National Social Security Institute (Rome). "Costi e relativi finanziamenti dei sistemi pensionistici nei vari paesi europei", in *Sistema Previdenza*, INPS monthly information periodical, Nov.-Dec. 1982, Special issue devoted to the INPS International Conference.

Rosanvallon P. *La crise de l'Etat-providence* (Paris, Seuil, 1981).

United States Department of Health and Human Services, Social Security Administration. *Social security programes throughout the world, 1981*, Research Report No. 58 (Washington, DC, United States Government Printing Office, 1982).

IXth World Congress of Sociology (Uppsala, 17 August 1978). *Social policies in comparative perspective*, Papers submitted, reproduced by the Danish National Institute of Social Research (Copenhagen, 1978).

Zakharov M.; Tsivilov R. *Social security in the USSR* (Moscow, Progress Publishers, 1978).

Articles

Aldrich, J. "The earnings replacement rate of old-age benefits in 12 countries, 1969-80", in *Social Security Bulletin* (Washington, DC, United States Department of Health and Human Services), Nov. 1982.

Blanchard, F. "Sécurité sociale: Une conférence internationale pour surmonter une crise générale", in *Le Monde* (Paris), 8 Apr. 1980.

Capian, A. "La socialisation du salaire", in *Revue économique* (Paris), Nov. 1981.

Canadian Conference of Catholic Bishops, Commission for Social Affairs. "Jalons d'éthique et réflexions sur la crise économique actuelle", reproduced by the *Catholic New Times*, Jan. 1983.

Crona, G. "Une voie révolutionnaire: La retraite partielle en Suède", in *Droit social* (Paris), Jan. 1980.

Delpérée, A. "Réflexions à propos de la réforme de la sécurité sociale", in *Revue belge de sécurité sociale* (Brussels), No. 3, Mar. 1980.

Feldstein, M. "Facing the social security crisis", in *Public Interest* (New York), Spring 1977.

Futuribles: Etats protecteurs en crise (Paris, Association internationale Futuribles), Special issue, May 1983.

Hautefeuille, A. "Le modèle suèdois sur la défensive", in *Futuribles* (Paris), July-Aug. 1981.

Perrin, G. "La sécurité sociale au passé et au présent", in *Revue française des affaires sociales* (Paris), Jan.-Mar. 1979.

Sachs, I. "The crisis of the Welfare State and the exercise of social rights to development", in *International Social Science Journal* (Paris, UNESCO), No. 1, 1982.

ILO bibliography on social security for migrant workers

Coëffard, A. "Regulations governing social security for persons moving within the European community", in *International Labour Review* (Geneva), May-June 1982.

Creutz, H. "The new Agreement on Social Security for Rhine Boatmen", in *International Labour Review* (Geneva), Jan.-Feb. 1981.

Moles, R. R. "Social security for migrant workers in Latin America", in *International Labour Review* (Geneva), Mar.-Apr. 1982.

Popescu, A. "Bilateral social security agreements concluded between European socialist countries", in *International Labour Review* (Geneva), Jan.-Feb. 1982.

Social security for migrant workers (Geneva, 1977).

Trier, A. "The Nordic Social Security Convention", in *International Labour Review* (Geneva), May-June 1982.

Villars, C. "Social security for migrant workers in the framework of the Council of Europe", in *International Labour Review* (Geneva), May-June 1981.

Voirin, M. "Social security for migrant workers in Africa", in *International Labour Review* (Geneva), May-June 1983.

Chapter 7

The impact of information technology on employment, working conditions and industrial relations

During the past few years there has been a series of developments of major importance in the field of information. Together they make up a powerful network of technology covering computers, telecommunications equipment and electronic components. The basic building blocks of this network are the miniaturised integrated circuits, microprocessors or microchips which store, handle and transmit information, and it is this convergence of recent innovations that has acquired the designation of "information technology".[1]

"Information" is used here in a very broad sense. It includes data of every kind that can be compiled, organised and transmitted. They may be quantitative or qualitative: signals transmitted to manufacturing, measuring and controlling apparatus, operations and calculations, bibliographical information, long-range transmission of messages, press items, transactions of every kind, management activities, office work, etc.

A 1980 ILO study, outlining some of the possible applications of the new technology, stated:

"The nature of the technology and its economic attractions means that it can be applied to a wide range of products and processes. It intervenes in both productive and administrative activities. It can be used to relate weight to price in a shop, control the cycles of a machine tool, guide an aircraft to a safe landing or optimise the mixture of fuel and air in the carburettor of a car. It will significantly alter production processes by increasing automation through micro-electronic controls and the development of robots. It will have a significant effect on the way services are produced, and on the way clerical work is performed, owing to the introduction of word processors, electronic storage systems and office automation in general. Thanks to micro-electronics, automation is penetrating liberal and artistic professions (e.g. medicine and design). It will bring about an exponential increase in scientific and technological research capacity. The technology will encourage the use of computer terminals in the home, the transmission of textual information through the telephone network and satellites, the development of electronic banking and remote control of factories and equipment." (Rada, 1980)

It can be safely assumed today that information technology is destined to spread to a vast range of economic activities, even though it may be impossible to foresee how fast this will happen. It will lead to the emergence of a large variety of new products and to changes which, on the one hand, will save capital, labour, materials and energy and, on the other, could bring about an even greater use of these factors of production.

In this chapter it is mainly the labour aspect that will be examined. Many people fear that the introduction of information technology will mean fewer and less interesting jobs and different relations between managers and workers. Others claim that the adoption of the new technologies and, particularly, the progress in micro-electronics are a necessary condition for maintaining economic growth and full employment. It is the aim of this chapter to bring some order to this debate and to examine whether there is empirical support for such claims.

First, however, a few general observations should perhaps be made which, in our view, suggest that considerable prudence must be brought to bear in assessing the situation and that it would be a serious mistake to make hasty generalisations.

There is evidence that during the past two centuries basic technical innovations have been associated with long-run cycles of economic activity: the steam engine in the late eighteenth century, railways and steelmaking in the mid-nineteenth century, the internal combustion engine at the turn of the twentieth century and, since the middle of this century perhaps, what we have dubbed information technology. These constellations of technical innovations normally have their origins in small enterprises with a high proportion of skilled technicians. They are the result of imaginative research and development geared towards practical applications and capable of exploiting hitherto dormant theoretical scientific know-how. During the "upswing" of the cycle, new products become standardised, economies of scale begin to be important, intense competition develops in the manufacture of better products, and prices fall. During the "downswing", research and inventive activity shift to cost-saving applications and lead to important labour-displacing investments. Each cycle lasts about 50 or 60 years. According to this theory, we are now somewhere on the downswing, when the information technology has matured and where concentration and competition are forcing enterprises to give increasing attention to cost-reducing technical change (Freedman, 1979).

That a "critical mass" of technological innovation should lead to profound economic upheavals and be associated with long and clearly discernible periods of economic development, though well attested by events, does not leave us with much in the way of practical guidance, at a given moment, as to the impact of these innovations on the creation or reduction of employment. The fact is that nobody is in a position to make any reasonable forecasts on the subject, and this for three reasons.

The first, and perhaps the most important, will come of something of a surprise to many observers. At the present time, we simply have no appropriate methodology for making such forecasts, since the technological change or progress in which we are caught up has not yet been clearly integrated in micro-economic analyses. Technology is not the kind of variable that can be isolated, nor does it have the kind of dimension of such classic factors of production as capital and labour. It is both everywhere and nowhere, and research into technical progress by economic sector, by undertaking or by occupation does not necessarily produce findings that are valid for the economy as a whole (Missika, 1980). Though productivity often depends on a combination of technological change and efficient management, the way in which its effects spread from one industry to another is not always easy to assess. These effects may in any case differ widely from one industry to another even while the general level of productivity of the economy is rising. Without going back too far in time, who was able to foresee the impact of the budding American automobile industry on the economic growth of the United States and the rest of the world? And, when the first huge American "electronic brains" made their appearance, was it not said by many that a dozen or so would amply suffice for the requirements of the United States?

The second reason is that, faced with the tangible effects of the introduction of new techniques, we are impressed more than anything by their immediate repercussions on the principal economic agents involved: workers threatened in their jobs, erstwhile prosperous undertakings now close to bankruptcy, regions dependent on an economic activity confronted with the prospect of decline. In fact, the spread of "major" technological innovations has often led in the longer term to the creation of entirely new industrial sectors, undertakings and jobs and has breathed new life into other regions. Economic history, indeed, is nothing more than the history of such changes. Of this trade union leaders today are fully aware, as we can see if we compare their attitude which is not in principle hostile to the new information technology with that of the workers' revolts of the nineteenth century – for example, the English Luddites and the silk workers at Lyons – when the machines were deliberately destroyed. The whole problem is one of assessing the potential scope of the new innovations – which brings us back to the first reason – and, above all, the pace of introduction. It is this that will determine the adaptations to be made: far-reaching adaptations if the change is unavoidable, minor adaptations if it is only transitory – though presumably in both cases never painless as far as certain undertakings, certain workers and certain regions are concerned. Yet how are we to set about the task of measuring these concepts?

The third reason has to do with the climate prevailing at the time of introduction of the new technology. During periods of rapid economic growth, the distribution of employment among various economic sectors changes but the new technology itself does not affect the general level of employment, which may even rise. In 1966 the United States National Commission on Technology, Automation and Economic Progress, which examined the relationship between technical change and unemployment for the country's economy, came to the conclusion that "technology eliminates jobs, not work" (*Technology and the American economy*, 1966). However, the situation may change completely if, as it is today, the background is one of economic recession, energy scarcity, concern about the environment and different attitudes towards work.

These general observations may serve to temper slightly the findings of the otherwise extremely useful research cited in this chapter, in which we analyse the impact of new technologies on employment, working conditions, skills and industrial relations. We shall begin with some general considerations concerning micro-electronics and the new economic sector of information.

Micro-electronics: the information sector

The basic element of micro-electronics technology is the so-called "chip" – a silicon wafer measuring a square centimetre or less which contains a multitude of transistors, integrated circuits and other components. The concentration or "printing" of components on these microchips has been constantly improved. While at the beginning of the 1970s component density per chip was about 10,000, the figure has now reached 250,000 and may soon exceed a million. To give an idea of what this represents, let us say that the processing capacity of a single microchip is greater than that of the first major computer marketed in the United States. Its advantages are obvious: more powerful, minimum space, reliability, reprogrammability, minimal energy consumption, extremely low cost.

One particularly important characteristic – and a definite advantage – of micro-electronic technology is that it can be incorporated in many products and processes, and not just in computers. Microprocessors are now used in more and more consumer durables such as household domestic appliances, entertainment products and personal products (pocket calculators and watches, for example). They are also playing an increasingly important role in industrial control technology, in which they are replacing other forms of electromechanical equipment and control systems (temperature control, traffic control, etc.). They are used

---

7.1

Some of the more common micro-electronic applications

Domestic appliances: washing-machines, sewing-machines, ovens, mixers.

Domestic regulators: central-heating control, lighting control.

Leisure: radios and television sets, hi-fi equipment, tape recorders, video tape recorders.

Personal: pocket calculators, watches, personal computers, teletex.

Cars: dashboard displays, fuel supply and ignition systems, braking systems, collision-avoidance devices, diagnostic systems.

Telecommunications: radio and television, electronic telephone, telephone exchanges, telex-switching systems, data transmission, electronic facsimiles, electronic mail transmission, remote terminals, teleprinters, paging systems, teleconferring, electronic news gathering, satellites.

Office: accounting computers, typewriters and word processors, copiers, computer microfilms, facsimiles, electronic archives and retrieval systems, recording, telephone-answering machines, dictation.

Trade: on-line ordering systems, automated warehousing and stock control, computer-planned distribution networks, point-of-sale equipment and terminals, automatic supermarkets.

Banking: automatic cash tellers, automatic transfer of funds, credit card systems, cheque processing systems.

Printing: linotype electronic systems, colour correction and storage, machine control.

Computers: mini-computers, microcomputers, input-output equipment, "intelligent" terminals, optical and laser character readers, printers and displays.

Industry (general applications): measuring and test equipment, devices for monitoring dimensions, temperature, weight and other factors; plant and personnel control, electronic clock-in; robots (programmed and self-programming devices) for welders, carriers, painters, etc.; monitoring and control of industrial processes in the nuclear and steel industries, for high-risk operations and for mass production; machine tools; smelting, welding and electro-plating equipment, textile machines, materials handling, etc.

Military and aerospace: air traffic control, radar system data processing, navigation systems, military communications, guided missiles, night-viewing equipment, microwave blind-landing systems, infra-red surveillance.

Design and construction: computer-aided design, civil engineering and related design and equipment.

Education: computer-assisted education, general educational techniques, audio-visual aids.

Health: filing, general hospital management, body scanners and advanced diagnostic equipment, heart pacemakers, patient monitoring system, kidney dialysis equipment, computer-produced speech, electronic aids and sight for the blind.

Public administration: centralised filing, police filing, traffic control, mail processing.

Other: meteorology, pollution control.

Source: J. Rada: *The impact of micro-electronics: A tentative appraisal of information technology* (Geneva, ILO, 1980).

---

in numerically controlled machine tools, industrial robots and material-handling equipment. They play a vital part in equipment employed by the State, such as aerospace, education, health and social security equipment. Needless to say, they are used first and foremost in the construction of computers of all sizes, data-transmission equipment and telecommunications systems (see box 7.1).

The new consumer products are often superior to the old in that they satisfy a greater variety of needs at a lower price. Moreover, the industrial processes are more efficient. The great advantage of micro-electronics, however, lies not so much in the products and processes themselves ("hardware") as in the way individual systems can be linked together. For example, computers can be linked with digital telecommunications equipment to allow instant access to information stored in various parts of the country or the world. The linkage of computer-aided design (CAD) and computer-aided manufacturing (CAM) makes it possible to integrate design, manufacturing and inventory operations in one system, and to produce at a much lower cost. Another aspect is that the linkage of word processors with electronic mail and filing systems may bring about the so-called "paperless office", where information would be exchanged, stored and retrieved at much greater speed and efficiency, with much less need for the intervention of secretaries and clerks.

A major development in micro-electronics technology is that "software" – i.e. the instructions which tell the computer or microprocessor

Figure 7.1
Employment in the four economic sectors (agriculture, industry, services, information) as a percentage of the labour force

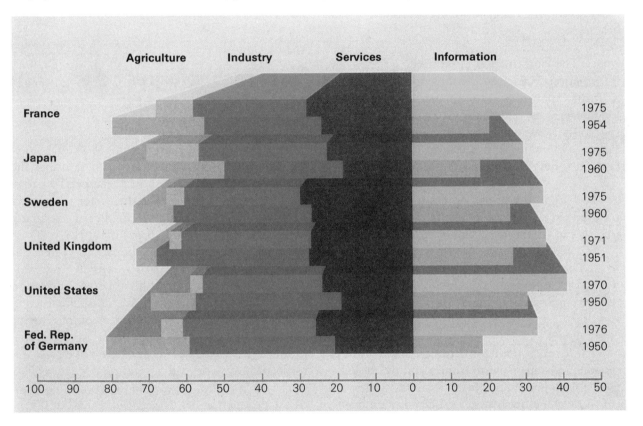

Source: OECD: *Information activities, electronics and telecommunications technologies: Impact on employment, growth and trade*, Information Computer Communications Policy No. 6, Vol. I (Paris, 1981).

what to do – is becoming much more important than the hardware. Software now frequently accounts for 50 per cent of total costs in many systems, a percentage which is expected to reach 80 to 90 by the end of the decade. For at least two reasons, this should not be surprising. In the first place, the linkages we have referred to – computer-aided design and manufacturing, integrated data processing and telecommunications operations – require a common language and instructions to allow the various systems to communicate with each other. Secondly, the products coming on to the market will have to be accessible to as many people as possible, be "user-friendly" and not require more technical know-how than is needed nowadays to operate a television or hi-fi set. It is in response to these requirements that software is

becoming more and more diversified and sophisticated.

The increasing importance of the production, storage, retrieval and distribution of information as defined at the beginning of this chapter has led some authors to believe that we are witnessing the birth of the information economy (Porat, 1977) or, at least, the birth either of a fourth economic sector that was previously considered to be part of the services sector (Gassmann, 1981)[2] or of new information activities or occupations in all sectors of the economy (Gershuny, 1978).

A recent OECD study provides an inventory of "information occupations" (OECD, Vol. I, 1981). Using the ILO International Standard

Classification of Occupations (the 1968 revised edition is scheduled to be brought up to date during this decade), the occupations are listed under four headings.

1. The information producers create new information or package existing information into a form appropriate to a particular recipient (engineers, agronomists, statisticians, market specialists, insurance agents, song and lyric writers, for example, but also all kinds of consultants including doctors and systems analysts.

2. The information processors receive and respond to information inputs (administrative, managerial, supervisory and clerical staff, etc.).

3. The information distributors primarily convey information from the initiator to the recipient (education and communication workers, journalists).

4. Information infrastructure personnel install, operate and repair the machines and technologies used to support information activities (telex and office machine operators, repair and maintenance staff, postal and telecommunications workers).

For the nine countries which participated in the OECD study, it was found that, on average, the share of information occupations in the labour force has increased since 1950 by nearly 3 per cent in each five-year period. In 1975 these occupations accounted for more than one-third of the labour force (see figure 7.1).

This already gives an idea of the role of such activities in economic life and, consequently, of the potential impact of the new information technologies with which they are bound to be concerned. Their role is in fact even more important than suggested by these findings: a further breakdown of national accounts into a primary and a secondary information sector reveals that they account for a growing share of gross domestic product at factor cost.[3]

Having seen the nature and applications of the new technologies and the scope of the information sector, we shall now discuss their impact.

New technologies and employment

We have already noted that it is to a large extent the economic environment which determines the employment effects of technical change. To gauge this climate, it may be useful to refer to a study published in the Federal Republic of Germany which distinguishes four types of situation (Dostal, 1982). The first type is innovation – a phase in which fundamental research results in new products or processes. Since this type of innovation creates, as it were, a new market, it usually leads to higher economic activity and thus employment, although it may compete with conventional products and processes (as in the case of digital and mechanical watches). A second type is rationalisation, which makes it possible to produce conventional products more efficiently while the use of production factors remains equal or diminishes. This is the case of the automobile and steel industries, where technical change is rapid, particularly as the result of robots. The third and fourth types are a reduction and expansion of activity without a change in technology or products; these phases depend on the general level of economic activity and on its position in the economic cycle.

Sectoral impact

In order to determine the importance of these four phases, the Institute of Labour Market and Occupational Research of the Federal Republic of Germany analysed technical change in six sectors of activity: synthetic material, wood, food processing, metalworking, printing and the retail trade. In 1,600 representative enterprises the Institute analysed about 3,000 technical changes subdivided

Table 7.1
Employment effects of four types of economic change in the Federal Republic of Germany (as a percentage of the 5-6 million persons employed in the undertakings analysed)

Reference year	Sector	Inno-vation	Ration-alisation	Expan-sion	Reduc-tion	Total
1970	Synthetics	+1.01	−0.05	+2.07	−0.20	+2.83
1971	Wood	+0.81	+0.09	+0.54	−0.21	+1.23
1972	Food processing	−0.06	−0.74	+0.92	−0.31	−0.19
1973	Metal trades	+0.43	−0.09	+1.40	−0.15	+1.59
1975	Printing	−0.38	−0.37	+0.24	−0.39	−0.90
1977	Retail trade	+0.21	−0.37	+2.16	−0.34	+1.70
Average		+0.34	−0.26	+1.22	−0.27	+1.03

Source: W. Dostal: *Bildung und Beschäftigung im technischen Wandel*, Beiträge zur Arbeitsmarkt und Berufsforschung No. 65 (Nuremberg, Institut für Arbeitsmarkt und Berufsforschung der Bundesanstalt für Arbeit, 1982).

into the four categories mentioned above: *(a)* innovation including new production installations and techniques, the use of new materials and the application of new energy sources and electronic data processing; *(b)* rationalisation including mechanisation, automation, organisational changes and transfer of production activities; *(c)* expansion; and *(d)* reduction of activities. The results are clear: innovation constituted 51 per cent of all technical changes in the six sectors, rationalisation 23 per cent and expansion 20 per cent. Table 7.1 gives an overview of the employment effects of the four types of economic change.

On the average, the employment effects of technical change are positive, but this is mainly accounted for by the expansion of activities. If one looks at the innovation and rationalisation variables alone, it is clear that such change has a fairly direct impact on employment within the sectors considered. The surveys end in 1977, however, and in recent years the combination of economic recession and accelerated introduction of new information techniques (in printing, for instance) would perhaps give a less positive overall picture, even at the sectoral level analysed.

Let us turn now to the employment effects of the introduction of robots. The Robot Institute of America defines a robot as a "reprogrammable, multi-functional manipulator designed to move material, parts, tools or specialised devices, through variable programmed motions for the performance of a variety of tasks". The world "population" of programmable industrial robots in 1980 was estimated at around 15,000 units, twice the 1978 total; some 40 per cent of these were located in Japan, 25 per cent in the United States and the rest in Western Europe. These are probably over-estimates, however, since the Japanese definition of robots is somewhat less strict than the American, which means that the proportion of Japanese robots also appears exaggerated. At the moment, most robots are installed in the automobile industry where they are used for welding and surface treatment. In future, they will be used more and more for assembly operations, if they can be equipped with adequate sensors.

Strictly sectoral studies on the employment impact of robots are pessimistic, albeit in varying degree. During the preparation of the Eighth French Plan (1981-85), it was estimated that the introduction of robots would lead to a loss of about 30,000 jobs, which was not even 1 per cent of the French industrial labour force in 1980. Forecasts in the Federal Republic of Germany are most sombre. Assuming that the utilisation of robots will increase from a mere 2 per cent in 1980 to 60 per cent of total potential in 1990, the result would be 200,000 lost industrial jobs – about 6 per cent of industrial employment (Volkholtz, 1981). This estimate is probably too high since it assumes a very rapid pace of diffusion. The trouble with these and other sectoral studies, as already pointed out, is their scope. Because they are restricted to a particular sector, they do not take into account the employment effects in other sectors of the economy, which are not necessarily negative.

The word processor is another application of information technology. It is a typewriter with a memory which, if linked with a computer and printer, permits simple, multiple corrections without the need to retype the entire text, a uniform layout, storage and filing of the text and its coding for photocomposition or reproduction. Word processors can be connected with data bases or banks and with different telecommunications equipment. Quite apart from their indirect functions (for example in the field of data acquisition and dissemination), they may involve the elimination of numerous repetitive tasks at the typing and reproduction stages and lead to greater efficiency.

An ILO study has come to the conclusion that the employment consequences depend on the way word processors are introduced (Werneke, 1983). In order to draw the maximum productivity benefit from word processors, IBM recommend the elimination of the one-to-one manager-secretary relationship. The secretarial function would be split between a centralised word-processing pool and an administrative assistance section which would take over all but the typing tasks, such as the routing of incoming telephone calls and messages (most of which would be done electronically through the office communications network). To date, few offices resemble this model. Generally speaking, word processors are being introduced gradually as a first step towards an automated office. There is no reason to believe that total employment of office staff will be reduced,

however. To begin with, some industry analysts find widespread resistance on the part of management to losing secretarial staff. Moreover, the declining cost of word-processing equipment and further technical developments may make it possible to decentralise and multiply such equipment rather than establish central pools of typists. Finally, by doing away with much of the repetitive work, word processors may bring about a different distribution of work design personnel and support staff, with the latter acquiring a broader range of tasks, rather than a reduction in employment. On the other hand, some secretaries and typists may lose their jobs as research workers, public servants, university staff and journalists learn to do without them by using word processors directly.

While the picture is uncertain as regards the effect of automated office equipment, it would seem somewhat clearer in the case of small and medium-sized enterprises resorting to innovation. These seem to have contributed significantly to the creation of employment (OECD, 1982). They are capable of exploiting the gaps left by large enterprises, which tend to increase profits by perfecting existing lines of production. Small enterprises can launch themselves on new, narrow or risky markets because they are more flexible and can often change production lines without too much extra cost. Most of these innovations result from the adaptation of existing technological elements such as microprocessors, using a wide variety of new materials, new forms of energy and telecommunications equipment. To mention just one example, micro-electronics are breathing new life into the toy industry.

Italy is a typical case in point (Pioré and Sabel, 1981). Conglomerations of more and more modern and competitive small enterprises are found, for example, in Emilia-Romagna and in and around Florence, Ancona and Venice. Many of these started out as subcontractors for large firms but are now operating with their own products on both the domestic and the international market. This development and its success were possible for three reasons. First, new machinery has been adapted to small productive units. In some cases this has taken the form of specially adapted numerically controlled machine tools; in other cases, artisanal techniques of smelting, enamelling, weaving, cutting or casting metal are designed into new machines, some of which are controlled by microprocessors. Secondly, the new product is born out of the firm's market expertise, especially its knowledge of the tastes of various groups of customers who are not satisfied with the standardised products turned out by large production lines. Because of the flexibility of production, products may be modified rapidly and easily so as to conform to or develop new tastes. Thirdly, the constant innovation in products and production technologies depends on and reinforces collaboration within and between firms.

The internal division of labour in these firms is very flexible, because owners, engineers, technicians, production heads and skilled craftsmen work in close contact with each other, without hierarchical formalities. The firms co-operate with one another by buying and sharing expensive capital equipment, by making large joint orders and by organising co-operative services for the purchase of raw materials and the obtaining of bank loans. Enterprises such as these create employment, sustain domestic demand and, to a certain extent, find ways round the relative saturation of markets for consumer goods.

While on the subject of the sectoral impact, we cannot afford to overlook the information industry itself. The most striking example of course is that of the United States, birthplace of electronic computers and micro-electronics. The success of such initially small undertakings as IBM, Hewlett-Packard and Motorola, which have now become giants, is well known. Employment in the information equipment manufacturing sector is thought to have grown at an average rate of about 4.4 per cent between 1970 and 1980, far faster than the national average. According to official projec-

tions, the annual growth rate for the industries producing electronic office equipment could be between 4.5 and 6.2 per cent between 1980 and 1990. The same is true of Japan, where the production of semiconductors, integrated circuits and microprocessors has created many new jobs, despite rapid progress in productivity. Because Europe is somewhat behind the United States and Japan in this respect, employment in the micro-electronic sector in the continent has grown rather more slowly.

National impact

Several countries have undertaken macro-economic studies to assess the overall impact of information or micro-electronic technologies on employment, especially so as to capture the indirect employment effects that are in addition to the sectoral impact. Such effects can occur for various reasons.

First of all, additional investment is needed for setting up the new technology. The pace of investment depends on the rate of diffusion of the technology, which depends in turn on the general economic situation (it is clear in the current circumstances that new investment does not take place easily and that, as a result, productivity does not increase fast, either). It is also important to know whether the investment will lead to more efficient production processes or to new products which may stimulate demand.

Secondly, the application of new technologies may lead to higher profits and wages, and possibly to a more unequal distribution of income. This has a major bearing on final demand, and thus on employment.

Thirdly, if not all the gain from a new process technology is taken up in wages and profits, price reductions should result. Moreover, new products are likely to lead to better price-quality ratios. The increases in real incomes should lead to increased demand.

Lastly, better price-quality ratios could improve a country's or a sector's competitive position on both the domestic and the international market, thereby favouring employment in the international sectors of the economy.

One needs a comprehensive macro-economic model in which to incorporate these data in order to establish the links between the various sectors of the economy. The model must include such variables as prices and wages, as well as the major aggregates of production, value added, employment, investment, private expenditure and the balance of payment.

The model developed by the Central Planning Bureau of the Netherlands has been used to assess the effects of technological change on employment. Two different scenarios were employed: rapid introduction of micro-electronics, and slower introduction in the Netherlands in comparison with the rest of the world. The first scenario shows a rapid increase in productivity and a decline in employment. Quite unexpectedly, the second also shows a poor employment situation which, in the long run, is even worse than in the first case because of the country's weakened international competitiveness. Nevertheless, under both scenarios employment as a result of technological changes would increase by about 150,000 work-years between 1980 and 1990 (current unemployment runs at about 700,000 work-years). It should be mentioned, however, that the effect on demand of lower prices or better-quality products was not taken into consideration.

The findings of an OECD study do not seem to point in the same direction (Stoneman et al, 1981). Reviewing a number of national studies (admittedly using different models) on the impact of information technology on aggregate employment, its authors tentatively conclude that the effect is rather small but that the distribution of employment by sector of activity changes drastically. The result is a mismatch between the supply of and demand for skills on the labour market. This sectoral redistribution of employment may also affect the distribution of employment between countries.

In fact neither the sectoral studies nor the overall analyses that are available point to any clear conclusion in one direction or the other as regards the impact of the new technologies on employment. In the long term and provided the process is accompanied by economic recovery, it is conceivable that the impact will be positive, though there is no proof that this is so. In the short and medium term, and leaving aside reductions in employment within sectors or undertakings (in favour of other sectors or undertakings), one must not overlook the effect of stagnating investment, a phenomenon brought about by the recession that is bound to slow down the diffusion of micro-electronics and other techniques. Once there are signs of sustained economic recovery, however, numerous undertakings will invest in numerically controlled robots and machine tools. Direct creation of employment as a result of such investment will therefore be less substantial than is generally believed.

International impact

We have already mentioned the different experience of the United States, Japan and Europe as regards employment in the information technology sector. It shows that jobs, at least at the sectoral level, are created above all where innovation takes place.

Let us turn now to the impact of micro-electronics on the international division of labour, particularly from the standpoint of the developing countries. A number of ILO studies provide a few pointers.

One of the earlier studies considers that, by decreasing the proportion of direct labour costs in total business cost, automation made possible by micro-electronics erodes the comparative advantage of labour-intensive sectors (Rada, 1980). Another study on the semiconductor industry shows that the value added outside the United States has been consistently declining, in the case of integrated circuits from 57 per cent in 1974 to 39 per cent in 1978 (Rada, 1982). There are several reasons for this. The first is that, owing to increasing capital and research and development needs, United States companies have become more vertically integrated. Secondly, automation is increasing the fixed cost of production and changing the skill mix within plants, with the result that investing in developing countries with low labour costs has become less attractive. Thirdly, increasing competition places more emphasis on the quality of the product and proximity to the consumer.

A third study on the garment industry points out that, given the relatively high cost of cloth in total costs (often up to 50 per cent), automation has integrated a whole sequence of tasks which used to be carried out manually, and separately, by highly skilled workers. It has not yet reached the sewing stage, however, which accounts for approximately 80 per cent of total labour and capital costs. The combined effect of higher wages in developing countries, increased protectionism in the countries to which their products are exported and innovations directed at rationalising labour-intensive tasks can be expected to lead to an erosion of comparative advantages in developing countries. On the other hand, international firms are likely to maintain their production in developing countries with large domestic markets. Moreover, many firms in the Third World are successfully competing on the high-fashion market, where profit rates are higher and tariff barriers lower. The study's conclusion is that it would seem impossible to make any generalisation in this sector (Hoffman and Rush, 1982).

Studies on other sectors seem to contradict Rada's findings in his 1980 study and to show that technological change may improve the position of developing countries. This may be the case with numerically controlled machine tools, particularly in newly industrialising countries (Jacobsson, 1982). These machines are easy to operate, do not require highly trained workers and permit economies by rationalising stocks, work in progress and factory space. Combined with relatively low wages and the introduction of shift work, this could improve a country's competitiveness. A recent ILO analysis qualifies this judgement by pointing out that such machines would be to the advantage only of newly industrialising countries and their biggest firms and that a stock of at least 20 machines would be needed to write off the cost of maintenance and repair (Watanabe, 1983). Newly industrialised countries would also seem to have an advantage for the production of software, as they have highly skilled computer programmers and system analysts generally working at lower salaries than elsewhere.

The growing availability of cheap satellite communications may also lead to significant changes in the international division of labour, though no general study has yet been made of its employment effects. What is clear is that the phenomenon of transborder data flows concentrates resources in the North. All the "control" data of international firms are centralised by the parent country and thereby diminish the autonomy of external branches, particularly in developing countries (Antonelli, 1981). Although this phenomenon may well increase the technological gap between North and South, it is not possible at this stage to gauge its impact in terms of employment.

It is in any case even more difficult to generalise about employment effects at the international level than it is to produce estimates or global simulations at the national level. There are at present simply no appropriate models, data or theoretical framework – an area where there is considerable scope for future research.

Working conditions

When new technologies are introduced, few managers or workers know in advance how to benefit most from the innovation, as regards either productivity or the quality of working life. The participation by all concerned in defining or redesigning their job is not only necessary for improving working conditions; it is in many cases an additional productivity factor (Kanawaty, 1981).

As far as information technology is concerned, this kind of co-operation can be particularly constructive since, in practice, the automation which the technology makes possible does not itself determine the profile and organisation of work. Managers, engineers, systems analysts and the workers concerned can collaborate in defining and applying a whole series of options.

Indeed, there is a considerable difference between the technical progress of the past, when mechanisation meant the substitution of machines for manual activities, and information technology in which micro-electronic control procedures take over from human intelligence functions. A recent ILO study draws attention to the diversity of situations to which the new "automation" can give rise and shows how much working conditions and skills can vary (Butera and Thurman, 1983). The study distinguishes four types of automation.

The first type includes computer-assisted isolated machines such as automatic packaging, automatic assembly and numerically controlled machines and simple industrial robots. In this case the work left to man is residual and ancillary to that performed by the machine. As a result, the quality of working life is poor because the main function of the operator is feeding and unloading the machine. He does not generally exercise control over the machine; in fact it can be said that he is controlled by the machine since it dictates the pace of his work.

The second type includes situations approximating the automatic factory: unmanned factories, refineries and power plants and driverless trains. The work is boring, the few workers employed feel isolated and stress is high because any error can have catastrophic consequences. The strategic skill required is not so much ability as reliability. Maintenance tasks are obviously more complex in such situations.

With the third type of automation, both the machines and the production unit are run automatically, but disturbances in input, conversion and output are frequent – for example in paper mills, printing shops, automatic transfer lines with a varied product mix, etc. The operator is actively involved in controlling the process and is able to operate manually or to change the process parameters. Active co-operation is necessary among the operators, designers and maintenance workers in order to manage the "memory" of the system (algorithm, parameters, technical integration, procedures, etc.).

The fourth type of automation is similar to the previous one but entails a great deal of manual work, such as in an automated rolling-stock mill or a partially automated chemical plant.

It is therefore difficult to generalise. To describe the new technology as improving or lowering working conditions can only be relevant in terms of the situation that existed before. Comparisons based on a typology such as that outlined above show that there are many possibilities for making working conditions better or worse and that the result is certainly not a foregone conclusion – any more than is, theoretically, the way the work will be organised as a result of the new technology.

This has been demonstrated in the case of flexible manufacturing systems (FMS) in a study carried out in the Federal Republic of Germany (Rempp, 1982). An FMS is a system of numerically controlled machine tools linked together by a transport information system. With this system the automation of small-batch production and complex processes has become possible. As the machines are reprogrammable, the system is extremely flexible, which leads to significant savings in fixed capital as it avoids the cost of retooling required by variable production lines or model changes.

An FMS may involve any one of five different organisation structures. At the one extreme, programming is done by the job planning division while setting up the machine tool is the joint responsibility of the job planning division and the shop and department foremen. The latter are responsible for optimisation and correction of programmes. The operators are responsible for loading and unloading as well as operating and monitoring; together with the shop foreman they check the finished product.

At the other extreme, all these activities are done independently by the operators and only quality control is carried out by inspectors. Obviously, this type of structure requires a maximum of training and experience as well as responsibility. From a production point of view, it entails some disadvantages as there is little feed-back between know-how acquired on the shop-floor and planning and a great deal of down-time due to changes in programmes. Advantages include lower costs in indirect activities, flexibility, on-the-job application of shop experience and more interest on the part of the workers.

The most common organisation structure is somewhere between the two. The operators are not responsible for the planning but set up the machine tools and operate and monitor them. Together with the job planning division, they also carry out optimisation and correction tasks.

The study concludes that the five organisation structures identified were used but that they were not always based on technical prerequisites, and the division of labour within the new system actually followed traditional patterns.

New automated systems can do much to improve working conditions. In the automobile and steel industries robots have now taken over strenuous and dangerous tasks such as welding, painting, sanding and molding. Automatic packaging and transport devices have eliminated many boring jobs. On the other hand, word processors that have been introduced in offices without preliminary study or appropriate precautions have caused eye strain, back fatigue, migraine and nausea (Werneke, 1983). A study in the United States reveals that 80 per cent of clerical users of visual display units (VDU) experience eye or muscle strain and nearly all experience abnormal fatigue (Working Women Education Fund, 1981). These findings are not unanimous, however. Studies conducted by works doctors and ophthalmologists consider that there is no evidence of any irreversible loss of vision and that muscular fatigue can be easily remedied provided workposts are properly designed and sufficient breaks allowed. According to some specialists, the danger of radiation is negligible. Be this as it may, and pending the findings of further research currently under way, the introduction of the new technology into offices makes it necessary to re-examine the equipment and its layout, ensure proper lighting and ventilation, provide "ergonomic" tables and seats and reorganise the work, all of which in any case means a whole new approach to secretarial work.

Another aspect of the new technology which is clearly illustrated by word processors is that it is conducive to keeping a closer check on workers, or at least on the work performed with machines. A secretary's typing speed, the number of pages "entered" each day and the time at which the operations are carried out can all be recorded without possibility of error. Similarly, in the case of numerically controlled machine tools and semi-automatic assembly lines, the speed of loading and unloading and the pace of work can be accurately measured. In judging such controls, much depends on what use is made of them and the general context in which they occur. If the management uses them to speed up the pace of work and set production standards that put too much strain on the workers or if they are used to promote maximum specialisation, they are not likely to elicit much co-operation from the workers. On the other hand, they would presumably not be opposed if they meant that the work was more varied, if the standards were acceptable and if keeping track of individual or group performance was used to improve the general management and productivity of the enterprise and, thus, remuneration and conditions of work.

The new technology generally entails a shift from directly operational activity to supporting and control functions. This has a twofold effect on working conditions. The work is less strenuous, but it tends to become boring and to cut the worker off from any direct contact with the actual production process. Several case studies listed in the aforementioned ILO survey (Butera and Thurman, 1983) make this point and warn against the danger of social isolation within undertakings. It is important to maintain a balance between manual and mental tasks when designing jobs for automated production processes and to incorporate opportunities for social interaction, which can be fostered in various ways: workshop discussions, exchanges of experience, increased participation in planning and control, and so on.

In many firms the introduction of new technology has on the whole had a positive effect on such important aspects of working conditions as pay, working hours and, frequently, job security. In the metal trades, for example, there have been many instances in which increased productivity has earned the workers higher wages or shorter working hours, particularly if they agree to be retrained.

Skills

A number of recent studies on relationship between new technology and skills have arrived at quite different conclusions. Some authors feel that there is a definite trend towards de-skilling. In the printing sector, for instance, photocomposition and facsimile satellite transmission can render much of the traditional know-how of the profession obsolete. The same is true in the metal trades, where highly skilled milling machine, lathe and grinding machine operators are replaced by numerically controlled machine tools, even though the latter are still less efficient for such operations as repoussé work (now taken over, though with a loss of quality, by numerically controlled stamping). Another point that is made is that the introduction of robots will lead to a general decline in qualifications because these machines take over not only manual but also intelligent human functions. Others, however, do not reach the same conclusion, arguing that the production and setting up of the machines require vast know-how and skills. Others, again, foresee a polarisation of skills with, on the one hand, an élite of designers, technocrats, controllers and repairers and, on the other, a large army of machine minders . . . and unemployed workers.

Such variety of opinion may not be so surprising. In the first place, the new technologies are only just beginning to be introduced and the occupational changes they entail are still quite unclear. Moreover, and above all, micro-electronics is applied in many different production processes and can therefore lead to very different skill patterns.

It is however possible here and now to foresee an unavoidable change: namely, that occupational activities will be less concerned with production processes than with control and support activities. We have already made this observation in connection with the many metalworking trades. Manual activities and craftsmanship will probably be

Figure 7.2
Qualitative changes in electro-technical occupations in the Federal Republic of Germany (1955-81)

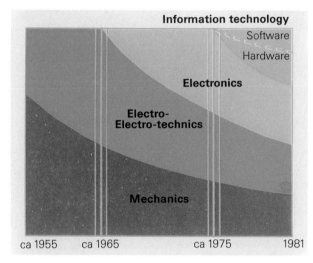

Source: F. Derricks et al., 1982.

transferred to maintenance and repair tasks, which will become more complex as the machines become more sophisticated. The very high degree of occupational skill required will need to be combined with a higher level of general and technical education.

Another definite trend is that, if the most important skill in an automated process becomes personal reliability, then again the general level of education will be a very relevant factor, not just so that the worker can understand the whys and wherefors of the limited operation for which he is responsible but so that he can absorb the successive training and retraining which the technical change is sure to entail – at the level of the factory, of the occupation and of the industry.

A third development is that, at least in certain occupations, information technology is playing an increasing role in skills from which it was totally absent only a few years ago. Figure 7.2 illustrates this point as it relates to electro-technical occupations in the Federal Republic of Germany.

Given these three trends, it seems safe enough to assert that broad basic education, in which a solid general initiation to the spirit and methods of science is very much to the fore, will be a valuable asset for future members of the active population who are called upon to work with the new technologies.

As regards the introduction of the technologies, the presence or absence of certain skills in the labour force has opposite effects. British firms at the beginning of the 1970s apparently decided to introduce numerically controlled machine tools because of an acute shortage of skilled metalworkers. On the other hand, the current shortage of computer programmers and software specialists in the Federal Republic of Germany, Switzerland and even in Japan is slowing down the diffusion of micro-electronics.

Industrial relations

As mentioned at the beginning of this chapter, it is noteworthy that by and large, though the degree of enthusiasm may vary, none of the social partners condemns the new technologies, despite the serious fears for employment provoked by the current economic climate, particularly in Europe.

The crucial issue raised by the new technologies as far as industrial relations are concerned has to do not so much with their content and their repercussions on conditions of employment as the precise stage at which workers and trade unions are informed of their introduction and the extent of their involvement in the decision. In most countries workers are informed only after the investment decision has been taken and only then do negotiations take place about wages and working conditions.

In Japan this procedure leads to less resistance on the part of the organised workers because large

189

7.2

Computer-aided design and the skills of draughtsmen

Computer-aided design (CAD) provides basic graphic software which speeds up the process of drawing and provides a wide variety of application programmes for use in engineering, cartography, business analysis, animation, statistics, research, etc.

By producing routine drawings very quickly, CAD increases the productivity of a draughtsman and helps designers to optimise their products (for example by reducing the wind resistance of motor cars). CAD also reduces the lead-time required to get a product onto the market. It can be linked to computer-aided manufacturing (CAM), thereby permitting fully automated production.

The impact of computer-aided design on skill requirement is varied. The technical skills required to operate CAD systems are about the same as those involved in manual systems. However, CAD de-skills the task of a draughtsman because it removes craft elements such as individually tailored layouts and individually developed lettering. On the other hand, the operator must know how to type, become familiar with visual display screens, learn terminal procedure and acquire a great deal of flexibility – characteristics that are often associated with youth. By contrast, the skill content involved in design has clearly increased. The skills required by supervisors and management have also changed. Managers need an overall view of the production process in order to reap maximum benefit from integrated information systems linking design, manufacture and inventory control. In other words, a certain amount of learning or relearning is involved for everyone.

The figure shows simulated learning curves for both management and operators.

As we can see, operators learn in stages. After three months, they are up to the productivity level of manual systems. After that productivity declines while they familiarise themselves with the use of the various "menus" (subroutines) incorporated in the CAD system (more sophisticated procedures, more intensive exploitation of the system's potential). After six months, operators are taking genuine advantage of the CAD's subsystems, and at the end of a

Simulated learning curves

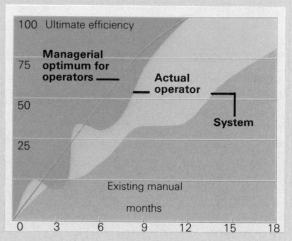

Source: Kaplinsky, 1982; Ebel, 1981.

year they are about as efficient as they could ever get. By that time, however, the maximum system-wide benefits have not yet been reached and management may need two or three years to master the system completely.

The learning process can be speeded up in a number of ways. One is to send both operators and managers on courses, either inside or outside the enterprise. A second strategy, generally pursued by enterprises for whom rapid progress is vital, is to poach existing expertise from other CAD users. A third way is for managers to gain important experience from the users' groups that are often organised by firms supplying turnkey CAD systems.

---

companies provide employment security and productivity increases are likely to result in higher real wages. A similar approach has been adopted in the United States, where the highly unionised sectors are able to guarantee employment security, although unions are not always able to bargain for higher wages (as can be seen today in the automobile industry). It is mainly in Europe that trade unions have been trying to negotiate "technology agreements".

In a few countries such as Denmark and Norway central agreements between the employ-ers' confederations and the trade union federations were concluded in 1981. These agreements stipulate that workers' representatives must be informed in advance about technical change. There are however slight differences, in that the Danish agreement provides that the information should be given before "management . . . brings into operation new, or alters existing, technology" while under the Norwegian agreement management must provide all the necessary information to employees, through their representatives, so that they can express their opinion before any decision is taken.

In the Danish agreement employers undertake to "endeavour to relocate individual employees in alternative jobs within the undertaking" and to pay course fees and any loss of wages to dismissed workers, in so far as these costs are not met by the State.

A draft agreement on new technologies was ratified in the United Kingdom by the Trades Union Congress (TUC) in 1980, but it was rejected by the Confederation of British Industry (CBI).

There are numerous agreements dealing with new technologies at the sectoral and plant levels. A 1978 newspaper settlement in the United States covering the principal New York dailies, for example, provides that the jobs of 1,500 regular printers are guaranteed until March 1984, while publishers are entitled to reduce manning levels through attrition and reduction of overtime. Post office workers in the United Kingdom negotiated in 1979 a security of employment agreement and a reduction in the working week to 37½ hours. In Ireland the Post Office Workers' Union negotiated in 1981 the payment of compensation to employees who are compulsorily transferred or made redundant following the closure of manual telephone exchanges.

In general, collective bargaining on new technologies is likely to include the following four elements: *(a)* security of employment – for example, for a fixed number of workers, by limiting workforce reductions to the rate of attrition or by reducing worktime; *(b)* training or retraining, sometimes also financed for workers who are dismissed; *(c)* financial compensation, in cases of voluntary separation or dismissal; and *(d)* profit sharing, explicitly linking pay and productivity.

In periods of economic crisis the introduction of new technologies poses a serious challenge for the social partners. Though it may be possible in isolated instances to resist innovations that seem superfluous, information technology as a whole has reached a point where it is useless or suicidal not to go along with the change, especially as it may provide a powerful contribution to economic recovery. The fundamental role of industrial relations, then, is to negotiate this change as painlessly as possible for each of the social partners and for the community at large. Here of course lies the rub, especially when the fate of a whole industry is at stake.

In practice the approach varies from one sector or country to another: direct state subsidies or protectionist measures to assist threatened industries; tripartite "management of decline" aimed at slowing down industrial contraction to allow for the creation of new employment opportunities in other industries; a "neo-liberal" response to change – in effect the deliberate adoption of measures to weaken trade unions and reduce social welfare. Perhaps the most promising and effective option is a tripartite productivity coalition in which employers and trade unions work together to increase an industry's productivity and competitiveness, in the interests of the long-term employment of the bulk of the workforce. The role of the State would then be limited to facilitating private investment, sponsoring research and development and providing various forms of assistance for workers adversely affected by the process of technical change.

In fact the role of the State does not end there. The NASA programme in the United States, the measures adopted by the Ministry of International Trade and Industry (MITI) in Japan and the more or less dynamic industrial policies pursued by certain European countries, for example, have actively stimulated the creation and diffusion of the new information technologies. But here we enter an area which is beyond the scope of this report. To conclude, therefore, let it suffice to point to three types of action in which government intervention, in co-operation with the social partners, would be beneficial: the laws and regulations governing working conditions in the new industries and with the new production processes; the definition of a legal framework for collective bargaining on new technologies, and perhaps even the establishment of international standards to be discussed within the ILO; and the development of effective and equitable ways and means of transferring these technologies to the developing countries.

[1] The concept of micro-electronics would seem to be broader in Europe than in the United States. In the United States the concept refers to the "microchip" itself, whereas in Europe it also covers its applications (OECD, 1981, Vol. I, p. 72, note 2).

[2] Chapter 2, note 9.

[3] The primary information sector includes all information goods and services which are sold on (established) markets, while the secondary information sector records the value added by domestic information activities produced and used by undertakings not operating within the primary information sector (OECD, 1981, Vol. I, pp. 34-40).

Selected bibliography

Antonelli, C. *Transborder data flows and international business: A pilot study* (OECD, 1981; mimeographed; doc. DSTI/ICCP/81.16; restricted).

Butera, F.; Thurman, J. *Automation and work design* (Geneva, ILO, 1983).

Conference of European Trade Union Centres. *Impact of technological change on working conditions and employment* (Geneva, ILO, 1981; mimeographed).

Denmark. Employers' Confederation (DA) and Danish Federation of Trade Unions (LO). *Technology agreement*, Supplementary Agreement to the Co-operation Agreement (Copenhagen, 1981).

Derricks, F.; Handel, C.; Meyer, N. "Auswirkungen der Mikroelektronik auf der Berufsbildung von Elektrofacharbeitern", in *Informationen* (Nuremberg, Bundesanstalt für Arbeit), 20 Jan. 1982.

Dostal, W. *Bildung und Beschäftigung im technischen Wandel*, Beiträge zur Arbeitsmarkt und Berufsforschung No. 65 (Nuremberg, Institut für Arbeitsmarkt und Berufsforschung der Bundesanstalt für Arbeit, 1982).

Ebel, K.-H. "The microelectronics training gap in the metal trades", in *International Labour Review* (Geneva, ILO) Nov.-Dec. 1981.

Freeman, C. "The Kondratiev long waves, technical change and unemployment", in *Stuctural determinants of employment and unemployment*, Vol. II (Paris, OECD, 1979).

Gassmann, H. P. "Is there a fourth economic sector?", in *OECD Observer* (Paris, OECD), Nov. 1981.

Gershuny, J. *After industrial society? The emerging self-service economy* (London, Macmillan, 1978).

Hoffman, K.; Rush, H. "Microelectronics and the garment industry: Not yet a perfect fit", in *IDS Bulletin: Comparative advantage in an automating world* (Brighton (Sussex), Institute of Development Studies), Mar. 1982.

ILO. *The effects of technological and structural changes on the employment and working conditions of non-manual workers*, Report II, Advisory Committee on Salaried Employees and Professional Workers, Geneva, 1981 (Geneva, 1980).

—. *New technologies: Their impact on employment and the working environment* (Geneva, 1982).

—. *The effects of structural changes and technical progress on employment in the public service*, Report III, Joint Committee on the Public Service, Third Session, Geneva, 1983 (Geneva, 1983).

Jacobson, S. "Electronics and the technology gap – The case of numerically controlled machine tools", in *IDS Bulletin*, op. cit.

Kanawaty, G. "Introducing and developing new forms of work organisation", in G. Kanawaty (ed.) *Managing and developing new forms of work organisation* (Geneva, ILO, 1981), Second (revised) edition.

Kaplinsky, R. "Is there a skill constraint in the diffusion of micro-electronics", in *IDS Bulletin*, op. cit.

Matheson, J. "Management and the challenge of technological change", in *Management* (Wellington, New Zealand Institute of Management), Dec. 1980.

Missika, J. L. "L'informatisation est-elle une unité d'analyse économique?", in *Informatique, travail et emploi*, Proceedings of the International Symposium on Information Technology and Society, Vol. II (Paris, La Documentation française, 1980).

—; Pastré, O.; Meyer, D.; Truel, J. L.; Larader, R.; Stoffaes, C. France. "IRIS – Document de préparation au VIIIᵉ Plan", in *Informatisation et emploi: menace ou mutation?* (Paris, La Documentation française, 1981).

Netherlands. *The social impact of microelectronics*, Report of the Rathenau Advisory Group (The Hague, Government Publishing Office, 1980).

OECD. *Microelectronics, productivity and employment*, Information Computer Communications Policy No. 5 (Paris, 1981).

—. *Information activities, electronics and telecommunications technologies: Impact on employment, growth and trade*, Information Computer Communications Policy No. 6, Vol. I (Paris, 1981).

—. *Innovation in small and medium firms*, Report by the Committee for Scientific and Technological Policy (Paris, 1982).

Piore, M.; Sabel, C. *Italian small business development: Lessons for US industrial policy* (Cambridge, Massachusetts Institute of Technology), Working Paper No. 288, Aug. 1981.

Porat, J.; Rubin, M. *The information economy* (Washington, DC, United States Government Printing Office, 1977).

Rada, J. *The impact of micro-electronics: A tentative appraisal of information technology* (Geneva, ILO, 1980).

—. "Technology and the North-South division of labour", in *IDS Bulletin*, op. cit.

Rempp, H. "The economic and social effects of the introduction of CNC machine tools and flexible manufacturing systems", in *European Employment and Technological Change*, New Patterns in Employment No. 2 (Maastricht, European Centre for Work and Society, 1982).

Stoneman, P.; Blattner, N.; Pastré, O. *An analytical review based on national reports*, Report presented to the OECD Second Special Session on Information Technologies, Productivity and Employment (Paris, OECD, 1981; mimeographed doc. DSTI/ICCP/81.29; restricted).

United Kingdom. "Robotics in the UK", in *Industrial Robot*, No. 1, 1981.

United States National Commission on Technology, Automation and Economic Progress. *Technology and the American economy*, Vol. I (Washington, DC, United States Government Printing Office, 1966).

United States: Working Women Education Fund. *Warning: Health hazards for office workers* (Cleveland, Ohio), Apr. 1981.

Volkholz, V. *Trends as regards the application of industrial robots in the eighties* (Paris, OECD, 1981; mimeographed doc. DSTI/ICCP/81.34; restricted).

Watanabe, S. *Market structure, industrial organisation and technological development: The case of the Japanese electronic-based NC-machine tool industry* (Geneva, ILO, 1983; mimeographed World Employment Programme research working paper; restricted).

Werneke, D. *Microelectronics and office jobs: The impact of the chip on women's employment* (Geneva, ILO, 1983).

193

Statistical annex

Introduction

The first volume of the World Labour Report 1983 is based on a large amount of data collected by the ILO in the course of its normal activities. Most of this statistical information is presented in the chapters dealing with particular topics. This statistical information is supplemented by tables presented in the Statistical annex.

In the first part, table A.1 presents the latest available information on the economically active population with a breakdown between the three major sectors (agriculture, mining and quarrying; industry; others) for 100 developing and industrialised countries. In addition to global figures, we also present separate figures for the male and female economically active population.

In the second part, data are given on income distribution by size for 33 countries. These newly available figures are the result of a joint ILO/World Bank project aimed at obtaining income distribution data with a higher degree of comparability than was the case with data available until now. Table A.2 shows the share of each of the ten deciles of households and a global indicator of inequality (the Gini coefficient) for each country.

In the third part, some basic information is provided about social security: the latest available data on the average social security receipts and expenditure per head of population, in national currency units (table A.3), receipts and expenditures of social security schemes as a percentage of GDP (or NMP) for 1965, 1975 and the latest available year (table A.4) and information on the normal age of retirement in developed and developing countries (table A.5).

1. Structure of the economically active population

The data presented in table A.1 on the sectoral distribution of the economically active population have been drawn from the latest available census or survey of the country concerned. They are taken from table 2A of the 1980-82 issues of the ILO *Year Book of Labour Statistics*. The symbol ★ means that the data are provisional; † refers to notes at the end of table A.1. For each country the date to which the data relate is given and the source of the data is indicated using one of the following abbreviations: C=complete census count; Cs=census sample tabulation, size not specified; C..%=census sample tabulation, size specified; LFSS=labour force sample survey; HS=household survey; OE=official estimates.

In interpreting these data, it should be borne in mind that there are important differences between countries as regards the treatment of such groups as armed forces, inmates of institutions, persons living on reservations, unemployed persons not previously employed, seasonal workers, persons engaged in part-time activities and family workers who assist in family enterprises, particularly females. In some countries all or part of these groups are included in the economically active population while in other countries they are treated as inactive.

The comparability of the data is further hampered by differences as regards details of definitions used, methods of collection and systems of classification. The reference period is also an important factor of difference, not only because of seasonal factors, but also because in some countries the reference period may refer to the actual position of each individual on the day of the census or survey (or during a brief specified period such as the week immediately prior to the census or

survey date), whereas in other countries it may refer to the usual position of each person, generally without reference to any given period of time (or else for a long specified period such as the preceding 12 months or preceding calendar year).

While most countries have supplied data on the basis of the International Standard Industrial Classification (ISIC), it should be borne in mind that the national industrial classifications on which the ISIC data are based present many points of divergence and that the actual content of industrial groups, though similarly labelled, may differ owing to variations in definitions and methods of tabulation. For example, even when using international classification schemes, national practices may differ concerning the classification of the unemployed who have previously worked. According to the international recommendations, such persons should be classified on the basis of their last or usual activity. When this is not feasible, they are often included in the residual category "activities not adequately defined".

Lastly, classifications in broad sectoral groups, such as shown below, also obscure fundamental differences in the industrial patterns of the various countries.

The sectoral classification shown in table A.1 encompasses the following major divisions of economic activity:

*Agriculture, mining and quarrying (ISIC 1-2):*Agriculture, hunting, forestry and fishing; mining and quarrying.

Industry (ISIC 3-5): Manufacturing; electricity, gas and water; construction.

Others (ISIC 6-9/10): Wholesale and retail trade, restaurants and hotels; transport, storage and communications; financing, insurance, real estate and business services; community, social and personal services; activities not adequately defined; not previously employed.

Table A.1. Structure of the economically active population

	Total			Agriculture, mining and quarrying			Industry			Others		
	M+F	M	F	M+F	M	F	M+F	M	F	M+F	M	F
Africa												
Algeria (II.77) C★†	3371023	3070706	300317	751872	743316	8556	637299	614519	22780	1981852	1712871	268981
United Republic of Cameroon (1982)OE†	3543000	2214000	1329000	2596380	1436200	1160180	225650	193500	32150	720970	584300	136670
Egypt (V.79) LFSS†	10023500	9244800	778700	4024800	3979400	45400	2046300	1949200	97100	3952400	3316200	636200
Liberia (1.II.74) C†	432871	316847	116024	332152	233991	98161	9913	9552	361	90806	73304	17502
Libyan Arab Jamahiriya (31.VII.73) C †	541174	504264	36910	122236	108005	25153	121090	119127	1963	286607	265891	20716
Malawi (1.X.77) C	2288351	1231812	1056539	1934296	938239	996057	134056	116711	17345	219999	176862	43137
Mali (XII.76) C★†	2235157	1856431	378726	1942254	1627621	314633	27005	15839	11166	265898	212971	52927
Seychelles (VIII.77) C†	25947	16362	9585	5058	3798	1260	6231	5461	770	14658	7103	7555
Tunisia (V.80) OE★†	1864220	1500680	363540	595940	477989	117951	559428	401358	158070	708852	621333	87519
Americas												
Barbados (1981) LFSS†	114300	62800	51500	9700	5900	3800	21900	13700	8200	82700	43200	39500
Bermuda (12.V.80) C†	31436	17232	14204	402	369	33	4061	3554	507	26973	13309	13664
Bolivia (29.IX.76) C†	1501391	1164619	336772	753648	661272	92376	229994	172883	57111	517749	330464	187285
Canada (IV.82) LFSS†	11665000	6859000	4806000	661000	516000	145000	2601000	2015000	586000	8403000	4328000	4076000
Colombia (1980) HS★†	8467000	6247000	2220000	2462153	..	..	1423159	..	..	4581688	..	..
Costa Rica (VII.80) HS★†	770272	578972	191300	206913	..	..	185541	..	..	377818	..	..
Chile (X-XII.80) LFSS†	3635600	..	..	873600	..	..	699300	..	..	2062700	..	..
Ecuador (VI.81) OE†	2808159	2057889	750270	1346244	..	..	445739	..	..	1016176		

Table A.1. (continued)

	Total			Agriculture, mining and quarrying			Industry			Others		
	M+F	M	F	M+F	M	F	M+F	M	F	M+F	M	F
El Salvador (I-VI.80) HS†	1593353	1039446	553907	641011	524802	116209	337391	232680	104711	614951	281964	332987
Greenland (26.X.76) C	21378	14234	7144	3539	3516	23	6075	4835	1240	11764	5883	5881
Guadeloupe (16.X.74) C†	107959	66418	41541	18611	14490	4121	19144	16834	2310	70204	35094	35110
Guatemala (1979) OE★†	2137642	1842658	294984	1225321	1207701	17620	386740	322537	64203	525581	312420	213161
Guyana (1977) LFSS★†	165031	122688	42343	52624	46311	6313	45125	38413	6712	67282	37964	29318
French Guyana (I.77) OE†	21740	12400	9340	3740	2240	1500	3830	3450	380	14170	6710	7460
Haiti (VIII.80) OE†	2317800	1232600	1085200	1320800	813400	507400	155900	111000	74900	841100	338200	502900
Honduras (1981) OE†	1124216	942467	181749	598067	..	..	166956	..	..	359193	..	..
Jamaica (XI.80) LFSS†	737300	448200	289100	280100	212500	67600	106400	83500	22900	350800	152200	198600
Martinique (16.X.74) C†	104484	60892	43592	15553	11838	3715	15997	13590	2407	72934	35464	37470
Mexico (VI.79) OE†	19650695	14843192	4807503	8174689	7439408	735281	4566821	3480728	1086093	6909185	3923056	2986129
Montserrat (12.V.80) C†	4872	2881	1991	485	355	130	1266	995	271	3121	1531	1590
Netherlands Antilles (XII.81) OE†	100048	65782	34266	829	..	..	17994	..	..	81225	..	..
Nicaragua (1980) OE†	863925	681089	182836	398529	..	..	135377	..	..	330019	..	..
Panama (11.V.80) C20%†	548460	396315	152145	145555	139760	5795	90510	76310	14200	312395	180245	132150
Paraguay (1981) OE★†	1290947	..	..	580891	..	..	253829	..	..	456227	..	..
Peru (V.82) OE	5977600	4270300	1707300	2364200	..	..	1005000	..	..	2608400	..	..
Puerto Rico (IV.82) LFSS†	1044000	681000	363000	55000	54000	..	295000	195000	98000	695000	430000	264000

Table A.1. (continued)

	Total			Agriculture, mining and quarrying			Industry			Others		
	M+F	M	F	M+F	M	F	M+F	M	F	M+F	M	F
St. Pierre and Miquelon (18.II.74) C†	2153	1604	549	126	126	..	551	505	46	1476	973	503
Trinidad and Tobago (VII-XII.80) LFSS†	430300	293600	136700	41300	30900	10400	163800	131600	32300	225200	131200	94000
United States (1981) LFSS†	110812000	63939000	46873000	4938000	4004000	934000	32169000	23629000	8542000	73704000	36306000	37397000
Uruguay (21.V.75) C†	1094599	783584	311015	177030	166923	10107	281577	214940	66637	635992	401721	234271
Venezuela (I-VI.81) HS†	4561043	3317340	1243703	704179	676587	27592	1211837	998958	212879	2645027	1641795	1003232
Asia												
Afghanistan (24.VI.79) C★†	3945591	3632155	313436	2428820	2416313	12507	485813	232656	253157	1030958	983186	47772
Bahrain (IV.81) C★†	142384	126179	16205	8487	8306	181	43502	42911	591	90395	74962	15433
Bangladesh (1.III.74) C†	20522592	19650597	871995	15824800	15214522	610278	986555	949647	36908	3711237	3486428	224809
Burma (1980-81) OE†	14098000	..	..	9103000	..	..	1275000	..	..	3720000	..	..
Cyprus (1981) OE★†	208100	135300	72800	46200	22300	23900	58100	38300	19800	103800	74700	29100
Democratic Yemen (14.V.73) C†	409742	333954	75788	168169	120583	47586	32636	30653	1983	208937	182718	26219
Hong Kong (9.III.81) C†	2503804	1618389	885415	48560	32469	16091	1191033	724852	466181	1264211	861068	403143
India (1.IV.71) C	180485006	149146069	31338937	130980918	104974044	26006874	19822763	17413451	2409312	29681325	26758574	2922751
Indonesia (1978) HS†	53097095	33884003	19213092	31668118	20752779	10915339	4674826	2734794	1940032	16754151	10396430	6357721
Islamic Republic of Iran (XI.76) C†	9796055	7810327	1985728	3705544	2877842	827702	2946010	2279859	666151	3144501	2652626	491875
Iraq (17.X.77) C★†	3133939	2589561	544378	980725	625782	354943	629281	574578	54703	1523933	1389201	134732
Israel (1981) LFSS†	1348500	852700	495800	78100	62000	16100	402900	329300	73400	867300	461400	406300

199

Table A.1. (continued)

	Total			Agriculture, mining and quarrying			Industry			Others		
	M+F	M	F	M+F	M	F	M+F	M	F	M+F	M	F
Japan (1981) LFSS†	57070000	34980000	22090000	5670000	2970000	2700000	19600000	13410000	6180000	31800000	18610000	13200000
Jordan (11.XI.79) CS★	377885	..	..	42703	..	..	88046	..	..	247136	..	..
Republic of Korea (1981) LFSS†	14710000	9213000	5496000	4930000	2823000	2107000	3780000	2585000	1194000	6000000	3805000	2195000
Kuwait (IV.80) C★	484106	422003	62103	16104	15807	297	146162	144813	1349	321840	261383	60457
Lebanon (1975) OE★	748000	..	..	128000	..	..	193000	..	..	426000	..	..
Peninsular Malaysia (1979) LFSS	4374500	2799800	1574700	1549100	..	..	1028700	..	..	1796700	..	..
Nepal (1976) HS	6197843	3869829	2328014	5571807	3409781	2162026	48969	39730	9239	577067	420318	156749
Pakistan (I.82) LFSS†	26635000	23381000	3254000	13562000	..	..	5187000	..	..	7886000	..	..
Philippines (X-XII.78) HS†	17362000	10939000	6423000	8769000	6455000	2314000	2451000	1521000	929000	6142000	2963000	3180000
Singapore (24.VI.80) C†	1115958	730606	385352	18101	14896	3205	404931	248447	156484	692926	467263	225663
Sri Lanka (1980-81) LFSS†	5714983	4109204	1605779	2356775	1703802	652973	807325	602610	204715	2550883	1802792	748091
Syrian Arab Republic (IX.79) LFSS†	2174225	1831370	342855	692545	492736	199809	669088	622058	47030	812592	716576	96016
Thailand (VII-IX.80) LFSS†	22728100	11988000	10740100	15979300	8076400	7902700	2284700	1464400	819800	4463300	2446500	2016600
United Arab Emirates (31.XII.75) C†	296516	286555	9961	20437	20207	230	117399	117040	359	158680	149308	9372
Yemen (1.II.75) OE†	1136000	..	..	877000	..	..	50000	..	..	209000	..	..

Table A.1. (continued)

	Total			Agriculture, mining and quarrying			Industry			Others		
	M+F	M	F	M+F	M	F	M+F	M	F	M+F	M	F
Europe												
Austria (1981) LFSS†	3147000	1930000	1217000	335000	181000	154000	1252000	965000	287000	1560000	784000	776000
Belgium (VI.81) OE†	4161328	2591563	1569765	137217	113583	23634	1197662	973497	224165	2826449	1504483	1321966
Bulgaria (2.XII.75) C	4447784	2365708	2082076	1133983	561079	572904	1816853	1071388	745463	1496950	733241	763709
Czecho-slovakia (1.XI.80) C†	7848867	4184481	3664386	1026386	601924	424462	3833608	2364496	1469112	2988873	1218061	1770812
Denmark (V.81) LFSS†	2674392	1485912	1188480	181767	144028	37739	806289	605634	200655	1686336	736250	950086
Faeroe Islands (22.IX.77) C	12808	4777	17585	3373	39	3412	4836	872	5708	4599	3866	8465
Finland (1981) LFSS*†	2402000	1280000	1122000	267000	165000	102000	801000	559000	243000	1333000	556000	777000
France (1981) OE*†	22970200	13940300	9029900	1941500	..	..	7238900	..	..	13789800	1012900	992400
Federal Republic of Germany (1981) OE*†	26936000	16577000	10359000	1873000	1081000	792000	11195000	8158000	3037000	13868000	7339000	6529000
Greece (1977) OE†	3318000	2307000	1011000	1104000	630000	474000	934000	754000	180000	1280000	923000	357000
Hungary (I.81) OE†	5014500	2761800	2252700	1109300	678500	430800	2046700	1239500	807200	1858500	843800	1014700
Iceland (VI.79) OE†	101400	..	..	12200	..	..	38400	..	..	50700	..	..
Ireland (VI.79) LFSS†	1235100	892000	343200	234000	213400	20800	357400	285900	71500	643700	392800	251000
Isle of Man (4.IV.76) C	23278	15479	7799	1278	1186	92	6770	5821	949	15230	8472	6758
Italy (1980) LFSS†	22804000	15215000	7588000	2925000	1870000	1055000	7772000	5949000	1823000	12108000	7397000	4711000
Malta (XII.80) OE†	123775	91867	31908	8505	7701	804	45828	31108	14720	69442	53058	16384

Table A.1. (continued)

	Total			Agriculture, mining and quarrying			Industry			Others		
	M+F	M	F	M+F	M	F	M+F	M	F	M+F	M	F
Netherlands (III-V.79) LFSS†	5 213 000	3 661 000	1 552 000	291 000	245 000	46 000	1 615 000	1 422 000	193 000	3 307 000	1 995 000	1 312 000
Norway (1981) LFSS†	1 971 000	1 150 000	822 000	164 000	116 000	48 000	575 000	467 000	108 000	1 233 000	567 000	666 000
Poland (7.XII.78) C	17 962 126	9 806 245	8 155 881	5 832 451	3 124 608	2 707 843	6 438 506	4 143 641	2 294 865	5 691 169	2 537 996	3 153 173
Portugal (VII.XII.81) LFSS†	4 366 000	2 554 000	1 812 000	1 065 000	509 000	557 000	1 519 000	1 067 000	452 000	1 796 000	978 000	818 000
Spain (X-XII.79) LFSS†	13 301 500	9 379 500	3 922 000	2 654 300	1 974 100	680 200	3 963 100	3 227 100	736 000	6 684 100	4 178 300	2 505 800
Switzerland (1980) OE†	3 018 500	1 963 900	1 054 600	223 900	..	..	1 191 300	..	..	6 300	3 700	2 600
Sweden (1981) LFSS†	4 332 000	2 342 000	1 991 000	251 000	188 000	63 000	1 309 000	1 014 000	295 000	2 775 000	1 140 000	1 633 000
Turkey (12.X.80) C1%†	19 026 885	12 614 100	6 412 785	10 661 983	5 226 916	5 435 067	2 892 604	2 597 089	295 515	5 472 298	4 790 095	682 203
United Kingdom (VI.80) OE†	26 350 000	16 034 000	10 315 000	1 002 000	851 000	151 000	8 948 000	6 763 000	2 184 000	16 402 000	8 422 000	7 980 000
Oceania												
Australia (II.82) LFSS*†	6 881 900	4 334 900	2 547 100	503 500	397 400	106 100	1 726 000	1 363 200	362 800	4 652 400	2 574 300	2 078 200
Cook Islands (1.XII.76) C	5 384	3 850	1 534	1 186	1 164	22	876	548	328	3 322	2 138	1 184
Fiji (13.IX.76) C	175 785	146 315	29 470	78 548	71 629	6 919	25 853	23 893	1 960	71 384	50 793	20 591
French Polynesia (27.IV.77) C†	43 058	30 748	12 310	7 604	6 812	792	7 949	6 995	954	27 505	16 941	10 564
Guam (XII.79) LFSS†	35 560	..	..	100	..	..	4 100	..	..	2 260	930	1 330
New Zealand (24.III.81) C13.6%†	1 331 210	875 500	455 710	146 200	114 900	31 290	416 650	323 340	93 320	768 380	437 260	331 110

202

Table A.1. (continued)

	Total			Agriculture, mining and quarrying			Industry			Others		
	M+F	M	F	M+F	M	F	M+F	M	F	M+F	M	F
Samoa (3.XI.76) C†	38 249	31 867	6 382	23 380	21 788	1 592	2 993	2 758	235	11 876	7 321	4 555
Tonga (30.XI.76) C†	21 435	18 077	3 358	9 545	9 478	67	1 653	1 501	152	10 237	7 098	3 139

. . not available.

AFRICA

Algeria

Excluding Algerians working abroad. "Others" also includes 345,067 persons seeking their first job and 325,760 unemployed with previous job experience for whom a distribution by sex, industry and status is not available.

United Republic of Cameroon

African population. "Others" includes 161,270 persons seeking work for the first time (119,100 males and 42,170 females.

Egypt

Egyptian population. Figures relate to persons 12 to 64 years of age. "Others" includes 424,500 persons seeking work for the first time (285,300 males and 139,200 females).

Liberia

"Others" includes 23,499 persons seeking work for the first time (17,476 males and 6,023 females).

Libyan Arab Jamahiriya

"Others" includes 9,774 persons seeking work for the first time (8,982 males and 792 females).

Mali

De jure population. "Others" also includes 8,913 apprentices (8,611 males and 302 females), and 41,991 persons seeking work for the first time (31,721 males and 10,270 females).

Seychelles

"Others" includes 764 persons seeking work for the first time (396 males and 368 females).

Tunisia

1958 ISIC. "Others" includes 233,100 unemployed (211,500 males and 21,600 females).

AMERICAS

Barbados

Excluding institutional households. "Others" includes 12,400 unemployed (4,600 males and 7,800 females).

Bermuda

"Others" includes 627 unemployed (341 males and 286 females).

Bolivia

"Others" includes 6,463 persons seeking work for the first time (5,286 males and 1,177 females).

Canada

Excluding Yukon, Northwest Territories, armed forces and Indians living on reserves. All figures are rounded to the nearest 1,000; consequently, the totals shown may differ from the sum of the component parts. "Others" includes 1,233,000 unemployed (744,000 males and 489,000 females).

Colombia

"Others" includes persons seeking work for the first time.

Costa Rica

"Others" also includes electricity, gas and water. "Industry" includes mining and quarrying. "Others" also includes 10,214 persons seeking work for the first time.

Chile

"Others" also includes 114,600 unemployed.

Ecuador

"Others" also includes 52,137 persons seeking work for the first time.

El Salvador

"Others" also includes 27,027 persons seeking work for the first time (8,498 males and 18,529 females).

Guadeloupe

"Others" includes 24,019 unemployed (13,775 males and 10,244 females).

Guatemala

Excluding institutional households. "Others" includes persons seeking work for the first time.

Guyana

1958 ISIC.

French Guyana

"Others" includes 1,080 persons seeking work for the first time (490 males and 590 females).

Haiti

"Others" includes 358,800 unemployed (228,000 males and 130,800 females) and 5,400 males members of armed forces.

Honduras

"Others" includes 111,745 unemployed.

Jamaica

Figures do not include unemployed.

Martinique

"Others" includes 11,532 persons seeking work for the first time (6,186 males and 5,346 females).

Mexico

1958 ISIC.

Montserrat

"Others" includes 298 unemployed (125 males and 173 females).

Netherlands Antilles

"Others" includes 20,173 persons seeking work for the first time.

Nicaragua

Economically active population figures do not include unemployed.

Panama

Including 16,380 persons working in the Canal Zone (13,330 males and 3,050 females). These persons are included in "Others". "Others" also includes 44,920 unemployed (26,855 males and 18,065 females).

Paraguay

"Others" includes 26,633 persons seeking work for the first time.

Puerto Rico

All figures are rounded to the nearest 1,000; consequently, the totals shown may differ from the sum of the component parts. "Others" includes 26,000 persons seeking work for the first time (14,000 males and 12,000 females).

St. Pierre and Miquelon

"Others" includes seven persons seeking work for the first time (six males and one female).

Trinidad and Tobago

All figures are rounded to the nearest 100; consequently, the totals shown may differ from the sum of the component parts. 1958 ISIC. "Others" includes 6,600 persons seeking work for the first time (2,700 males and 3,900 females). "Industry" includes mining and quarrying.

United States

Economically active population figures relate to persons 16 years of age and over. All figures are rounded to the nearest 1,000; consequently, the totals shown may differ from the sum of the component parts. "Others" includes 982,000 persons seeking work for the first time (472,000 males and 510,000 females) and 2,142,000 members of armed forces (1,964,000 males and 178,000 females).

Uruguay

"Others" includes 17,131 persons seeking work for the first time (9,220 males and 7,911 females).

Venezuela

"Others" includes 40,168 persons seeking work for the first time (22,495 males and 17,673 females).

ASIA

Afghanistan

"Others" includes 77,510 persons seeking work for the first time (66,057 males and 11,453 females).

Bahrain

De jure population. "Others" also includes 4,492 unemployed (2,958 males and 1,534 females).

Bangladesh

"Others" includes 502,706 unemployed (471,254 males and 31,452 females).

Burma

"Others" includes 512,000 unemployed.

Cyprus

Including Cypriots working temporarily abroad. "Others" includes 1,065 persons seeking work for the first time (865 males and 200 females).

Democratic Yemen

"Others" includes 71,522 unemployed (55,593 males and 15,929 females).

Hong Kong

"Others" includes 99,737 unemployed (66,946 males and 32,791 females).

Indonesia

"Others" includes 1,316,736 unemployed (978,945 males and 337,791 females).

Islamic Republic of Iran

"Others" includes 297,990 persons seeking work for the first time (160,553 males and 137,437 females).

Iraq

"Others" includes 74,725 unemployed (64,278 males and 10,447 females).

Israel

Including data relating to certain territories under occupation by Israeli military forces since June 1967. Economically active population figures do not include armed forces. All figures are rounded to the nearest 100; consequently, the totals shown may differ from the sum of the component parts. "Others" includes 34,300 persons seeking work for the first time (15,200 males and 19,100 females). "Industry" includes mining and quarrying.

Japan

All figures are rounded to the nearest 10,000; consequently, the totals shown may differ from the sum of the component parts. "Others" includes 1,260,000 unemployed (790,000 males and 470,000 females).

Republic of Korea

Excluding armed forces. "Others" includes 661,000 unemployed (526,000 males and 135,000 females).

Peninsular Malaysia

"Others" includes 250,600 unemployed.

Pakistan

Excluding Jammu and Kashmir (the final status of which has not yet been determined), Gilgit and Baltistan, Junagardh and Manavadar. "Others" includes 944,000 unemployed.

Philippines

Economically active population figures do not include armed forces and institutional households. All figures are rounded to the nearest 1,000; consequently, the totals shown may differ from the sum of the component parts. "Others" includes 694,000 unemployed (262,000 males and 433,000 females).

Singapore

"Others" includes 38,868 unemployed (24,089 males and 14,779 females).

Sri Lanka

Owing to independent estimation, the totals shown may differ from the sum of the component parts. "Others" includes 1,165,457 unemployed (738,630 males and 426,827 females).

Syrian Arab Republic

"Others" includes 49,731 persons seeking work for the first time (38,442 males and 11,289 females).

Thailand

All figures are rounded to the nearest 100; consequently, the totals shown may differ from the sum of the component parts. Economically active population figures do not include unpaid family workers who, during the survey week, worked less than 20 hours. "Others" includes 204,200 unemployed (121,600 males and 82,500 females). 1958 ISIC.

United Arab Emirates

"Others" includes 3,990 persons seeking work for the first time (3,568 males and 422 females).

EUROPE

Austria

Excluding institutional households.

Belgium

"Others" includes workers in vocational training. "Others" includes 399,093 unemployed (170,174 males and 228,919 females) and 31,639 males members of armed forces.

Czechoslovakia

Economically active population figures do not include 1,185 unpaid family workers for whom a distribution by sex and age is not available.

Denmark

Economically active population figures relate to persons 15 to 74 years of age.

Finland

Economically active population figures relate to persons 15 to 74 years of age. All figures are rounded to the nearest 1,000; consequently, the totals shown may differ from the sum of the component parts. "Others" includes members of armed forces.

France

Excluding persons on compulsory military service. "Others" includes 1,696,000 unemployed (713,400 males and 982,600 females) and 309,300 professional members of armed forces (299,500 males and 9,800 females).

Federal Republic of Germany

All figures are rounded to the nearest 1,000; consequently, the totals shown may differ from the sum of the component parts. "Others" includes 104,000 persons seeking work for the first time (48,000 males and 56,000 females) and 535,000 males members of armed forces.

Greece

"Others" includes 56,000 unemployed (28,000 males and 28,000 females).

Hungary

"Industry" includes mining and quarrying.

Iceland

"Industry" includes mining and quarrying. "Others" includes 400 unemployed.

Ireland

All figures are rounded to the nearest 100; consequently, the totals shown may differ from the sum of the component parts. "Others" includes 84,800 unemployed (69,100 males and 15,700 females) and 13,800 members of armed forces (13,500 males and 300 females).

Italy

Economically active population figures do not include persons on compulsory military service. All figures are rounded to the nearest 1,000; consequently, the totals shown may differ from the sum of the component parts. "Others" includes 1,698,000 unemployed (715,000 males and 982,000 females) and 535,000 males members of armed forces.

Malta

"Others" includes 4,039 unemployed (3,455 males and 584 females) and 798 males members of armed forces.

Netherlands

All figures are rounded to the nearest 1,000; consequently, the totals shown may differ from the sum of the component parts. "Others" includes 274,000 unemployed (139,000 males and 134,000 females) and 88,000 males members of armed forces.

Norway

Economically active population figures do not include persons on compulsory military service. Economically active population figures are rounded to the nearest 1,000; consequently, the totals shown may differ from the sum of the component parts. "Others" includes 40,000 unemployed (17,000 males and 23,000 females).

Portugal

Owing to independent estimation, the totals shown may differ from the sum of the component parts. "Others" includes 164,000 unemployed (49,000 males and 115,000 females) and 97,000 males members of armed forces.

Spain

"Agriculture, mining and quarrying" also includes the milling of minerals. "Industry" also includes the extraction of fuels. "Others" includes 1,348,500 unemployed (891,900 males and 456,600 females).

Sweden

Economically active population figures do not include persons on compulsory military service. Economically active population figures relate to persons 16 to 74 years of age who have worked at least one hour per week. All figures are rounded to the nearest 1,000; consequently, the totals shown may differ from the sum of the component parts. "Others" includes 108,000 unemployed (55,000 males and 52,000 females).

Switzerland

"Others" includes 6,300 unemployed (3,700 males and 2,600 females).

Turkey

"Others" includes 839,930 persons seeking work for the first time (684,160 males and 155,770 females).

United Kingdom

De jure population. All figures are rounded to the nearest 1,000; consequently, the totals shown may differ from the sum of the component parts. "Others" includes 1,660,000 unemployed (1,132,000 males and 527,000 females) and 323,000 members of armed forces (307,000 males and 16,000 females).

OCEANIA

Australia

All figures are rounded to the nearest 100; consequently, the totals shown may differ from the sum of the component parts. "Others" includes 484,400 unemployed (251,700 males and 232,700 females).

Guam

"Others" includes 2,260 unemployed (930 males and 1,330 females).

New Zealand

Including Maoris; excluding armed forces overseas. Economically active population figures relate to persons who have worked at least 20 hours per week. "Others" includes 10,270 persons seeking work for the first time (4,530 males and 5,740 females).

French Polynesia

Economically active population figures do not include unemployed.

Samoa

"Others" includes 45 unemployed (29 males and 16 females).

Tonga

"Others" includes 2,809 persons seeking work for the first time (2,194 males and 615 females).

2. Income distribution in selected countries

Most of the income distribution estimates shown in this part are the result of a joint ILO/World Bank project. Estimates for nine developing countries (Argentina, Brazil, Chile, Costa Rica, Honduras, Peru, Republic of Korea, Sri Lanka, Venezuela) were taken from various studies undertaken within or for the World Bank. The estimate for the United States was taken from an article by Radner and Hinricks.[1] The income concept used for these estimates is as close as possible to household available income as defined by the United Nations.[2] According to this definition household available income includes wages and salaries, in cash and in kind (excluding social security contributions both by employers and employees), net income from self-employment (including consumption of own produce), income from personal property and investment (including imputed rent of owner-occupied housing), transfers from social security, social assistance and pensions, minus personal income and property taxes. Owing to data limitations, it was not always possible to use the precise concept of available income in estimating the income distributions.

Most estimates shown in table A.2 are based on household surveys, although some of them are based on tax surveys (France, for example). The original data from these surveys have been adjusted for inconsistencies with national accounts and reliable population data (such as population censuses). The two main adjustment procedures for inconsistencies with national accounts are adjustment of income by income sources and the adjustment of consumption expenditure by different items to which is added an estimate of savings.

Table A.2 shows the distribution of household available income for deciles of households, as well as the Gini coefficient calculated from the decile distribution. In principle, it would be better to

show the distribution of available household income per capita for deciles of household members. This is so because small households derive higher welfare from a given level of income than large households. However, information on the distribution of per capita income exists only for a limited number of countries. Moreover, the advantage of showing the distribution of income per household is that they are comparable with most previous income distribution estimates.

Full information on the sources of statistical data, on methodology and adjustment procedures is contained in the forthcoming ILO publication describing the ILO/World Bank project: W. van Ginneken and J. Park: *Income distribution estimates for 23 countries* (Geneva, ILO; forthcoming).

---

[1] D. B. Radner and J. C. Hinricks: "Size distribution of income 1964, 1970, and 1971", in *Survey of Current Business* (Washington, DC, United States Department of Commerce), Oct. 1974.

[2] United Nations Statistical Office: *Provisional guidelines on statistics of the distribution of income, consumption and accumulation of households* (New York, 1977). Sales No.: E.77.XVII.II.

Table A.2. Income distribution (adjusted available income per household)

Country	Year	Percentage share of household income, by decile groups of households										Gini coefficient
		1st (lowest)	2nd	3rd	4th	5th	6th	7th	8th	9th	10th (highest)	
Argentina	1970	1.5	2.9	4.3	5.4	6.3	7.8	10.3	11.2	15.1	35.2	0.44
Bangladesh	1973-74	2.7	4.1	5.1	6.3	7.6	8.5	10.2	13.3	14.8	27.4	0.35
Brazil	1972	0.6	1.4	2.1	2.9	4.0	5.4	7.1	9.9	16.0	50.6	0.61
Chile	1968	1.5	2.9	3.9	5.1	6.2	7.6	9.5	11.9	16.6	34.8	0.45
Costa Rica	1971	0.9	2.4	3.7	5.0	6.1	7.2	8.8	11.1	15.3	39.5	0.49
Denmark	1976	2.9	4.5	5.6	7.0	8.5	9.8	11.3	12.9	15.1	22.4	0.30
Egypt	1974	2.1	3.7	4.9	5.8	6.8	7.9	9.5	11.3	14.9	33.2	0.40
Fiji	1977	1.1	2.6	4.0	4.8	6.0	7.4	9.4	11.5	15.5	37.8	0.47
France	1975	1.8	3.5	4.9	6.2	7.4	8.6	10.0	11.8	15.3	30.5	0.39
Federal Republic of Germany	1974	2.9	4.0	5.0	6.0	7.1	8.3	9.9	12.0	16.0	28.8	0.37
Honduras	1967	0.7	1.6	2.2	2.8	3.5	4.5	6.4	10.5	17.8	50.0	0.61
India	1975-76	2.5	3.4	4.5	5.8	6.4	7.5	9.0	11.5	15.8	33.6	0.42
Islamic Republic of Iran	1973-74	1.4	2.4	3.3	4.2	5.6	6.5	8.3	10.9	15.8	41.7	0.52
Ireland	1973	2.5	4.7	5.3	7.8	8.2	8.4	10.4	13.3	14.3	25.1	0.32
Kenya	1976	0.9	1.8	2.6	3.7	4.9	6.6	8.9	10.3	14.6	45.8	0.59
Republic of Korea	1976	1.8	3.9	5.0	6.2	7.1	8.3	9.9	12.5	17.8	27.5	0.38
Mexico	1968	0.7	2.0	2.8	3.6	4.5	5.7	7.5	10.6	15.9	46.7	0.56
Nepal	1976-77	1.8	2.8	3.4	4.6	5.2	6.5	7.5	9.0	12.7	46.5	0.53
Panama	1976	0.7	1.3	2.0	3.2	4.7	6.3	8.4	11.6	17.6	44.2	0.57
Peru	1972	0.7	1.2	1.9	3.2	4.6	6.4	8.9	12.1	18.1	42.9	0.57
Philippines	1970-71	1.9	3.2	4.1	4.9	5.8	7.0	8.5	10.5	15.3	38.8	0.46
Sierra Leone	1967-69	2.0	3.6	4.5	5.1	5.8	6.9	8.8	10.8	14.7	37.8	0.44
Spain	1973-74	1.9	3.8	5.1	6.5	6.9	8.9	10.2	12.7	16.0	28.0	0.37
Sri Lanka	1969-70	3.1	4.4	5.4	6.3	7.3	8.4	9.8	11.9	15.1	28.3	0.35
Sudan	1967-68	1.2	2.8	4.0	5.0	6.5	8.5	10.0	12.5	14.9	34.6	0.44
Sweden	1979	2.6	4.6	6.1	6.7	7.5	9.9	11.8	13.6	16.0	21.2	0.30
Tanzania	1969	2.1	3.7	4.9	5.3	6.4	7.5	8.9	10.8	14.8	35.6	0.42
Trinidad and Tobago	1975-76	1.6	2.6	3.8	5.3	6.5	7.4	9.5	13.3	18.2	31.8	0.45
United Kingdom	1979	2.8	4.5	5.5	6.9	8.2	9.5	10.9	12.5	15.5	23.8	0.32
United States	1971	1.6	3.4	4.7	6.1	7.5	8.9	10.6	12.6	15.6	29.0	0.39
Venezuela	1970	1.0	2.0	3.1	4.2	5.6	7.3	9.8	13.0	18.3	35.7	0.49
Yugoslavia	1978	2.4	4.2	5.4	6.7	8.2	9.4	11.6	13.4	15.8	22.9	0.33
Zambia	1976	1.0	2.4	2.9	4.5	5.2	6.0	7.6	9.3	14.8	46.3	0.56

3. Social security

The three comparative tables concerning social security refer respectively to the average annual receipts and expenditure per head of population in national currency units (table A.3), receipts and expenditure of social security schemes as a percentage of GDP–or where applicable, the net material product–(table A.4) and the normal age of retirement in most countries which have set up a social protection scheme for the aged (table A.5).

The first two tables are based on the results of the international surveys on the cost of social security which the ILO has been carrying out at regular intervals since the beginning of the 1950s (the eleventh survey covering the years 1978-79 is now under way and the results of the tenth–for 1975-77–were published in 1981). Thus, 1977 is the latest year for which international data are available on social security financial operations; however, a few countries have already replied to the eleventh survey which explains why in some cases it has been possible to take account of a more recent year.

These two tables present data of the social security schemes falling within the scope of the surveys, that is to say schemes or services which fulfil the following three criteria:

(i) the objective of the scheme must be to provide curative or preventive medical care, to guarantee means of subsistence in the event of the involuntary loss of income from work or a significant part thereof, or to grant supplementary income to persons with family responsibilities;

(ii) the scheme must be set up by an act of legislation which confers specific individual rights or which imposes definite obligations on a public, semi-public or autonomous body;

(iii) the scheme must be administered by a public, semi-public or autonomous body.

However, any scheme for the compensation of occupational accidents or diseases is included in the survey, even if it does not fulfil criterion (iii) above, when the compensation for occupational accidents and diseases is directly borne by the employer.

In the final analysis the following types of schemes are thus included: compulsory social insurance; optional social insurance within the limits of criterion (ii) above; employer's liability in the event of occupational accidents and diseases; special civil servant schemes, whether contributory or non-contributory; special schemes applicable to certain branches of activity or certain occupations; family benefit schemes; medical care dispensed under public health services; benefits granted to war victims within the limits of criterion (i) above; schemes or arrangements concluded by agreement between employers and workers, provided that the resulting obligations for the employers have been approved by law and that these schemes or arrangements also satisfy criteria (i) and (iii) above. On the other hand, account is not taken of private schemes, that is to say those which are not established under the law and which offer protection against ordinary contingencies, either to groups or to individuals. The most striking example of such schemes is that of company pension funds or insurance contracted by employers for their staff and which, in some countries, account for a considerable proportion of social security resources. Further information concerning the scope covered by tables A.3 and A.4 is contained in the introduction to the study *The cost of social security: Tenth international survey, 1975-1977* (Geneva, ILO, 1981).

Table A.5 was prepared on the basis of official documentation available to the ILO in November 1981.

Table A.3. Average annual social security receipts and expenditure per head of population (in national currency units) (latest available year)

Country and currency units	Financial year	Receipts	Expenditure Total	Benefits
Africa				
Benin (CFA francs)	1977	1 126.3	975.5	887.4
Ethiopia (dollars)	1976-77	6.39	5.13	5.08
Kenya (dollars)	1977	3.90	2.15	2.09
Libyan Arab Jamahiriya (dinars)	1977	73.36	48.75	46.92
Mali (francs)	1977	994.8	775.3	636.3
Mauritius (rupees)	1976-77	382.9	335.4	332.0
Morocco (dirhams)	1977	50.1	36.4	34.1
Niger (CFA francs)	1976-77	538.2	417.6	393.0
Rwanda (francs)	1977	135.90	43.81	38.63
Senegal (CFA francs)	1975-76	2542.2	1961.6	1792.3
Sierra Leone (leones)	1976-77	3.32	3.18	3.18
Togo (CFA francs)	1977	1597.0	1519.1	1288.5
Tunisia (dinars)	1977	21.2	11.5	10.4
Upper Volta (CFA francs)	1977	583.3	412.5	373.3
Zambia (kwachas)	1976-77	23.11	17.26	16.46
Americas				
Argentina (pesos)	1977	57 081.6	49 198.6	47 560.1
Barbados (dollars)	1977	300.5	236.6	230.9
Bolivia (pesos)	1980[a]	694.1	702.2	573.4
Brazil (cruzeiros)	1977	1 292.0	1 275.0	1 105.4
Canada (dollars)	1979-80[a]	1 944.4	1 705.6	1 662.8
Chile (pesos)	1977	3 971.0	3 035.3	2 822.9
Colombia (pesos)	1980[a]	2 278.9	1 979.8	1 619.7
Costa Rica (colones)	1977	947.8	746.4	677.0
Dominican Republic (pesos)	1977	23.6	23.2	22.0
El Salvador (colones)	1977	57.4	49.0	33.4
Guatemala (quetzales)	1977	17.6	13.4	12.4
Guyana (dollars)	1977	60.3	30.7	24.9
Haiti (gourdes)	1976-77	12.8	11.1	10.3
Jamaica (dollars)	1976-77	77.46	57.13	50.73
Nicaragua (cordobas)	1977	192.4	155.9	140.3

Country and currency units	Financial year	Receipts	Expenditure Total	Benefits
Panama (balboas)	1977	120.5	95.7	85.3
Trinidad and Tobago (dollars)	1977	253.8	188.4	181.5
United States (dollars)	1979-80[a]	1 762.9	1 581.2	1 492.0
Uruguay (pesos)	1977	790.2	717.8	636.2
Venezuela (bolivares)	1977	545.8	488.7	459.6
Asia				
Bangladesh (taka)	1977	5.64	5.45	5.38
Burma (hyats)	1976-77	10.85	10.63	10.55
Cyprus (pounds)	1980[a]	73.9	63.7	62.8
India (rupees)	1975-76	50.08	28.95	28.48
Iraq (dinars)	1976-77	9.3	6.1	5.7
Israel (pounds)	1976-77	4 501.3	4 124.3	3 694.5
Japan (yen)	1979-80[a]	266 564	210 568	188 687
Malaysia (dollars)	1977	115.7	56.0	51.5
Singapore (dollars)	1980[a]	1 305.6	476.2	447.4
Sri Lanka (rupees)	1976-77	81.0	50.9	50.3
Europe (Countries with a market economy)				
Austria (schillings)	1977	22 699.9	22 187.6	21 167.6
Belgium (francs)	1980[a]	91 697.8	93 579.1	88 290.1
Denmark (crowns)	1980[a]	20 169.5	19 644.9	19 117.5
Finland (marks)	1980[a]	8 459.2	7 248.2	6 991.5
France (francs)	1980[a]	14 285.3	13 827.7	13 160.8
Federal Republic of Germany (marks)	1980[a]	5 836.7	5 793.5	5 581.2
Greece (drachmas)	1979[a]	21 756.5	18 671.5	17 775.6
Iceland (crowns)	1977	303 590.9	237 381.8	217 300.0
Ireland (pounds)	1977	308.8	308.4	291.6
Italy (lires)	1977	638 222	698 495	627 276
Luxembourg (francs)	1980[a]	100 340.3	90 446.9	86 747.2

209

Table A.3. (continued)

Country and currency units	Financial year	Receipts	Expenditure Total	Benefits	Country and currency units	Financial year	Receipts	Expenditure Total	Benefits
Malta (pounds)	1976–77	81.52	73.47	67.42	Bulgaria (leva)	1977	296.6	284.8	270.3
Netherlands (florins)	1980[a]	8035.5	6735.4	6498.0	Czechoslovakia (crowns)	1980[a]	5963.9	5963.9	5942.4
Norway (crowns)	1977	9760.8	9225.2	9010.6	German Democratic Republic (marks)	1977	1495.2	1495.2	1488.7
Portugal (escudos)	1976	5870.0	5292.5	4853.9					
Spain (pesetas)	1980[a]	66431.1	67124.0	64275.6	Hungary (forints)	1980[a]	10126.0	10063.7	10028.0
Sweden (crowns)	1980[a]	22124.2	20134.3	19628.9	Poland (zlotys)	1980[a]	9147.1	8561.0	8459.0
Switzerland (francs)	1980[a]	4557.4	4219.1	3970.2	Romania (lei)	1980[a]	2666.7	2323.5	2323.5
Turkey (liras)	1977	1326.2	839.0	675.1	Ukrainian SSR (roubles)	1977	201.3	201.3	201.3
United Kingdom (pounds)	1979–80	638.8	608.5	579.6	USSR (roubles)	1977	209.6	209.6	209.6
Europe (Countries with a centrally planned economy)					*Oceania*				
Byelorussian SSR (roubles)	1978[a]	204.1	204.1	204.1	Australia (dollars)	1979–80[a]	1319.7	1217.7	1174.6
					Fiji (dollars)	1977	76.7	39.9	32.3
					New Zealand (dollars)	1979–80[a]	1257.6	1119.1	1096.3

[a] Provisional figures.

Source: United Nations: *Demographic Yearbook 1980*. Government replies to the ILO inquiry on the cost of social security for the years 1978–80. ILO: *The cost of social security: Tenth international inquiry, 1975–1977* (Geneva, 1981).

Table A.4. Receipts and expenditure of social security schemes as a percentage of GDP[a] for 1965, 1975 and 1977 (for some countries, the most recent year has been taken instead of the year 1977)

Country	Financial year	Receipts	Expenditure Total	Benefits	Country	Financial year	Receipts	Expenditure Total	Benefits
Africa					Libyan Arab Jamahiriya	1969–70[b]	2.8	1.8	1.7
Benin	1975	2.6	2.5	2.3		1975	4.1	3.1	3.0
	1977	2.5	2.1	1.9		1977	3.4	2.2	2.1
Ethiopia	1971–72[b]	1.7	1.3	1.3	Mauritius	1969–70[b]	7.4	6.7	6.6
	1974–75[b]	2.1	1.9	1.8		1974–75[b]	4.7	4.2	4.1
	1975–76[b]	2.5	1.8	1.8		1976–77[b]	6.8	5.9	5.9
Kenya	1970	3.0	1.9	1.9	Morocco	1970	2.9	2.6	2.5
	1975	3.3	2.1	2.0		1975	1.9	1.6	1.5
	1977	2.9	1.6	1.6		1977	2.0	1.4	1.3
					Rwanda	1975	0.8	0.3	0.2
						1977	0.8	0.3	0.2

Table A.4. (continued)

Country	Financial year	Receipts	Expenditure Total	Benefits
Senegal	1969-70[b]	3.6	3.3	3.2
	1974-75[b]	2.9	2.3	2.1
	1975-76[b]	2.8	2.2	2.0
Sierra Leone	1971-72	1.5	1.5	1.5
	1974-75	1.6	1.5	1.5
	1976-77	1.3	1.2	1.2
Togo	1965[b]	3.0	2.4	2.3
	1975	2.4	1.9	1.6
	1976	2.5	2.3	2.0
Tunisia	1965[b]	3.4	3.1	2.6
	1975[b]	3.8	2.4	2.1
	1977[b]	5.6	3.2	2.8
Upper Volta	1975	2.5	2.0	1.9
	1977	2.2	1.6	1.4
Zambia	1965[b]	2.1	1.9	1.9
	1974-75	4.3	3.1	2.9
	1976-77	6.2	4.6	4.4

Americas

Country	Financial year	Receipts	Expenditure Total	Benefits
Argentina	1977	8.0	7.3	7.0
Barbados	1971[c]	6.4	3.6	3.5
	1975	6.7	4.9	4.8
	1977	7.9	6.2	6.1
Bolivia	1961[b]	4.3	3.6	3.0
	1975[b]	3.4	3.1	2.8
	1979[d]	3.3	3.1	2.7
Brazil	1965[b]	4.5	4.3	3.4
	1975[b]	6.1	5.7	4.9
	1977[b]	6.2	6.2	5.3
Canada	1964-65	10.7	9.4	9.1
	1974-75	16.7	14.7	14.0
	1979-80[d]	17.4	15.2	14.9
Chile	1965[b]	13.9	12.1	9.8
	1975[b]	11.7	9.3	8.5
	1977[b]	13.2	10.1	9.4
Colombia	1965[b]	1.1	1.1	1.0
	1975	3.6	3.0	2.8
	1979[d]	3.8	3.3	2.7

Country	Financial year	Receipts	Expenditure Total	Benefits
Costa Rica	1976	3.8	2.3	1.9
	1975	6.8	5.1	4.6
	1977	7.4	5.8	5.3
Dominican Republic	1970	2.9	2.7	1.8
	1975	2.5	2.4	2.3
	1977	2.6	2.5	2.4
El Salvador	1965[b]	2.4	2.2	2.1
	1975[b]	3.9	3.3	2.4
	1977[b]	3.4	2.9	2.0
Guatemala	1965[b]	2.0	2.0	1.8
	1975[b]	2.0	2.0	1.8
	1977[b]	2.1	1.6	1.5
Guyana	1965	4.3	4.3	4.2
	1975	3.6	1.9	1.6
	1976	4.0	2.1	1.7
Haiti	1974-75	1.0	0.9	0.8
	1976-77	0.9	0.8	0.7
Jamaica	1964-65[b]	2.9	2.7	2.5
	1974-75	4.1	3.1	2.5
	1976-77	5.9	4.4	3.9
Nicaragua	1965	2.6	2.1	1.9
	1975	3.4	2.8	2.5
	1977	2.8	2.3	2.1
Panama	1965[b]	7.3	6.0	5.6
	1975[b]	9.2	7.2	6.1
	1977[b]	9.9	7.9	7.0
Trinidad and Tobago	1965[b]	3.0	2.8	2.8
	1975[b]	3.2	2.3	2.2
	1977[b]	3.4	2.5	2.4
United States	1964-65	8.1	7.1	6.5
	1974-75	14.4	13.2	12.4
	1978-79[d]	15.0	13.2	12.4
Uruguay	1975	11.1	10.4	8.2
	1977	11.3	10.3	9.1
Venezuela	1965[b]	3.0	3.1	3.0
	1975	4.2	3.7	3.5
	1977	4.5	4.1	3.8

Table A.4. (continued)

Country	Financial year	Receipts	Expenditure Total	Expenditure Benefits
Asia				
Bangladesh	1975[b]	0.3	0.3	0.3
	1977[b]	0.4	0.3	0.3
Burma	1964-65[b]	1.0	0.9	0.9
	1974-75[b]	1.5	1.4	1.4
	1976-77[b]	1.2	1.2	1.2
Cyprus	1965[b]	3.3	2.3	2.3
	1975[b]	6.5	7.1	7.0
	1979[d]	5.6	5.0	4.9
India	1964-65[b]	1.9	1.3	1.3
	1974-75	3.4	2.0	2.0
	1975-76	4.2	2.4	2.4
Iraq	1964-65[b]	1.1	1.0	1.0
	1974-75[b]	2.3	1.9	1.8
	1975-76[b]	2.3	1.7	1.6
Israel	1964-65[b]	6.9	6.0	5.2
	1974-75[b]	11.9	10.0	9.4
	1976-77[b]	14.6	13.4	12.0
Japan	1964-65	6.6	5.1	4.6
	1974-75	10.4	7.6	6.6
	1979-80[d]	14.1	11.2	10.0
Malaysia	1965[b]	5.4	3.0	2.9
	1975	5.3	3.0	2.8
	1977	4.5	2.2	2.0
Singapore	1965[b]	5.4	3.6	3.6
	1975	9.3	3.0	3.0
	1979[d]	12.4	4.9	4.5
Sri Lanka	1964-65	4.1	3.4	3.2
	1975	3.6	2.4	2.4
	1977	3.6	2.3	2.3
Europe (countries with a market economy)				
Austria	1965	18.2	17.7	16.6
	1975	20.5	20.2	19.3
	1977	21.5	21.1	20.1

Country	Financial year	Receipts	Expenditure Total	Expenditure Benefits
Belgium	1965	17.2	16.1	14.6
	1975	24.4	23.6	22.1
	1979[d]	25.5	25.9	24.4
Denmark	1964-65	12.8	12.2	11.9
	1974-75	23.0	22.4	21.9
	1979[d]	25.9	25.3	24.6
Finland	1965[b]	12.5	10.6	10.2
	1975	18.4	16.1	15.5
	1979[d]	21.2	18.9	18.3
France	1965[b]	15.5	15.6	14.7
	1975	24.5	24.1	20.9
	1979[d]	26.4	26.0	24.7
Federal Republic of Germany	1965	17.2	16.6	15.7
	1975	23.3	23.5	22.6
	1979[d]	23.5	23.9	23.0
Greece	1965[b]	10.3	9.2	8.8
	1975[b]	12.1	10.8	10.2
	1979[d]	14.6	12.5	11.9
Iceland	1965[b]	8.8	7.2	7.0
	1975[b]	17.2	13.3	12.0
	1977[b]	17.1	13.4	12.2
Ireland	1964-65	10.4	10.3	9.8
	1975	19.6	19.7	18.9
	1977	18.4	18.3	17.3
Italy	1965	15.9	14.8	13.8
	1975	19.9	23.1	21.0
	1977	20.8	22.8	20.5
Luxembourg	1965	17.4	15.1	14.6
	1975	23.6	21.6	20.8
	1978[d]	26.5	24.5	23.6
Malta	1964-65	9.0	9.0	8.9
	1974-75	14.4	14.2	12.5
	1976-77	13.2	11.9	10.9
Netherlands	1965[b]	18.2	15.5	14.8
	1975	31.7	26.8	25.9
	1979	33.9	29.2	28.3
Portugal	1965[b]	6.9	5.3	4.6
	1975[b]	12.2	11.0	10.2
	1976[b]	12.2	11.0	10.1

Table A.4. (continued)

Country	Financial year	Receipts	Expenditure Total	Expenditure Benefits
Spain	1975	12.2	11.7	11.0
	1979[d]	15.5	15.7	14.9
Sweden	1965	16.6	13.6	13.3
	1975	29.4	26.2	25.6
	1979[d]	33.9	30.7	29.9
Switzerland	1965[b]	10.1	8.5	8.0
	1975[b]	15.8	15.1	14.3
	1979[d]	17.2	16.0	15.1
Turkey	1965	3.1	1.7	1.6
	1975	6.2	3.5	2.9
	1977	6.5	4.1	3.3
United Kingdom	1964-65	12.1	11.7	11.0
	1974-75	17.7	16.2	15.2
	1979-80[d]	18.9	18.0	17.1

Europe
(countries with a centrally
planned economy)[e]

Country	Financial year	Receipts	Expenditure Total	Expenditure Benefits
Bulgaria	1965	11.2	10.0	10.0
	1975	16.4	16.0	14.9
	1977	16.9	16.2	15.4
Czechoslovakia	1965	18.2	18.2	18.2
	1975	17.2	17.2	17.1
	1979[d]	18.7	18.7	18.6

Country	Financial year	Receipts	Expenditure Total	Expenditure Benefits
German Democratic Republic	1975	15.3	15.3	15.3
	1977	16.2	16.2	16.2
Hungary	1965	10.7	10.7	10.6
	1975	14.8	14.8	14.7
	1979[d]	16.5	16.5	16.4
Poland	1965	9.6	9.3	9.3
	1975	11.9	11.0	11.0
	1979[d]	14.6	13.6	13.4
Ukrainian SSR	1965	10.6	10.6	10.6
	1975	13.8	13.8	13.8
	1977	13.6	13.6	13.6
USSR	1965	11.6	11.6	11.6
	1975	13.8	13.8	13.8
	1977	13.4	13.4	13.4

Oceania

Country	Financial year	Receipts	Expenditure Total	Expenditure Benefits
Australia	1964-65	9.0	8.3	8.0
	1974-75	11.1	10.7	10.2
	1976-77	15.1	14.1	13.6
Fiji	1975	5.2	2.9	2.4
	1977	6.5	3.4	2.7
New Zealand	1964-65	12.0	11.5	10.9
	1974-75	13.6	12.5	12.3
	1979-80[d]	18.6	16.6	16.3

213

[a] Gross domestic product in accordance with the new system of national accounts adopted by the United Nations in 1968 (unless otherwise indicated). [b] As a percentage of the gross domestic product computed in accordance with the old system of national accounts. [c] As percentages of gross domestic product at factor cost. [d] Provisional figures. [e] As percentages of net material product.

Source: United Nations: *Yearbook of National Accounts Statistics* (New York, 1980). Government replies to the ILO inquiry on the cost of social security for the years 1978-80. ILO: *The cost of social security: Tenth international inquiry, 1975-1977* (Geneva, 1981).

Table A.5 Normal age of retirement. System of protection: social insurance – general scheme (situation in November 1981)

Country	Males	Females	Males + Females	Country	Males	Females	Males + Females
Africa				Dominican Republic	–	–	60
Algeria	–	–	60	El Salvador	65	60	–
Benin	–	–	55	Guatemala	–	–	65
Burundi	–	–	55	Honduras	65	60	–
United Republic of Cameroon	–	–	60	Mexico	–	–	65
Central African Republic	55	50	–	Nicaragua	–	–	60
				Panama	60	65	–
Congo	–	–	55	Paraguay	–	–	60
Egypt	–	–	60	Peru	60	55	–
Gabon	–	–	55	United States	–	–	65
Guinea	–	–	55	Venezuela	60	55	–
Ivory Coast	–	–	55				
Liberia	–	–	60				
Libyan Arab Jamahiriya	65	60	–				
Madagascar	60	55	–	*Asia and Oceania*			
Mali	–	–	55	Australia	65	60	–
Mauritania	60	55	–	Israel	65	60	–
Mauritius	–	–	60	Japan	60	55	–
Morocco	–	–	60	New Zealand	–	–	60
Niger	–	–	60	Philippines	–	–	60
Rwanda	–	–	55	Syrian Arab Republic	–	–	60
Senegal	–	–	55				
Sudan	60	55	–				
Togo	–	–	55				
Tunisia	–	–	60	*Europe*			
Upper Volta	–	–	55	Austria	65	60	–
Zaire	–	–	58	Belgium	65	60	–
				Bulgaria	60	55	–
				Czechoslovakia	60	53-57	–
				Denmark	67	62	–
Americas				Finland	–	–	65
Argentina	60	55	–	France	–	–	65[a]
Bahamas	–	–	65	Federal Republic of Germany	–	–	65
Barbados	–	–	65	German Democratic Republic	65	60	–
Bolivia	55	50	–				
Brazil	65	60	–				
Canada	–	–	65	Greece	65	60	–
Colombia	60	55	–	Hungary	60	55	–
Costa Rica	–	–	57	Iceland	–	–	67
Cuba	60	55	–	Ireland	–	–	65
Dominica	–	–	60	Italy	60	55	–

Table A.5   (continued)

Country	Males	Females	Males + Females	Country	Males	Females	Males + Females
Luxembourg	–	–	65	Spain	–	–	65
Netherlands	–	–	65	Sweden	–	–	65
Norway	–	–	67	Switzerland	65	62	–
Poland	65	60	–	USSR	60	55	–
Portugal	65	62	–	United Kingdom	65	60	–
Romania	62	57	–	Yugoslavia	60	55	–

[a] 60 years (Ordinance of March 1982).